IN AMAZONIA

IN AMAZONIA

A Natural History

HUGH RAFFLES

PRINCETON UNIVERSITY PRESS
PRINCETON AND OXFORD

COPYRIGHT © 2002 BY PRINCETON UNIVERSITY PRESS
Published by Princeton University Press, 41 William Street, Princeton,
New Jersey 08540
In the United Kingdom: Princeton University Press, 3 Market Place, Woodstock,
Oxfordshire OX20 1SY

Library of Congress Cataloging-in-Publicaton Data
Raffles, Hugh, DATE
In Amazonia : a natural history / Hugh Raffles.
p. cm.
Includes bibliographical references and index.
ISBN 0-691-04884-3 (alk. paper) — ISBN 0-691-04885-1 (pbk. : alk. paper)
1. Ethnology — Brazil — Igarapé Guariba. 2. Ethnology — Amazon River
Valley. 3. Indigenous peoples — Ecology — Brazil — Igarapé Guariba.
4. Indigenous peoples — Ecology — Amazon River Region. 5. Estuarine
ecology — Brazil — Igarapé Guariba. 6. Estuarine ecology — Amazon River
Region. 7. Natural history — Brazil — Igarapé Guariba. 8. Natural history —
Amazon River Region. 9. Igarapé Guariba (Brazil) — History. 10. Amazon
River Region — History. 11. Igarapé Guariba (Brazil) — Social life and
customs. 12. Amazon River Region — Social life and customs. I. Title.

GN564.B6 R34   2002
306'.09811 — dc21   2002016909

British Library Cataloging-in-Publication Data is available

This book has been composed in Sabon.

Printed on acid-free paper. ∞

www.pupress.princeton.edu

Printed in the United States of America

10 9 8 7 6 5 4 3 2 1

FOR SHARON

Pará, December 15, 1928. Mouth of the Amazon.

A young woman who was on our boat, coming from Manaus, went into town with us this morning. When she came upon the Grand Park (which is undeniably nicely planted) she emitted an easy sigh.

'Ah, at last, nature,' she said. Yet she was coming from the jungle.

—HENRI MICHAUX, *Ecuador: A Travel Journal*

CONTENTS

ACKNOWLEDGMENTS

Many people have read and commented on either single chapters or larger portions of a manuscript that has been in progress for several years; others have made more informal but no less valued contributions. My appreciation runs deep to all—including those whose names have somehow escaped this list: Arun Agrawal, Noriko Aso, Iain Boal, Bruce Braun, Graham Burnett, Jim Clifford, Steve Connell, Bill Denevan, Amity Doolittle, Kate Dudley, Carla Freccero, Jody Greene, Carol Greenhouse, Jimmy Grogan, Donna Haraway, Gill Hart, Julie Harvey, Emily Harwell, Amelie Hastie, Cori Hayden, Gail Hershatter, David Hoy, Jake Kosek, Jean Lave, Celia Lowe, Joe McCann, Doreen Massey, Bill Maurer, Ben Orlove, Miguel Pinedo-Vásquez, Anna Roosevelt, Vasant Saberwal, Suzana Sawyer, Candace Slater, Janet Sturgeon, Neferti Tadiar, Liana Vardi, Michael Watts, Antoinette WinklerPrins, Karen Tei Yamashita, and Dan Zarin. In addition, Don Brenneis, Susan Harding, Susanna Hecht, Dan Linger, Christine Padoch, Nancy Peluso, Michael Reynolds, Jim Scott, K. Sivaramakrishnan, Kristiina Vogt, Eric Worby, Heinzpeter Znoj, and an anonymous reviewer from the Press have made major contributions by reading and responding to one or another version of the entire work. In this regard, I owe particular thanks to David Cleary, who twice provided exceptionally detailed, insightful, and generous readings that considerably advanced the project. I am also more than normally indebted to Don Moore, whose sustained commentary has pulled both me and this book further into Pacific Time than would otherwise have been possible. The book has benefited greatly from the attention of two outstanding copy editors—Maria E. DenBoer and Annie Moser Gray—and from the production skills of Brigitte Pelner and Sarah Green. My thanks also to Lys Ann Shore for preparing the index. Mary Murrell has been everything I hoped for in an editor and more: smart, sensitive, imaginative—and an inimitable lunch companion!

Individual chapters have been presented at seminars and conferences at Irvine, Santa Cruz, Philadelphia, Washington, D.C., the University of Delhi, the University of London, and Yale, and I thank audiences and commentators at these events, particularly Amita Baviskar, Teresa Caldeira, Fred Damon, Rebecca Hardin, Gísli Palsson, and Adriana Petryna. In London, I remain grateful to James Dunkerley, Stephen Nugent, and the late Michael Eden for providing a home at the Institute of Latin American Studies, enabling my return to academia and departure for Brazil.

In the United States, I have had the great fortune to work in remarkable institutional settings on both coasts. At Yale, Jim Scott, Kay Mansfield, and the Program in Agrarian Studies welcomed me to what became a formative location. As for Santa Cruz: this book would have been very different and, I am certain, far poorer, had it been written anywhere else. I have learned from all my colleagues, and working at close quarters in particular with Don Brenneis, Jackie Brown, Nancy Chen, Susan Harding, Dan Linger, Ravi Rajan, Lisa Rofel, and Anna Tsing has been equal parts humbling and inspiring.

In Brazil, I am indebted to Jaime Rabelo and Marcirene Machado, Fernando Rabelo and Lúcia, Moacir José Santana, Mary Helena and Fernando Allegretti, Hélio Pennafort, Waldiclei Pereira Ramos, Waldir Pereira, the staff at the SEPLAN library, the Museu Histórico do Amapá, the public library in Macapá, and the Archivo Público in Belém, to Trish Shanley, Célia Maracajá, Toby McGrath, Harry Knowles, and to Dora, Lene, and Walmir, who always found room for my *rede*. I am also grateful to Joe McCann for the memorable visit to the Arapiuns basin that is recorded in Chapter 2, and to Michael Reynolds for his friendship on that and other journeys. Above all, though, I owe a permanent debt of gratitude for the extraordinary generosity, kindness, patience, and humor of those I name only by pseudonym: the residents of Igarapé Guariba, Rio Preto, Fazendinha, Macapá, and elsewhere in Amazonia, whose lives animate the pages of Chapters 2, 3, 6, and 7.

The research on which this book is based was funded by the Joint Council of Latin American and Caribbean Studies of the Social Science Research Council and the American Council of Learned Societies with funds provided by the Ford Foundation; the National Science Foundation; the Program in Agrarian Studies at Yale University; the Yale Center for International and Area Studies; the Yale Tropical Resources Institute; and by faculty research funds granted by the University of California, Santa Cruz. I was able to complete the writing thanks to the award of a University of California President's Research Fellowship in the Humanities and an S.V. Ciriacy-Wantrup Fellowship in Natural Resource Studies at the University of California, Berkeley. I am grateful to Michael Watts for acting as my faculty mentor at Berkeley and to all the above institutions for their generous support.

In addition to the people who figure in its pages, I have written this book for my family in Britain and Ireland, especially for my parents. I dedicate it to Sharon Simpson, lifelong best friend, partner-in-crime. So many years sharing our dreams, anxieties, and passions. Always talking, always thinking, never stopping! So many distances traveled. And always together, even when apart. In every respect, this book is the outcome of our two lives entwined.

IN AMAZONIA

1

IN AMAZONIA

Dreams of Avarice — My Heart Goes Bump! — Landscape as Text
. . . and as Biography — Igarapé Guariba — Another Discovery —
Environmental Determinisms and Narrative Acrobatics — Spaces of
Nature — A Natural History — Collecting and Reflecting — Traces of
Trauma — Sawdust Memories

Let's begin in 1976. It was late summer that year when a crew from the
Companhia de Pesquisas e Recursos Minerais, the geological survey of
the Brazilian Ministry of Mines, shot this infrared aerial photograph of
the Rio Guariba, by then almost a river. They didn't find what they
were looking for, at least not here, although there was plenty of gold
and magnesium close by. But their image is worth treasuring anyway. Its
tactility holds this book in place — exactly where it should be.

It was a famously hot summer in London. I was working in a gray
stone warehouse in the East End docks, loading and unloading delivery
trucks and stacking crates of beer and wine in tall towers on wooden
pallets. That building is still standing, but like most of the warehouses
down there it's been transformed: gutted, scrubbed, and converted into
luxury condominiums. Back then, every Thursday, all the workers —
transients like myself and those hoping for the long haul — formed a
snaking line up a narrow, deeply shadowed stairwell to a battered door-
way on the top-floor landing. Every week, as the person ahead exited, I
would knock on the closing door, enter the cramped office, and say my
name to the company accountant seated behind a desk piled high with
tumbling stacks of papers. And every Thursday, with the same motions
and with the same half-smile, the accountant would calculate my wages,
shuffle the money into a new brown envelope, and, as if to himself,
repeat the same unsettling phrase: "Beyond the dreams of avarice. . . . "

That same summer, an ocean away, in a world of which I still knew
nothing, the Brazilian dictatorship was chasing avaricious dreams of its
own. Late in 1976, as I grappled with an irony beyond my sensibility,

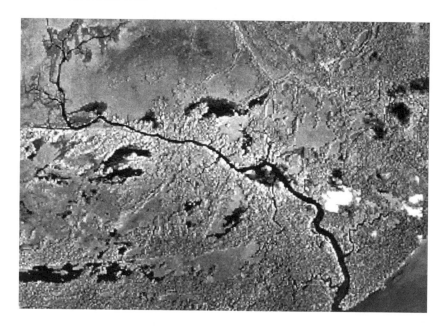

the generals were forcing convulsive inroads into their northern provinces, brushing aside Indian, peasant, and guerrilla resistance, creating fortunes, chaos, and despair. It was an aggressive territorialization, one that would radically change the dynamics and logic of regional politics and produce an unforeseen geopolitical re-siting that the military and their civilian successors have ever since struggled to disavow, a now-familiar ecological Amazonia subject to planetary discourses of common governance.[1]

Meanwhile, between the contours of the military maps, people were making new worlds of their own. The survey image does not lie. Though we cannot see it yet, that river is growing, and in growing it transforms the lives that transform it. And the water that flowed past as I piled boxes by the Thames at Wapping Stairs where Jeffreys the Hanging Judge once attempted flight disguised as a sailor, that lapping water on which Ralegh was finally captured, his pockets stuffed with talismans of Guiana, and on which young Bates and Wallace, heading to Kew in 1848, talked of tropical travels soon to come, that murky water is the same rushing tide that washes in and out, a monstrous pump, sweeping the land out to sea and remaking this place I have called Igarapé Guariba.

I arrived in Igarapé Guariba in 1994 looking for oral histories. I was in the northern Brazilian state of Amapá and was captured by the landscape, its blatant physicality and its enduring imaginaries. It was especially thrilling to be in an airplane here on a cloudless flight and to be held by that iconic view of dense and boundless forest veined by sharply golden rivers, by a long-anticipated panorama that was already part of my experience well before I saw it for myself.

On the ground, of course, although the consciousness of vista never really dissolves, it all looks different — a matter of ethnography and the practice of history, and a rationale for this book. There is a passage in Walter Benjamin's *One-Way Street* about this, written in an age when commercial air travel was still exotic, a meditation on embodied experience, on the perspectival dislocations of new technologies and the traditions of Judaic scholarship. Benjamin, alive to the materialities of practice and to the liveliness of objects, compares the difference between passing over and walking through a landscape to the difference between reading a text and copying it. But it is the first term of his analogy that catches my attention:

> The power of a country road is different when one is walking along it from when one is flying over it by airplane. . . . The airplane passenger sees only how the road pushes through the landscape, how it unfolds according to the same laws as the terrain surrounding it. Only he who walks the road on foot learns of *the power it commands*, and, of how, from the very scenery that for the flier is only the unfurled plain, it calls forth distances, belvederes, clearings, prospects at each of its turns like a commander deploying soldiers at a front.[2]

Benjamin draws his European landscape with a mind's eye trained on the darkening horizon that presages his own suicide. His country road leads inexorably to 1940 and his death at the Franco-Spanish border. And the mood of detachment affected by his passenger is also of a time and place. When the clouds part unexpectedly to reveal a glimpse of the deep green forests of Pará receding to a haze, my heart goes bump — just like that! — and a visual lexicon I hardly knew I possessed takes over. Laid out below is the Amazon as seen in a thousand picture spreads, an entity already grasped whole, a planetary patrimony, about which I have no sense of what I bring and what I find.

In Igarapé Guariba, I asked people about where they lived—the rivers, trees, and mudflats, the fishes, birds, and mammals—searching for signs of the potent environmental Amazon of contemporary imagination. In answer, as conversation turned to the past, their memories called up another place situated right here in this same geographical location but unmistakably different, another place entirely; a place distinct not only in its sociality but also in its physical characteristics. Slowly, through the months of talking, a biographical landscape, at once material and fantastic, one born from the politics of history and molded out of everyday life, began to take shape.

When the four founding families of Igarapé Guariba sailed across the endless expanse of the Amazon delta in the late 1950s, passing between islands and hugging the shore, they found only a stream running out of the forest to meet their boats and announce their new home. The water from which the community took its name was, as Pedro Preto put it, a "*besteira*," a joke, a silly little thing. A creek not a river, an *igarapé* not a *rio*, it must have been no more than a mile long, narrowing from about 50 yards where it met the open sea of the Amazonas to less than 20 yards at its headwaters in the rocks of a shallow waterfall.

They were soon followed by Raimundo Viega, the owner of forest and savanna that stretched between three rivers and the boss for whom they had crossed the estuary from the islands of Afuá. Raimundo built a sawmill, and he hired men in Macapá, the state capital, to come out and work it for him. The settlers, meanwhile, collected timber and seeds and they planted fields of banana and watermelon. And they sold it all to Raimundo, always the Old Man, in his white-painted store on the bluff at the mouth of the stream.

Igarapé Guariba was a beautiful place, with a magical abundance of wildlife and trees. In that twinkling time, the fish found their own way into your nets. But how could it last? Soon any wood worth cutting was gone. The closest now was in the distant forest lining the horizon above the waterfall, the same area returning hunters reported rich with game and forest fish, and with truly fertile bottomlands. To get there meant pushing and dragging a canoe for hour after hour, opening the heavy curtain of tall papyrus grass that closed behind as you went forward, camping upstream for weeks on end.

It was Raimundo Viega who ordered the streams cut and the channels dug. It was Pedro Preto, Benedito Macedo, and the others who pushed themselves day after day, summer after summer, and year after year through the fields and swamps, hacking and digging, opening waterways, engineering what would turn out to be a whole new world.

Using canoes and motorboats to navigate Igarapé Guariba, traveling this impressive and mercurial river along which the village straggles, emerging on the broad, often choppy lake into which its waters empty, following the disorienting tracery of channels and creeks that vanish into the upstream forest, it was impossible for me to believe this landscape had existed for less than thirty-five years. It was so massive. So perfect in its limpid beauty. So complete in its deep surfaces and crowded banks. So resonant in its towering *buriti* palms, its lazy flocks of pure white egrets. So deeply green and forested. So *natural*.

Yet, time and again people told the same story: when we arrived, there was just a little stream, so shallow children could wade its mouth. It ended at a waterfall. Beyond, there were only fields. Then we cut the channels. Now look at it!

Such a simple story. But astonishing nonetheless. There had been no warning of this in the scholarly or popular literature. The accounts of manipulations of rivers and streams in Amazonia were scattered, minor, and largely unknown.[3] I wouldn't find them until I returned to the United States and dedicated myself to the task. It was not just that nothing of such a scale had previously been reported: the idea that the rivers and streams of the region were subject to systematic human ma-

nipulation had never been seriously entertained. Here was something new. Yet the story presented an awkward irony, and telling it placed me in the very tradition of European discovery I had intended to challenge. For, in many places, despite the drama of their scale and emotional resonance, these streams would be fairly unremarkable. But because they were made in Amazonia, they have a special status. In Amazonia, they immediately run up against sedimented histories of a primal nature, histories that have circulated and multiplied ever since Europeans first came here in the sixteenth century, situated their geographical imaginations, and returned home with wide-eyed accounts of their adventures. In Amazonia, visitors have struggled to locate new experiences on old intellectual maps, returning again and again to discover the region, as if for the very first time.

From those initial early modern accounts, European travelers offered northern South America as a place of excessive nature, and they began to imagine a region in which lives were dictated by the rhythms and exigencies of their surroundings, and where emotions, moralities, and technologies were subject to a natural logic.[4] It was a region where social conditions could be explained according to a fiercely hierarchical notion of the relation between people and their landscapes, a notion that became more stable as the distinction between culture and nature secured its footing in European thought.

By the time nineteenth-century naturalists found their way across the Atlantic, they were able to interpret what they saw as social stagnation and agricultural backwardness in terms of the indolence-inducing effect on race of an over-fecund nature, of the corruptions of a land where the fruit falls ripe from the tree. More than 100 years later, by the middle of the twentieth century, archaeologists, anthropologists, and natural scientists were describing the apparently identical social effects of an environment that they saw as having the *opposite* characteristics: a harsh setting of nutrient-poor soils and inadequate protein. For Victorian explorer-scientists, Amazonians were seduced into decadence by the ease of the tropical life; for post–World War II cultural ecologists, the harshness of the tropics imprisoned Amazonians in the primitive. It is no accident then that the transfigured landscapes of Igarapé Guariba and others like them have only recently begun to appear in accounts of Amazonian realities. It is no surprise either that their history is so hard to fully comprehend. We are entering a space of nature: nature pristine, nature overwhelming, nature violated and in danger.

A Natural History

But neither Amazonia nor its nature is so easily contained. The natures I describe in this book are dynamic and heterogeneous, formed again and again from presences that are cultural, historical, biological, geographical, political, physical, aesthetic, and social. They are natures deep within everyday life: affect-saturated affinities, unreliable and wary intimacies.

It is difficult to write densely constituted worlds filled with things that can, without naïveté or reductionism, be termed nature. Such nature calls for a natural history, an articulation of natures and histories that works across and against spatial and temporal scale to bring people, places, and the non-human into "our space" of the present.[5] This is less a history of nature than a way of writing the present as a condensation of multiple natures and their differences.[6] And such natures, it should be clear, resist abstraction from the worlds in which they participate.

As the foregoing suggests, I am caught up in the reworking of scale through attention to the entanglements of time, space, and nature in particular sites. This is all about the specificities of Amazonia — its regions, localities, and places — and the ways these spatial moments come into being and continue being made at the meeting points of history,

representation, and material practice.[7] At the same time, I am preoccupied by a range of questions in the politics of nature that draw me to
explore the fullness and multiplicity of nature as a domain marked both
by an active and irreducible materiality and by a similarly irreducible
discursivity — a domain with complex agency. In addition, this is a book
of intimacies, an account of the differential relationships of affective
and often physical proximity between humans, and between humans and
non-humans. Such "tense and tender ties" are themselves the sites and
occasions for the condensations I examine here.[8] Indeed, they are the
constitutive matter of these locations. And, in the intimacies of memory
and on-the-ground complicities and yearnings, affective relations encompass the work of fieldwork and writing, making this book an extended reflection on the ethnographic.

I have grounded this study in the practices through which particular
categories and subjects (Amazonia and Amazonian nature) are formed
and enacted, and I have drawn from four broad sets of sources. From
the sixteenth-century nature experienced by Sir Walter Ralegh (Chapter
4), I take the logic of embodied intimacy, the unstable engagement with
a world of correspondences, and a resistance to classificatory hierarchy.
From Henry Walter Bates and the natural historical explorations of the
mid-nineteenth century (Chapter 5), I hold onto a dialogic, vernacular
nature that encompasses multiple local knowledges, and I rediscover the
politics and agency of even the humblest of animals, the insects, alive
and dead. Paul, Ana, Moacyr, and the forest ecology research team at
Fazendinha (Chapter 6) show me that nothing stands still in a forest,
that trees and people create each other, that the histories produced in
nature are biographical, unpredictable, and deeply affective, and that,
as a location for modern managerial science — for a traveling governance — nature is extraordinarily generative. From the people of Igarapé
Guariba and elsewhere in the region (Chapters 2, 3, and 7), I learn that
nature is always in the being-made, that it is indissoluble from place,
that it is multiply interpellated in active and vital politics, that its brute
materiality cannot be denied, and that it resides in people as fully as
people reside in it. Out of all this I have written a natural history
grounded in micropolitics and power, one that I offer as a supplement
to contemporary interventions in Amazonia — those of the social sciences, the natural sciences, and of "development" — interventions that
too often segregate and diminish both the natural and the social.[9]

A particular inspiration has been the convergence of two recent

bodies of work: one that seeks to reconfigure the logic of the modern
(to dissolve nature/culture binaries, for example) and one that excavates
the ontologies of Renaissance nature.[10] Communing with the latter no
longer means taking facts, to use Mary Poovey's helpful term, as "deracinated particulars." Nor does it require relying on the opposition of
the particular (the Aristotelian "historical") to the universal (the "philosophical"), nor on the hierarchized division of labor between natural
history and natural philosophy that this distinction underwrote. Modern facts, including "natural" facts, contain and speak from theory — a
position that natural historians eventually came to acknowledge.[11] But
there are many ways through which the thickness of facts can be ac-
complished. With its resistance to regularities and its emphasis on "diversity more than uniformity, and the breaking of classificatory boundaries more than the rigors of taxonomy,"[12] pre-Baconian natural history
persists as a reminder of the dynamic and unsettled variety of modes of
knowing, a trace of other ways of imagining, experiencing, and investi-
gating nature.

Reading back into earlier natural histories, I have reimagined this
book as a collection — although one committed (so far as writing allows) to keeping its objects alive and in motion. Unlike the collection of
the nineteenth century, in which "the object is detached from all its

original functions in order to enter into the closest conceivable relation to things of the same kind,"[13] this is an ecumenical assemblage for which I have gathered, cared for, arranged, and displayed small pieces of a world of difference breathing life into the husks of their connections, finding new meanings and possibilities through juxtaposition. Yet, as with Henry Walter Bates' Amazonian collection, mine too is marked by incompleteness as much as wholeness. And it is held fast in various elsewheres by the attachments that objects, however violated in their recontextualization, retain to place and biography. A collection is a work of affinity, intensity, and excess, "a form of practical memory" that binds us skin to skin with the richly real.[14] Describing his own collecting of books, Benjamin noted that "every passion borders on the chaotic, but the collector's passion borders on the chaos of memories."[15] The chaos of memories from which I draw this book is one of identifications and seductions. It is not only the natures that hold me. I like the people here too much as well.

When I first took up this project, I pictured it forming around a more familiar politics of agency and restitution: the story of anthropogenesis in the space of wilderness. As I have already indicated, some of that story remains. But I was hijacked, and the book followed. Now it feels closer to the real, all entanglements, cross-talking, and open ends. And now it has to begin again, this time with the remains of a trauma that shadows every page.

A few short years ago, two of my sisters, still young, died suddenly and unexpectedly and within just fifteen weeks of each other. Twice, 3,000 miles away in New York City, I answered the phone. *In an instant*, twice, I learned that when such things happen (things that are both unbearably particular and profoundly universal) nothing that will happen or has happened is ever the same. New lines appear, cleaving the lives of all who survive. At such times of crisis, affect has a materiality so overwhelming that nothing else matters. Crisis, I found, crushes time and space, exploding their assumptions, until scale — the very ordering logic of everyday life and the most comfortable of accommodations — becomes a visceral and destabilizing problem, no longer convincing as ideological fantasy ("structuring our social reality itself").[16] At such moments of ontological and epistemological excess, everyday coordinates are suspended and the world is experienced as if everything were up for grabs.

Within a few months of these deaths, I found myself, as if shell-shocked, washed up on the banks of the Rio Guariba, introverted and self-absorbed, miserable, and inflicting my misery on those unlucky enough to be my hosts. With my growing understanding that the *extremis* of sudden loss was a familiar condition here, the encounter — as should be evident — developed a happier and more encompassing intensity. But the arbitrariness and particularity of fieldwork could not have been more apparent. The peculiar optic through which I discovered Amazonia, my hypersensitivity to the affective, to the purposive politics of trust and complicity, to the inconstancies of time and place, to a world of dense and dynamic materialities, all this — though now fading fast in the face of life's relentless normality — has overdetermined, structured, shaped, and textured this project. Its mark is indelible. It seeps through cracks, forcing them open, forcing remembrance.

I last visited Amazonia in 1999. Not long before leaving, I spent a few days in the logging town of Paragominas with Moacyr, whom I introduce more fully in Chapter 6. He was showing me how, even though the timber industry has moved west from there, its traces linger, as material as can be: mills disused and giant heaps of sawdust abandoned in the midst of flimsy wooden housing. The piles smolder, threatening to ignite, but children play on them anyway, now and again sliding down through the shifting surfaces, badly burning their bodies.

It was a hot afternoon and we crisscrossed the sprawling town, thirsty, walking up and down, far and wide. At one point — we were talking about foreign researchers — Moacyr asked me how it was that foreigners could come here, get to know maybe one or two places, perhaps a couple more if they stayed a long time, and then return to their universities, stand in front of roomfuls of students, and teach about somewhere they called Amazonia. What, he asked, with a mixture of bafflement, irony, and refusal, allows them to make such a claim: to pretend that they know *Amazonia?*

Despite his then strained circumstances, there was no animus in Moacyr's question. It was, rather, a grappling out loud with the profound asymmetries that allowed his life to be so easily circumscribed. It was a struggling that had come to reside in a particular, cosmopolitan sense of wonder, a marveling that this complicated world of condensed and generative intimacies could be so contained by language, travel, and science. That it could be collected and displayed as if nothing were lost in translation.

2

DISSOLUTION OF THE ELEMENTS
The Floodplain, 11,000 BP–2002

"Where do correct ideas come from?" Mao Zedong asked his revolutionary cadres in May 1963. "Do they drop from the skies? . . . Are
they innate in the mind?" Many certainties collapsed in the second half
of the twentieth century, but Mao's answer is still entirely unimpeach-
able. "They come from social practice," he states without equivocation,
"and from it alone."[1]

What do we know about Amazonians and Amazonian nature?
There are two closely related ways of knowing, both of which arise in
and are themselves practices. One is evidentiary, one genealogical. Let's
begin with the evidence.

THE CANAL DE IGARAPÉ-MIRI

I was reading a crumbling pocket edition of *Travels on the Amazon and
Rio Negro*, Alfred Russel Wallace's account of his tragic journey to Brazil.[2] It was Wallace's first trip outside England, four unhappy years during which he lost a beloved brother to yellow fever and an entire collec-

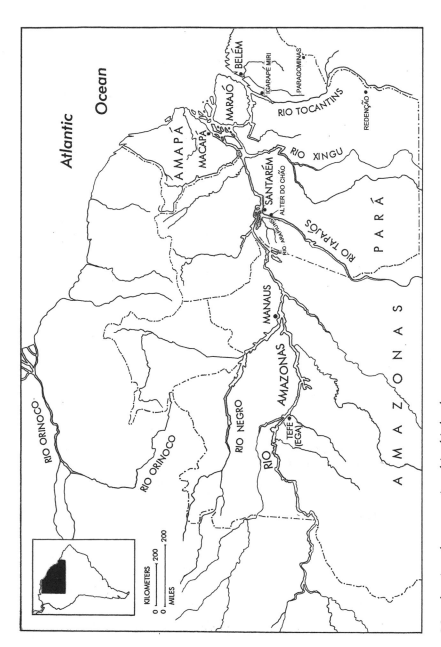

Map showing places mentioned in this book

tion of specimens and drawings to a catastrophic shipboard fire that left him drifting ten days in mid-Atlantic. Finally back in Britain, he published his *Travels* to an indifferent response. The book is flat, despite its adventures, cobbled together from letters, the few notebooks that survived, and a disconsolate memory. Darwin, in an uncharitable moment, wrote: "I was a *little* disappointed in Wallace's book on the Amazon, hardly facts enough."[3]

Darwin and Wallace's relationship was too intimate for innocent criticism, of course.[4] Not only would they compete for ownership of the theory of natural selection, but Wallace, a complicated maverick who paid the professional and personal price for unorthodoxy, would finally depend on Darwin to petition Prime Minister Gladstone for the pension that would keep him one step from destitution.[5] In August 1848, though, he was still an ambitious young autodidact from the artisan class. It was a paragraph in the second chapter that caught my eye. I must have read it before more than once without pausing, but this time canals were on my mind. Wallace is describing a boat journey from the state capital Belém to the Rio Tocantins:

> At nine A.M., on the 28th we entered the Igarapé Mirí, which is a cut made for about half a mile, connecting the Mojú river with a stream flowing into the Tocantíns, nearly opposite Cametá; thus forming an inner passage, safer than the navigation by the Pará river, where vessels are at times exposed to a heavy swell and violent gales, and where there are rocky shoals, very dangerous for the small canoes by which the Cametá trade is principally carried on. When about halfway through, we found the tide running against us, and the water very shallow, and were obliged to wait, fastening the canoe to a tree. In a short time the rope by which we were moored broke, and we were drifted broadside down the stream, and should have been upset by coming against a shoal, but were luckily able to turn into a bay where the water was still. On getting out of the canal we sailed and rowed along a winding river, often completely walled in with a luxuriant vegetation of trees and climbing plants.[6]

The perils of the journey are clear enough, but the character of the "cut" is ambiguous. Wallace had arrived in the Amazon just three months earlier, and he was sailing with his close friend Henry Walter Bates. After frustrating delays in Belém, the two naturalists had eagerly accepted an invitation from Charles Leavens, a Canadian timber merchant, to join him as he scoured the unmapped upper Tocantins for valuable "cedar." It was on the outward leg of this expedition that the party passed through Igarapé-Miri. Soon after, unable to contract guides or porters, Leavens cut short the proposed three-month trip and within five weeks of departing they were all back in the city, somewhat deflated. Bates, unfailingly scrupulous, records the same journey — though marking it for the next day — and describes the waterway unequivocally as "a short, artificial canal."[7]

Such a tame spot for two explorers to almost lose their lives. A popular shipping route, in fact. And, as you might expect, it turned out that Wallace and Bates were by no means the only published authors to pass through the canal at Igarapé-Miri. Trawling nineteenth-century travel writing, a literature of chorography and social commentary, I found that the radical railroad engineer and poet Ignácio Baptista de Moura had been here too.

Baptista de Moura's account is quite different from either Wallace's or Bates'. Local political economy had gone through some drastic changes in fifty years. But isn't it also because of his connection to the fledgling Socialist Workers' Party of Pará that, where the British naturalists marveled at walls of luxuriant vegetation, Baptista de Moura looked from the deck of his boat to see a desolate scene of barely functioning sugar mills lining the banks of the canal?[8] In the 1840s, Atlantic steam transport had been introduced, boosting the internal export markets in the south of Brazil. The competitive advantage gained by the sugar planters of the Brazilian northeast had more or less wiped out the Amazon trade in white and brown sugar and cane-honey. The factories Baptista de Moura described in 1896, their original water- or animal-powered motors often replaced by British steam engines, were scraping by, distilling *cachaça*, white rum, for the local market.[9]

A few years later the geographer Manoel Buarque saw similar signs of decline. Buarque, though, has an ear for anecdote, and in the account of his travels along the Tocantins and Araguaia rivers in 1905–6 the canal starts to come alive.[10] The "Canal de Igarapé-miry," he writes, was opened by a certain Carambola, a prominent local landlord and slaveowner who was also the largest regional supplier of timber to Belém:

Carambola was illiterate, but he had a slave who could read and write. One day he got it into his head to learn to read. He made this slave his teacher and every day they had classes.

When Carambola made a mistake and his instructor pointed out the error, the former responded by seizing his wooden cane and striking the hapless teacher on the hand, upbraiding him with the words: *"Nigger, are you correcting me?"*[11]

According to Buarque, this had all happened in the 1820s, before the explosion in rubber prices that was to transform many of these riverine towns, and at a time when the sugar economy dominated the southern channel of the Amazon estuary.[12] The petulant cruelty exhibited in this slapstick vignette of colonial life — in its topsy-turvy ironies like a scene from a period-dress *telenovela* — was, Buarque establishes, anything but random. With a sudden shift in tone, he leads us from this framing episode to the story of the canal itself:

There's more to tell about this Italian. When he opened the Canal it was those slaves that he didn't like that he put to work on the last stretch. So when the Mojú poured into the Mucajatuba there were those unfortunate souls, swept away by the rush of the waters and dragged into the fearsome abyss.[13]

All at once, Buarque sweeps us up in the rushing stream of modern Amazonian history, the story of the canal collapsing into tragedy. We are in *terra anfíbia*, an amphibious universe, where the lines between earth and water, between living and dying, are friable and fluid.[14] Or look at it another way: he has taken us to a place where the casual waste of life in pursuit of overbearing engineering schemes is almost a trope, with its own eclectic genre — read, for instance, Márcio Souza's *Mad Maria* or H. M. Tomlinson's *The Sea and the Jungle*, stories of the building of the Madeira–Mamoré railroad, a famously gruesome episode from the rubber period invoking corruption, disease, brutality, and the perverse utopianism of the metropolitan tycoon; or watch Werner Herzog's delirious *Fitzcarraldo*, or better still, Les Blank's disbelieving commentary, *Burden of Dreams*.[15] Or a third way to hear what Buarque is saying: how, as a liberal modern, he calls up the now-standard geographical metaphor, the canal as another instance of the lawless workings of capital on the periphery, looking too similar to recent massacres of landless workers at Corumbiara and Eldorado de Carajás (close, as it happens, by road as well as history to Igarapé-Miri). And the rationalization that often emerges as the palliative corollary to such willful brutality arrives with abruptness — again — in Buarque's account, although this time as anticlimax. "On the other hand," he writes, "this barbarian provided a great service to the region, protecting the little vessels from the furies of the Bay of Tocantins."[16]

But Buarque's is not the last word on the canal either. Eladio Lobato's *Caminho de canoa pequena*, a very different kind of book, tells the official story of Igarapé-Miri: an institutional history of its founding, an annotated genealogy of its elite, a tour of its natural wealth, and a chronicle of the municipality's steady progress toward modernity. The canal holds a special place in this story and Lobato retells Buarque's narrative in a very different register:

> The work was started from the Rio Igarapé-Miri on May 21st 1821, and it was only on the seventh of August of the following year, when there were just slightly more than a hundred meters to go, that excavation began from the Rio Moju side. However, it so happened that the team of slaves working from the Rio Igarapé-Miri left a fragile bank of about four meters standing in the middle of this narrow passage, when, on November 23rd 1823, while the slaves were digging, the Moju flooded suddenly and violently, at the same time that a swollen tide provoked the so-called phenomenon of the POROROCA, which tore down the bank.[17]

Lobato goes on to list the eighteen slaves who died in this tragedy (out of the thirty-seven put to work by Carambola — presumably the entire group working from the Rio Moju).

The *pororoca* is indeed a phenomenon: an intense tidal reflux occurring in summer, most notoriously on the Amapá coast near the mouth of the Rio Araguarí. In L. H. Myers' melodramatic novel *The Clio* (1925), Professor Brown, the mysterious traveling scientist who offers commentary on the region's *physique générale* as he steams into tropical intrigue with an assorted party of rich adventurers and vacationers, succeeds in capturing its mythic force:

> The great estuary up which we have been steaming all day is little more than a backwater of the main stream of the Amazon, which flows north of Marajó. There the current fights with the Atlantic tides and creates a dangerous bore. Three waves which are sometimes as much as twelve feet high rush up the river, sweeping over the low islands with devastating force. No-one

lives in those parts. . . . This part of the earth is not yet ready to be the abode of man.[18]

In Lobato's narrative, the pororoca is the town's alibi as well as Carambola's, transmuting crime into fate at this formative moment of municipal history. But right at the end of Lobato's list of slave victims, there is a clue that tips the scales toward Buarque's account. The last-named casualty is Pedro Salgado, "called Salgado [Salty/Spicy], [because he] was constantly whipped owing to his defiance of his master and overseers."[19]

Neither Buarque nor Lobato leaves much doubt about the local economic importance of the canal. When Buarque visited Igarapé-Miri in April 1905, he found it a depressing backwater of a place, the future of which, he thought, depended entirely on the widening of the canal to allow free passage for large ships bound between Belém and the Rio Tocantins. In this era of highly active commerce in the eastern Amazon, all kinds of vessels were carrying Brazil nuts from Marabá and rubber (and later the inferior *caucho* latex) from Conceição do Araguaia and stations along the Rio Tocantins out into the Bay of Tocantins and on to Belém for distribution around Brazil and overseas. Yet Buarque's boat was too large to get through the canal, and he had to switch to something smaller, suggesting that Carambola's channel had closed over considerably by this point.

Buarque saw that the potential benefits of the canal were not washing up on the bedraggled waterfront at Igarapé-Miri. Although it should have brought profits to the town through service industries, taxes, and toll payments, income from the canal was instead flowing out past the small interior community to arrive in Belém. When they did use the canal, boats carrying sugar from the interior mills and Brazil nuts and rubber from the Tocantins sailed straight on through, heading directly for the Moju and the capital. There seemed to be little in Igarapé-Miri to detain them. In a tale characteristic of both the sugar trade and the historically important extractive economies, Igarapé-Miri, the provincial municipality with little political clout, failed to capitalize on its costly engineering triumph. Profits from forest and farm either stayed in the interior or drained out to the capital.

But it is Carambola, the engineer, the canal-dreamer, the vindictive slave master, who captures my imagination. Lobato, by no means a straightforward apologist, points out that this nickname came from the

star fruit—of which the engineer was so fond that he would order brutally flogged any of his slaves found picking it on his land without permission. Yet, where Buarque talks of Carambola as an arbitrary tyrant,
Lobato portrays him also as a fugitive outsider. Carambola, he tells us,
was to live out much of the latter part of his life afflicted with leprosy,
alone in a shack at the mouth of an isolated creek, excommunicated for
ordering the beating of the local priest, shunned even by travelers passing by his remote homestead, visited by a single black man, Felisberto,
"the only person who had the courage to see him."[20] Nevertheless, in a
discreet gesture, public history and the municipality of Igarapé-Miri
have perhaps been more generous: the contemporary visitor who knows
that a star fruit was once also a man finds the immigrant immortalized
in the principal thoroughfare leading off the town square: Avenida
Carambola.

Carambola's biography makes compelling reading. As a small child,
he was one of the 11,000 Portuguese colonists evacuated from Morocco
when the garrison at Mazagão fell to the Moors in March 1769. These
340 families were shipped first to Belém, from where most were sent off
to strategic outposts of the Brazilian colony. Some stayed in the capital;
a large number crossed the estuary to the recently founded garrison
town of Macapá, and almost half of these went farther into the forests
of Amapá to settle the rice colony of a new Mazagão.[21] There are, however, no records that I have seen of refugees from this debacle heading
into the hinterlands south of Belém and no accounts of how the child
Carambola, the illiterate son of a Portuguese man and an African slave,
grew up to become the largest producer of timber in this part of the
Amazon.

At the very least, Carambola's mercantile universe would have
stretched between his immediate forests and the fast-growing city of
Belém, the regional market nexus and administrative center of the vast
province of Grão-Pará. Although he lived in the municipality of Igarapé-
Miri and married from the town's society register, the nature of the
extractive economy in Amazonia would have compelled Carambola to
establish debt-credit relationships in Belém that effectively bypassed a
dependence on local commerce. The canal promised safe passage of forest products to his urban *patrões* (patrons/buyer-suppliers) and it must
have seemed a presumptuous venture for a local merchant. But Carambola, we know, had already crossed oceans.

Regional mercantile networks extended well beyond the individual.

In fact, each person in the municipality would have been caught at different points and in different ways in the tangle of economized personalist relations called *aviamento* (from the verb *aviar*, to supply).[22] But, as well as imposing constraints, such relationships always offer opportunities. In Carambola's case, those reciprocal dependencies expressed in his links to powerful interests in Belém may have been what enabled him to establish his fractious autonomy from the normative morality of his municipal peers. Did he die out there on the creek, racked by disease, fine clothes in tatters, only Felisberto to berate? With a finely understated irony, Lobato completes the tale:

> After many years, the excommunication was finally lifted by Father Caetano Brandão, the bishop of Pará and interim governor, who was constructing a large warship in Belém, and who needed a quantity of timber that only Carambola was able to supply.[23]

Despite its individualist inception, once opened the canal was effectively public property. Successive provincial governments funded a series of improvements and maintenance works, some on a quite significant scale. In 1841, for example, only twenty years after its inauguration, thirty workers spent sixty days clearing the canal of wood and debris and shoring up its banks with stakes. Around this time, the municipality began levying a toll on vessels taking the route.

Although the Canal de Igarapé-Miri was the most important artificial waterway in this part of Pará, it was far from being the only one. Lobato comments that public money was readily forthcoming from a state administration that always showed itself willing to help such engineering projects ("sempre se faz constar as ajudas às escavações").[24] His review of funding for public works affecting the municipality makes this clear. Local and provincial government officials were preoccupied with maintaining free access through a number of canals and streams in the area during the second half of the nineteenth century. Relatively large-scale works were financed throughout this period: in 1849, along with the canal at Igarapé-Miri, maintenance money was given for the same purpose to the town of Salinas; in 1899, the year following the very grand opening of the Teatro Amazonas in Manaus, Governor José Paes de Carvalho signed a law providing money to clear not only the Canal de Igarapé-Miri, but streams at Suruú, at Soure on Marajó Island, and to drain a swamp close to the town of Porto de Mós near the mouth of the Rio Xingu. Lobato, concerned only with laws and decrees that included money specifically earmarked for his municipality, details ten projects of this type between 1841 and 1899. Then nothing for fifty years, as the region sank into decline in the aftermath of the rubber frenzy, and the canal rapidly shrank to the sorry state in which it was encountered by Buarque.[25]

Having read about the canal in Wallace, Bates, Buarque, Baptista de Moura, and Lobato, I was happy to reach Igarapé-Miri and see that, yes, the cut was still there. Nowadays, though, the journey is much easier, and I arrived in just a few hours, a crowded ferry ride and bus trip from Belém.

Igarapé-Miri is still a small town, a staging post for even smaller interior settlements such as the irresistibly named Rio das Flores (known for the local clay that supplies its roofing tile factories). There is a lively waterfront crammed with brightly painted riverboats brimming with paying passengers and goods coming from Belém, waiting for the tide to carry them upstream from the modern municipal jetty. These days, though, it seems that most traffic reaches Igarapé-Miri by road, and behind the jetty is a cavern of a bus station. There is also a handsome white church, a conveniently central place for teenagers to hang out. A few stalls selling beer, snacks and sweets line one side of the dusty plaza. Behind these, the town extends a few hundred yards along the river with one-story wooden houses standing back from the slatted boardwalk. Walking this way in the mid-afternoon sun, I first passed a row of busy workshops turning out boats of various sizes and then overgrown, muddy fields as the riverbank curves off to follow the course of the canal.

Boat-building with local timber is clearly one of the main economic activities in Igarapé-Miri today. But there are still fifty-two sugar mills in the municipality, some sending cane to Belém to be crushed into sweet juice, most producing cachaça. This is the bitter residue of a healthy market in artisanal liquor that collapsed when manufacturers of cheap, industrial rum from São Paulo established road contact with Belém and, repeating the pattern of Brazilian sugar history, drove local producers even farther into the margins. More important now for Igarapé-Miri and many of the other towns that line the estuary and dot the coast of Marajó within striking distance of Belém and Macapá are the trades in the fruit and heart-of-palm of the *açaí* palm, a floodplain staple and an urban fancy whose cultural and economic role in the contemporary estuary is hard to overestimate. Despite its immersion in the açaí boom, Igarapé-Miri has little of the bustle of its larger neighbor, Abaetetuba, a town that is working this expanding market with a vengeance.

On making the obligatory hour-long homage through the canal, I was impressed by the amount of traffic. After a number of restorations, the canal is now fully as wide as the Rio Igarapé-Miri Velho into which it flows. Workers from town were on their way to and from the large sawmill on the Rio Moju, cargo boats and barges of all sizes were heading downstream to Belém laden with Brazil nuts, sawn timber, and sacks of açaí, returning weighted down with household goods for sale here and along the Rio Tocantins. Everyone was keeping to their side as if on a two-lane highway. Nowadays, it seems, there is no need for maintenance work on this route: the huge timber barges clear any debris out of the channel as they push their way through. Vessels of this size must play havoc with those residents of Igarapé-Miri who intensified fishing and shrimping activity on the canal, even moved out here to live, in response to the evaporating job opportunities caused by President Fernando Henrique Cardoso's *Plano Real* currency stabilization. If you look carefully, there are low breaks in the forest wall where people have cut narrow channels to take them by canoe to houses and fields set back from the main stream.

Something else you may notice traveling through the canal is a change in its microgeography. Starting at Igarapé-Miri, the broad channel meanders gently in a beguilingly natural manner. The forest on each side is characteristic of the estuarine floodplain: a confusion of species often associated with human occupation—açaí, *buriti*, *imbaúba*, *pau mulato*, and, less decoratively, bamboo. Once in a short while there is a wooden house, typically raised on low stilts to stand above the flood. Then, about ten minutes before you reach the Rio Moju, there's a subtle change. The width, the vegetation, and the houses remain consistent, but the channel stops meandering, and, for the first time, takes on the aspect of a *canal*: it runs straight, like a Roman road. Geraldo, the boat owner piloting us through, explained that from here on in the channel had been dug out of the forest. From Igarapé-Miri up to this point, the slave workers had followed the course of a tiny, seasonally navigable creek, cutting, clearing, digging, and widening as they went. But from here, it was an "*escavação*," an excavation. Indeed, he said, pointing down over the side of the boat, at low tide you still need to beware of the strong currents from the submerged waterfall that marks the headwaters of this stream.

So it would have been here that the mud caved in, sweeping away those eighteen slaves sent to die by Carambola. And that story of the slave deaths (with its evocative coda in the turbulent waters that mark their graves) was the recurring motif that had sedimented in popular commentary, preserving the troubled memory of Carambola, and fixing at least one meaning of the canal among the people I talked to in Igarapé-Miri: "Muita gente morreu . . . Aquela época dos escravos era dura" ("So many people died . . . Those days of slavery were really hard").

THE ARAPIUNS BASIN

More than 500 miles upstream, on the floodplain that surrounds the city of Santarém, economic history has been quite different from that in the estuary where Igarapé Guariba and Igarapé-Miri are located. Rather than the sugar trade giving way to timber and açaí, as at Igarapé-Miri, here the trajectory has been from jute, introduced in the 1930s by Japanese immigrants, to extensive cattle and buffalo pasture, and the human depopulation that follows in its wake.[26]

In their typology of Amazonian floodplains, botanists João Murça Pires and Ghillean Prance distinguish these "true" várzea floodplains washed by the Andean sediments of the whitewater rivers from the flooded igapó forests of clear and blackwater rivers such as the Tapajós, the Arapiuns, and the Rio Negro.[27] This is a helpful clarification if you want to map an economic geography of the region, as the links among rivers, soil, and vegetation can be almost linear in Amazonia.[28] Classification based on optical properties of rivers is standard here, in both academic and local notations, and the terminology is more than descriptive. The turbidity of whitewater rivers indicates their high silt and biotic content. Clear water rivers, generally flowing from the harder pre-Cambrian shields, are transparent because of a lack of particulate nutrients. Blackwater rivers take their color from the often toxic humic and fulvic plant acids that leach in soil organic matter from their terra firme (upland forest) watersheds.[29] Logically enough, these blackwater and clear water rivers, the so-called rivers of hunger, have greatly reduced animal populations, and, as one indication of this, on arrival there is immediate relief from the armies (and air forces!) of biting flies and mosquitoes that make life on the whitewater Amazon so uncomfortable.[30]

Three rivers converge in the glistening bay in front of Santarém: the whitewater Amazon, the clear water Tapajós, and the clear water Arapiuns. It is a wonderful place to see the *encontro das águas*, the meeting of the waters—bands of different-colored water flowing parallel to each other for mile after mile, barely mixing because of their distinct sediment loads and densities. The more famous contrast between the Amazon and the blackwater Rio Negro just below Manaus is certainly impressive, but here at Santarém, several bands of water are clearly visible—Amazon *café-au-lait*, Tapajós green, and the blacker tones of the Arapiuns. Often, during the low summer tides, one stream will part on meeting an island or sandbar, somehow another will slip into the breach, and this cosmopolitan river will flow on in an ad hoc pattern of four or five stripes. Yet despite such natural drama, it was Manaus (under the aggressively entrepreneurial Governor Gilberto Mestrinho) that captured the eco-tourist itinerary of the Amazon, and visitors to Santarém are often surprised to find that this town too is a site of fluvial spectacle.

As all this might lead us to expect, ecological conditions on the várzea of the Amazon River and the floodplains of the Tapajós and Arapiuns are significantly different. It would be a mistake to assume, however, that edaphic poverty leads automatically to human poverty. It is true that the white and reddish sand igapós found bordering the Tapajós and Arapiuns support a distinct and, to my eye, lackluster vegetation with a scrubby Mediterranean look, and few of the tall, graceful palms that lend such vitality to the estuarine várzea. But the Arapiuns is sprinkled with small villages and there is an active trade with Santarém in those Amazonian carbohydrate staples *farinha d'água* and *farinha de tapioca*, gritty manioc products that are produced only with difficulty on the inundated floodplain. Mapping the lower Arapiuns basin in the 1920s, the pioneering German anthropologist Curt Nimuendajú—the inspirer of Claude Lévi-Strauss' South American inquiries—reported compacted trails known as *estradas*.[31] Farmers still use these as routes to deep and extensive deposits of *terra preta do índio*, fertile black soil, probably of pre-Columbian anthropogenic origin, on which they maintain productive agricultural colonies. These deposits were commonly found in dry upland forest and linked by the estradas to riverine settlements, often several miles away. People travel back and forth between these locations along this remarkable network of trails, many of which, worn deep and tunnel-like into the ground, also evoke an ancient history.[32]

Leaving Santarém, it takes a full four hours to cross the mouthbay of the Tapajós and reach the Arapiuns. Even here, so far from the estuary, the volume of water in this river system is astonishing. The vast bay resembles an inland sea or one of the North American Great Lakes, and is subject to the same restless weather. Henry Bates, returning from a voyage on the Tapajós in 1852, almost died here as well:

> We were driven back on the first night (October 3rd) by a squall. The light terral was carrying us pleasantly round the spit, when a small black cloud which lay near the rising moon suddenly spread over the sky to the northward; the land breeze then ceased, and furious blasts began to blow across the river. We regained, with great difficulty, the shelter of the point. It blew almost a hurricane for two hours, during the whole of which time the sky over our heads was beautifully clear and starlit. Our shelter at first was not very secure, for the wind blew away the lashings of our sails, and caused our anchor to drag. Angelo Custodio, however, seized a rope which was attached to the foremast and leapt ashore; had he not done so, we should probably have been driven many miles backwards up the storm-tossed river. After the cloud had passed, the regular east wind began to blow, and our further progress was effectually stopped for the night. The next day we all went ashore, after securing well the canoe, and slept from eleven o'clock till five under the shade of trees.[33]

Bates might have expected something similar. The dry season, the period Amazonians call *verão*, acknowledging it as a form of summer, is a time of unpredictable winds, sudden storms, and dangerous tides. In Santarém, there is a 36-foot drop in water levels between the height of the seasons, and sandbars, islands, and beaches migrate, to reappear almost out of nowhere, challenging the reflexes of local sailors. Vegetation standing on dry sand at this time of year may have been completely submerged in the long, wet *inverno*, the Amazonian winter, and how it manages to photosynthesize for months on end under such conditions is still not entirely clear.

This landscape of the middle Amazon has a chimerical quality all its own, a bewildering instability different from that of the estuary. In those lower deltaic reaches, people sit on front porches overlooking the water and watch giant fallen trees and big chunks of riverbank flow out to sea with the tide. In winter, with the heavy rains and swollen rivers, an eerie long-distance procession forms, and the estuary takes on a surreal aspect, filled with floating islands of long *canarana* grass descended with small animals and clouds of insects from who-knows-where, possibly hundreds of miles upstream—the very same islands I saw bobbing quietly at the mouth of the Tapajós outside Santarém, readying themselves for the long voyage down to the sea.

Unlike the Tapajós and the Amazon, the Arapiuns moves unnervingly slowly, especially in its broad lower course, where, as Harald Sioli, the eminent limnologist who first worked here in the 1950s, observed with descriptive precision, the river represents "an elongated lake."[34] Upstream, above the Cachoeira do Aruá (a wide and violent set of rapids beyond the division of the Arapiuns into the Rio Aruá and the Rio Maró), the dark water coils around in great meanders, doubling back on itself, passing silently between steep walls of high forest. To evade the rapids in summer when the waters are low, people take one of the estradas, the land trails described by Nimuendajú. These paths take them past fields planted with manioc and by huddles of clay-and-thatch houses built close to the low, swampy bank of the Aruá. The people who rely on these routes maintain them with machetes and *enxadas* (heavy, sharp-edged hoes) in organized annual *limpezas*, or cleanings, keeping them wide enough for oxcarts and smooth enough for bumpy bike rides, scraping off the accumulated litter from a broad passage that sinks lower each year.

Still, if you are paddling a canoe between the dispersed settlements on its banks, a river like this is hard work. And the big, slow bends that lead almost nowhere are particularly frustrating. On the Rio Aruá, residents have made their lives easier by cutting short channels that chop off a loop, allowing a canoe to pass in a more or less straight line through a forest tunnel and out again onto the open river. People living beside the Aruá also describe communal limpezas that serve to maintain these canals. I arrived here with my friend Michael Reynolds and we met up with Joe McCann, who has been conducting research on the history and uses of terra preta in this area. An elderly man told us that he himself had cut one of these channels across the river from his house, digging out the tree roots through the forest with an enxada to access a tiny, seasonal *rego*, a creek. The slow current gradually stripped away the heavy clay *tabatinga* soil, he said, and opened a channel 3 or 4 yards wide. He lent us a canoe, so we followed his directions and paddled up to take a look. Sure enough, there was a narrow break in the forest wall, and we left the almost silent river to slip into a coolly shaded atrium about 50 yards from end to end, where the transparent, shallow water flowed rapidly before scooting us out into the bright sunlight once again.

People here used the word *varadores*, a term I had not heard before, to identify these anthropogenic channels.[35] As you might expect from those who live in a landscape dominated by water and tides, their vocabulary, like that of other *ribeirinhos*—as people who live along the rivers are sometimes known in the region—is particularly rich in designations for watercourses. Precise distinctions are drawn between waterways according to length, depth, type of water, seasonality, and other relevant factors. At least, so it would appear at first glance. As well as igapé, rego, rio, canal, várzea, and igapó, words I have already used in this chapter, after a few days in a village on the Amazon floodplain, a visitor might also have heard *rio-mar*, *riacho*, *atalho*, *mupéua*, *furo*, *paraná*, *córrego*, *caminho*, *água grande*, *água pequena*, *água parada*, *reponta*, *préamar*, *pacuema*, *lancante*, *remanso*, and *mondongo*. Many of these, especially those derived from Tupi, are regionally endemic. Others are more generally Brazilian but have specific local associations. All are likely to be complicated by their diminutives: *regozinho*, for instance, or, even, *águazinho*, little water.

I found guidance in Vicente Chermont de Miranda's *Glossário Paraense*, a slim dictionary of rural Amazonian usages that I spotted (in a moment of obsessive but serendipitous distraction) in a stall selling used books at a lively open-air party during the annual Festas Juninhas in Belém.[36] Chermont de Miranda compiled his glossary in 1904, the same year W. H. Hudson's best-selling fable *Green Mansions: A Romance of the Tropical Forest* went on sale in London. Hudson deploys the standard device of the enchanted faery glen to evoke the types of magical forest recesses created by the diggers of the varadores, and he employs it without restraint, conjuring a tropical idyll in the midst of the forest:

> I spent several hours in this wild paradise, which was so much
> more delightful than the extensive gloomier forests I had so

often penetrated in Guayana: for here, if the trees did not attain
to such majestic proportions, the variety of vegetable forms was
even greater; as far as I went it was nowhere dark under the
trees, and the number of lovely parasites everywhere illustrated
the kindly influence of light and air. Even where the trees were
largest the sunshine penetrated, subdued by the foliage to ex-
quisite greenish-golden tints, filling the wide lower spaces with
tender half-lights, and faint blue-and-grey shadows. Lying on
my back and gazing up, I felt reluctant to rise and renew my
ramble. For what a roof was that above my head![37]

Chermont de Miranda's investments were expressed rather differently. I like to think of the contrast between his classificatory logic and
Hudson's extravagant Romanticism not as one between a modern scientific sensibility and something now archaic, but rather as a measure of
the awkward but not unhappy coexistence of disparate and contradictory ways of knowing Amazonian nature. Very often, for instance, and
without having to look too hard, we find the pantheistic in the scientis-
tic. But Chermont de Miranda's glossary is interesting in its own right.
Surprisingly, despite immediate appearances, his book leads us to think
about everyday life on these Amazonian rivers.

When he returned from his studies in Lisbon to sell his parents'
loss-making sugar mill on the Rio Capim, not far from Igarapé-Miri in
eastern Pará, Vicente Chermont de Miranda made a highly satisfactory
marriage into the Dutch upper class, and entered Paraense society envi-
ably situated, a scientist-politician, wanting neither money nor cultural
capital. He would eventually complete a series of studies on the natural
history of nearby Marajó Island, but his particular triumph was the
Glossário Paraense. In it he provides comprehensive definitions for
most of the watery terms I listed above, and he includes others: *arroio*,
repiquete, *baixas*, and *perau*. As a luminary of the Liberal Party, Chermont de Miranda would have had little sympathy for his socialist contemporary Baptista de Moura, the engineer-poet who had passed through
the canal at Igarapé-Miri less than ten years before. Somehow, though,
in his writing, political elitism does not prevent him from combining
pedantic hauteur with a less expected dialogic sensitivity, frequently
clarifying terms by including examples of their usage in local speech. He
is rigorous too. Here is his discussion of rego, which I earlier rashly
translated as "creek":

REGO, n.m. — Gullies, fed by rain water, start as shallow streams; while they are snaking their way through the savanna [*campo*], exposed to the atmosphere, they dry up, becoming narrower and more shallow, and take the name *regos*. Where they are shaded by trees at the margins, they are known as *igarapés*. During the severe dry season the shallow streams and *regos* dry up, leaving only the *igarapés* in their upper reaches, receiving river water at full tide, becoming dry at low tide. On the savannas of Marajó, perennial water does not exist, as has been erroneously reported by Professor Orville Derby. *A Ilha de Marajó, by Professor Orville Derby, Boletim do Museu Goeldi, vol. II, p. 170.*[38]

Clearly, Chermont de Miranda can find plenty to say about streams. His definition of igarapé, which focuses mostly on questions of etymology, takes up a full page. And there is no doubt that his text was unique in its day, a labor of dedication and connection, still fascinating for those of us trying to come to grips with vocabulary that rarely find its way into standard Portuguese dictionaries.[39] Moreover, the *Glossário Paraense* embodies an affection and regard for ribeirinho culture, a persistent current in urban Amazonia but one that is often, although not here, sentimentalized, and that is neither universal nor, necessarily, unambiguous.

Chermont de Miranda sent me to Igarapé Guariba with an anticipatory sense of the complexity of native cognitive categories. However, in my attempts to fix these categories, to tie words to definitions and definitions to concrete examples, I rapidly found myself at sea on this expanding river. The terms existed in popular usage, and I had no trouble identifying a declamatory context, much as had Chermont de Miranda himself. But there was nothing fixed about that context, and words refused to be tied down. It was not only that different people used the same word with different meanings; it was more that these supposedly highly specific terms seemed largely interchangeable.

"Mupéua" is a case in point. This was a word that became important to me, partly because it was unusual (Chermont de Miranda does not list it), but more because, for some people, it signified the work of humans. A friend, a middle-school teacher, who was transcribing interview tapes for me in Macapá, knit her brow when she heard this strange word and sought out her boyfriend's father, a man who had

spent most of his life living and working on rural Marajó. The definition he gave her was exact and, at the same time, intriguing: "A small,
shallow river, a streamlet (riacho), opened by manual labor in upland
forest" ("aberto pelo mão do homen em terra firme"). Yet, this clarification threw no new light on the portion of the tape that had confused
her, a conversation between two elderly men in Igarapé Guariba:

> *Seu Benedito:* When we arrived here, what was it like . . . it
> was narrow.
>
> *João Preto:* It was a mupéua.
>
> *Seu Benedito:* There was a . . .
>
> *João Preto:* It was a mupéua.

A few days later I asked Seu Benedito what a mupéua was. "Just a
rego," he said, without much interest, "a little furo."

I turned to the classics. Valentin Vološinov's *Marxism and the Philosophy of Language*, a revolutionary revision of linguistic theory written in the 1920s, is marked by both precision and creativity. Vološinov
(most likely the great Russian linguist Mikhail Bakhtin writing under a
politically expedient pseudonym) reconfigures Saussure's linguistics
by considering what happens to the structural formalities of language
when it is thrown around in the rough-and-tumble of social speech. For
Vološinov, "the meaning of a word is determined entirely by its context.
In fact," he tells us, "there are as many meanings of a word as there are
contexts for its usage." While also possessing an intrinsic unity, a word
has what he calls "polysemanticity."[40] Resolving this paradox is a task
for which Saussure, with his stiff and unconvincing models of social
interaction, is ill-equipped. Vološinov's solution is characteristically
elegant:

> Actually, any real utterance, in one way or another or to one
> degree or another, makes a statement of agreement with or a
> negation of something. Contexts do not stand side by side in a
> row, as if unaware of one another, but are in a state of constant
> tension, or incessant interaction and conflict.[41]

Vološinov gives us a theory of language-in-motion, a theory in
which the very act of plucking a word from its relational moment in
time and space to extract a general definition is both utopian and

wrongheaded. Which is not to say that the *Glossário* is useless, only that the definitions won't work unless some serious thought is given to the context in which the words are being used and to the relationship of the speakers to each other and to their broader surroundings.

A rego and an igarapé, an igarapé and a furo, a riacho and a canal. At times these become equivalent pairs. At others, their distinct meanings are contextually apparent, and, like a glossary, we can allocate and codify them as if they represented the substance of an indigenous knowledge.[42] But such definitions will be shattered in speech, as when a long-suffering interlocutor finally lost patience: "Look, this is the Amazon. You know, we're very easygoing about this kind of thing; we're very flexible. Sometimes it's a furo, sometimes it's an atalho. That's the way it is."

Chermont de Miranda does not include varador in his glossary. But he does have an entry for the closely related *varadouro*.[43] This he defines as a shortcut across the várzea — ironically enough, in his text, both a "canal" and an "atalho." Indeed, atalho, which can be any kind of shortcut, by water, road, boat, or foot, is a word that people in the Arapiuns often use when pressed to redefine varador. Varador is related to the feminine noun, *vara*, signifying the long pole used to propel canoes through muddy or swampy passages, or to guide river launches in or out of moorings. "Vara" also leads to the transitive verb *varar*, which means to travel through or into, either with or without the aid of a vara, but which, in my understanding, connotes a certain degree of difficulty, the way in English you might say "we made it home." However, while varar accurately expresses the function of the Arapiuns varadores as places through which a person travels, it glosses their heterogeneity.

The same elderly man who directed us to the varador on the Rio Aruá described a large number of such passages along the length of that river. Several dry up in summer when the water level in the river drops, forcing people to take the long route. In these months, however, there is less river traffic anyway, as people use the estradas of the terra firme to move between their houses and fields.

A couple of hours downstream from here, near a small Protestant community on the Rio Arapiuns called Monte Sião (Mount Zion), there is a broad zone of what Pires and Prance call igapó, flooded blackwater forest that grows up from the muddy depths. Here, an energetic woman we met described interventions at the mouth of a swampy stream called

Igarapé Nazário. It made a useful route to a terra preta colony, she explained, and was kept open by chopping with machetes as you guided your canoe through the grasses, vines, and sprouting aquatic plants, easing past the branches and fallen trunks that rose, spectral, piercing the dark, reflective surface of the river.

Many of the dry season walking and oxcart trails in the Arapiuns basin double as canoe routes in winter, and there are some that have a brittle feel underfoot where the water has retreated, leaving a ghostly scum on the leaves. Other channels are small natural openings that local people work at until they become viable waterways. One example, the Varador Comprido (Long Varador), a channel wide and deep enough to pass through in a sizable boat, has stretches of a vicious, knife-like sedge called *tiririca* that closes over and has to be repeatedly cut back by teams of men and boys.

People showed me channels in the Arapiuns that they had manipulated to facilitate transport and open up areas for fishing and perhaps hunting. Although modest on an individual scale, the streams as a whole appeared to make a significant contribution to people's capacity to get by in this relatively resource-poor environment. Such practices, and, in this case, the associated use of terra preta, undermine the attempts of scholars to produce causative models in which it is nature, even if in the last instance, that determines culture and political economy. This might seem rather obvious, but I offer it in response to those ecologically derived frameworks that use such concepts as "carrying capacity" to characterize the relationship between people and their landscapes and which seem often to lead into non-specific and authoritarian arguments about population limits and control, arguments that have been profoundly influential in recent debates on globalization and international development.[44]

All of the anthropogenic channels in the Arapiuns were called varadores, but not all varadores had been manipulated. In this sense, the term "varador" was analogous to canal, atalho, and mupéua, words that may signify anthropogenesis but that by their ambivalence also work to hide the human dimensions of the fluvial landscape. For convenience, and as an appreciative gesture to Vicente Chermont de Miranda, etymologist and dialogician, I divide the Arapiuns channels into two broad categories according to geomorphological context and type of intervention:[45]

1. Passages dug with hoes, scythes, and machetes that shorten routes

along upland streams and rivers. These are often high-water routes only and may not exist in summer when travelers would have to follow the meander.

2. Routes cut through above-ground igapó vegetation that shorten travel distance for watercraft of various types and that allow people to enter an area to fish or to reach a house or settlement. These may be seasonal routes through the floodplain that serve as dry trails in summer and canoe paths in winter. They are maintained by people with machetes as they pass through.

THE RIO NEGRO

Sitting on the edge of the sandy sidewalk in Alter do Chão one perfect evening in June 1996, waiting for the bus to Santarém and suffused with that warm sense of well-being that comes so easily from a day spent on the beach and in the water, I started talking to Vitor. In 1853, Henry Walter Bates, fighting losing battles against bats, cockroaches, fire ants, and spiders, called Alter do Chão "one of the most wretched, starved, ruinous villages that could be found on the earth."[46] But in 1995, *Veja*, the leading weekly Brazilian news magazine, featured this tiny town, an hour by road from Santarém, as a hideaway of outstanding beauty, bathed by the crystal waters of the mighty Tapajós, an essential destination despite the long flight from Rio or São Paulo. In summer, when the tides drop to expose a chain of sparkling white sandbars, jeweled stepping-stones to the green hill with its spectacular views over the confluence of the Tapajós, Amazon, and Arapiuns rivers, it's easy to share the travel writer's enthusiasm.

Vitor was tall, affable, and disarmingly good-looking in an outdoorsy way. Like me, he was waiting for the bus back to the city. He asked what I was doing in the Amazon, what my research was about, and then made that familiar metamorphosis from a chance acquaintance to what social scientists, like detectives, call an "informant," tacitly acknowledging the moral ambiguity of the trade in information: "So they cut channels and the land changes. So what? Everyone does that. Those things are everywhere. It's hardly a big deal."

Vitor worked at the reception desk of a fancy hotel in Manaus, but previously, it turned out, he had been an eco-tourist guide on the Rio Negro, far upstream from Alter do Chão. He was full of engaging anecdotes about irascible foreigners stranded overnight on sandbanks and getting closer to tropical nature than they might have wanted. His stories reminded me that in the climax to *The Clio*, L. H. Myers had grounded the cruise ship just below Óbidos and kept his world-weary aristocrats and scheming *arrivistes* helplessly trapped as Latin American revolution swirled around and the forest inexorably engulfed them.[47] And, later, thinking back, I remembered Manoel, working on a small boat that sat helpless at anchor for twelve hours in midstream on the Rio Arapiuns with a broken piston. Manoel, who had sought out Michael and myself on deck especially to say: "So I guess this is your Amazon adventure, *né?*"

Vitor's job had involved taking tourists out of Manaus in diesel-powered covered launches and transferring them to large canoes driven by outboard motors. From this more mobile but less sturdy transport, they could view wildlife and vegetation up close in the narrow igarapés off the Rio Negro. He had enjoyed this active life more than the hotel work to which he was confined when we met, and he was puzzled as to why I was wasting time researching something as commonplace as stream-making in the Amazon. "All the igarapés up there are man-made," he explained with what I took to be hyperbole. "People dig them out to get to their fields or to make shortcuts, to cut out a bend in the river or something. They cut them right through the high forest. You know who did it by the name: Igarapé Maria, Igarapé Joaquim. . . . It's the name of the person who cut it."

Vitor's comments were casual and imprecise, a weak form of data. But they signaled a structure of feeling and added to an accretive order of evidence, a situated, expanding facticity. It was the sense of anticlimax in Vitor's narrative, his easy affirmation of intimacy with the fluvial landscape — the assertion that *everybody* knows about this stuff — that gave his comments such power.

It is partly because of conversations like these that I have come to see labor in every Amazon stream. Now, when I look at the landscape, I imagine histories of creativity. When I travel along rivers, I picture the multiple agencies of human and non-human actors. When I hear talk of nature, the words have a specific resonance, a lived referentiality. But I also remember John Berger's warning, double-edged now: "Landscapes can be deceptive."[48]

It is the impression of stasis that beguiles. They may look secure, but landscapes are always in motion, always in process. In Igarapé Guariba, the energy of the non-human is so excessive that it forces recognition. The river will not allow you to ignore it. The land shifts of its own accord. The banks crumble, the fields flood, the orchards float off to the horizon. This is not saying anything new about Amazonia. On the contrary, discourse on the region has so strongly claimed the dominance of nature and the correlative subjection of people that statements of this type can be perilous. Because of this, they have to be situated in that other form of fluvial practice, the genealogical, deep in the evidentiary, the space where facts get made out of history, theory, and strategy.[49]

Deeply informed by Malthusian notions of natural limits and in dialogue with emergent Spencerian ideas of social progress through struggle, mid-nineteenth-century commentary on what was becoming "the tropics" often relied on a racialized variant of environmental determinism. As we will see in Chapter 5, Victorian travelers found the super-fecundity of Amazonian nature nurturing a population corrupted by the indolence of daily life in a land of such potential that the failure of productivity was doubly offensive. By the time of Julian Steward's massive *Handbook of South American Indians* (1946–50), this assessment had undergone a stark reversal—yet without displacing the encompassing episteme. Evolutionary models still underwrote social theory and continued to be tied to an environmental causality.[50] The absence of progress was still deeply troubling. Nature and race were again the principal culprits. But the motor was now negative circumscription: it was the overwhelming poverty of the natural environment that determined social life. Human agency was again radically restricted in a region that, as Steward put it, "imposed many serious difficulties on all activities."[51]

Steward divided South America into four "culture areas," binding people and place through the reifications of material culture.[52] This was a model underwritten by eighteenth-century theories of race and culture, particularly those of Kant and Herder, and funneled through Friedrich Ratzel's anthropogeography and its North American expression in the work of Ellen Churchill Semple.[53] It relied on "cultural adaptation," a key category that was to exert a long-term and baleful influence on subsequent anthropological work in the Amazon. Steward animated research on the region—much of it directly via his students at Columbia University and later at the University of Illinois. Northern South America became a favored location for the elaboration of "cultural ecology," and the 1960s and 1970s saw the focusing of considerable energy around a single problematic: What were the environmental limiting factors that produced such restricted cultural development and inchoate forms of social organization in the region?[54]

This narrow preoccupation with the constraints of given biophysical conditions provoked some exasperatingly protracted debates in the North American Amazonianist literature — most famously that concerned with the limitation on "social development" enforced by a supposed lack of protein available to native populations.[55] It also led directly to the work of Betty Meggers, a research associate in South American archaeology at the Smithsonian, who elegantly glossed the adaptationist position that was to drive her own investigations for almost half a century: "The level to which a culture can develop," she declared, "is dependent upon the agricultural potentiality of the environment it occupies."[56] Invoking Steward — but more suggestive of the later cultural materialism of Marvin Harris[57] — Meggers allocated the tropical forest environment to the "Type 2 culture area . . . [a region] of limited agricultural potential," suitable only for swidden agriculture, and, accordingly, restricting society to the "tribal level of organization."[58] Agricultural potential was reducible to soil fertility, itself understood as a fixed set of conditions. Not only was the environment dominant and determining, but its cultural effects were predictable.

Meggers offered a stripped-down version of cultural ecology. In her hands, Steward's evolutionism became resolutely unilinear and his willingness to countenance flexibility between natural constraint and sociocultural organization was largely discarded. In other respects, though, Meggers was faithful. With her husband Clifford Evans, a Smithsonian curator, she conducted extensive research in the Amazon estuary at habitation mound-sites of the Marajoara settlement phase.[59] In her interpretation of these data she reiterated the diffusionist position of the Handbook. Without the ecological conditions for transformative technology to develop endogenously through intensification, she argued, evidence of more complex culture within the tropical forest zone could only be explained as intrusion from the Andean "hearth."[60] Indeed, any more "advanced" group — such as the people of the Marajoara phase — unfortunate enough to find themselves within such an impoverished environment were doomed to decline.[61]

At the time Meggers was publishing her most widely read work, the monograph *Amazonia: Man and Nature in a Counterfeit Paradise* (1971), researchers were documenting pre-Columbian initiatives that included monumental irrigation earthworks, raised fields, and long-distance trading networks, indigenous projects that looked considerably more like transformative labor than simple adaptation.[62] Scholarship of this type and its successor work of the 1980s pointed to a decisive shift toward environmental possibilism, a looser, more agnostic form of causation. Indeed, by the 1980s a significant reconfiguration of Amazonianist cultural ecology was under way, most obviously in the highly influential work of William Balée, William Denevan, Darrell Posey, and Anna Roosevelt.[63] Through paying close attention to biotic and geomorphological variation, dynamics, and plasticity, and to the associated ecological knowledges of local residents, these scholars began to imagine a radically distinct account of regional history. Roosevelt, for example, constructed a powerful and restitutive narrative of pre-colonial Amazonia around ethnohistorical readings of the early chronicles of European exploration and her own excavations of urban scale sites on the lower and middle Amazon, settlements that radically transgressed the presumed limits of the Stewardian tropical forest culture area.[64]

Roosevelt has argued strongly against "ethnographic projection," the reading of historical Amazonian social relations from the modern context.[65] Instead, she has reinserted the demographic collapse that accompanied colonial encounter, presenting data to support the eyewitness descriptions of dense settlements lining the rivers in the sixteenth century. Similarly, she and her collaborators have established a far deeper temporal frame than had previously been allowed, their dating of 11,000-year-old rock paintings and other material from a cave near Monte Alegre suggesting an entirely new sequence for the occupation of the Americas as a whole and challenging the Clovis hypothesis with evidence of a parallel and distinctive human presence in Amazonia by the late Pleistocene.[66]

Other scholars have emphasized the ability of contemporary and historical Amazonian populations actively to produce new environments at a variety of scales. Posey's careful documentation of the Kayapó forest islands — species-rich "gardens" that the Kayapó assemble by foraging over a vast territory — was groundbreaking in this regard.[67] And, through attention to species composition and density, as well as to the presence of terra preta, Balée has argued convincingly for the "biocultural" origins of at least 12 percent of the region's contemporary landscape and for the continuing significance of such sites to forest and savanna populations.[68]

Long before these studies, cultural ecologists, including Meggers and Evans, had encountered similar manipulations. Even in the *Handbook*, Alfred Métraux had documented interfluvial anthropogenic channels connecting Mojo villages in the Bolivian Amazon.[69] Yet, these scholars provided little interpretative space for the analysis of their finds. Such phenomena were either downplayed, ignored, or, where too significant to disregard, attributed to Andean or Mesoamerican diffusion. The explicit emphasis in the work of Balée and others on the dynamic co-production of people and landscape thus represents a significant shift away from the hegemony of determinism and offers the basis for an overdue rethinking of the orthodoxy of adaptation. It presumes a strong notion of human agency, yet continues to emphasize the materiality of the biophysical, the agency of the non-human. It foregrounds history, while moving us toward the practices of intimacy that produce and sustain everyday life, those differentiated and contingent socialities that Laura Rival—writing out of this emergent literature—has glossed as the "social relationships" that bind "human groups and living organisms."[70] It is, as Mao insisted, all about social practice: practices of meaning, production, representation, and politics. The practices of landscape-makers and the practices of researchers.

AMAPÁ

The stories proliferate. Nowadays, so far from Alter do Chão, I know of these channels throughout the Amazon, and friends make me into an archive, sending messages about varadores, canais, and atalhos they have followed from Maranhão all the way to Acre.

Once alive to the textures of fluvial intervention the signs are everywhere. In Amapá, I find them at every turn. One time, on the Rio Pedreira, the deep, dark river from which Indians hauled stone to build the fort at Macapá in the mid-eighteenth century, I stopped at a ranch house that sits at the mouth of an igarapé on a grassy plain of cattle pasture and spoke to a guarded woman who took me by surprise, assuming that I wanted a channel like hers. "You couldn't do it these days," she confided, arms folded across her chest. "You could never afford to pay what these peasants want." But why had she and her husband invested so much in digging out this broad stream that now

links up with the next river, 2 miles away? "Because we wanted an
igarapé and there wasn't one." And then, speaking as one who knew
her catfish: "Now we can catch *filhote*."

Time and again, these managed waters percolate in chance conversation, as on that tense day I ferried poor crazy Lene with her three
crosses of malaria to the clinic at Santo Antonio, pale, unnaturally still,
and, we feared, near death in the bottom of the boat. As I squatted
outside in the shadeless sun, the elderly bar owner from across the clearing offered me lunch and talked in a soothing monologue about his
capital plan for the business and its centerpiece, a *viveiro*, a fish-trap for
raising fish and river-turtles, 15 yards wide and 150 yards long, dug out
mechanically in an extended "L" parallel to the river. Or again: discuss-
ing buffalo over dinner one evening with a friend whose father owned a
ranch on Ilha Caviana, I heard for the first time that years before he had
worked with his brothers to dig a mile-long channel to drain winter
pasture: "It rots the animals' hooves to stand too long in the flood," he
explained between mouthfuls of barbecue.[71]

Then there are the stories told by maps. Like the one drawn of
Amapá in 1808 on which a river is marked *Obstruido*, with the explan-
atory note: "Furo Araguarí blocked off on the orders of Conde de V$^{\underline{a}}$
Flor."[72] And, of course, place-names are cultural histories in themselves.[73]
A few hours downstream toward the ocean from Igarapé Guariba is
Igarapé Novo, which, we might speculate, may not have been there
long. People in Igarapé Guariba could not say much about Igarapé
Novo except that the original stream was cut in the 1960s or 1970s as
part of the local landlord's campaign to exploit the timber market, and
that it is now about as wide as the Rio Guariba. One man I know has a
cousin there: "When you return, we'll go," he promised. "With that
outboard motor, we could be there and back in a day."

Just one more. I called Octávio da Gama on the recommendation of
his ex-boss, for many years a logger, now an expert in reforestation who
manages the rolling recuperation of the vast Trombetas bauxite strip
mine in the middle Amazon. Octávio was friendly and seemed eager to
meet. I found his spacious white bungalow, tucked away in Santa Rita,
a prosperous neighborhood of Macapá, without difficulty. As always in
September, it was a blistering day, and we sat out on Octávio's shaded
patio and drank cokes and ate cookies that the maid brought us on a
silver tray. Gradually, Octávio warmed to his subject: the glory days of

Amazon logging. He had plenty of time to talk. I doubt he was much more than fifty, but his career was already over, and it was only too obvious that unemployment was not a life to which he had taken well.

Octávio had been a manager for Bruynzeel Madeiras S/A (BRU-MASA), a Dutch company whose domination of the Amapá timber trade can be readily gauged by a glance at any of the Ministry of Planning's annual statistical almanacs during the 1970s. At the foot of each page of data on timber extraction, processing, or export, there's a one-word note on the source: "BRUMASA."

Like Indústria e Comércio de Minérios S/A (ICOMI), a North American mining company that in the 1920s captured access to the considerable local magnesium deposits, BRUMASA's Brazilian operation was eventually bought out by Grupo CAEMI, a national consortium that had benefited significantly from federal disbursements under the POL-AMAZONIA development program of 1974. Unlike ICOMI, however, BRUMASA, along with Octávio's job, was liquidated once the supply of easily accessible estuarine timber had disappeared.

BRUMASA's main sawmill was in Santana, a booming port 20 miles from Macapá. But their operations extended to Marajó, both channels of the estuary as far upstream as Gurupá, and, according to Octávio, they even owned land and contracted collectors west of Manaus. In their efforts to get the big trees, BRUMASA combined their muscle with imagination. To really appreciate their operation, it helps to remember just how inhospitable the estuarine várzea can be. As well as the disease, insects, and animals that trouble everyday experience, industrial extraction has to contend with a radically unstable terrain. The earth moves. It makes and remakes itself with the twice-daily tides. At low tide it sucks you down into waist-deep mud; by high tide, much of the forest is a swamp. There are plenty of trees lining the banks of rivers and streams, but many more deep in the woods. Under such conditions, how do you get in there and bring them out?

Octávio had a flair for the dramatic. Without explanation, he left the patio, returning with a small stack of bleached-out color photographs. They had been taken during one of his field operations. The first showed bare-backed ribeirinhos working on what looked like a railroad through flooded várzea forest. This, he told me, with pleasure at my amazement, was a *madeiravia*, a wood-road. The company brought in the rails pre-sawn from *maçaranduba*, a highly resistant terra firme timber, and the locally recruited temporary workers cut trees on-site for the ties. It was simple. They hacked their way into the forest and laid the wood-road across the swamp as far as an interior clearing to which other men were dragging the felled trees. Then they rolled the rail trucks off the boats and pushed them, inch by inch, out and then back along the tracks, weighed down with the giant logs cut deep in the forest.

Their other strategy was to dig canals. Octávio's second photograph was of a sizable barge, more like a motorized raft, a vessel Amazonians call a *balsa* and which you often see plying the big rivers loaded with logs, containers, or vehicles. Like most balsas, BRUMASA's came with a cabin and sleeping quarters and it was flat-bottomed, designed with minimal draft to pull right up to the shoreline and navigate shoals and sandbars. But there were a couple of significant differences: at the front it had a giant mechanical digger, and at the rear a large horizontal rectangular slab of wood. It was an adapted dredger.

During the late 1970s, BRUMASA's balsa saw a lot of action. The company used it to bludgeon nearly 20 miles of channels in the municipality of Breves in the southwest of Marajó. They tore up the land at the rate of 100 yards a day, carving a ditch 6 yards wide and 3 yards deep into which the rivers poured. They plowed straight through the forest, slicing at the trees with chainsaws as they went. An unstoppable juggernaut. "We could go wherever we wanted," said Octávio.[74]

It would really be something to visit those places today. The channels must still be there, although wider and deeper, the powerful estuarine tide continuing the work of the loggers. I imagine the people there living along the crumbling banks of the canals just like people in Igarapé Guariba and Igarapé-Miri, the streams now deeply part of a world of hunting, fishing, and canoes that the water makes possible, a world in which people manage the açaí to which BRUMASA, without thought for the lives or landscapes it was invading, gave access.

It is easy to drown in all this movement among earth, people, and water, to sink in its ubiquity and idiosyncrasies. But didn't Chermont de Miranda always keep his head above the tide he never tired of defining? And even though to me these channels finally all mean the same, that won't stop them from sliding in and out of categories.

Although the urge to typology seems to diminish this Amazonia of restless landscapes and practical people, of the foundational intimacy of multiple materialities, the urge itself has an irresistible aesthetic that intensifies its logic. The seductions of classification should not be denied. Think about technology and capitalization: comparing channels stripped with mechanical diggers and customized barges to ones cut by men struggling through mud with enxadas and machetes. Or the question of initial motivation and subsequent utilization: whether the channel is primarily seen as a shortcut to somewhere else or as a site of resource extraction in its own right. There is the matter of the environment in which the intervention is made: its soils, vegetation, and water qualities. Or, a more sociological approach: an examining of the roles in canal production of discretely analyzable social actors. We could identify channels initiated by individuals and collectivities with principal allegiances at a community level, others opened by members of the provincial elite, others by corporate elements of the regional economy with secure links to national and international capital circuits, and still others cut by organized sectors of the state itself. And, always historical conjuncture: associating interventions with particular moments in Amazonian history — the eighteenth- and nineteenth-century slave economies, the nineteenth- and early-twentieth-century rubber trade, the timber and cattle frenzies of the 1970s. Or, archaeological conjecture and links to pre-Columbian economies. And what about the country and the city, a distinction between urban and rural manipulations, including in the former those giant projects of damming, channeling, and draining igarapés carried out during the construction of Belém and Macapá?

The value of classificatory categories lies in more than their dismantling. Sometimes, the juxtaposition of taxa gives a shock of illumination. At other moments, there are other satisfactions, albeit more prosaically heuristic. The anthropogenic channels of Amazonia — great and small, old and new — are moments in the life of a region. Like grains of sand, their presence lies in their spectacular multiplicity; yet, they are also little gems, self-contained and faceted histories of counterpoint and relief. They signal other worlds, so normal, commonplace, and everyday, yet also unfamiliar, and, in the persistence of that difference, revelatory of the boundaries that circumscribe inquiry.

The porosity of the borders between earth and water in this terra anfíbia marks another order of fluidity. It offers an opportunity to reflect on both the insubstantiality of categories and on the work that they accomplish: on the instrumental logic that holds apart the everyday from the historical, the natural from the artificial, the local from the global, the human from the non-human. We can follow these channels, swim in their waters, float in their currents. We can suffer their intimacies as they take us to places in a different region, on another set of maps. Another place, right here, yet unmistakably different. Another place entirely. The Amazonian waters I know best run through Igarapé Guariba. We have barely broken their surface.

3

IN THE FLOW OF BECOMING
Igarapé Guariba, 1941–1996

How Did This Place Come into Existence? — Octávio, Race, and
Nature — Timber and the Political Economy of Place-Making . . .
and Unmaking — The River That Time Forgot — The Patrão, the
Caboclo, and the Cultural Politics of Aviamento — The Simple
Man — Onto the Maps of Modernity — Hard Work and Discursive
Practice — Imprinting Locality on Landscape — Heavy, Fat Fish —
Above the Waterfall — Digging, Digging, Digging — And More
Digging — They Knew Where They Were Going — Two Aerial
Photos — The Story of O Centro — Long Unraveling and Systemic
Collapse — A New Regime — Many Natures, Many Places — These
Truly Are the Things That Matter!

I walked on shimmering pavement to meet Octávio da Gama, the ex-
logger whose dredger ate the islands of Marajó. By night, Macapá is a
party town for some, and a dance club marks the line of the equator.
But under the relentless summer heat all is flat, dusty-red, and shadeless,
and Octávio's leafy patio was cool relief.

Inevitably, it was our current selves that met that afternoon, "all the
earlier phases of development continu[ing] to exist alongside the latest
one," as Freud once said, remembering Rome.[1] Octávio seemed bound
in frustration, forced retirement leaving no outlet for the decisive mind
and powerful body that had once traveled rivers and commanded men.
And I was newly obsessed by the landscapes of Igarapé Guariba, worrying constantly at one expanding question: How did this place come into
existence?

"How did this place come into existence?" It was Octávio who
revealed the question's possibilities. Perched in the BRUMASA offices
above the port of Santana, he had received wood for many years from
Raimundo Viega's sawmill in Igarapé Guariba. And, although he had

never actually set foot in Igarapé Guariba, he was not about to let that be an impediment to theory-making.

BRUMASA controlled the Amazon timber trade from the beginnings of the logging boom in the early 1960s through to the 1980s. They bought up vast stretches of the estuary and built a state-of-the-art sawmill at Santana. They processed high-value timber for export, either to the south of Brazil, to the United States, or to Europe, and they sold cheaper lumber for construction in the local market. They operated largely by contract, buying logs from independent third parties who set up poorly capitalized, inefficient, and mostly short-lived sawmills at the mouths of distant rivers. BRUMASA's operations extended from Santana past Manaus, nearly 1,000 miles upstream. They bought wood cut in Igarapé Guariba until there was no more worth buying, and, from his dealings with residents, Octávio, a senior manager in those years of dynamism, felt secure in asserting the place's typicality and confident about describing its history and future.

Octávio began by explaining that he, too, was an *índio*, an Indian. His blood was just as contaminated, his spirit just as base, as those who lived in the countryside and whom, he told me, I could find drinking themselves stupid down by the docks or wandering through town looking lost. In fact, everyone here in the Amazon, he told me, was índio. The *patrões* — the landowners — were the same, he said, even if they did not look it. What I should realize was that he, Octávio, had escaped in a way that these other wealthy men had not: they may be bosses, but they were of the interior, the hinterland, and they had never fully broken away. He, however, had been moving in a completely different world — working for a major international corporation, running the largest sawmill in the eastern Amazon, transforming his thinking and his character. He had, as Amazonians say, "*mudou a cabeça*," he had "changed his head."

Octávio was unabashed in his characterization of the *ribeirinhos*, the people who live along the Amazonian rivers. "They spend 90 percent of their time looking for food. They don't work. They put up their little houses, make their little fields, get themselves a woman, have a bunch of kids, and *pronto*! When they're 65," he concluded with vigor, "they get their pension from the government and they live like kings — *vagabundos!*"

Although lively — and familiar — enough topics, race and destiny formed little more than an ambient agenda. As we sat sipping Cokes in the easy shade of his walled garden, what Octávio really wanted me to acknowledge was that there was nothing special about Igarapé Guariba, nothing that made it worthy of a foreigner's attention.

"The story of Igarapé Guariba," he explained, carefully, so I could not fail to understand, "is the standard Amazonian story. Some guy puts up a sawmill in the interior. There's never enough labor out there so he builds a bunch of shacks and contracts workers from somewhere else. After a while, there's no more wood left to cut. The sawmill closes down, but there's still this remnant of a town and so people stay on. They collect their fruit, catch their fish, hunt their animals; and soon there's nothing left. Then they pack up and move to the city." He worked up a satisfied cadence of inevitability, far from resignation: "Igarapé Guariba won't be there for long. You'll see."

Octávio was determined I not be naïve. There were certain realities here that needed affirming. But his language was disorienting. He was bringing me abruptly face to face with a new Igarapé Guariba, a place that at once seemed starkly opposed to, but no less realized, than the ones I encountered daily on the banks of the river itself. I tried to tell him it wasn't at all this way! But then I started to think about the effects of a story like his — an account that described lives quite concretely and asserted a deep and specific connection between location and social life, that, in fact, made it clear that place, as much as race, class, and gender, was itself a social relationship. I started to think about what it meant when stories like this were set loose upon the world. Octávio's Igarapé Guariba was not just nostalgia filtered through the bitterness of prejudice. His timbre, the crisp and absolutist structures of feeling he called upon, were naggingly similar to tones I knew from conversations in Igarapé Guariba itself. I saw it was a mistake to assume that the familiar ribeirinho style of assertive self-negation, with those knowing tales of how it had all gone to the dogs around here, was simply an expression of political maneuvering internal to this place.

On the face of it, Igarapé Guariba is very much a "small place," to use Jamaica Kincaid's deliberate term.[2] Just twenty-five houses strung along a river, no roads to take you there or back, no electricity to speak of, poor sanitation and the diseases that it brings, intermittent schooling, no health services within easy reach, a priest who stops by once a year to sanctify birth, death, and marriage, an economy of farming, fishing, hunting, and the sale of forest fruits. A village of the Amazon interior.

Dora, my best friend there, the one at whose kitchen table I sat kvetching for more than a year, and a woman of formidable aspiration, regularly and evocatively referred to herself as living on "O Rio Esquecido" — The Forgotten River — as if this were all a waking nightmare from some tacky jungle movie. It was a phrase she launched with great acidity but very little irony, despite my discomfort. The language, of course, has its personal histories. For Dora, the overwhelming backwardness of Igarapé Guariba springs from her intolerable sense of out-of-placeness, her almost insupportable desire to return to the urban life in which she spent her teenage years and in which she still feels complete. Her favorite adjective, *triste*, evokes something deeper and more systemic than ordinary sadness, and she uses it deliberately to describe this place, making of the wooden house and its scattered neighbors a metaphor for her life.[3]

It was her ability to travel across psychic and cartographic boundaries that gave such intensity to what Dora experienced as the parochialism of Igarapé Guariba. It was the fated inevitability of return from her trips to Macapá — the inability to overcome her husband's control of transport — that always generated her dismay, and the cascade of wishes, promises, schemes, and threats that betrayed it. Yet it is her voluble travels, her explosive coming and going along the networks that take her from Igarapé Guariba through Macapá, Santana, and occasionally Belém, her own charismatic cantankerousness, that are themselves the things that guarantee this river is not forgotten.

Dora would have cursed Octávio for his arrogance had she heard our conversation that afternoon, but she would also have understood him. They had in common the terror of being circumscribed by lack of possibility, of being cast outside and behind the stream of history. The local as cosmopolitan horror story, the city as home. If the local was a pocket of exclusion, here were two people who refused to live within its compass. Dora never needed to spell it out directly: strong places can be so alienating, their pull of conformity so withering.

Yet places are never still, and they are never finished. Instead, like people, they are always in process, always in "the flow of becoming," always on the move.[4] Igarapé Guariba forms and unravels, it comes together and disperses, constantly, unendingly, at particular moments in the service of particular projects. And everyone who speaks of it or who listens to its stories or who believes they know it in some otherwise analogic or associative way has their own changing idea of what Igarapé Guariba, this small place, actually is.

Octávio can explain this. Most of the middle-class urban Amazonians I know affirm their strong kinship connections with people in the countryside through talk that casts ribeirinhos in sentimentally nostalgic terms, as nobly folkloric, if deeply flawed figures. Octávio had other ideas. He considers blood ties subject to transcendence and locates himself on an uneasy border. Though his body be saturated with the genetic stain of the indigene, his spirit can soar, taking flight, south to São Paulo, north to Miami, perhaps east across the Atlantic. His conversation contains echoes of the Amazonian travel accounts of Victorian natural historians, with their descriptions of the easefully decadent life of the interior and the inability of rural people to perform what, in post-Enlightenment terms, was the definitively human action of asserting their will over nature through transforming it into culture. And I also hear traces of the Amazonianist anthropologists and archaeologists of the 1950s, 1960s, and 1970s — famous names: Julian Steward, Alfred Métraux, Betty Meggers, Daniel Gross — with their parallel depictions of a descent into nature, although here it is the draining enervations of Steward's "tropical forest culture area" rather than race or psychology that determines decline. There are important distinctions, but there is also an epistemic correspondence. Both these share with Octávio what literary critic David Spurr has recognized as a familiar Rousseauian-derived hierarchy of differences: one that "identifies non-European people with . . . nature, and then places nature in opposition to culture."[5]

Octávio's account was in many ways more sophisticated than either of these influential narratives. He, at least, understood that the making of places was hard, unremitting work, and, moreover, that it was characterized by tenuousness and insecurity. He demonstrated a rare understanding of the instabilities and incertitudes of global transformations, of the fact that space produced can later be erased, that marks on a map often have little permanence. This awareness stemmed partly from his rootedness in Amazonian localities. Here was a man who, although based in a comfortable office, had spent a good part of his thirty-year logging career on expeditions in the estuary searching for timber. Here was a man who had dragged his own cosmopolitan self through rural communities, trekking into forests, sleeping in the open, grappling with the logistics of timber extraction in difficult, uncomfortable, and technically and emotionally challenging terrain.

Octávio clearly had a local knowledge, and it was one that involved a certain sensitivity to the insecurities of rural life. But it was positioned in such a way that it obscured the slightest notion of rural agency. As in the European narratives of jungle nature, his account locates Amazonian ribeirinhos as living *on* and *off* the land, scratching parasitically at its superficial layer, subject to its vicissitudes, and destined finally to succumb, driven to flee once the shade of the patrão's protective economic order has been withdrawn. Locality, for Octávio (in this case, Igarapé Guariba), was no more rooted than those ribeirinhos who were now its sole, inadequate markers. With the timber all gone, Igarapé Guariba had no meaning beyond its pitiful residue of abandoned peasants, whose commitment to this piece of land Octávio knew to be entirely transitory.

Unlike most Victorian naturalists and many post-war Amazonianist anthropologists, Octávio understood that rural Amazonian places assume at least some of their particularity through the transnational mobility of political economy. He had, after all, personally directed a sizable chunk of extra-local capital as it made its blundering way into the interior, chopping down forest and hauling out trees. These extractive projects of the 1970s did not just represent modernity, they actually were modernization in his eyes. And he was hardly alone in viewing the arrival of large-scale capitalist enterprises as the vehicle that would drag Amazonia and its reluctant peasantry into the modern world. This had been a strong-state project premised, like so many others in so many places, on the notion that new subjects would be created through the making of a new nature.[6] It would be through the transformation of the Amazonian landscape that those debilitating bonds holding rural people captive to nature finally would be severed.

After the timber ran out along the northern channel of the estuary and BRUMASA was taken over and liquidated in the late 1980s, Octávio passed into that premature career twilight in which we met. In so doing, he received brutal confirmation that there is nothing permanent about Progress. In his world of unforgiving nature, in which constant vigilance was needed just to stay civilized, rural places could fall out of locality far more easily than they could come to exist within it. And, he believed, once those networks of bourgeois political economy that had wrenched it into history were dissolved, there was nothing standing between Igarapé Guariba and the unforgiving jungle from which it had temporarily emerged.

THE PATRÃO

Especially compelling in Octávio's account of Igarapé Guariba was his conflation of rural society into a single, undifferentiated *caboclo*, a countryperson, a hick. What people in Igarapé Guariba expressed as a foundational cleavage—the line between ribeirinhos and patrão—was eclipsed in his narrative. Instead, Octávio offered a view of the world in which the site of irreducible difference was the gulf between the modernization project of BRUMASA and that of the patrão of Igarapé Guariba, Raimundo Viega, the Old Man.

Until a few years before he died in 1983, Raimundo Viega was *O Patrão*. This did not mean that he was simply the landowner. He had purchased the land in the 1940s after working his way as a cowboy, a rubber-tapper, a small farmer, a boat-builder, and, by some accounts, as a *regatão*, an itinerant trader sailing between the settlements that dot the rivers and coastline around Macapá.[7] He had accumulated a little capital, married, bought his first piece of land in the municipality of Afuá on Marajó Island, and cultivated a network of ribeirinho clients— or "partners," as his wife Dona Rita once corrected me. In explaining the underpinnings of life in Igarapé Guariba when his father was in control, Nestor, Raimundo's son, suggested why his mother might have made this distinction:

> It was a type of exchange. You have some land. You put in someone who these days we'd call a *freguês*, a client. The responsibility of the patrão is to make land available to the freguês without the obligation of paying rent. . . . He plants his crops and takes them to the [patrão's] store and, with the produce he's bringing, grown on that land, the freguês buys merchandise. It was an exchange of work for goods.

Powerful emotional ties and obligations fostered and underwrote this transactional framework. Nestor is making explicit the often unspoken intimacies of *aviamento*, that intricate, persistent, Amazonian system of credit that emerged during the nineteenth-century rubber boom and involved large numbers of intermediary merchants moving capital (in the form of a variety of transformable goods) from places like Liverpool to other places like Igarapé Guariba, and back again.[8] To Viega's family, real leadership of Guariba involved more than merely managing economy. It was an experiment in modernist social engineering, an enactment of enlightened humanitarianism, and a continuance of traditional forms of Amazonian solidarity. The terms in which Nestor and his mother frame the story of Igarapé Guariba were powerfully expressed twenty-five years earlier in a local newspaper column written by Edinaldo Gomes, a journalist and family friend:

> It was only because of Raimundo Viega's *fibra*, his will, that people came to help with the occupation of Igarapé Guariba, an area unknown until 1940. That was when the brave pioneer, impelled by circumstance, resolved to drag it from a state of abandonment and exploit the potential that was already there only awaiting courage and the absolute willingness to work — two virtues Viega possesses even today.[9]

For Gomes, this effort was a collaboration. The people who "came to help" were the ribeirinhos, who, I was told many times, by residents of Igarapé Guariba as well as by members of the Viega family and their associates, prospered under the paternalist regime that was soon established.

The great Brazilian historian of Amazonia, Arthur Cézar Ferreira Reis, writing in the 1950s, described the Amazon patrão as follows:

> He is neither an opportunist nor someone who has got where he is by dint of birth or money. Originally, he was a backwoods scout, a forest explorer, who succeeded through possession of the virtues and qualities needed for victory. Experienced in the forest, ambitious, capable of imposing himself to willfully discipline men, successful in gaining the confidence of his suppliers. Sometimes he was the founder of a plantation, a *seringal*, sometimes an ex-worker who had managed to climb among his comrades and substitute himself for the former patrão, inheriting, by legal means, ownership rights to the plantation.[10]

Reis is talking specifically about the rubber trade. But his militaristic construction of the patrão in self-made heroic terms corresponds remarkably with the language used by Gomes and by Viega's family. The discourse of struggle is not just tied to that of enlightenment, it constitutes it. Viega understands his fregueses because he himself was once where they are now. Moreover, their dependence on him imposes responsibility. As Nestor told me:

Papai always said: "One hand washes the other, and both wash the face." So if you help me, I'll help you. In those days when he was helping [his fregueses], papai understood that everybody needed each other. There's no mystery in this.

Reis continues his discussion by outlining another characteristic of the patrão: his violence. This was a politics repudiated by the Viega family. In a well-run community, there is no need for heavy-handed enforcement. Yet, in describing this side of what he effectively conveys as the self-fashioning dualities of the emergent peasant boss, Reis throws light on Octávio da Gama's account of undifferentiated rurality:

> We need to understand the social milieu from which [the pa-trão] came and in which he lived. In contact with only men, subject to the anguish that comes from isolation in the forest, he is hardly going to be the drawing-room type, with refined gestures and perfect manners. . . . He has to be dynamic, crude, perhaps tyrannical. Any weakness, any indecision could spell disaster. He needs to exercise power without the least hesitation.
> . . . When we are trying to understand him, we need to remember that he generally has little education, and has not spent time in refined environments. . . . He is a friend to his *companheiros*. He stands shoulder to shoulder with them in difficult times. He feels their problems, problems he himself experienced when he too was a simple worker. Brave in the times of most uncertainty, he knows how to face the natural and social world [o meio geográfico e social].[11]

This is the expressive ambivalence of the "simple man," the *pessoa simples*, the salt of the earth. It is a masculine idiom with strong regional roots, through which many successful traders I met in Macapá define themselves, at least in commercial contexts. Used by middle-class urbanites in relation to the ribeirinho, it has a sentimental flavor implying an artless honesty coupled with lack of education. Used by ribeirinhos to describe city-folk, it is a categorical compliment, though with the potential for the ironic deflation of those who imagine they can rise above their class without compromise. Used by self-fashioning urban merchants to construct their own identities, it enables the simultaneous assertion of authenticity and rurality against the fact of urban prosperity, affirms their ability to communicate with the ribeirinho man to

man, and announces their willingness to engage faithfully in the personalist obligations of aviamento economics.

Viega's surviving family emphasize his roots in poverty, and the self-
less devotion and love for place, the *carinho*, that tender affection
through which he built up Igarapé Guariba and, with it, the lives of his
fregueses. In these accounts, the index of devotion is the obstacles overcome, and the greatest of these was Amazonian nature. Dona Rita,
Raimundo's wife, told me that when she first went to Guariba, "there
wasn't even a stream there. It was just forest and dense grassland."
Lene, her daughter, picked up the theme:

> When papai bought that land it was *mata virgem*, virgin forest.
> It was really wild, dense forest, so dense that a person couldn't
> penetrate it. There was an area of thorny scrub that would just
> cut you up all over. . . . All the boats had to stop at the en-
> trance [to the stream] because they couldn't get in. It was closed,
> so narrow that there was no way for a large boat to get down —
> only those tiny little canoes that you can take right into the
> forest, bending down and dragging them. That's what it used to
> be like.

We already know something about how Raimundo Viega and his
fregueses remade the nature of Igarapé Guariba. In the process, the patrão built a store, a school, and a chapel out of the commodified resources taken from the forest and rivers. And he blessed his *vila*, the
commercial complex at the river's mouth, with electric light. Incremen-
tally, steadily, Igarapé Guariba seemed to be finding its way onto the
maps of modernity. Yet the apparent success of the Old Man's project
only masked the contradictions that were finally to drive him out. The
social contract collapsed. The Macedo family — ribeirinhos, emblematic
pessoas simples who had come from Afuá to work with their patrão on
his new property — changed the rules. Viega's community came crashing
down, and the meaning of place and nature in Igarapé Guariba was
revealed as bitterly contested and disturbingly ambiguous.

PLACE-MAKING, NATURE-MAKING

So how *did* this place come into existence? I have to say that it was all
about work, the work of place-making and, inseparably, the work of

nature-making. Some of this has to do with belonging, with finding ways to become local and with getting caught up in the elaboration of what Raymond Williams called a structure of feeling.[12] Much of this is the work of discursive practice, in this case, of the stories people tell over and over again that reinforce personal connections to this particular local.

There is, for example, the one about a huge snake, an anaconda, that was killed in 1993 during the demarcation of land controlled by the newly formed Residents' Association. It was long enough for the large group of men hacking a trail through the swampy grassland with the land reform agency official to stand in a line and fix the moment — posing for a photograph, one behind the other, with this monster held up, stretched above their heads in dramatic gesture, using a moment of assertion over landscape to draw the boundaries of difference that excluded unwelcome nature and uninvited land grabbers.

With José Macedo as president and Antônio, his brother, as secretary, the Association was an explicit institutional consolidation of a de facto political leadership. Backed by the Rural Workers' Union of Amapá, it emerged as residents temporarily cohered to challenge the right of Raimundo Viega's heirs to cut heart-of-palm on what both parties considered their land.[13] The implications of legal victory and the act of boundary-drawing that followed were not entirely satisfactory to all the people living in Igarapé Guariba. Accustomed to hunting and fishing freely over a large area, residents were now under court order to restrict their activities to the demarcated area or else be reclassified as invaders and poachers. The anaconda, the most hostile, the least transformable to economy of the landscape's animal occupants, became an appropriately ambivalent metaphor for a victory that created a new set of concerns and initiated a new series of external definitions of "community."[14]

Ten years previously, a bitter saga of confused land dealings, contested indemnification, and the threat of physical violence had led everyone to abandon their homes and gardens on the north bank of the river and relocate to the south side, ferrying over what they could in canoes and motor-launches. Viega had recently died, and his children, squabbling over their inheritance, went back on a commitment residents claim he had made: within months of their father's death his heirs had sold the land on which his fregueses were living, leaving these caboclos no choice but to move.

People sometimes dramatized this history by showing me the structural beams of their new houses, decay-resistant wood they brought with them from Afuá forty years earlier and which won't grow in swampy Igarapé Guariba but which provides imaginative and emotional continuity within a narrative of dislocation. These knotted beams have come to express the persistence of place, even as they embody the trials of eviction and forced mobility. In this story, so different from Octávio's, locality resides in people rather than in economy or geography. And it is rooted in shared experience.

Although shared, it's no surprise that this story of departure from what people always call "the other side" has no unified consensual narrative: it is always crosscut by a language of betrayal and opportunism, and it continues to conjure bitterness in its telling. People talk diplomatically about their *falta de orientação*, their lack of political sophistication at the time. But it's hard not to hear this as coded critique of those who broke ranks first and set sail across the river. These memories are profoundly diagnostic of local division, and whatever shared-ness there is in the experience seems to have settled in as a shared shame, continually fueled by the proximity of the formally inaccessible opposite bank, where their fruit trees have long since been cut down and their gardens gone to seed, just there, across the river.

That shame can be tied up in local subjectivity is hardly surprising for a class of people who are popularly known in Amazonia by the pejorative term "caboclo."[15] Caboclo is often wielded with assertive irony in Igarapé Guariba, but the pervasive awkwardness in this narrative of eviction allows no such play. Instead, these memories become a stick with which to beat the present community leaders, people then active in union politics but nonetheless ineffective, and whose families, some imply, were the main beneficiaries of the indemnification. In this way, through their circulation and repetition, people use such stories to intervene in the often acrimonious politics surrounding the Association, and to advance arguments for the pursuit of one out of several potential futures. The conflictual and ongoing work of place-making is here expressed through the idiom of shared pasts.

Stories of this type call on nature to reinforce belonging, and they anchor place, yet dispute its meaning. Another, the story of the remaking of nature in Igarapé Guariba, the story I introduced in Chapter 1, describes an originary moment in local history. And it involves, in radical form, the imprinting of locality on landscape.

Raimundo and Rita Viega bought the area that included Igarapé Guariba in 1941. By this time, Raimundo was a well-known businessman who owned a large store in Macapá that sold hardware and the tools needed for settlement in the interior. He had three or four boats, a venture close to the port of Santana where he processed rice, and several landholdings on the islands that form the municipality of Afuá. When you look at him in photographs—smartly but casually dressed, taller and more powerfully built than his companions, his whiteness accentuated by his shiny bald skull—you meet a self-assured patrão who stares straight into the lens with the combative proprietorial eye of the man of action evoked by his son Nestor.

Everyone who knew Igarapé Guariba in these early years agrees that its attractions were obvious. The woods were packed with valuable timber, and the river was teeming with fish and wildlife. When you set fire in the fields, "turtles ran from you like cockroaches," one longtime resident told me. The chatter of scarlet macaws and the bellowing of howler monkeys were so intense you might not get to sleep. "You just had to lean down and dip a basket in the river to bring it up full of heavy, fat fish."

But at first this abundance was only potentiality. What dominates accounts of those days is wilderness, the menacing wild forest into which only the very brave would venture and into which strode Raimundo Viega, a patrão driven by a transformative vision.

There was a long period during which he did little with the land. A guard was living at the mouth of the stream, and Viega's boats sailing between Macapá and Afuá stopped off with supplies to keep him going. Viega took out timber now and again, and the guard tapped rubber and grew bananas. But the Old Man was just letting Guariba tick over. His real interest at the time was in the next river, the Rio Preto, purchased in the same deal, where he had a rice plantation employing 140 wageworkers.

It was only when the project on the Rio Preto faltered that Viega turned his attention to Igarapé Guariba. He harvested just one crop of rice and then had his workers plant pasture for cattle. His men cut narrow trails through the forest and savanna and drove the animals to pasture, close to what was then the creek at Guariba. Then he began recruiting fregueses from his land on Afuá.

It was 1958 when the Viegas finally arrived in Guariba. They built a tile-roofed house on a low bluff at the mouth of the river, and they brought in their son Chico, a man of imposing bulk, to uphold their law. They built a warehouse to receive forest and agricultural products, a store which, as somebody in this roadless world joked, sold "everything except cars," and they assembled the single-blade sawmill. Their boats began stopping off with manufactured goods bought on credit from one of the Viegas' own patrões in the city of Belém, up to seven days by sail across the bay. And after stocking the store, the boats would head off with the contents of the warehouse, making a circuit of the couple's properties and trading in Macapá on their way back across the estuary.

Four families moved at first from Viega's properties on Afuá to Igarapé Guariba. They included Benedito and Nazaré Macedo and their eight children. They built a house near the store and cleared a garden. They planted their first year of bananas and watermelons. They mapped out new rubber trails, and they worked in the forest, hunting, collecting oilseeds, and cutting timber. It was not that different from Afuá. Igarapé Guariba, though, Benedito Macedo remembers, was *farto*, a land of plenty. There was more timber, as much fish and meat as you could want, and the soil was fertile. The Macedos settled once more into the type of clientelist arrangement that had spread through the Amazon during the nineteenth-century rubber boom and that is still a widespread form of social organization. As their fregueses arrived, the Viegas advanced them materials to build, hunt, and farm. In return, they would sell all the products of their labor only through the Viegas and their agents. Anything these clients needed to purchase, they could find in the store, available on terms of exchange that were monopolistic but not unusually punitive.

Longtime residents describe the Rio Guariba of the early 1960s as a *besteira*, a joke, a silly little thing. It was a short and narrow river, probably about 50 to 75 yards wide at its mouth, where it met the Amazon, and shallow and safe enough for children to wade or swim across at low tide. It ended in a waterfall—a feature usually described in the diminutive, a *quedazinha*, a *cachoeirazinha*. Hunters would haul their canoes over or around the rocks to arrive in the midst of an open grassy landscape of flooded savanna. Such areas are often dominated by the papyrus-like *pirí*, from which people in poorer families in Guariba make mats that sell in bundles of ten for R $1 (then U.S. $1) to the Macedos and other local boat owners. Above the waterfall, the pirí formed a dense barrier, a *pirizal*, in association with *aninga*, a woody aroid that can easily stand 6 or 7 feet high. The pirizal was near-stationary, shallow, and entirely dried out in summer, yet residents called it a lake, the *lago*.[16]

Within a few years of the families' arriving and the sawmill starting up, it became clear that the valuable resources at the mouth of the river — animal skins and timber particularly — would soon be exhausted. Moreover, the difficulty of communicating among expanding Igarapé Guariba, Viega's upstream cattle post, and the property on the Rio Preto had become a source of considerable frustration for the land-owner. Above the waterfall, beyond the the pirizal, hunters reported an upstream forest well-stocked with valuable hardwoods and animals. To get there, hunters would spend hours crossing the swampy lake, push-ing and dragging their unladen canoes. On the way back several days later — if everything went according to plan — they would have salted meat strapped to their backs or be carting sacks of seeds or fruit. The forest, although productive and desired, was a largely non-functional source of value.

Raimundo Viega was proactive and thoroughly instrumental in the face of this dilemma. He organized the men of Guariba into teams. He handed around cane-liquor, gave his orders, and, in the most elaborate accounts, climbed a large tree to supervise the work.

Benedito Macedo and the other men broke through the waterfall. On the far side, they were faced with densely packed barriers of aninga and pirí. Slowly, with axes, hoes, and machetes, they dug out a narrow channel, maybe 4 to 6 feet wide, all the time enduring insects and the threat of larger animals. And, from his vantage point high above the flat landscape, Raimundo Viega kept them on track for the forest in the distance.

For close to ten years, the digging in Igarapé Guariba continued during the lean, dry summer months. Once the headwaters had been breached and the lago had been opened, the huge volumes of water that enter the northern channel of the Amazon estuary with the twice-daily tides rapidly swept soil and vegetation out into the main river — into what people here, in poetic recognition of its vastness, call the *rio-mar*, the river-sea. Without a definable watershed and surrounded by land too flat for a drainage area, the Rio Guariba is a long, narrow inlet, repeatedly scoured by the erosive tidal action of the Amazon. With the barrier of the waterfall removed and a passage opened into the low-lying *campo*, the flood of the Amazon poured into the upstream basin, excavating and widening the main channel. Today, people recline on the wooden boards of their front porches and watch as fallen trees, big chunks of riverbank, and islands of grass flow evenly out to sea on the tide.

Transport to the upstream forest soon became possible not only by canoe, but also by sail and motorboat. And it was then that the residents of Igarapé Guariba, independently of the Old Man, and often without his knowledge, began to cut their own routes. They formed communal work teams, and they maintained the openings by taking his buffalo and driving them repeatedly through the new gullies. Two of the Macedo brothers who had done much of the digging told me that this was the only reason they consented to Viega's punitive project in the first place. They had known where they wanted to go from the outset, they claimed. While women worked downstream — fishing, collecting forest products, managing children — men camped in the upstream forest, cleared fields on good-quality land, dug out more and more canals into the forest for themselves and their neighbors, and created the storied expeditionary spaces I am describing.[17]

The landscape within which these activities took place was radically transformed. The narrow mouth of the river now gapes open more than a half mile across where it meets the Amazon, capsizing motorboats on a windy day. The swampy pirizal — unmistakably a lake now — is a sweeping expanse of water itself nearly a mile wide. The closed upstream forest is threaded with a dense tracery of creeks, streams, and broad channels.

Take a look at the images on pages 60 and 61. The first is the infrared aerial photograph made by CPRM that starts this book. It was taken as part of a mineral survey of the eastern Amazon at a moment when the region was in the grip of unrestrained speculative development. This was late summer 1976, well after work had first begun in Guariba, and it shows the Rio Guariba with the Rio Preto below, and just a glimpse of the mass of the Amazon flowing by.

CPRM first mapped this part of the region in the late 1950s, but for some reason their splendid archives in Rio de Janeiro presented only a gap where I had hoped to find the Igarapé Guariba of that time, with its four families at the river-mouth, its waterfall, its obdurate pirizal, and what must have been the skinnier, shorter stream then flowing through the forest. The image on page 60 is from 1976 and is therefore the first, a commanding view of the scene some fifteen years after the digging

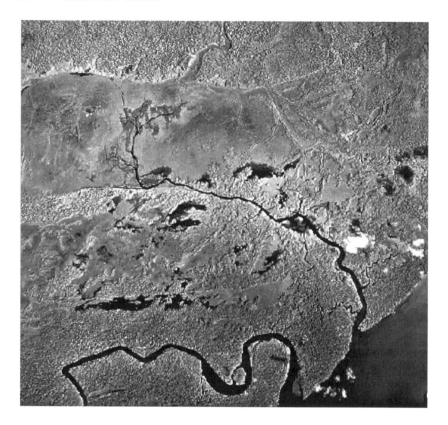

began. It is a classic landscape picture in the terms of Raymond Williams' famous observation that the genre is underwritten by the erasure of the labor through which nature is made — not to mention the effacement of landscape's own work of nature-making.[18] Actually, this image goes even further, offering a land without social relations or history, a land of potentiality. In this sense, its abstraction makes it a classic Amazonian landscape, one in which the implied view is both entrepreneurial and extractive.

Yet even here, it is the broader blackness of the Rio Preto that draws the eye. The Rio Guariba is quite narrow, and the upstream area where it fragments into smaller channels is tentative and anemic. But look at this next image, taken in 1991, another fifteen years on, a Landsat TM composite satellite image to the same scale.

Same scale, same time of year, same point in the tidal cycle.[19] But when tied to its predecessor, this image creates a disruptive juxtaposi-

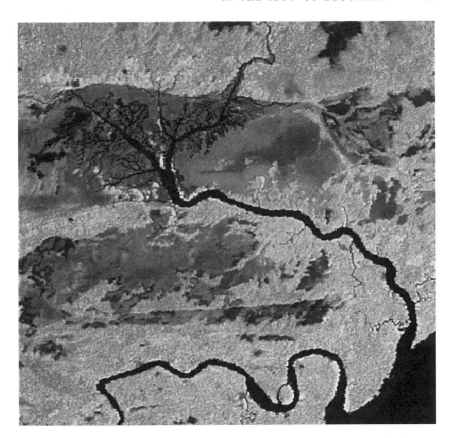

tion, proposing a radical shift in narrative. Not only is the expansion of the river quite clearly apparent, but it has come alive, no anemia here. Instead, its channels proliferate, enveloping the forest like capillaries of the alveoli, at once engulfing and absorbing the terra anfíbia of which it is a part.

There is a simple point here. Places and what passes for nature have a consuming materiality. And so do place-making and nature-making, makings that make no sense without attention to practice. So, again, how did this place come into existence?

In the midst of attention to discursive practice, we have to resist eliding the materiality of those concrete transformations that people actively undertake and remember to pay attention to fathoming events at the juncture of ideas and practices. Discourses of place and nature in Igarapé Guariba are grounded, literally. People here actually did these things: place, nature, and locality were transformed — remade, invented even — through physical, corporeal action.

Yet, in recovering practice, we need to recognize that despite its brute tactility, the digging of channels was not narrowly material. It rested on old understandings of what nature is, and it created new ones. It drew energy from political-economic and cultural projects that tied Igarapé Guariba into temporarily coherent transnational commodity circuits — the timber trade of the 1970s, for example — and it reinvigorated embedded networks of short-distance trade, such as those in palm-fruits and other forest products. The cutting of channels relied on a shared story of a nature in Igarapé Guariba that began impossibly wild but could be made to surrender its abundance. And, in enabling a present that relies for legitimation on constructions of the past and projections of the future, a discursively and physically plastic local nature became subject to co-optation and incorporation into the mobile practices of contemporary politics.

THE CABOCLO

During the course of twenty-five careful years, Benedito and Nazaré Macedo and their family succeeded in displacing the Viegas, strategizing to exploit the spaces implicit in their personalist regime, discovering pathways between subjection and subversion.

That densely ramified upstream area in the Landsat image is where we're headed now. It was this part — known as *o centro*[20] — that was to become the focus of the engineering activity I am describing. This is what it looks like at low tide today. The two tall stakes to the left are fishing markers, barely visible when the river rises. Behind us and in the far distance is forest. We're looking out from Tomé's retreat, a location of some significance in the unfolding of this story.

Who knows why Old Man Viega really wanted to cut these streams? There seems no doubt he was aiming to tie this rich landscape to Macapá and Belém, via both the downstream Igarapé Guariba community and the Rio Preto. Nestor Viega says that all this activity was driven by his father's need to get buffalo to the slaughterhouses in Macapá in good condition. Raimundo's widow and daughter are less instrumental: it was his "curiosity to see what was there" that drove him on, they insist.[21] It was to get bananas to Macapá, says his grandson Miguelinho.

Old Dona Terezinha, gripping my arm, by herself now that her husband has run off again, standing there in rags by the hand-dug igarapé that links the centro with the Rio Preto, remembers something else: he did it to carry his family in style by motorboat from the sawmill to the road they were building from Macapá that passed by the Rio Preto. No, states Benedito Macedo matter-of-factly, he did it to get the timber.

Viega knew the commercial potential of this good-quality land for bananas, corn, watermelon, and the marrow-like *maxixe*, and he understood the value of the forest resources that visiting hunters had reported. His fregueses were similarly informed and participated in the same project, recognizing the same potential. Yet, many of them denied the legitimacy of his claims to governance, and they used these upstream lands to generate the income that enabled them to free themselves of the burden of debt and as a basis for their subsequent land claim that pushed the patrão off the river.

Viega should have been prepared. José Macedo, Seu Benedito's son, had accumulated formidable expertise in years as a traveling representative of the *Comunidades de Base*, the Catholic base communities that preceded the rural workers' unions in Amapá.[22] And he was not alone. Igarapé Guariba had produced a generation of sophisticated political operators, including Martinho the Goat, the union leader, who had learned the mechanics of the Viegas' operation from the inside—as the teenage clerk in the store and receiver at the warehouse—before studying populist Marxism and refashioning himself as feudal landlordism's relentless nemesis.

The Macedos dug channels. While Viega mapped out a route for the Rio Preto, they headed for the centro, pushing their way toward the shiny crops they envisioned growing in the mata virgem.

There was no inherent conflict in these coinciding projects. One hand was still washing the other, and, for a while at least, both were washing the same face. Better land effectively meant higher rents, as more produce entered the warehouse and more goods left the store. But the Macedos knew something Viega did not know they knew, and may perhaps not even have known himself. Through their political contacts in Macapá, José Macedo and Martinho the Goat had accessed the landlord's files in the Macapá offices of the Instituto Nacional de Colonização e Reforma Agrária (INCRA), the federal land reform agency, investigated his holdings, and confirmed their suspicion that he was exaggerating his claim. The *título definitivo*, the outright title he had bought in the deal that gave him the Rio Preto and Igarapé Guariba, extended only 2,200 yards from the confluence of the Rio Guariba and the Amazon, nowhere near the land upstream toward which the canal-diggers were steadily heading. What was more, in an affirmation of the concrete significance of abstract argument about invisibility and anthropogenesis, this upstream land had the legal status of unoccupied land, open to petition from the state as *terra requerida*, that is, petitioned or petitionable land.[23]

It seems that for some time no one in Igarapé Guariba breathed a word to the patrão. In June 1969, one of the original fregueses, Seu Tomé, announced that he was petitioning INCRA for a large parcel of land, a forest island upstream on which he had built a simple workpost. Viega reacted angrily, dismissing Tomé, asserting his own right to land that he had legally and honorably purchased, whether he had written title or not. Tomé went straight to Macapá and stayed until he had extracted the requisite documents from INCRA. He returned to Igarapé Guariba. Raimundo again dismissed him, this time giving him written notice to remove himself and his pigs from the property within sixty days. Tomé left again, but soon returned with INCRA officials in tow. Viega backed down. Miguelinho, Raimundos' grandson, ended this dra-

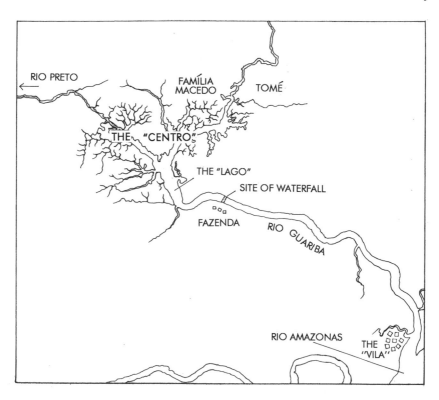

matic narrative on a sour note: "This is our land, this land of [Tomé's]. It was land that we bought. There was nothing *requerida* about it." Nestor Viega, in a commentary on the long unraveling that begins with Tomé and that reads like a threat, but which was delivered with a re-signed bitterness, told me — and I am sure he is right — that in the south of Pará they would have settled this business by killing the whole lot of them: "But the Viega family are not that kind of people."[24]

Within a few years, Viega had lost control of most of the area up-stream. Following Tomé's success and the absence of violent repercus-sions, Benedito Macedo filed for title, multiplying his holdings by claim-ing in the names of his sons. The other families also petitioned, but for those who approached INCRA after the Macedos, pickings were slim.

When I was first told about these events, I assumed they represented a radical shift of power in Igarapé Guariba. Yet things continued much as before. Although they now had land, the fregueses continued to treat the vila with its store and warehouse as their principal commercial entrepôt. Chico Viega continued to police the river, inhibiting all the outside trade he could. The families continued to live downstream on his father's land. And the bonds between the patrão and his fregueses appeared to deepen. When this upstream land produced bumper crops of watermelon and bananas too large for his transport capacity, the Old Man brokered deals for his fregueses with other merchants. And he did something else: he advanced Tomé the money to buy the motor for a boat.

As Martinho the Goat informed me when I expressed surprise, there was nothing so strange about enforcing indebtedness. It took Tomé twelve years to pay off the money, and, in the meantime, he continued to sell through his patrão. His boat, on which Viega was earning rent, became an addition to the landlord's fleet at a time when he needed the extra volume. It was clear that transport in itself was not the key to political-economic authority. Although a transport monopoly—never entirely complete in any case, given the resourcefulness of the river trader—was a powerful technology, it could be surrendered with no immediate loss of hegemony. What was critical was the use to which a boat was put.

Viega still had his eye on upstream timber. He had access, but he no longer had the land. The wood he wanted was a tall grove of *andiroba* on the Macedos' new property. Raimundo and Benedito talked. They had an intimacy that came from thirty years of association. Viega bargained, Macedo balked. Viega offered a good price, Macedo rejected it. The patrão asked him what he wanted. Without hesitation, Benedito replied: a riverboat.

Viega advanced the money at low interest. Benedito and his family cut the trees and carried the wood and boatload after boatload of bananas they had grown on those upstream bottomlands direct to Macapá. Within two months they had cleared the debt and started to buy produce from their neighbors. This, then, was the formal collapse of monopsony. I had to ask Nestor about it:

Hugh: So what happened between you and the Macedos?

Nestor: What happened was that they ... well, today ... they're there. It's their land, isn't it?

Hugh: So they buy from the community then?

Nestor: That's right. It looks to you like the community's going nowhere, right? You think society doesn't grow with this type of business? I know what you want to say: you think this is all just a vicious circle. Am I right?

Hugh: No, not really. Look, so far as I can tell . . . it's hard to explain. . . . It looks to me like the Macedo family has more or less occupied . . .

Nestor: . . . the space the Viegas used to occupy! But that's it exactly!

They linger so raw, the wounds from this story of justice and betrayal, this tale of social transformation woven through narratives of the transformation of nature. The physical and imaginative remaking of nature has been central to the re-siting of locality in the context of the sociological and discursive reinvention of Igarapé Guariba. This new Igarapé Guariba that was brought into being through the machination of political intrigue and the rhetoric of resistance relied on a transformed nature both materially, by underwriting the struggle for political control with the cash crops that paid off debt, and discursively, as the battlefield on which was played out an historic drama of liberation. As Igarapé Guariba gradually re-emerged in the form of a juridically secured "community," the web of translocal relationships within which it had traveled through the person of Raimundo Viega were largely thrown off by the family of Benedito and Nazaré Macedo. Instead of the middle-class social clubs mined by Viega, Igarapé Guariba circulates now through the offices of the Rural Workers' Union and across the desks of land reform administrators at INCRA. Instead of residents carrying their forest products to exchange in Viega's family store, the Macedo family distributes them along reconfigured clientelist networks in Macapá. Igarapé Guariba, then, has in certain ways become an entirely different place, requiring a different order of local self-consciousness, and, at the same time, another locality, situated in and constituted through a changed set of translocal cultural and political economies.

Nevertheless, what I — and the Viega and Macedo families — consider to be the new Igarapé Guariba is no less differentiated than the old version. And, what is more, it is a place in which, retaining an affective link with the former patrão, the dominant emotional register for more than a few is not progressivism, but nostalgia.

PROLIFERATING LOCALITY

Place-making in Igarapé Guariba still relies on the hard work of nature-making. This is partly because nature, in its biophysicality, is never in stasis, and forces a constant reinvestment and reinvention of labor, debate, and knowledge.[25] But it is also, in a fuller sense, because nature is both a dynamic actor and a decisive ground in the contemporary politics of place-making and the ongoing struggle over everyday life. As different claims on nature proliferate, so different Igarapé Guaribas come into view. As individuals travel, narrating this placed nature and its associated histories, so these proliferations spread, becoming mobilized simultaneously in different contexts and with disparate meanings. Let me return briefly to Raimundo Viega.

I described Viega as a well-known businessman from Macapá. But that doesn't tell us much. Before he purchased Guariba, Viega, then a young man, had set up a rice-processing plant at Fortaleza, close to the port of Santana. He had some luck because, just as the business was failing, huge manganese deposits were discovered inland and the state stepped in, expropriated his parcel, and paid compensation. He spent part of the money buying the estuarine no-man's-land that included Igarapé Guariba, provisioning his store, and setting up the sawmill. He used part to build a three-story house on the main street of Macapá. He inserted himself in an emergent local society that sensed the winds of opportunity blowing through the region as the military government intensified its campaign to open up the Amazon, and foreign capital, through companies like BRUMASA, once more began reaching into the interior. He sent his sons away to college to come back as doctors and lawyers and to run for political office. And he found a place for himself among a sympathetic group of nonconforming, hard-drinking, self-consciously Amazonian middle-class men, a group who has since started a social club they call the Brotherhood of the Marauni, after the once powerful indigenous occupants of the area. Aside from drinking and collegiality, their energies go into the recovery and promotion of what they identify as local culture and folklore.

Nestor Viega socializes with the Brotherhood and so does Edinaldo Gomes, the journalist who took Viega out of the forest and into his newspaper column. Apart from a short stint as a political aide to the conservative Governor Annibal Barcellos in the early 1980s, Gomes has based his career on writing rural life. He enchants the countryside for his urban readers through a rhetoric of stunning immediacy and authenticity. He treats his audience to firsthand accounts of his adventures in the interior, stealing across borders with clandestine migrants, hunting crocodiles and jaguar by flashlight—etching finely drawn encounters with ribeirinhos that emphasize their cautious wisdom and wily quirkiness.

When Gomes talks about Igarapé Guariba, he vividly recalls the day sometime in the early 1970s when he traveled there with a different governor to inaugurate the new school Viega had built. Residents of Guariba still remember the unexpected sight of the politicians' plane touching down at the mouth of the river. Gomes describes a thriving community grateful to its patrão, and a table groaning under the weight of rural delicacies—*paca, tracajá, açaí, tambaquí, maniçoba, tacacá, bolo de macaxeira*—delicious foods that signify a plentiful Amazonian Arcadia.[26] Through Gomes' tales of Raimundo Viega and the evocative black-and-white photos he ferrets out to show me, I enter an Igarapé Guariba thoroughly located in regional political and social networks, an affluent, modern community, a center in the area, with electric light flowing from an oil-fired generator, a medical post, a new school, and the largest and best-stocked store on any of the proximate rivers.

For Gomes, as for the surviving members of Viega's family, such moments stand at the pivot of a history of subsequent decline, of the unmaking of locality. Indeed, the same can be said for those residents of Igarapé Guariba who now find themselves hemmed in by the new (albeit leakier) Macedo monopsony—a regime made even more irksome by the absence of glamour in a leadership possessing none of the aura that comes from ownership of a big house in Macapá and children in the professional class.[27]

The old-time Igarapé Guariba evoked by Edinaldo Gomes, the surviving family of Raimundo Viega, and these dissident residents felt secure as a place and as an embedded locality. It had traveled through the mobile bodies of the Viega family to the highest offices in the territorial administration, and it was tied into the types of social patronage networks that form the only guarantee of public-sector credit in the region, and that can gain the ribeirinho a not-too-hostile hearing behind the doors of a government ministry. While still not written into the formal cartography of Amapá, it figured, albeit peripherally, on the cognitive maps that mattered.

Yet, to Octávio da Gama, the ex-logger who locates himself trans-regionally, never captured by the interior and having somehow transcended Amazonian society, such networks were never more than chronically provincial. To Octávio, Raimundo Viega was never more than an índio. And, by pointing to what he sees as the corrupting parochialism of Amazonian society, Octávio reminds us that the logic of locality is a hierarchy of retreating communities: Igarapé Guariba, (the backwoods of) Amapá, (which is a byword for backwardness in) Brazil, (which is in a Third World part of) the world. From the local to the global, each representation is more abstract than the one before. Individuals within any one of them emerge through a mobile emplacement—at once self-determined and over-determined—at particular points in what is commonly both a chain and a series of ever-widening concentric circles.

The making of place and nature in Igarapé Guariba, then, must also be understood as a production of modernity—at a time when Amazonia's status in the national imagination was of a fearfully backward region destined only to be dragged (kicking and screaming, índios and all) into the time-space of the modern world and in which the key to modernity was integration in the nation-state. Amazonia's backwardness was signified by the indistinguishable wildness of its nature and of its Indians. And, as Octávio points out, anybody who lived there was an índio.

For Octávio, Igarapé Guariba never approached either modernity or effective locality. For the survivors of Raimundo Viega, for Edinaldo Gomes, and for a number of its residents, Igarapé Guariba passed through a sparkling moment of possibility, only to revert temporally and spatially to a shadow of a remote hinterland.[28] For these people, the nature brought into being during this brief experience of modernity is even today highly problematic. Gomes, the urban journalist, for example, ascribes the changes in the landscape to a series of violent tidal episodes that, he insists, nearly wiped out the community, but which no one living in Guariba at the time now considers of any significance. Dona Rita, Raimundo's widow—elderly, dressed permanently in nightclothes, hesitant behind thick, dark eyeglasses, living upstairs in her bedroom in Macapá as if in final exile—also downplays the importance of human intervention in the changes to the land. Protective of her husband's memory, sensitive to international environmental discourse, she imagines a foreigner's reading of landscape reorganization on such a scale as brutally destructive of the wonder that is Amazonian nature.[29]

When her daughter Lene tells me that "most of that destruction in Guariba wasn't done by people, it was done by nature itself," Dona Rita agrees. "It was only pirizal there," she says, "no one cut any *trees* down." Her son Nestor, flirting good-naturedly over drinks with the weary prostitutes in the town square, has a slightly different explanation: there was only one channel cut on his father's orders, the one that links Igarapé Guariba to the Rio Preto. The others were the work of those "tremendously destructive" buffalo. Orlando, another son — in an interview a few days after he lost his job as the resident doctor at the land reform agency — concurs: "If it did happen, it was those caboclos who did it," he complains, going on to remind me of the hundred head of buffalo mysteriously spirited off his ranch alongside the lago.

To today's disgruntled residents of Igarapé Guariba who work to circumvent the Macedo family's economic reach through tying themselves to new patrões in Macapá, who remember the Old Man's community as a bustling, vibrant center, and who now characterize the place as a "cemetery,"[30] nature is unappeasable. The chain of ecological effects set in motion in the name of progress is causing houses to fall in the river, fields to turn to swamps, fruit trees to sink into muddy banks, and fish to pick up and move to other rivers.[31] Nature is complicit in an ongoing tale of decline, and its recalcitrance is grist to the millstone of political intrigue.

Yet, for those people I have identified as contemporary leaders, the transforming of the land is a foundational epic. As if viewing their critics' history in negative, for them Igarapé Guariba is even now emerging from the darkness of "slavery" to make a place in the light of a modern future. The project of these leaders is to transform past structures of locality through the wrestling of this place onto alternative routes among the networks that tie the retreating circles of intersecting localities one to another. They want to position Igarapé Guariba in a forward-looking Amapá, and move through the resources of Amapá to Brazil the nation-state. They intend to connect via Brazil to the world. From the union office in Macapá, they can jump scale and link by e-mail directly to NGO and academic contacts in the United States and Europe. Through alternative political patrons they can negotiate to reconstruct the electricity grid and health post that collapsed after Viega's departure. Through union-brokered talks in Santana they can strike deals with the new palm-fruit cooperative that is large enough to take all the produce they can ship from Guariba, and promises to send their

fruit to Rio, São Paulo, even Japan, side-stepping the seasonal bot-
tlenecks and sharp practice at the quayside in Macapá.

So, while for some of its interlocutors Igarapé Guariba is a place
that has fallen out of locality, for others, it is, for the first time, beginning to locate itself. Whereas for some, Igarapé Guariba surrendered its
ties to the modern world when it broke with Viega, for others, it is only
through self-location that it can enter within the compass of modernity.
While at first blush the material contours of modernity may appear
strikingly similar in both narratives — health, education, transport, electricity, TV, refrigerators — for the Macedo family there is also this exis-
tential component: modernity and locality (both) are embodied self-
determination, underwritten and secured by the transformation of wild
nature.

As I have suggested, though, the locality of Igarapé Guariba is both
too shared and too contested to be so easily appropriated. The compli-
cation for the Macedo family is that the new, remade nature of Igarapé
Guariba, although dramatic, inspirational, and, arguably, utilitarian,
was fundamentally vitiated at the moment of its coming-into-being.
And it seems impossible for its inheritors to construct the foundational
story of its transformation as one of renewal. Even when Benedito Macedo tells me that he didn't take "one *centavo*" in payment from old
Raimundo Viega for the work of digging canals, he says it with the
uncertain vehemence of one who knows the power in blind Dona Rita's
bitter charge of *sacanagem*, of betrayal, of getting fucked over by these
comrades, these peasants. Such are the wages of slaveholding, Seu Benedito might well say. But even this would not disguise the fact of collaboration and the problem of authorship: the pervasive sense that even
now, fifteen years after he died, this landscape and the locality it embodies belong as much to Viega, the pioneer, as they ever will to Macedo; that in the very acts of their making, place and nature were
marked by collaboration, dissent, and deceit.

THE MAJESTIC AMAZON

These thoughts have grown slowly out of my troubling meeting with
Octávio da Gama that summer afternoon in Macapá. Even though he
did not know about the remaking of nature in Igarapé Guariba, Octávio would not have cared much anyway. He saw Guariba as already

on a one-way slide into the estuary mudflats. It was the cynicism in Oc-távio's erasure of people and place that pushed me to think about the fullness of the existence into which this place came, about what that state of "being Igarapé Guariba" might mean.

As places take shape in the world, not only multiple places, but multiple natures come into view and become implicated in the claims and counterclaims of contemporary politics. Octávio's tale of BRU-MASA, for example, describes the production of locality as the technology of extraction passes through the estuary and Igarapé Guariba is pulled and pulls itself into the re-emerging networks of timber transnationalism. Yet, pursuing coherence, Octávio denies both the possible pre-existence and the persistence of rural society. Indeed, such a recognition would require an admission of ribeirinho agency. Nature is subject only to the Company in his telling. Successful intervention both defines and is predicated on a certain level of personhood that he expresses in strict racial-hierarchical terms.

Is this an assumption shared by Edinaldo Gomes—advocate for the legitimacy and integrity of rural culture and connoisseur of all things caboclo—who studies the map of Amapá on the wall of his study in Macapá, shakes his head, and points to where the *pororoca* attacks the coastline and causes rivers to change course? My suggestion of local interventions produces agitation, irritability, and a lecture on the power of the Amazon—"O Amazonas majestoso," the majestic Amazon, as a friend of mine murmurs with awe and pride every time we turn the corner at the top of the hill in Macapá and see its sluggish brown mass filling the view to the horizon. For Edinaldo, at least, there is a thoroughgoing autonomy inhering in nature, far greater than the petty determinations of race and class.

A few days later and a couple of miles across town, when I raise the same issue with Dona Rita and her daughter Lene in the presence of their two elderly family servants, the response is again uneasy. Dona Rita loved Guariba with that same intense carinho she attributes to her dead husband. Even though it has been more than ten years since she visited, that affective link is simultaneously a territorial claim and a mark of the injustice of her banishment. It is the natural beauty, the wildlife, the river, that she recalls most vividly. Dona Rita is willing to acknowledge fluvial manipulation, but she is also keen to establish its limited character. She too talks about tides and the pororoca. But her language is more guarded: nature is prepared to undergo all kinds of alterations by all kinds of people, and, yes, she says, she has seen the drastic changes. But, she adds, this is no way to think about my husband and what he built in Igarapé Guariba. *These are not the things that matter.*

Let's pause here, just for a moment. Let's stop momentarily to ask what on earth you do with a statement like this. The blunt declaration that these are not the things that matter. A statement with which it is impossible not to both agree and disagree, fundamentally. We all guard our loved ones' memories, defend them from calumny, resist unjust representation and narrative. Dona Rita was telling me to honor this man, to give respect to someone who still stirred such tangled feelings in all who remembered him. Because Raimundo's remaking of nature had become too compromised — not by its unanticipated radical outcome, but by the transformed context in which it now found meaning. Dona Rita knew full well that in the power-laden geometry of international politics, the triumph of the pioneering will over Amazon nature was no longer a script that sold. Despite our differing locations, we both understood that once it began to travel the story of Igarapé Guariba would read instantly as one of deforestation and a hapless Amazon peasantry. And here we agree: this truly is not the thing that matters!

But, Dona Rita's refusal is also itself the sign of significance, revealing that what does count here is the very vitality of this contentious politics of nature. The incontrovertible fact is that people actually did these things, that, in Igarapé Guariba, place, nature, and locality were transformed — invented, even — through embodied practice. These micropractices of locality, these very things in which Octávio, Edinaldo, Dona Rita, the Macedos, and everyone else here are so profoundly invested, are precisely the natural-cultural histories to which this book cleaves. And for good reason. Because, as the travels that follow suggest, it is largely by the elision of the multiple agencies through which places are made that the Amazon itself, the Amazon that many of us know only as the space of a very particular nature, has come into existence.

4

A COUNTREY NEVER SACKT
Guiana, 1587–1631

Guiana and the Wild Coast — Correspondence of Native and
Colonial Mappings — Ralegh, Hakluyt, and the Imperial Project —
His Rapid Rise and Vapid Tumble — Failures of Science, Civility,
and Knowledge — A Politics of Restraint and Equivalence —
Circulations — Dialogue without Communication — The Rape of
Guiana, Its Promised Lands — Difference and Similitude, Proof and
Credence — The Ralegh Circle, Vernacular Science, and Scientific
Imperialism — A Pullulating World — Faced with Such Nature,
Words Fail Him — The Germ of the Tropical — The Plaines of
Sayma Are Not What They Seem — Violence, Subjection, and the
Displacement of Guiana

A river not a region. On the edge of a place, rather than the place itself. The Amazon entered Europe as a liminal space in an unsettled
cosmography.

It hardly mattered that the Spanish had long since witnessed popu-
lous hierarchical societies as they sailed downstream and out into the
Atlantic. At the end of the sixteenth century, the Amazon's principal
significance to Europeans was as the southern margin of Guiana, a region whose boundary reached from the mouth of the Orinoco, along
the shore of what is now Amapá, down to the Canal do Norte.[1] This
was what Europeans knew as the Wild Coast, the eastern seaboard of a
still mysterious territory that stretched an uncertain distance inland — at
times, depending on imperial hubris, all the way to the Pacific.[2] For the
English who fill the pages that follow, there was little reason to distinguish between the Amazon and the Orinoco. Edmund Spenser, for example, celebrating Sir Walter Ralegh's return from his first voyage to the
Orinoco in search of El Dorado, locates the "land of gold" on the Ama-

zon, "that huge Riuer, which doth beare his name / Of warlike Amazons, which doe possesse the same."[3]

This was not simply vague geography. The two rivers melded as
sites of the spectacularly indeterminate, and both their main channels
and the great landscapes between figured centrally in colonial-entrepre-
neurial design. For nearly fifty years, from the late 1580s to the 1630s,
English, Irish, Dutch, French, Portuguese, and Spanish maneuvered to
establish secure footing in a region that none could convincingly claim,
and to which they were drawn not only by gold, but by hardwoods,
dye-stuffs, tobacco, and a more general sense of abundance.[4] It was this
latter that Ralegh detailed to James I in strikingly domesticated terms in
his *Apologie* of 1618, a long, involuted letter written from Salisbury
while feigning illness following his catastrophic second voyage to Guiana:

> [B]esides the excellent air, pleasantness, healthfulness, and riches,
> it hath plenty of corn, fruits, fish, fowl (wild and tame), beeves,
> horses, sheep, hogs, deers, conies, hares, tortoises, armadiles,
> [ig]wanas, oils, honey, wax, potatoes, sugar canes, medica-
> ments, balsamum, simples, gums, and what not.[5]

Although Ralegh's prose would draw him into other modalities, this
was a nature that invited colonization rather than mere plunder. And it
was consistent with a defining characteristic of his Guiana: the compe-
tence of its native population, their self-conscious and developed political subjectivity, their recognition of the virtues of English restraint and
protection, and their unjust subjugation beneath the feet of the Spanish
intruder.

Indeed, it was not just in European cosmography that this expansive Guiana achieved cohesion. Beyond the wild coastline lay a complex
of shifting indigenous polities that spanned the Pakaraima uplands dividing the watersheds of the Amazon and Orinoco.[6] Formed out of
long-distance trade, as well as by conquest and kin-based and military
alliance, here was a parallel region deeply sedimented in traveling narrative and "politically integrated in native conceptions."[7] It was a realm
of active politics, sharpened by the intensifying presence of Europeans
that followed Orellana's descent of the Amazon in 1540. To the English,
it was an unexpectedly volatile realm, and they were wrong-footed by
the leadership and territorial changes that took place between Ralegh's
visit in 1595 and Lawrence Keymis' return a mere six months later—
reconfigurations that left them scrambling to reassemble a native alliance.

There is, of course, no mystery to the correspondence between indigenous and European mappings. Exploration was both dialogic and textual, a fundamentally ethnographic practice.[8] Ralegh, who learned Spanish specifically to read the accounts of the early expeditions, and who twice had the opportunity to test his skills on captive *conquistadores*, is explicit about this. His enterprise, he makes plain, is accretive and cumulative, building on the experience and authority of the Iberians who forced their way through the forests in search of El Dorado.[9] And how did these ill-equipped men chart this world? Through the stories of their native interlocutors, through the calculations of encounter and the tales of invasion and flight, through the same local narratives of history and nature in which Ralegh himself would participate, through stories inhabited by the immanent spatial logic of the region.

Guiana was the focus of English ambition in South America at a time of much-fabled English ascendancy. Between 1550 and 1630, a London-based alliance of merchants, gentry, and scholars effectively reinvented the English nation, creating an emergent imperial power out of an island backwater on the cold periphery of a disdainful Europe — an island barely present in the centers of continental trade and whose own domestic commerce was largely controlled by outsiders.[10] Yet, although the Elizabethan age is today recalled in national narratives as a triumphal era of maritime expansion, this was a period marked by political vacillation and by the reluctance of the queen and her successor, James I, to respond materially to the efforts of the imperialist lobby. As a result, English ventures in the New World were to suffer repeated failure and personal disaster.

Of all the failures, the most conclusive was Guiana. Of the personal disasters, the most compelling was that of Ralegh, which it contained. When the elderly courtier's flight to France was intercepted on the Thames and his captors rifled his pockets before removing him to the Tower, it was, symptomatically, mementos of Guiana that they discovered — maps, ingots, a spleenstone, an "idol of Gold" — the fetishes of obsession.[11]

Yet, to many contemporary and modern observers, Ralegh's two voyages to Guiana were of little moment. The first, wrote Vincent Harlow in 1928, "merely consisted in traversing the Orinoco from its estuary to the cataract on the Caroni, a journey with which every Spanish soldier at Trinidad was perfectly familiar."[12] The second, in 1617–18,

although involving a substantial force, was even less effectual, and Ralegh himself spent most of the time cabinbound off Trinidad, feverish
and exhausted, anxiously awaiting word from the expeditionaries.
No gold was recovered, no settlement founded, no enduring alliances
established.

It is true that Ralegh returned from South America with insufficient
material rewards to win his argument at Court. And it may well be that
to imperial dreamers the eventual claiming of British Guiana was, as
Pablo Ojer puts it, no more than a consolation prize.[13] But there is much
more here than such narrowly instrumental assessments would suggest.
Ralegh's voyages and his vivid 1595 account, *The Discoverie of the
Large, Rich, and Bewtiful Empire of Guiana*, proved an enduring colonial inspiration. In the decades around the turn of the seventeenth century, they guaranteed that the mouths of the Orinoco and Amazon were
thrown into violent and messy imperial competition, a definitive disaster for those already living in the region. Reinvoked in the nineteenth
century, they stood for lyrical precedent, the lineage through which the
English renewed their territorial claims within reconfigured geographies.[14]
At a moment when Europeans were still formulating a language through
which the New World would enter the vernacular imagination, Ralegh
issued an invitation to a region and a nature at once familiar and
strange, an unsettling yet alluring vision of what would become tropical
America.[15]

DESTINY AND DESIRE

From the defeat of the Spanish Armada of 1588 to the accession of
James I in 1603, English activity on the high seas was almost entirely
dedicated to privateering. Ralegh's complementary roles as a principal
sponsor of English maritime "picory" and chief architect of the Virginia
and Guiana campaigns indicate the extent to which trade and plunder
were entwined in these early imperial ventures.[16] Northern South America and the Antilles were prime sites for opportunistic pillage, and in the
Discourse of Western Planting (1584), a foundational appeal to the
Crown to stand behind American exploration and settlement, Richard
Hakluyt the younger drew particular attention to the Wild Coast:

> All that parte of America eastwarde from Cumana vnto the
> River of *Saint* Augustine in Bresill conteyneth in length alongest

to the sea side xxj C [2,100] miles, In whiche compasse and tracte there is neither Spaniarde, Portingale nor any Christian man but onely the Caribes, Indians, and saluages. In which places is greate plentie of golde, perle, and precious stones.[17]

Hakluyt wrote the *Discourse* "at the requeste and direction" of his patron, Ralegh. It was an important state paper, initially intended for the most restricted audience, and it represented the programmatic expression of the expansionist party at Court. It is here that Hakluyt introduces the two arguments repeatedly marshaled in support of the Guiana enterprise: absence of prior possession and presence of wealth beyond measure. In advancing these claims to the queen and Privy Council, the members of the influential circle gathered around Ralegh sought to formalize English maritime practice, and simultaneously to disrupt the aura of Spanish invincibility that underwrote national marginalization prior to the defeat of the Armada.[18] They understood clearly that without significant state financing the prospects for New World colonization were slim. Yet, with a nervous eye to future Spanish wars, Elizabeth was diffident. She rewarded Ralegh with a knighthood and Hakluyt with a prebend. But that was all.

Ralegh would repeat these same claims, again and again, right up until his silencing in late 1618. Even after Elizabeth had died, as if refusing to admit the changed circumstances of the Jacobean era, he continued to press a policy that could lead only to confrontation with a Spain whose ambassador now had the run of the English Court and a king deep in negotiation to marry the Infanta. At the last, both the logic and substance of Guiana eluded him. Having failed for so long to deliver on their promise, the claims he promoted with such bluster became themselves the basis of the charges used to justify his execution. Hadn't he intended war with Spain from the beginning? Didn't he know all along that the gold of El Dorado was just for fools?

The second voyage to Guiana came at the end of a long period of imprisonment. Sentenced to death by James for conspiracy and consigned to the Tower, Ralegh wrote his monumental *History of the World* (1614) to demonstrate the vanity of kings. His return to the Wild Coast took the form of a parole, and it was James who set the terms. In concluding the Treaty of London with Spain in 1604, the king had withdrawn Crown protection from any English who trespassed into Spanish-held territory. English adventurers might sail to the Wild Coast — a region of ambiguous sovereignty — but were then subject to Spanish attack and, should they retaliate, to charges of piracy on their return.[19] Only a highly profitable outcome could revise this calculus. In Ralegh's case, rehabilitation was possible only should he both find the gold mine he promised and avoid confrontation with the Spanish soldiers billeted in its approach.

In the event, the expedition, a large-scale affair involving at least a thousand men, was even more of a disaster than anticipated. No mine was found, the Spanish garrison of San Thomé was unprofitably sacked in the inglorious episode that claimed Ralegh's eldest surviving son, and as the *Destiny* limped home, in a clumsy and pathetic coda, Lawrence Keymis, his closest aide, first shot, then stabbed himself to death, adrift in love, loyalty, and humiliation.

Persuaded by a mutinous crew that flight for France, Newfoundland, or other potential safe harbor was out of the question, Ralegh returned to London and, with hair disheveled and clothes unkempt, climbed the awaiting scaffold. The decapitation scene, as a number of biographers have pointed out, was among the finest that he played, even if, by its nature, it simultaneously denied him the opportunity to savor the laudatory reviews.[20] No matter, it seems the death of the sustaining dream had killed him even before he faced the executioner's axe.

The failure of the second voyage to Guiana casts the trials of the first into tragic relief. But we should resist any sense of gathering futility. There was nothing to tell Ralegh and his associates that the fatal vision of unlimited wealth in Guiana was a chimera. Indeed, the lesson of the still recent sackings of the Aztec and Inca empires was that treasures inconceivable in their vastness awaited men bold enough in spirit.[21] As Ralegh himself reasons: "although these reportes [of El Dorado] may seem straunge, yet if wee consider the many millions which are daily brought out of *Peru* into Spaine, wee may easely beleeve the same."[22]

Interest in the Americas reflected a late realization that the bulldog strategy of intercepting and harrying the Spanish treasure fleet as it passed through the Caribbean was a poor substitute for the possession of equivalent sources of specie.[23] Despite the decline in New World gold and silver exports in this period, the inflationary instability of the Spanish economy, and the rapidity with which American bullion flowed from Castile to the finance houses of northwest Europe (and thence, in Fernand Braudel's chilling phrase, to the "necropolis" of Asia), the ambitious and patriotic Ralegh circle remained dazzled by the glint of precious metal and dedicated to usurping the Spanish monopoly.[24]

It was Hakluyt who provided this project's most public expression. His massive *Principal Navigations* (1589) was a striking embodiment of global ambition, conjuring imperial precedent from the English failure to capitalize on the fifteenth-century fishing voyages to the Brazilian coast from Bristol and on Cabot's trips to Newfoundland. His work was the earliest English institutional welding of science, commerce, and empire, part of the effort to pressure a Crown happy to benefit from private initiative but unwilling to venture its own diplomatic or financial resources. More decisively, Hakluyt brought together merchants and adventurers in a textual juxtaposition that materialized concretely in the innovative joint-stock companies of the period.[25] As a propagandist for expansion, he integrated the rhetorics of economy and travel with such skill that he was to begin the nineteenth century lionized as a prophet of free trade and to end it as the equally vaunted giant of imperial ambition.[26] In an important sense, this malleability of Hakluyt's reputation merely demonstrated the capacity of the Elizabethan "golden age" to function as a shifting signifier of nostalgic glory in later British politics. But it also accurately reflected the ties between commerce and militarism in Hakluyt and Ralegh's aggressively imperial mercantilism.

In March 1584, soon after the disappearance of his half brother Humphrey Gilbert off Newfoundland in the first concerted English attempt at American colonization, Ralegh received royal charter to find and settle what would ultimately become Virginia. It was the year before war broke out with Spain, and the queen's letters patent urged him

> at all times for euer hereafter to discouer, search, find out and view such remote heathen and barbarous lands, countreis and territories, not actually possessed of any Christian prince, nor inhabited by Christian people, as to him, his heires and assignes, and to euery or any of them as shall seeme good . . . to have holde, occupy & enjoy to him, his heires and assignes for euer with all prerogatiues, commodities, jurisdictions, royalties, priviledges, franchises and pre-eminences, thereto or thereabouts by land or sea, whatsoeuer we by our letters patent may grant.[27]

It was a lucrative prospect and Ralegh was prepared. Within two weeks a small expeditionary force set sail from the West Country, bound for a coastal reconnaissance of what are now Florida and North Carolina.

This was a moment of striking ascendancy for Ralegh. It was to

The queen's favorite, c. 1585

reach a climax with the destruction of the Spanish Armada of 1588, which followed the fateful settlement of Roanoke and left him awash in royal sinecures and with title to vast estates in Munster. We should set this achievement in gaining the queen's ear — and, as the schoolbooks tell us, her heart — in the context of an unlikely pedigree. Because he was the son of impoverished Devon gentry, Ralegh's background ensured his subjection to the encircling snobbery of the English elite,[28] and it is perhaps to explain his remarkable ascent that, with rare exception, biographers emphasize his charm, his energy, and his extravagant and strategic dandyism. Equally important, though, was the ceiling English society imposed on a man of his social origins, however seductive. As he undoubtedly knew and ultimately discovered, Crown indulgence, easily bestowed, could be withdrawn with even greater facility. Irrespective of the level of patronage he achieved, Ralegh's inheritance left him without clear manorial title and bereft of both dependable income and the possibility of establishing a landed dynasty. In this respect, England was stifling to his ambition—as was Spain to Cortés and Pizarro—and the best hope for a radical transcendence lay in the promise of perpetuity made by the letters patent and the prospect of vast lands and treasures overseas.

His ready participation in massacres of Irish and Spanish prisoners shows Ralegh to be ruthless, cold-blooded, and deceitful where national and self-interest coincide. Moreover, his business and personal dealings reveal a man frequently vain, amoral, and duplicitous. But it is also hard to resist the conclusion that, at critical moments, he found himself beyond his depth in the treacherous waters of the Tudor and Jacobean Courts. In 1592, just four years after the triumph of the Armada, he was to suffer a drastic reversal with Elizabeth's discovery of his secret marriage to Elizabeth Throckmorton and the birth of their daughter. Ralegh's bride was not only a maid-of-honor at Court, she was a member of a prominent Catholic family that had been held responsible for the 1584 plot to replace Elizabeth with her cousin, Mary, queen of Scots. His fall was as stunning as his rise. Temporarily banished to the Tower with his wife, he was reduced to pleading for petty favor through intermediaries. The discovery of Guiana held out the promise of redemption.

ARRIVAL

Ralegh was out-of-shape by the time he got to Guiana. He was forty-three years old, already past the flirtatious prime of the Elizabethan courtier, and we find him struggling, bitterly. No matter the flights of Arcadian lyricism he might achieve at times, the daily experience of travel in Guiana seems to have been overwhelmingly grueling.

Realistically and intimately, physical and spiritual ordeal is a recurring feature of the Guiana narratives. Indeed, in Ralegh's El Dorado quest, in the tribulations undergone in its pursuit, and in his characterization of the voyage as a "paineful pilgrimage,"[29] there is a reaching back to the legend cycles of King Arthur and Lord Owen Madoc, early Britons claimed by Hakluyt and John Dee as prior conquerors of America, legitimation for the still notional British Empire.[30] Travel on the Orinoco was grim:

> We carried 100 persons and their victuals for a moneth in the
> [open boat], being al driven to lie in the raine and wether, in the
> open aire, in the burning sunne, & pon the hard bords, and to
> dresse our meat, and to carry al manner of furniture in them,
> wherewith they were so pestred and unsavery, that what with
> victuals being most fish, with the weete clothes of so many men
> thrust together and the heate of the sunne, I will undertake
> there was never any prison in England, that coulde be founde
> more unsavory and loathsome, especially to my selfe, who had
> for many yeares before beene dieted and cared for in a sort
> farre differing.[31]

The double irony of this analogy would have been lost on neither
Ralegh nor his readers at Court. As they knew, he had recently been in
prison, but the Tower was less brutal than this voluntary hardship, a
suffering that by any measure proved his loyalty to a queen and nation
indivisible. But as well as conveying endurance, the physicality of the
language—the hard boards, the burning sun, the winds and rains that
punish the cramped sailors—is calculated to mark the materiality of
Guiana and its nature.

As the men cross the mouth of the Orinoco and travel farther into
the estuary, they without warning enter a region of undecidability. It is a
physical and narrative passage into the unknown and, as if to demonstrate their transgressing of an unseen border, the Indian pilot they
kidnapped as they crossed the bay is suddenly as bewildered as the
Englishmen:

> [T]his *Arawacan* promised to bring me into the great riuer of
> *Orenoque*, but indeed of that which we entred he was utterly
> ignorant, for he had not seene it in twelve yeeres before, at
> which time he was very yoong, and of no judgement, and if
> God had not sent us another helpe, we might have wandred a
> whole yeere in that laborinth of rivers, ere we had found any
> way, either out or in, especiallie after we were past the ebbing
> and flowing, which was in fower daies: for I know all the earth
> doth not yeeld the like confluence of streames and branches, the
> one crossing the other so many times, and all so faire and large,
> and so like one to another, as no man can tell which to take:
> and if we went by the Sun or compasse hoping thereby to go
> directly one way or another, yet that waie we were also caried

in a circle amongst multitudes of Ilands, and every Iland so
bordered with high trees, as no man could see any further than
the bredth of the river, or length of the breach.[32]

This is one of several memorable passages in *The Discoverie* in
which Ralegh captures his disorientation in the face of the unprecedented, a loss of psychic balance both terrifying and elating. This is
a landscape of "broken Ilands and drowned lands," "of many great
stormes and gusts, thunder, and lightnings," and of forests "thicke and
spiny, and so full of prickles, thorns, and briers, as it is impossible to
creepe thorow them."[33] Ralegh's panic rises. His strategies for mastering
space collapse around him. He has no reliable maps of the estuary. Instead, he plans to use this exploration and the abducted pilot's expertise
to make a map. But his forcible appropriation of local knowledge back-
fires: not only is this man unable to help them, his confusion only adds
to the English disarray. Even worse, the new science on which the imperial project is based dissolves within this indecipherable landscape.
Their navigational calculations and technologies fail them. They cannot
see far enough, or, if they can, they are unable to differentiate one from
another these labyrinthine channels in their maze-like routes between
indistinguishable islands. Techniques painstakingly developed in Renaissance libraries to plot longitudes and distance are as worthless for finding their position as are their clothes for protecting their persons. And,
like their clothes, their science turns out to be a hindrance, trapping
them into thinking they were prepared, that they could conquer uncertainty through method. It is the first defeat for empiricism, and, in its
symbolic leveling, it is also the first sign that Ralegh will encounter
native people in the spirit of Montaigne as well as that of Cortés; that
he will see these new worlds with both the relativizing eye of the *liber-
tins erudits* and with the "cold gaze of the soldier."[34]

THE WILD COAST

Ralegh's engagement with Guiana may have begun as early as 1587.
Historian Joyce Lorimer has uncovered documents suggesting his involvement in a murky affair aimed at establishing an outpost on the
Orinoco under the flag of the Portuguese pretender, Dom Antonio, prior
of Crato.[35] Though tentative, this venture already showed the strategic

interests at play. The Wild Coast was unprotected, "open to all and sundry," and it lay to windward of the Spanish main, relatively safe haven for ransack, encampment, and trade.[36] A base here could render vulnerable both the pearl fisheries of La Margarita to the north and the Atlantic treasure fleet itself. Moreover, Spain and its enemies shared a belief that descent of the Amazon could be reversed and that usurpers might travel upstream, exposing the Andean mines to attack from the east.[37]

But the project was also driven by the prospect of more dazzling reward. Just a few months earlier, two of Ralegh's privateering ships had returned from the Azores with Spanish prisoners. Among them was Pedro Sarmiento de Gamboa, famous through Europe as the colonist of the Straits of Magellan and a scholar of Incan history. Ralegh entertained him lavishly, and, in return, found himself enchanted into the ranks of the *doradistas*.[38]

In El Dorado, Europe found its second center of South American civilization and an incitement to exploration. Somewhere between the Amazon and the Orinoco lay the golden kingdom of Manco Capac, built by the defiant Inca after his repulsion from Cuzco in 1533.[39] It was a potent imaginative topography that drew Orellana down the Amazon in 1540 following his separation from Gonzalo Pizarro's starving band of conquistadores.[40] It also impelled the calamitous venture of Pedro de Ursúa, a project of conventional brutality until it surrendered to Lope de Aguirre's transcontinental terror, that stripped-down metaphor of colonial extremity captured in Werner Herzog's film *Aguirre, Wrath of God* (1972). Amazon exploration was a repeated debacle, attaining symbolic exhaustion in Aguirre's hallucinatory letter to Madrid:

> I advise thee not to send any Spanish fleet up this ill-omened river; for, on the faith of a Christian, I swear to thee, O king and lord, that if a hundred thousand men should go up, not one would escape, and there is nothing else to expect.[41]

As Amazon gold failed to materialize in the desired quantity, El Dorado migrated, and its elusiveness provoked a progressive inflation. From the early tales of a native king ritually anointed with gold dust, in Ralegh's *Discoverie* it became a Guianan kingdom of golden warriors "al shining from the foote to the head."[42]

Renewed Spanish attempts were led by Antonio de Berrio. In 1579, already fifty-three years old, Berrio inherited the governorship of a huge territory east of the Andes from Gonzalo Jiménez de Quesada, his uncle and the conqueror of New Granada. Quesada's brother, Hernán Perez de Quesada, assuming command in Bogotá, led a brutal campaign into the lowland forests of modern Colombia in search of the golden kingdom, returning with appetite unsatisfied and dying soon after—struck down by a lightning bolt in a widely appreciated signal of divine displeasure.[43] In 1583, following the trail downslope, Berrio marched eighty men as far the upper Orinoco, and by 1591 he was certain he had located El Dorado on Lake Manoa, at the headwaters of the Rio Caroní, close to the Orinoco estuary.[44]

Rumor of this activity filtered back to Europe in quayside conversations, seized documents, and chance meetings like that between Ralegh and the scholar-conquistador Sarmiento. And it is clear that the voyage of 1587 took place in the midst of increasing Europe-wide interest in the region's possibilities. The English contribution to the expedition was small. But it included four anonymous young men, two of whom were set ashore in Trinidad and two on an island in the Orinoco delta. They were the first of several to be planted in this way, and their task was to learn native languages and establish informal alliance, opening the way to a more substantial presence. Their fate is unknown. But their assignment is the first indication of the dialogic form of the Guiana enterprise, its simultaneously strategic and open character as a series of calculated yet affective negotiations and exchanges.

As the promise of his North American enterprise fades, we see Ralegh's attention turning increasingly to Guiana.[45] In 1594, released from the Tower but out of favor, he outfitted two ships under Jacob Whiddon, the captor of Sarmiento. Whiddon returned from Trinidad with the news that Berrio had built a fort on the island, securing the critical supply route to the Wild Coast, and that he was preparing a further expedition to the land of gold.

Speech Acts

Ralegh's fleet of five ships left Plymouth with one hundred men in February 1595. Unlike many of the overseas ventures of the time, his expedition was underwritten almost entirely by investors from the landed gentry, the absence of merchant interest an indication that its material prospects were viewed as less promising than its patriotic ones.[46] As if to

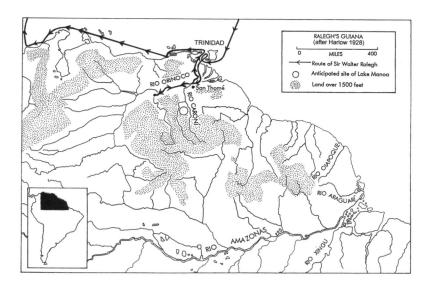

refute such judgments, Ralegh stopped off en route to raid Trinidad. The unexpected booty he netted turned out to be Antonio de Berrio. It was what A. L. Rowse has aptly called "a fatal stroke of luck."[47] In spite of the conquistador's dark admonitions, the long shipboard interviews only intensified Ralegh's commitment to the El Dorado quest, kindling the fire set by Sarmiento and inspiring the extraordinary tales of native kingdoms and thwarted knights that fill the early pages of *The Discoverie*. The closure of the region to competitors assumed ever greater urgency.

As we have seen, the Tudor letters patent granted property rights to the New World in a context of geopolitical maneuver. The legalistic phrasing carefully avoided acknowledging competing claims. All lands "not actually possessed of any Christian prince, nor inhabited by Christian people" were open to broad categories of exploitation. Yet, although dominion was extended to landscapes formally figured as empty terrain, the imagination of such territory as "heathen and barbarous lands" showed the elision of native people to be far from complete.[48] Despite the explicit absence of non-Christians in these grants, it was self-evident to Crown and colonizer that the meaningful production of colonial space required effective sovereignty over regional populations. By the late sixteenth century, Europeans knew that indigenous politics could not be taken for granted. Unsettling instances of local resistance and rebellion made it clear that the outcome of colonial encounter could be bloody and uncertain, and that the allegiance of native elites was often a decisive prize.[49]

Despite disavowal, then, relations with indigenous Americans were the cause of tremendous anxiety. For Ralegh, they demanded the politics of embodied restraint, a moral and strategic continence that was also the measure of his leadership:

> I suffred not anie man to take from anie of the nations so much as a *Pina*, or a *Potato* roote, without giving them contentment, nor any man so much as to offer to touch any of their wives or daughters: which course, so contrarie to the Spaniards (who tyrannize over them in all things) drew them to admire hir Majestie, whose commandement I told them it was, and also woonderfully to honour our nation. But I confess it was a very impatient worke to keepe the meaner sort from spoile and stealing, when we came to their houses, which bicause in all I could not prevent I caused my Indian interpreter at every place when we departed, to know of the losse or wrong done, and if ought were stolen or taken by violence, either the same was restored, and the party punished in their sight, or els it was paid for to their utmost demand.[50]

This remarkable behavior had two self-conscious reference points, both immediately recognizable to Ralegh's readers. The first was personal: Ralegh's ragged reputation as a sexual adventurer, his estrangement from the queen following his marriage, and his attempt to recover his favored status — a complex cluster to which I return below. The second association was with the *leyenda negra*, the Black Legend of Spanish barbarity in the Americas. Humanist Catholic texts such as Las Casas' *Breuissima relacion de la destruycion de las Indias* (1552) had demonstrated to the English that the divine right to empire could be forfeited on moral grounds — reasoning that Hakluyt appropriated in support of the manifest destiny of Protestant colonization.[51] This was a serviceable but highly contingent ethics, absent, for example, from the Irish campaigns and selectively applied where it might create tactical advantage. Temperance was part of a larger strategic practice: Spanish conduct provided an opening to the more self-controlled outsider; successful alliance with disaffected but still dependent elites required the sustained work of diplomacy.

The key relationship Ralegh establishes in Guiana is with the aged "king" Topiawari, an ally he presents as the most reliable client of the Crown. Topiawari's territory offered access to the borders of El Dorado, and treaty with him was a central goal of the expedition. It was also Ralegh's only clear accomplishment and, accordingly, is described in careful and sympathetic detail. It is this sympathy that has led Mary Campbell to praise Ralegh for the "widening of consciousness" he achieves in his representation of native Guianans, people who most often enter his account as individualized interlocutors, emerging through reported speech as multidimensional subjects.[52] Campbell explains this in terms of the structural position of such people as Topiawari in Ralegh's campaign and narrative. They are his informants, providers of the vital data he needs to accomplish his mission. Ralegh introduces them through events in which they themselves are central actors. It is a rhetoric designed to convey the credibility of his sources, as well as the authenticity of his own presence. *The Discoverie*, above all, is an argument for intervention: an argument based not only on the existence of El Dorado, but on the military vulnerability of Guiana and on the authority of the narrator himself.

But there is a certain delicacy here. For his project to succeed on either side of the Atlantic, Ralegh's informants should themselves be convincingly authoritative and substantial. As allies, they must be capable of delivering arms and resources. They must also be moral beings, appreciative of the superior English virtues. Yet, at the same time, neither his field practice nor its reporting can leave any doubt as to Ralegh's own mastery of encounter. Thus, at the outset of their first meeting, Ralegh explicitly subverts Topiawari's local authority, managing the idiom of courtliness to claim for himself the rights of host. In a show of condescending deference to the "king of *Arromaia*," Ralegh establishes the ground for their interview by raising a tent and allowing Topiawari, now the visitor in his own domain, to rest in its shade. Eventually, with the aid of Ralegh's interpreter, they talk:

> I asked what nations those were which inhabited on the further side of those mountaines, beyond the valley of *Amariocapana*, he answered with a great sigh (as a man which had inward feeling of the losse of his conntrey and liberty, especially for that his eldest sonne was slain in a battel on that side of the mountaines, whom he most entirely loved), that he remembred

in his fathers life time when he was very old, and himselfe a
yoong man that there came down into that large valley of *Guiana*, a nation from so far off as the *Sun* slept, (for such were his
own words,) with so great a multitude as they could not be
numbred nor resisted, & that they wore large coats, and hats of
crimson colour, which colour he expressed, by shewing a piece
of red wood, wherewith my tent was supported, and that they
were called *Oreiones*, and *Epuremei*, those that had slain and
rooted out so many of the ancient people as there were leaves
in the wood upon all the trees.[53]

There is something quite out of the ordinary here: an ethnographic
sensibility rare in the contemporary literature. Despite Ralegh's controlling of the terms of the interview, the passage is striking for its labor of
empathy, the resolve to break the barriers of language and capture the
voice, gesture, and historicized subjectivity of Topiawari, less an indigene than a fellow noble. It is a narrative of doubling. Ralegh offers us
the inner life of an outsider, his "inward feeling," a tale of dispossession
made real through the immediacy of reported speech and by the appeal
to the universality of the emotionally specific—the loss of homeland,
parent, and, as Ralegh himself had recently experienced, child. He shows
a willingness to allow the equivalence of rank, with its embedded con-
fusions of sentiment and honor, to transcend difference.[54] As such, the
account of their meeting is intended to impress upon his status-
conscious readers the wonder of similitude, within an environment of
difference:[55]

> This *Topiawari* is held for the proudest, and wisest of al the
> *Orenoquopeni*, and so he behaved himselfe towards me in all
> his answers at my returne, as I marvelled to finde a man of that
> gravity and judgement, and of so good discourse, that had no
> helpe of learning nor breed.[56]

The familiar bustle in Topiawari's camp takes Ralegh back to "a
great market or faire in England," and, when he again meets the old
king on his return downstream, the deferential visitor "desires" him to
"instruct me" some more about Guiana.[57]

Although by now we sense that this discoverie will be little more
than a scouting trip, Ralegh uses the authority of the old man's detailed
advice as the premise on which to abandon his planned march on El

Dorado. Finally, they undertake what Ralegh presents as a symbolic exchange of kin:

> [H]e freely gave me his onelie sonne to take with me into England, and hoped, that though he himselfe had but a short tyme to live, yet that by our meanes his sonne shoulde be established after his death: and I left with him one *Frauncis Sparrow*, a servant of captain *Gifford*, (who was desirous to tarry and coulde describe a cuntrey with his pen) and a boy of mine called *Hugh Goodwin*, to learne the language.[58]

We have to be wary of reading too much of Topiawari through Ralegh. It is, however, clear that native leaders were faced with a number of competing options at this moment of sudden involvement in imperial competition. Topiawari, too, is negotiating an ally at these meetings, and their exchange patterns the relationship in a manner notable for its formal mutuality. We might regard this transaction as an inaugural moment in the relationship between Guiana and Europe. Ralegh, with no apparent sense of the potential ambiguities of such an act, offers it as a moment of purity: a ceremonialized meeting of distinct societies, untainted by cultural or — thanks to his vigilance — sexual miscegenation. We know that native Americans were already long marked by commercial and political intercourse with Europeans.[59] Here though, we meet exchange of a different order. True, Ralegh presents a highly specific contract embodying strategic and affective association between the English and the "Arromaia." But this transaction also transcends such individualities, signaling a new transoceanic regime as human bodies circulate, securing the cultural and genetic hybridization that has become axiomatic in local discourse on modern Amazonia. It is one of the starting points for a complex history of institutionalization and counter appropriation that today is often figured too easily as a tragic endgame of cultural extinction. Topiawari sent several men to London: of these, two will later assist Ralegh with botanical experiments during his imprisonment in the Tower, and it seems plausible that a third is the Anthony Canabre who serves as Robert Harcourt's interpreter on the Oiapoque in 1609, returning to mediate between what are no longer two worlds.[60]

Yet, even such elaborate dialogue cannot guarantee communication. Ralegh had failed to hear what Topiawari was telling him. The Guianan requested a body of fifty armed men as defense against the Spanish. The

Englishman demurred, leaving just Sparrey and the sixteen-year-old Goodwin. The following year, when Lawrence Keymis sailed out to consolidate the alliance, he found that Topiawari had fled ahead of a small force of Berrio's men and was now dead. Compounding disaster, Berrio had established the fort of San Thomé on the strategic site of the old man's port, blockading the gateway to El Dorado.[61] This was the garrison where Wat Ralegh, the eldest son, would be killed under Keymis' command in 1618 and the reef upon which the El Dorado adventure was finally wrecked.

Perhaps it is useful here to recall Stephen Greenblatt's comment that the "overriding interest" of these chroniclers of New World encounters was "not knowledge of the other but practice upon the other."[62] Clearly, the separation is not so clean and, as I have emphasized, there are also reciprocities: local people were involved in a set of practices that were no less tied up in the political economy of exploration than were those of the Europeans whose invention it was. Yet, the emphasis on practice is rewarding. For Topiawari, practice on the other, however disadvantageous the terms, extended across the Atlantic to the Elizabethan Court. For Ralegh, it also stretched beyond Guiana to London, and, similarly, to the reception of *The Discoverie* in the chambers of state and the joint-stock companies. Both men knew that the return voyage carried the burden of the colonial future. However much he may elide the structural asymmetries, Ralegh infuses his text with this powerful intimation that, like himself, Topiawari and the other Guianan leaders are involved in a high-stakes game for personal and political survival. It is with a sense of ontological equivalence that he creates these recognizable Americans, as circumscribed by calculation and micropolitics as any Tudor courtier or statesman.

But this is shifting ground. And there is another, radically different language in which Ralegh tells the story of Guiana. It is, unmistakably, what Michel de Certeau has called "*writing that conquers*," writing that uses the New World as "a blank, "savage" page on which Western desire will be written."[63] It is writing that draws the lines of difference and spells out their consequences. And it arrives most jarringly at the end of Ralegh's narrative in a vision of violation, a proposition that colors all that came before:

> To conclude, *Guiana* is a Countrey that hath yet her Maydenhead, never sackt, turned, nor wrought, the face of the earth

hath not been torne, nor the vertue and salt of the soyle spent
by manurance, the graves have not been opened for gold, the
mines not broken with sledges, nor their Images puld down out
of their temples.[64]

Complicated figures. But conventional also. George Chapman, in *De
Guiana carmen Epicum*, his epic poem that commemorates Ralegh's
first voyage, imagines the English conquerors with "their glad feet on
smooth Guiana's breast."[65] For Lawrence Keymis, Guiana is also a
woman, and similarly enticing, although no longer so innocent. Her
lands "do prostitute themselves unto us," he writes in his account of
1596, "like a faire and beautifull woman in the pride and floure of
desired yeeres."[66]

Sexual conquest was already a commonplace metaphor for colonial
subjugation, drawing on the long-standing symbolic alignment of nature and the feminine.[67] The figuring of Guiana as woman—in the context of the male expedition—extends the logic of contemporary gender
relations, feminizing Guianan landscapes and Guianans, naturalizing
the politics of dispossession. For the Elizabethan Englishman, it also has
its more specific referent: an assertion of subject masculinity in an age
of peculiar ambivalence.[68] Ralegh's virgin Guiana, the site of his own
sexual restraint, is a too-transparent metaphor for his virgin queen, and
its symbolic violation at the close of his account can be read as a mark
of his recent humiliations, a textual response to his banishment, wounded
and nasty. His tone turns threatening, the wheedling diminishes. If Elizabeth is not willing to "invade and conquere"—to perform the rape in
her own name—she will forfeit dominion to "men worthy to be kings
thereof" who "will undertake it of themselves."[69] He resolves the ambivalence around his vaunted continence but in a manner dangerous
and self-defeating. His parting shot becomes a further instance of *The
Discoverie*'s failure as a persuasive text. It strikes the wrong tone, as if
he suspects the limits of his writerly powers and has tired of this game,
as if he knows already that Elizabeth will not be seduced into support-
ing this extravagant American fantasy.

The potential assaults on Guiana's virtue that Ralegh lists here—
rape, theft, ransack—are the very activities from which he and his men
so self-consciously refrain. It is their rejection that separates English
civility from Spanish barbarity, enabling Keymis' fantasy of Guiana, the
eager colonial vassal, inviting his entry. Other actions however—the

working, turning, and planting of the land — are the foundation of a putatively different type of colonial enterprise, and the selfsame projects that have only recently failed Ralegh in Roanoke. This conflation of plantation and violation is thus an uneasy coupling. It implies that all along disavowal has been merely deferral, a further incitement. Plantation will take place, the land will be worked and turned, and the riches of the country will be pillaged without restraint. The character of English imperial command is not so different from that of the Spanish after all.

In this discourse of Guianan planting, the value of the region derives not just from the temporary stay of colonial depradation but, equally, from the lack of industry of native people. When, in the following decades, the English achieve their brief settlement of the Oiapoque and Amazon, it is, inevitably, to turn the soil, to plant tobacco and sugar, and to undertake manurance. With his usual bluntness, Keymis captures the logic of Ralegh's conceit, and he does so with an inversion that domesticates the territory to emphasize its appeal. In Guiana, he tells potential investors, there are "whole shires of fruitfull rich grounds, lying now waste for want of people."[70] It is an invitation that will echo down the centuries: a land poor in people but rich in resources; a land of indolence awaiting only industry; a pristine landscape on which the marks of culture are rendered invisible, invalid, unproductive.[71]

DISCOVERY

A full century had passed since Columbus' landfall in the Caribbean, yet at the time of Ralegh's outfitting of the El Dorado venture, Europe was still in the midst of a long and uneven process of intellectual assimilation. Rather than a definitive intellectual watershed, the discovery of the New World had turned out to be an extended, uncertain, and incomplete process, one that as readily enlivened medieval thought as overthrew it. Debates on such questions as the character of native humanity and the distinctiveness of New World nature were to sustain their urgency well into the seventeenth century and beyond, and it was not only in relation to definitions of America that local hierarchies were destabilized.[72] In the most famous examples — Montaigne's "Of cannibals" (1580) and "Of coaches" (c. 1585) — scathing satire of the civilized was combined with precise, conventionally idealized depictions of reported native American mores, and drawing on the tradition recently initiated by Las Casas, the conduct of New World colonialism was taken as a measure of European debasement.[73]

American novelties were not, as often supposed, a fatal challenge to a coherent system of Old World tradition and belief.[74] Among Renaissance scholars, familiarity with the classical texts had brought with it a rich sense of human, geographical, and historical difference — as well as strategies for rendering difference intelligible. Moreover, any philosophical coherence had long since fragmented, and the accounts of discovery entered Europe as supplements to the lively antagonism between humanists and scholastics in which many of the chroniclers themselves participated. The foundational texts, the geography and natural history of Herodotus, Strabo, and Pliny, among others, had proved fluid and adaptable and, taken together as a complex and frictional corpus, had been subject to appraisal in a dissenting atmosphere that substantially predated the American voyages.[75] By the late sixteenth century, Lorraine Daston and Katherine Park tell us, European scholars were engaged in a bruising "intellectual free-for-all."[76]

For humanists, New World discoveries could enrich and strengthen the traditional schema while simultaneously demonstrating the foolishness of a dogmatic reliance on the ancient corpus. Once landfall in the Americas was confirmed, it was the Bible that often emerged as the most secure authority, and reconciliation among the scriptures, the ancients, and the discoveries was a familiar struggle — one in which Ralegh was to engage repeatedly in the *History of the World*.[77] Travelers to America could experience firsthand the falsity of the Aristotelian *klimata* underlying the Renaissance map's division into habitable *oikoumene* and outlying antipodean, boreal and torrid zones, the preserves of the marvelous races. The Bible, on the other hand, with a versatile imprecision, records that God instructed Adam and Eve to go forth and multiply. This is the starting point for the official Spanish chronicles of the New World, the *Decades* (1511–30) written by the Milanese humanist, Peter Martyr. In 1587, Hakluyt dedicated his edition of the *Decades* to Ralegh, who read the chronicles before setting out for Guiana and who shared Martyr's "critical skepticism,"[78] as well as the pre-evolutionary conviction in a global nature, invented by God and intact since Creation.

Notwithstanding creationist unity, early modern scholars — especially those who crossed the Atlantic — found ways of making sense of

American difference without reductionism, although without resolving the tension between difference and resemblance, novelty and the familiar. Accounts are laden with the hyperbole of difference — "I know all the earth doth not yeeld the like confluence of streames and branches." Yet, interpretation often demanded a falling-back on personal experience. Ralegh manages novelty via its refraction through pre-existing aesthetic conventions, a comparative method in which familiar precedent is invoked through historical as well as geographical analogue, through reference to ancient Rome as well as to English parkland.[79] Even his Amazons show appropriate Tudor virtues: "cruell and bloodthirsty" in war, so courtly in love that they "cast lots for their *Valentines.*"[80]

Ralegh's reports of such New World marvels are worth considering in some detail. He takes care to establish that his interest in Amazons, oyster-trees, and the headless Ewaipanoma is a curiosity born of science. Unable to meet any Amazons for himself, yet "very desirous to understand the truth," he "made inquirie amongst the most ancient and best traveled of the *Orenoqueponi.*"[81] He proceeds according to a hierarchy of proofs: textual authority (at various points he cites such familiar figures as Pliny, Mandeville, Thevet, and Martyr), reliable hearsay (often gained in conversation with local leaders), and, the only unequivocal test, the evidence of his own eyes.[82] This was an empiricist methodology derived from the experimental, a logic through which the discoveries were becoming reinterpreted as the ground of a modern science, distinct from prior knowledges: "I am aware," wrote the astronomer Kepler in 1610, "how great a difference there is between theoretical speculation and visual experience; between Ptolemy's discussion of the antipodes and Columbus's discovery of the New World."[83]

A methodological distinction of this type was entirely consistent with Ralegh's larger contribution to the English maritime effort. At once patron, student, and pioneer of scientific navigation, he assembled a collaborative network of practitioners and scholars caught up in the associated development of cartography, logarithms, and optics, practices explicitly conceived as applied sciences.[84] As well as veterans of the recent Irish subjugations — a proving ground for would-be conquistadores — this select circle of Americanists included merchants, mariners, and instrument-makers, the prominent astronomer-mathematicians John Dee and Thomas Hariot, and the artists Theodore de Bry and John White, whose images of native American life were to have

lasting influence on European ideas of geographical and historical difference.[85]

This was a comprehensive attempt to found imperial expansion on
a systematic, empirical basis. And, with some justification, it has been
said that Ralegh made of each of his voyages a scientific expedition.[86] By
this, we should not imagine the type of extravagant data-collecting regime famously imposed on James Cook by Joseph Banks in 1768.[87] Although Ralegh's interests in New World botanicals and mineralogy might
anticipate those of later colonial travelers, his principal energies were
devoted to the foundational task of placing navigation on a scientific
footing.[88] Held in the Tower from 1603, Ralegh read Copernicus and
Galileo (as well as Machiavelli), and he equipped a workshop where,
assisted by the Puritan Lady Apsley and Arawak men who had returned
with him from Guiana in 1595, he experimented with ways of keeping
meat fresh at sea, of curing scurvy, of distilling fresh water from salt
water, and of deriving medicinals from various New World plants.[89]

This utilitarian experimentation fits squarely within the broader
context of what Christopher Hill has called "a greedy demand for scientific information" in sixteenth-century England.[90] The Ralegh circle aggressively promoted a vernacular science, seeing in it the basis for a new
expansionist maritime politics. Merchant recognition that effective navigation, mining, and surveying relied on modern mathematics and as-
tronomy created the conditions for a potent alliance of capital, craft,
and scholarship outside the Aristotelian bulwarks of the academy. Indeed, the laboratories of the period were not in Oxbridge, but in London, in the workshops developing new techniques to process glass, paper, dyes, metal, and sugar.[91] The intellectual energy of this coalescence
of popular scientific production—a rash of books aimed at merchants,
craftsmen, mariners, and surveyors—was fueled by a popular nationalist anti-Spanish politics that embraced economic liberalism and was expressed most succinctly in the Hakluytian demand for free commercial
access to the Spanish-American empire. It was to be seen clearly in the
sponsorship of Gresham College, an urban, merchant-founded, adult
education institution, providing free lectures in the vernacular and self-
consciously organized as an alternative to the universities.[92]

Yet, we should be cautious about mapping sixteenth-century science
as coherently prefigurative of our own. This was a world in which the
phenomena of nature were "bursting and pullulating," animated, and
brimming with cosmic meaning.[93] Although Ralegh's was an instrumen-

tal experimentation, it was also a product of the surge of interest in natural history and natural philosophy expressed in the eclectic encyclopedia of the *Kunst- und Wunderkammer*, the cabinets of curiosity.[94] Manifold new territories, scientific as well as geographic, were on the horizon. Ralegh may have approached his marvels with circumspection, but he was by no means immune to their substance, and, as a mode of inquiry, the non-compartmentalized natural philosophy he debated with Dee and Hariot has few corollaries in the post-nineteenth-century distribution of art, religion, and science. There was no incongruity to the pairing of imperial hardheadedness with fabulous non-headedness: the reincarnation of the ancient world's acephalous Blemmyes as the Guianan Ewaipanoma. Such juxtaposition speaks to an epistemological ordering in which "the conventional antinomies of visionary and down-to-earth, romantic and practical, have little meaning."[95] In John Dee, we meet an energetic imperial scholar whose translation of Euclid's *Elements* (1570) was part of a modernist program of extending the methods of quantitative analysis to natural questions, and whose mechanistic view of the universe would be familiar to Kepler, Galileo, and Descartes.[96] Yet, Dee's knowledge was also divine revelation, communicated in his long-running conversations with angels, and his remarkable technical contribution to modern navigation was bound up with his desire to reach Cathay and find Initiates to the secrets of the Philosopher's Stone and Elixir of Life.[97]

Nonetheless, in the chatter surrounding Elizabeth, Ralegh's reports of the marvels of Guiana contributed to a general disbelief in the reliability of his narrative, which was received locally as a work of the literary imagination.[98] In this time of growing skepticism, when a readership capable of scrutiny and comparison was being formed from the glut of travelers' narratives, authorial credibility was no longer a given, and Ralegh's qualification and hedging were inadequate defense.[99] Amazons and Acephali—as well as creatures that did not appear in *The Discoverie*, such as dog-headed Cynocephali and the Sciopodes whose one foot was so large they could rest in its shade—were traceable through Pliny to Greek reports of their fifth-century B.C. Persian and Egyptian neighbors.[100] Just as they demeaned the paltry financial rewards of his voyage, accusing him of having returned via Barbary to buy the ore he presented at Court, Ralegh's opponents ridiculed the narrative extravagances of *The Discoverie*.

Yet, animated by the overseas voyages, the medieval vogue for the

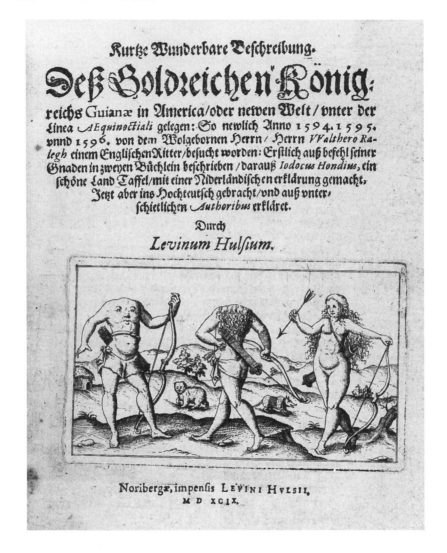

Kurtze Wunderbare Beschreibung.

Deß Goldreichen Königs

reichs Guianæ in America/oder newen Welt/ vnter der
Linea Æquinoctiali gelegen: So newlich Anno 1594. 1595.
vnnd 1596. von dem Wolgebornen Herrn/ Herrn VValthero Ralegh einem Englischen Ritter/besucht worden: Erstlich auß befehl seiner
Gnaden in zweyen Büchlein beschrieben / darauß *Iodocus Hondius*, ein
schöne Land Taffel/mit einer Niderländischen erklärung gemacht.
Jetzt aber ins Hochteutsch gebracht/vnd auß vnter-
schietlichen *Authoribus* erkläret.

Durch

Levinum Hulsium.

Norbergæ, impensis LEVINI HVLSII.
M D XCIX.

wondrous in nature was still flourishing in late-sixteenth-century Europe,[101] and Ralegh's marveling was fashionable and tactical, as well as
epistemological. *The Discoverie* was an immediate literary success. It
ran through three editions in 1596, was rapidly translated into Latin
and German, and circulated internationally in several of the popular
compendia of discovery narratives—Hakluyt's *Principal Navigations*,
Hulsius' *Voyages*, and the Latin, French, and German editions of De
Bry's *Americae*.[102] It produced echoes in the literature of the seventeenth

century and stayed in print in various European languages throughout the eighteenth. From Othello's bitter memory of the "Anthropophagi and men whose heads / Do grow beneath their shoulders" (1604) and De Bry's and Hulsius' foregrounding of Amazons and Ewaipanoma in their engravings — (left, Hulsius' title page of 1599) — it seems clear that the same sensations for which *The Discoverie* suffered at Court were not only a source of its wider appeal, but also diagnostic and constitutive of the early modern European imaginary of Guianan nature.

ON THE NATURE OF GUIANA

When Ralegh claimed that nowhere else on earth was there such a confusion of streams, "the one crossing the other so many times, and all so faire and large, and so like one to another, as no man can tell which to take," it was not an excuse for his disarray. Rather, he was underscoring difference to emphasize his ultimate achievement in overcoming it. Yet, in this passage and in many others like it, what Ralegh succeeds in conveying above all is the radical and protean otherness of Guianan nature. Rhetorically, on the heels of a long and scholarly preamble appealing for investment and patronage on the basis of the failures of previous El Dorado expeditions, what he offers is a characteristically self-defeating contradiction, one that undermines his own strategic interests. Because why should an investor risk dearly held capital to enter a world of such prodigious unpredictability?

American nature was psychically as well as physically unsettling. New nature demanded new vocabulary. *Waterfall, cataract, lagoon, whirlpool, swamp, hurricane, tornado,* and *thunderstorm* all entered the English language in the first hundred years of exploration.[103] Ralegh gropes for neologisms, twisting existing terms to fit unfamiliar phenomena. Words, literally, fail him. He settles on *overfals,* "the turbulent meeting of contrary currents," to capture what we now recognize as the spectacular Caroní Falls. But his usage will not survive past 1613.[104]

New referents demanded new signifiers. Peter Hulme has traced the steady displacement of the English vernacular "tempest" by "hurricane," from the Arawakan *hurakan.* The English language seemed incapable of describing such alien terror, only the American word would do. The hurricane was "an attribute of native savagery, a fact confirmed by its tendency of attacking . . . the marks of civility: the building of towns and the practices of tillage and husbandry."[105] The otherness of such phenomena was only meaningful when tied to its geographical and human context. It was through such congruencies and correspondences between the natural and the human that Ralegh and his contemporaries found order in their pullulating world, and regulated — E.M.W. Tillyard's word is "tamed" — the anomalies of New World nature.[106] Yet Ralegh consistently avoids the negative conflation of human and natural menace. Rather than between European and native, his principal arenas of conflict in Guiana are those between English and Spanish, and between humans — English, Spanish, and native — and nature.

The unpredictable logic of this nature is at times unfathomable to the European traveler. Tides, currents, islands, winds, rains, and hills circumscribe travel and open its potentialities. But they do so firmly on their own account, not as embodiments of human difference. Looking through the eyes of his native pilots, Ralegh sees a landscape that is intensely mercurial, as frequently inimical as it is harmonious. Even at its most familiar, this animate New World remains more exotic than the indigenous Guianans with whom he is able to converse and whose signs he can claim to interpret. This nature, he knows, is profoundly meaningful, but too often its meanings elude him, to the point that his entire enterprise is under threat.

The heightened imaginative pitch of the opening scenes on the Orinoco establishes a tension between the invaders and nature that Ralegh never fully succeeds in ordering. Although he manages to acquire a knowledgeablc pilot, he can never relax because "many times the old man himselfe was in great doubt which river to take."[107] The traumatic crossing of the estuary shakes Ralegh's confidence, and *The Discoverie* is peppered with commentary on the punishments he and his men endure from waters and climate. It is a struggle that continues right up until their nail-biting departure from the delta:

> [W]hen we were arrived at the sea side then grew our greatest doubt, and the bitterest of all our journey forepassed, for I protest before God, that wee were in a most desperate estate: for the same night which we ancored in the river of *Capuri*, wherc it falleth into the sea, there arose a mighty storme, and the rivers mouth was at least a league broad, so as we ran before night close under the land with our small boates, and brought the Galley as neere as we could, but she had as much a doe to

live as coulde be, and there wanted little of her sinking, and all those in her.[108]

Much like the storm through which Shakespeare was to deposit Antonio, Ferdinand, and the rest on Prospero's Island in *The Tempest* (1611), Ralegh's bracketing of his time on the Orinoco in this way is an effective device to dramatize the distinctiveness of the New World. Like those of Shakespeare's shipwrecked Italians, the torments undergone by Ralegh and his men pervade the narrative, potent auguries that enliven natural phenomena and bring them to life as actors, center stage in the drama of discovery, a nature that colonizes consciousness and manipulates mortality.

Such anxiety here. Part stems from the enforced dependence on local people that these unnerving natural conditions create. Three days after capturing their new guide, a man familiar with this stretch of the river, their galley hits a sandbar. They haul it off and press on. But the next day finds them rowing hard against the swiftly running current:

> [W]e had then no shift but to perswade the companies that it was but two or three daies worke, and therfore desired them to take paines, every gentleman and others taking their turns to row, and to spell one the other at the howers end. . . . When three daies more were overgone, our companies began to despaire, the weather being extreame hot, the river bordered with verie high trees that kept away the aire, and the currant against us every daie stronger than other: But we evermore commanded our Pilots to promise an end the next daie, and used it so long as we were driven to assure them from fower reaches of the river to three, and so to two, and so to the next reach: but so long we laboured as many daies were spent, and so driven to draw our selves to harder allowance, our bread even at the last, and no drinke at all: and our men and our selves so wearied and scorched, and doubtfull withall whether we should ever perform it or no.[109]

These are desperate straits. Weak from hunger and heat, Ralegh is reduced to pleading with his men to keep going lest "the worlde . . . laugh us to scorne."[110] At this moment of despair, suddenly, unannounced, Guianan nature shows its other face:

> On the banks of these rivers were divers sorts of fruits good to eate, flowers and trees of that varietie as were sufficient to

make ten volumes of herbals, we releeved ourselves manie times with the fruits of the countrey, and sometimes with foule and fish: we saw birds of all colours, some carnation, some crimson, orenge tawny, purple, greene, watched [pale blue], and of all other sorts both simple and mixt, as it was unto us a great good passing of the time to behold them, besides the reliefe we founde by killing some store of them with our fouling peeces.[111]

This is the first intimation Ralegh gives us that nature in Guiana can be as paradisaical as it is nightmarish. It is a decisive moment, but hardly unexpected. One unspoken premise of the voyage to Guiana has always been "the literalization of the celestial Jerusalem" in El Dorado's gilded hallways.[112] This, of course, is merely one migration of many in this period: Berrio has moved El Dorado from the upper Amazon to Guiana; Montaigne's natural savage has relocated to Brazil from Cicero's Scythia and Tacitus' Germany; and, here, with Columbus and Ralegh, Mandeville's missing paradise of the east finds an American home.[113] What is significant is the need to fix these places geographically as well as imaginatively, to find in them objects of exploration, discovery, and possession. Ralegh, we know, consistently comes up short of his stated goal and must always resort to finding substance in the mostly inconsequential. He does not discover El Dorado or even its outliers. He fails to secure meaningful alliances, and the meager treasure with which he returns nowhere approximates the cost of his voyage. But there are numinous moments in *The Discoverie* when he comes close to finding earthly paradise.

It is not just an image of effortless plenty in the above passage; it is the experience of surfeit, thrilling for minds that find science in the blatantly sensuous (*ten* herbals!). And at the very moment the writing convinces that all human needs could be met right here, Ralegh organizes a reconnaissance party and they are off once again—this time to a village where the pilot has told them they can find more familiar foods: "bread, hens, fish, and . . . countrey wine."[114] Having reached this enchanted place after such suffering, they leave so soon; despite its abundance such exotic nature is inadequate—an early anticipation of Buffon's thesis on the inferiority of the Americas. The Eden of Ralegh's imagination will be more pastoral.

There is a further anticipation here. In the recurrent ambivalence toward Guianan nature resides the germ of the tropical—the equatorial colonial world of natural excess, sensual and brutish, that will come to saturate European geographies of northern South America.[115] With no looking back, in what will eventually be a well-worn trope of tropicality, Ralegh leads his men out of the haven of domestic security, and the expedition again plunges into the uncanny waters of illegibility and distrust. The pattern is repeated. Rowing endlessly and without food on the pitch-black river, using their swords to hack through the branches that bar their path, they suspect treason and "[determine] to hang the Pilot" who, in a startling reversal tells his captors that their goal is just a little farther, just one more reach of the river.[116] At the moment all hope seems lost, they hear dogs barking and spy a light. They find bread and hens. They almost meet the local chief who, laden with gold "came so neer us" while they rode at anchor in the night "as his *Canoas* grated against our barges."[117] And the next morning, elation, epiphany. "On both sides of this river, we passed the most beautifull countrie that ever mine eies beheld." It is the same leap from despair to rapture, the same vertiginous lunge between unstable poles:

> [A]nd whereas all that we had seen before was nothing but woods, prickles, bushes, and thornes, heere we beheld plaines of twenty miles in length, the grasse short and greene, and in divers parts groves of trees by themselves, as if they had been by all the art and labour in the world so made of purpose: and stil as we rowed, the Deere came downe feeding by the waters side, as if they had been used to a keepers call. Upon this river there were great store of fowle, and of many sorts: we saw in it divers sorts of strange fishes, and of marvellous bignes[s] but for *Lagartos* [alligators] it exceeded, for there were thousands of those uglie serpents.[118]

Unlike the terrifying country through which they had just passed, this is an eminently legible scene, a thoroughly civilized prospect — at least, that is, until the irrupting *memento mori*, the serpents in paradise. What distinguishes this place, as Ralegh makes clear in emphasizing the contrast, is the sense of space and perspective it allows the relieved travelers. Claustrophobia is gone, and all of a sudden they behold the landscape stretching in a great plain to the horizon. In this visual reckoning there is, for the first time, the possibility of possession, and a glimmer of what Ralegh will see in his final figure of Guiana, never sackt.

It is this sympathetic landscape's ability to offer itself as a prospect

that makes it so ripe for colonization. The forests and mountains beloved of modern guerrilla armies are anathema to an invading force;
open space allows for defensive encampment as well as advance. And
the prospect allows possession in other ways: by virtue of its familiarity
and its naturalness. The short green grass, the tame deer, the attractively
arranged groves of trees, the abundant fowl (ready for a gentleman's
sport)—if it weren't for the reptiles it could be the same Thames
"Meadow, by the Riuers side" where Edmund Spenser "a Flocke of
Nymphes . . . chaunced to espy" in *Prothalamion*, his neo-pastoral
wedding allegory of the following year.[119]

But what else? It was Raymond Williams who pointed out that Philip Sidney's definitive *Arcadia* (1590) "was written in a park which had
been made by enclosing a whole village and evicting the tenants."[120] In
England, such landscapes had to be manufactured from nature's craggy
raw materials. Ralegh, who devoted time and money to the planting of
his gardens at Sherbourne in Dorset, knew the aesthetic, social, and
moral value of such improvement. The revelation here is that such a
landscape could apparently simply exist. Rather than having to undertake the labor of recreation, this scene offers the prospect of a simple
occupation of the idyllic picturesque—a prospect that is not just a view,
but a projection into a domesticated future.

An Englishman could stop and settle in these Guianan plains. They
were places to create a future out of the reminders of a faraway life,
places to know that peaceful "sensation of suddenly being at home in
the world."[121] Why should Ralegh be immune to this prospective nostalgia of the traveler? Overlooking "the valley of *Amariocapana*," he
shades his eyes to view the savanna receding into the far distance:

> [A]s fayre grounde, and as beawtifull fieldes, as any man hath
> ever seene, with divers copses scattered heere and there by the
> rivers side, and all as full of deare, as any forrest or parke in
> England, and in every lake and river the like abundance of fish
> and fowle.[122]

At moments such as these, *The Discoverie* is suffused with familiar
analogy. Ralegh sees a mountain as "a white Church towre," and hears
bells clashing in the sound of cataracts. The "town of *Toparimaca* . . .
standing on a little hill, in an excellent prospect, with goodly gardens a
mile compasse round about it, and two very faire and large ponds of
fish adjoyning" could be in his own Mendip Hills.[123] The exotic land-

scape resonates with Englishness: the inevitable point of reference and the sign of the latent materiality of colonial transformation.

Yet, where we could expect triumphalism in the imperial vision, Ralegh's prose suggests insecurity and doubt, the worry that such Arcadian landscapes may not be quite what they seem. De Bry's engraving captures this hesitation well, the river a heaving mass of classical monsters through which they must pass to enter the garden. It picks up on the textual anxiety that emerges through Ralegh's disbelieving subordinate clauses: "*as if* they had been by all the art and labour in the world so made of purpose . . . *as if* they had been used to a keepers call." Surrounded by serpents in paradise, the intruders have their first casualty. One of the crew, "a very proper yoong fellow," is beguiled by the scenery to dive in for a swim and at once, before their eyes, is savagely dismembered by alligators.[124] *Et in Arcadia Ego.*

As if to confirm Ralegh's unease, recent archaeological research presents these Orinoco savannas and the immense Venezuelan *llanos* of the "plaines of the *Sayma*" surveyed by his scouting party as areas of intense pre-Columbian manipulation, gridded by networks of raised and ridged fields, mounds, and causeways, and deep in a native history of cultivation.[125] Similar grasslands cover huge expanses of the region—perhaps 15 to 20 million hectares of the Amazonian *terra firme*—and there is considerable uncertainty about their origins.[126] Even if, as botanists João Murça Pires and Ghillean Prance maintain, these areas predate the arrival of people in tropical South America, it seems inconceivable that their extent and ecology have not been greatly modified by the human use of fire in their management.[127] Writing in 1596, Keymis describes such practices south of the Orinoco in the context of native defensive action against the Spanish, observing that "the Iwarewakeri have nourished grasse in all places, where passage is, these three yeeres, and . . . it is at this present so high, as some of the trees; which they meane to burne, so soone as the Spaniard shall bee in danger thereof."[128]

In addition to the direct material aid that native leaders like Topiawari gave Europeans—food, shelter, orientation, and military information and support—there was also a less obvious indigenous contribution to the colonizing process. By planting and burning, by flood-control and earthworking, by attracting game animals such as deer, by concentrating valued plant species in accessible sites, native Americans created a landscape that Europeans were able to recognize and understand, a place that offered the sudden sensation of being at home in the world.[129]

Early modern European travelers were already halfway there. The erasure of people and labor that begins in the letters patent drew spontaneously on the eagerness of voyagers to locate the earthly paradise. Philip Amadas and Arthur Barlow, the captains of Ralegh's 1584 reconnaissance of the Carolinas, find that "the earth bringeth foorth all things in aboundance, as in the first creation, without toile or labour."[130] Where Montaigne's cannibals lived, "the whole day is spent in dancing."[131] Ralegh's Tivitivas "never eate of anie thing that is set or sowen."[132]

But how to avoid fatalism? There was nothing inevitable about the terrible disaster that befell native Americans. Although so much was ranged against them, the future was still unwritten, and—hard as it is—we must try to imagine the anxieties of the irresolute moment. Nevertheless, there was classical tragedy on the Plaines of Sayma: Guianans achieved the English ideal of rendering the artifice involved in the manufacture of these virgin landscapes entirely invisible. Free of both the epistemological dichotomization of nature and culture, and of English notions of Arcadia, indigenous Americans produced a landscape that fulfilled the colonialists' nostalgic yearnings for nature at its most amenably pristine. In doing so, they unwittingly created the conditions for the imaginative and material dispossession of their own golden land.

I have a favorite passage in *The Discoverie*. Reading it now confirms what I have suspected all along: that at some point, like so many others, I fell for Ralegh's charms. I fell for his charms and I fell for his frailties. And his Guiana became a part of my Amazon.

I include the passage at length here, partly because it is such wonderful writing and partly because it is perhaps the one moment in which Ralegh finds a unity in his experience of Guianan nature, a moment when the angels and the demons, the rapture and the horror, collapse into each other's arms, creating their own kind of terrible peace. It is the closest he will get to El Dorado, the farthest point he reaches in Guiana, and it is not really very far. He must transform defeat into accomplishment, to make the text somehow confound the failure of the voyage. It is a passage of complex beauty. As always, the language is tactile and immediate, and Ralegh draws us skillfully into his experience, sharing the excitement, the trepidation, the comradeship, the vulnerability, the wonder, and the inevitable disintegration. He is tired, but he is running up the hill:

> When we ronne to the tops of the first hils of the plaines adjoyning to the river, we behelde that wonderfull breach of waters, which ranne down *Caroli*: and might from that mountaine see the river how it ran in three parts, above twentie miles of, and there appeared some ten or twelve overfals in sight, every one as high over the other as a Church tower, which fell with that fury, that the rebound of waters made it seeme, as if it had beene all covered over with a great shower of rayne: and in some places we took it at the first for a smoke that had risen over some great towne. For mine owne part I was well perswaded from thence to have returned, being a very ill footeman, but the rest were all so desirous to goe neere the said straunge thunder of waters, as they drew me on by little and little, till we came into the next valley, where we might better discerne the same. I never saw a more beawtifull countrey, nor

more lively prospectes, hils so raised heere and there over the
vallies, the river winding into divers braunches, the plaines adjoyning without bush or stubble, all faire greene grasse, the
ground of hard sand easy to march on, eyther for horse or
foote, the deare crossing in every path, the birds towardes the
evening singing on every tree with a thousand several tunes,
cranes & herons of white, crimson, and carnation pearching on
the rivers side, the ayre fresh with a gentle easterlie wind, and
every stone that we stooped to pick up, promised eyther golde
or silver by its complexion . . . and yet we had no meanes but
with our daggers and fingers to teare them out heere and there.[133]

It is the earthly paradise, home of the gold for which they have
endured so many trials. And, as so often, Ralegh gives us an image of
irresistible potentiality, spiraling into defeat. It is a prophetic and self-
negating scene, it is the death of all pretense: the language continues to
promise possession, but the adventurers merely grovel in the dirt, their
aspirations pitifully base, framed by the transcendent glories of the New
World.

NEVER SACKT

In the late sixteenth and early seventeenth centuries, James Williamson
has usefully told us, an interested observer "might well have predicted
that Guiana was the destined chief sphere of English colonization."[134]
That energies would then turn so decisively to Virginia had much to do
with the lack of Crown support and the (minimal but sufficient, given
James' policy) Spanish response. In the face of such uncertainties, merchants put their capital firmly behind the northern ventures — despite
the potential returns from Guianan tobacco, a considerably more profitable item than its Virginia equivalent.[135]
    Although Guiana was still of interest in 1617, by choosing to enter
via the Orinoco, Ralegh was already sailing against the tide of colonial
enterprise. In the twenty years since *The Discoverie* had captured the
attention of English, Dutch, and Irish adventurers, interest had drifted
to the southern part of the region, and settlers were now heading to the
Rio Oiapoque — the present border between Amapá and French Guiana —
and to the Canal do Norte.[136] Spanish power was less evident in this

In the Tower, c. 1615

area, and settlers negotiated and traded among themselves in an atmosphere free from military engagement and the constraints of the chartered companies. As this suggests, the commodities that attracted the settlers were more mundane than those promised by El Dorado. John Wilson, one of the ten survivors of Charles Leigh's failed Oiapoque colony of 1604–6, included timber, dyes, pepper, cotton, flax, oils, gums, wax, tobacco, sugar, and feathers "such as Ladies doe weare in their hats" in his list of tradable resources of the area.[137] Although the golden kingdom had not disappeared from mental maps, it was being steadily displaced by more conventional enterprise.

Leigh had followed the transatlantic route established in 1596 by Keymis and by Leonard Berry, another Ralegh captain, in the following year. The standard crossing, a relatively short and easy one, now ended with landfall at the mouth of the Rio Araguarí, just north of the Amazon itself. Initially, this southern route had been determined by the effort to find unguarded access to Lake Manoa, but it also brought the entire Wild Coast and its resources to the attention of the settlers. John Ley, a "lone trader," who had trailed Keymis out in 1597, visited the Oiapoque but also turned south, entering the Canal do Norte on an exploration that took him all the way to the mouth of the Xingu.[138]

It was voyages like this, and the increasingly ambitious attempts to secure strategic landmarks by building forts and defense works, that would finally attract the attention of the Portuguese. Having recently displaced the French from Maranhão, they established the fort of Belém-do-Pará in 1616. Their suppression of the native population both near São Luís and around their new base sparked a general Indian rebellion that spread rapidly to Marajó and the Amazon estuary.[139] The ferocious response of Bento Maciel Parente, the Portuguese governor, was doubly effective. His destruction and enslavement of the Tupinamba and other native groups between 1616 and 1621 inspired such widespread terror among native Amazonians that it removed the logistical basis for northern European settlement. Native Americans were no longer prepared to risk collaboration with English, Irish, or Dutch. The sack of Trinidad and capture of Berrio that had stood Ralegh in such good stead with Topiawari had been drastically superseded. The politics of nominal equivalence were dead and irrecoverable. In the decade after 1623, a ruthless Portuguese campaign led by Pedro Teixeira forced all foreign rivals out of the estuary.[140]

For all intents and purposes, this was also the end of Guiana. Its

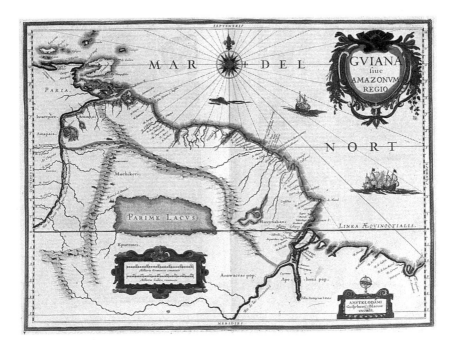

imperial rationale displaced, we can trace its gradual disappearance from European cartography and incorporation within an expansive, if variable, Amazonian regionalism. Although the boundaries seem secure and the dark blob of Ralegh's Manoa still fills the central space, the inscription on the cartouche of Blaeu's map of 1638 reads "The Region of GUIANA or Amazon," an index of ambivalent and shifting territory.[141] This is the beginning of a long retreat as Guiana falls back behind the borders of the northerly nation-states, leaving only a vestigial persistence as an arcane usage in scholarly ethnohistory.[142] When the English finally return to northern South America 200 years later, it is again in the idiom of discovery, following Ralegh's gloried footsteps yet beginning anew, with histories rewritten and landscapes pristine, arriving once more to claim the riches of a virgin land.

5

THE USES OF BUTTERFLIES
Bates of the Amazons, 1848–1859

A Hydrographic Region — The Cabanagem, Another Region —
Multiple Taxonomies and Taxonomic Immanence — "Where Are
the Horrors?" — The Mimesis for Which He Is Famous —
Unglamorous Beginnings but a Presumptuous Agenda —
Destabilizing Scientific Hierarchy — Popular Science — A
Programmatic Landscape — Race, Nature, and Difference — Liberty,
Independence, and Yearning — Centers of Calculation, Cycles of
Accumulation — The Collection as Region-Maker — The Power of
Numbers — Overdeterminations of Spatial Practice — Mimesis and
Epistemological Hybridities — Those Pervasive Instabilities

In 1863, when Henry Walter Bates published the now famous account of his eleven years in northern South America, there was still no obvious way of naming the spaces from which he had recently returned. Bates opted to call his book *The Naturalist on the River Amazons*, revealing just how much the great river had captured contemporary imaginations.

By tying himself so firmly to the river, Bates laid claim to its most alluring quality: the capacity to transgress and remake not only space, but the boundaries of geography, biology, culture, and politics. As the maps he commissioned to accompany his narrative made clear, in doing so he was swept away in the currents of an irresistible hydrography.

When Bates first crossed the Atlantic in 1848 on the barque *Mischief*, the Amazon was still largely unmapped beyond the estuary and only spottily occupied by non-Indians.[1] For the second time, European explorers found themselves — in Humboldt's phrase — on "the New Continent," a world reborn by the collapse of Iberian influence in the Americas and the coincident re-visioning of matter through the optic of the natural sciences.[2] By no means, though, was this unimagined territory. The northeastern reaches of what Bates sketched as "the Basin of

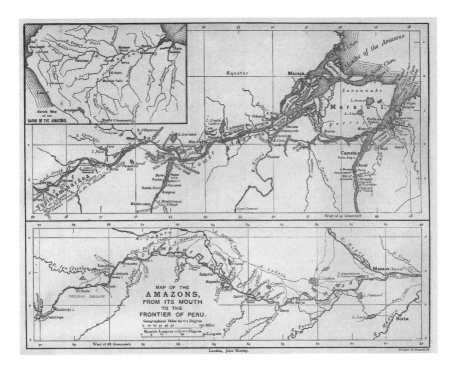

the Amazons" were emerging as a semi-autarkic economy with particularly close ties to Europe, and, as we know, they had long been present
in metropolitan consciousness as the ambiguous location of rich and
seductive resources, of a super-abundant nature, and of potential settlement. They had also, since Brazilian independence in 1822, fostered an
intensifying political regionalism that in 1835 spilled over into revolt,
rapidly setting fires raging throughout the countryside as a chaotic and
fluctuating alliance of Indians and slaves plunged the huge province
of Grão-Pará into the vortex of the Cabanagem rebellion. This latter,
though, was not the region-making in which Henry Bates participated.[3]
More than many contemporary travelers, Bates acknowledged the continuing shock of the Cabanagem, and its after-tremors regularly agitate
his narrative. Yet, the region in which he saw himself traveling and that
he brought back with him to Europe was only tangentially formed from
these histories. Instead, Bates' Amazons was nourished in a matrix of
his own moral and philosophical formation, the institutional and epistemological tensions of Victorian natural science, and the everyday
practices of natural historical fieldwork.

Nineteenth-century naturalists traveled through a world of emergent taxonomies, a world in which nature's superficial disorder merely masked its immanent logic. New ways of figuring the distinctions between humans and nature that had developed in Europe in the seventeenth and eighteenth centuries and had been powerfully expressed in Linnaeus' *Systema naturae* (1753), had underwritten innovation in the physical and chemical sciences, agriculture, navigation, and allopathic medicine to make the alien and unsettling nature that had so troubled Ralegh increasingly pliant and predictable.[4] Bates set out on his adventure from a Europe flush with new habits of thought. Innovative classificatory schema were sweeping up race as well as the non-human biologies of botany and zoology and were simultaneously plotting new global geographies through the hierarchical taxa of spatial scale.[5] Despite being a process that relied on and, in fact, created particularity and difference, Victorian region-making emerged from the contradictions of a self-consciously universalizing and domesticating metropolitan science. It is in the context of these transformations that we can understand Bates' disappointment on arrival in Brazil. "Where are the dangers and horrors of the tropics?" he wrote home to his friend Edwin Brown. "I find none of them."[6]

MIMESIS AND ALTERITIES

It was Amazonian butterflies and beetles that turned Henry Bates into the leading entomologist of his day and created a man who, along with his friend and temporary traveling companion Alfred Russel Wallace, still dominates the story of European entanglement in the region. Bates spent the eleven years from 1848 to 1859 in the forests, towns, and savannas of northern South America, frequently working in places no European scientist had previously set foot, assembling and cataloguing a vast natural history collection that was dominated by insect and bird specimens, but that also promised other treasures — human hair, for one thing — with a more ethnological appeal. On his return to England, he wrote *The Naturalist*, an account widely considered the pre-eminent Victorian narrative of Amazonian natural history, and he secured the coveted position of assistant secretary at the recently formed Royal Geographical Society (RGS), a post he held for the remainder of his life. This final, metropolitan phase of Bates' career placed him squarely at

Back from the Amazons, c. 1859

the institutional center of British imperial science (as well as of nascent academic geography) and makes explicit some of the connections between imperial policy and biological fieldwork that are often submerged in the celebratory narratives of Amazon exploration.[7]

Bates is well known to modern biologists as the discoverer of

"Batesian mimicry." He was collecting at Óbidos, not far from Santarém on the middle Amazon when he noticed that unusual and vulnerable butterflies were often effectively identical to common, unpalatable
species and varieties that predators avoided. In Bates' view, expressed in
a famous paper given at the Linnaean Society in November 1861, the
protective mechanism leading to mimetic resemblance provided "a most
beautiful proof of the truth of the theory of natural selection," and
Darwin enthusiastically seized upon this solution to a delicate puzzle for
the definitive sixth edition of the *Origin of Species* (1872).[8]

Darwin, Bates, Wallace, Joseph Dalton Hooker, and T. H. Huxley
were prominent members of an assertive alliance that was to succeed in
establishing the unsettling hegemony of evolutionism in the natural sciences. And there is much to be learned about the workings of British
science at this formative moment from tracing the letters and specimens
passing between these and other scholars as they falteringly assemble
the elements of a convincing theory of natural selection and strategize
on the most effective means for its deployment.

Bates was an unlikely figure to be keeping such elevated company.[9]
Rising from unglamorous beginnings as a provincial amateur naturalist,
he trained himself in the rudiments of scientific methodology by stealing
time from apprenticeship in a hosiery warehouse. He worked the long
but standard hours of artisans and the lower middle class — arriving to
sweep out at 7:00 A.M. and finishing at 8:00 in the evening, six days a
week — and he read and studied voraciously, closely following ideas current in the social theory, politics, and natural history of the day.[10] With
Wallace, he debated Malthus' *Essay on the Principle of Population* (1798),
Lyell's *Principles of Geology* (1830–33) and its appended summary of
Lamarck's theory of the transmutation of species, Robert Chambers' *Vestiges of the Natural History of Creation* (1844), Humboldt's *Personal
Narrative* (1816–34), Darwin's *Voyage of the 'Beagle'* (1839), and, eventually — and decisively — William H. Edwards' *A Voyage Up the River
Amazon, Including a Residence at Pará* (1847).[11] By the time they left
Liverpool in April 1848, ambitious and energized and bound for Pará,
the two young naturalists had definite ideas about the possibilities of
tropical adventure: their journey would solve the mystery of the origin of
species.

Science was a recognized avenue of social mobility at a moment of
unprecedented upheaval in industrializing British society.[12] Nonetheless,
for men in their early 20s with little formal education, few connections,

and no money to speak of, this was a presumptuous agenda. The established scientific hierarchies sanctioned a clear and subordinate role for the self-educated enthusiast, the amateur lacking the cultural capital to penetrate the elite institutions then proliferating professional procedure. Needless to say, there was little encouragement to theory-making. Field-naturalists like Bates and Wallace were infantrymen in the taxonomic war on natural disorder, their spoils supplying armchair savants with the exotic specimens that crowded the natural history cabinet. And, as we might expect, the achievement in crossing class lines was to be recurrently complicated by compromise. Once Bates took up his post at the RGS, his original writing was largely restricted to narrowly focused (although massive) exercises in insect classification. The remainder of his scholarly work was editing. He compiled a richly illustrated six-volume compendium of travel and natural history vignettes, managed the Society's two journals, made newly available a number of classics of Victorian geography, and oversaw the publication of other people's exploration narratives.[13] Writing Bates' obituary in *Nature*, Wallace complained that onerous administrative duties had impeded his friend's ability to contribute to natural history and had destroyed an already frail constitution.[14]

Despite lacking formal qualifications, Bates was a graduate of the rich tradition of popular education flourishing in early-nineteenth-century Britain. Although he left school at age 13 to enter apprenticeship, he managed to assemble the basis of a natural historian's education by attending night classes at the Leicester branch of the Mechanics' Institutes. Bodies such as these formed the most visible expression of a vigorous culture of radical self-improvement among English artisans during the first half of the nineteenth century, a period in which, in E. P. Thompson's words, "the towns, and even the villages, hummed with the energy of the autodidact."[15]

Part of this energy was invested in the spread of provincial popular science and, in particular, in the growth of local natural historical field societies emphasizing informality and low subscription rates. Open to men and women, these clubs rapidly became both popular and fashionable, and their outings as much social as scientific events. Botanical collecting and the pleasurable field excursion, previously rather eccentric occupations, became increasingly acceptable ways of spending free time as field equipment was produced in more affordable forms, and the democratic implications of Linnaean binomialism became apparent in field guides that came out in portable editions.[16] Bates explored Charnwood

Forest with a homemade butterfly net, foraging with his brother Frederick on the property of the Earl of Stamford, "who did not strictly preserve for game," and steadily building his private natural history cabinet.[17]

Bates' parents were staunch Unitarians, and their four sons grew up in the midst of the Dissenting tradition that throve with particular vitality in the northern and Midlands textile trades. Strongly ethical, solidaristic, and experimentally communitarian, rational in its theology, progressivist in its enthusiasm for science, and activist in its commitment to civil and religious liberties, Unitarianism was also wracked by internal division and subject to political appropriation by more orthodox reformist tendencies in the rising middle class.[18] If Thompson has justly celebrated the tumult of the industrializing period from 1780 up to the reforms of 1832 as revelatory of the crosscutting cultural richness of class-in-the-making, we should not forget that the succeeding decades of the 1830s and 1840s were when the hatches were battened down, grueling depression set in, and we witness the destruction of "pre-industrial traditions [that] could not keep their heads above the . . . rising level of industrial society."[19] As local clubs and societies lost their economic base, popular scientific education became increasingly sporadic and dependent on middle-class patronage.[20] By the 1830s, the locally set curricula of the Mechanics' Institutes tended to reflect the aspirations of Noncomformist manufacturers, and orthodox political economy was displacing artisan Radicalism. The Leicester Institute seems to have hung on longer than most — at least judging by its ability to generate opprobrium. In the early 1830s, offended local clergy could still be roused to castigate it as a school "for the diffusion of infidel, republican, and levelling principles."[21]

Wallace, whom Bates befriended in Leicester public library in 1844, was a follower of Robert Owen, the charismatic and paternalist socialist. Owen's utilitarian and rigorously rational social engineering materialized in the cooperative movement that transformed itself into the organized trades union confederation, and it also inspired and directed the influential utopian "communities of equality" at Orbiston in northern Britain and New Harmony, Indiana. Wallace remained consistently vocal about his Owenism, speaking and publishing on socialist themes throughout his life. Bates' political convictions were more circumspect, but marginality was similarly a part of his self-fashioning: "A scientific man," he wrote in his journal, "is not expected to be otherwise than heterodox."[22] And, when it came to sponsoring Peter Kropotkin, whom he met after the charismatic anarchist-geographer's release from prison in Clairvaux in

1886, Bates could be direct. In his active encouragement of the project that led to *Mutual Aid* (1902), there is the explicit reassertion of an early cooperative politics in the face of the rising influence of Huxley's and Spencer's individualist interpretations of natural selection.[23]

As we might expect, then, idealistic political consciousness suffuses the Amazonian accounts of both young naturalists. One way in which it manifests is through the appearance of programmatic and utopian communitarianism in repeated visions of ordered, cooperative European settlement. Wallace, for example, imagines forest plots converted into prosperous mixed-cropping and livestock farms in a tropical version of European smallholder agrarianism. This is no mere reverie, but rather a small-scale blueprint for colonial settlement on the lines of the experimental Owenite communities: "two or three families, containing half-a-dozen working and industrious men and boys, and being able to bring a capital in goods of fifty pounds." The Radical tenor of the plan is barely concealed:

> The idea of the glorious life which might be led here, free from all the money-matter cares and annoyances of civilization, makes me sometimes doubt, if it would not be wiser to bid [England] adieu forever, and come and live a life of ease and plenty on the Rio Negro.[24]

The rationalist utilitarianism of their early ideological formation also feeds a recurring anti-nostalgia that pervades the travel writings of both men. Something approaching poignancy appears in narratives grappling with the need to conventionally understate yet somehow communicate emotional excess. Bates, at the climactic moment of departure from Amazonia, has a sudden moment of brutal clarity:

> During this last night on the Pará river, a crowd of unusual thoughts occupied my mind. Recollections of English climate, scenery, and modes of life came to me with a vividness I had never before experienced, during the eleven years of my absence. Pictures of startling clearness rose up of the gloomy winters, the long grey twilights, murky atmosphere, elongated shadows, chilly springs, and sloppy summers; of factory chimneys and crowds of grimy operatives, rung to work in early morning by factory bells; of union workhouses, confined rooms, artificial cares and slavish conventionalities. To live again amongst

these dull scenes I was quitting a country of perpetual summer, where my life had been spent like that of three-fourths of the people in gipsy fashion, on the endless streams or in the boundless forests.[25]

This is an untenable contrast, and it is one to which I will return. Bates moves quickly to defuse this tension with a passage that at once signals the progressivist and determinist limits of a mid-century Radical consciousness saturated by racialized identifications.[26] "It was natural to feel a little dismayed at the prospect of so great a change," he continues,

but now, after three years of renewed experience of England, I find how incomparably superior is civilized life, where feelings, tastes, and intellect find abundant nourishment, to the sterility of half-savage existence, even though it be passed in the garden of Eden. What has struck me powerfully is the immeasurably greater diversity and interest of human character in a single civilized nation, than in equatorial South America, where three distinct races of man live together.[27]

The end of a narrative can be even more diagnostic than those calculated ethnographic moments-of-arrival to which Clifford Geertz has drawn attention.[28] Bates' contrast between (temperate) intellect and (tropical) sensuality was both conventional and definitive, and, as we see below, registers an allegiance to the evolutionism of climatic determinism as well as a susceptibility to the long-standing belief in the "weakness" of America.[29] Native Americans, who bathed "as dogs may be seen doing in hot climates," were simply not in the right place:

The impression gradually forced itself on my mind that the red Indian lives as a stranger or immigrant in these hot regions, and that his constitution was not originally adapted, and has not since become perfectly adapted to the climate. It is a case of want of fitness; other races of men living on the earth would have been better fitted to enjoy and make use of the rich unappropriated domain. Unlike the lands peopled by Negro and Caucasian, tropical America had no indigenous man thoroughly suited to its conditions, and was therefore peopled by an ill-suited race from another continent.[30]

Here was an explicitly formulated environmental determinism that we can readily associate with the simplified materialist theoretical procedure of the Darwinian emphasis on the physical determinants of speciation; a contemporary scientific common sense that gained a persuasiveness and coherence from the alignment of natural selection with the familiar biological hierarchy of race already regulated by Linnaeus, among others. Indeed, it was a reasoning that enabled Bates to find ample evidence that native Americans were constitutionally unsuited to what Humboldt would have considered the encompassing *physique générale* of the Amazon.

In contrast, tropical nature is a thing of wonder. Writing to his brother Frederick just two years before he finally left these rivers, Bates apologizes for the brevity of his unflattering description of people in Ega, but "they are so uninteresting and unamiable a set of animals that you must excuse my giving any further account." Instead, and with deliberate emphasis on the opposition, he continues:

> The charm and glory of the country are its animal and vegetable productions. How inexhaustible is their study! . . . It is not as in temperate countries (Europe), a forest of oak, or birch, or pine — it is one dense jungle: the lofty forest trees, of vast variety of species, all lashed and connected by climbers, their trunks covered with a museum of ferns, Tillandrias, Arums, Orchids, &c. The underwood consists mostly of younger trees, — great variety of small palms, mimosas, tree-ferns, &c., and the ground is laden with fallen branches, — vast trunks covered with parasites, &c. . . . One year of daily work is scarcely sufficient to get the majority of species in a district of two miles circuit.[31]

With its elegantly heightened language and cascading detail, this is an unmistakably Humboldtian conceit. And it is one that resonates with more than just rhetoric. In a famous passage introducing the *Personal Narrative*, Humboldt contrasts the experience of voyagers to the New and Old Worlds. He is, he confesses, "fully sensible of the great advantages enjoyed by persons who travel in Greece, Egypt, the banks of the Euphrates, and the islands of the Pacific, in comparison with those who traverse the continent of America."

> In the Old World, nations and the distinctions of their civilization form the principal points in the picture; in the New World,

man and his productions almost disappear amidst the stupendous display of wild and gigantic nature.[32]

Bates, too, sees Amazonians fading away in the shadows of a forest that is alternately "interminable," "glorious," "sombre and oppressive," "strange and wonderful," and "teeming with valuable productions."[33] Yet his understanding of the relationship between people and nature is explicitly contingent on ideas of race and class and modulated by an associated vision — to which only rarely do native Amazonian farmers conform — of the way a rural landscape should be organized. Bates' imagination dwells in a potent aesthetic of European settlement: individual holdings, fences, gardens, geometric space, monocultural rows, ornamental flowers, and domesticated animals. Resonant images of a simple but honest frontier life build an agrarian narrative that calls up a tradition of European family farming in alien environments — Australia, New Zealand, North America — while, as we have seen, simultaneously incorporating the utopian aspirations of petit-bourgeois dissent. The coherence of this notion of a tamed, morally acceptable nature reordered along utilitarian lines is such that on those occasions Bates does recognize horticultural practices he assesses them by how closely they approximate this regimented norm. Necessarily, such criteria privilege the prosperous. Wealthy farms, and what are considered well-organized holdings, meet with approval. Struggling cattlemen, in contrast, invite scorn for their self-inflicted distress:

> The lazy and ignorant people seem totally unable to profit by these [natural] advantages. The houses have no gardens or plantations near them. I was told it was useless to plant anything, because the cattle devoured the young shoots. In this country grazing and planting are very rarely carried on together, for the people seem to have no notion of enclosing patches of ground for cultivation. They say it is too much trouble to make enclosures.[34]

Poor Amazonians' inability to transcend local nature signifies a moral crisis, and the landscape through which Bates passes references their degeneracy.[35] Bates ties what he sees as agrarian disorder to Amazonians' inability to resist a decadence generated by the easy fertility of nature and the super-abundance of life's necessities. "The lower classes," he tells us, "are as indolent and sensual here as in other parts of the province [Pará], a moral condition not to be wondered at in a country where perpetual summer reigns, and where the necessaries of life are so easily obtained."[36]

Nevertheless, there was considerably more to Bates' Amazonian experience than repetitious complaint might propose. And there are times, even in the retrospection of *The Naturalist*, when the apparent certainties dissolve and representational hierarchies collapse. In Ega, where he lived long enough to become a familiar sight around town, Bates experiences the dislocation of what Michael Taussig has called "second contact,"[37] a moment of carnivalesque subversion that here occurs during a local *festa*:

> One year an Indian lad imitated me, to the infinite amusement of the townsfolk. He came the previous day to borrow of me an old blouse and straw hat. I felt rather taken in when I saw him, on the night of the performance, rigged out as an entomologist, with an insect net, hunting bag, and pincushion. To make the imitation complete, he had borrowed the frame of an old pair of spectacles, and went about with it straddled over his nose.[38]

It is the sense of disappointment, of trust betrayed and community rebuffed, that makes this moment so troubling—especially so when we realize that these are the very same people whom he has described to Frederick as "taciturn, idle, and phlegmatic; so apathetic that they never appear to feel any of the emotions or affections."[39] As the closing passage of *The Naturalist*, with its longing invocation of days spent in "gipsy fashion" suggests, his personal engagement is more complex than his theoretical architecture can allow. There is, he had written to his brother, "liberty and independence [in] this kind of life," and, at times, he is able fluidly to evoke his sense of a hard-won freedom with palpable conviction and an empathy for his Amazonian associates that brings a submerged relativism welling up to the surface of his text.[40] We find it in his adoption and subsequent burial—preceded by a controversial public baptism—of a kidnapped Indian child in Ega.[41] It is there in his undisguised pleasure on his excursions with local hunters, in the intimate camaraderie and his fascination with their skills. It breaks through in his sensitivity to the generosity of poorly provisioned rural hosts who scramble through their minimal resources to assemble meals for an unexpected guest. It has sufficient substance to signify an alternate structure of feeling that endows his account with the layered richness that can come so powerfully from uncertainty. One such occasion finds him at night sailing on the Rio Tocantins toward the town of Cametá. He has been dozing on deck, wrapped in a sail, listening to the crew talk and sing:

> The canoe-men of the Amazons have many songs and choruses, with which they are in the habit of relieving the monotony of their slow voyages, and which are known all over the interior. The choruses consist of a simple strain, repeated almost to weariness, and sung generally in unison, but sometimes with an attempt at harmony. There is a wildness and sadness about the tunes which harmonise well with, and in fact are born of, the circumstances of the canoe-man's life: the echoing channels, the endless gloomy forest, the solemn nights, and the desolate scenes of broad and stormy waters and falling banks. . . . I fell asleep about ten o'clock, but at four in the morning John Mendez [the pilot] woke me to enjoy the sight of the little schooner tearing through the waves before a spanking breeze. The night was transparently clear and almost cold, the moon appeared sharply defined against the dark blue sky, and a ridge of foam marked where the prow of the vessel was cleaving its way through the water. The men had made a fire in the galley to make tea of an acid herb called *erva cidreira*, a quantity of which they had gathered in the last landing-place, and the flames sparkled cheerily upwards. It is at such times as these that Amazons travelling is enjoyable, and one no longer wonders at the love which many, both natives and strangers, have for this wandering life. The little schooner sped steadily on, with booms bent and sails stretched to the utmost. Just as day dawned, we ran with scarcely slackened speed into the port of Cametá, and cast anchor.[42]

There is, for sure, a loneliness in this gipsy life, but it nonetheless has a special appeal for Bates. How should we understand its charms? We need to think again about his feelings on the eve of departure from Pará or, at least, his representation of them as he closes *The Naturalist* and meditates on the appeal of a vagabond existence. In the aftermath of so many complaints about the indolence of Amazonian people, in the midst of his stark vision of industrial England, and as a conclusion to an account that can have left no reader in doubt as to the heroic character of his collecting efforts, his wistful appeal to another way of life finds him looking both apprehensively forward and fretfully back. On this last evening on the Amazon, Bates' anti-nostalgia draws on the grim figure of the industrial Midlands landscape that embodies so many anxieties about his future prospects. It is a gloom brimming with tentative, defeated forebodings that even should he escape the hosiery workshop for which he has been raised, the scientific reward he craves for these eleven years of Amazonian hardship is no more than a sweetly poisoned chalice, promising only a life forever cut off from the entomologizing pleasures from which he is to sail in the morning. At this moment of crisis, there is — just for an instant — a final chance to reconcile with that transcendent yearning insistently loosening the clutch of his stubborn reproduction of alterity. For one final moment, he frees himself from his disdain for indolence and envies that fabled three-fourths of Amazonians living free of slavish conventionality. Then, with the shudder of presentiment, he hammers the lid down tight on the last of his collection and strides on board the ship for Liverpool.

THE LIVES OF SPECIMENS

When Bates finally left the interior it was at the insistence of a local riverboat owner appalled at the deterioration in his health and at his rapid loss of weight and strength. His sustaining dream — to reach the Andes and maybe the Pacific — was deferred, indeed abandoned. Reading his notebooks, letters, essays, and monograph, the isolation and vulnerability of his experience are striking. From them comes a powerful sense of contradiction: not simply ambivalence, but, as we have seen, articulate, contradictory expressions of attachment and dislocation, of identification and indifference. Yet the crudeness of his racialized caricatures is jarring and seemingly belied by the considered character of his conduct in the field. And it appears that his internal struggle is with conventionality, that his journey, no matter where it takes him, is haunted above all by the commonplaces of middle-class England — by his own institutional aspirations, by the confines of his familiarity with geographical and ethnological thought, and by the anxious letters from home urging his return to the family business, that, despite its audacities, his life is already unfolding as a series of unheroic compromises.

Bates' insecurities were fueled by his continuing status as little more than a professional collector. We know already that this was the role for which, from an elite perspective, he was best equipped. It is also clear that it was one neither he nor Wallace particularly relished. Despite their reservations, however, it was only through entering the Banksian networks of commercial science that these independent, although not independently wealthy, travelers were able to finance their expedition.[43] Before finally resolving on the Amazon as a destination, they visited William Hooker at Kew and Edward Doubleday in the Lepidoptera Department of the British Museum, arranging commissions for plants and rare insects and receiving assurances that demand for the fauna and flora of the Amazon was still strong despite the work of naturalist predecessors. More important, they engaged an agent, Samuel Stevens, an amateur entomologist and brother to a noted London natural history auctioneer. Stevens earned his commission: he successfully disposed of their collections, reliably forwarded money to Pará, and acted as a local booster, enticing metropolitan savants with extracts from Bates' letters, which he published at regular intervals in the *Zoologist* and other leading journals.[44]

Clearly, even for such rank amateurs there were locations on the networks of science and geography waiting to be accessed. The key nodes — sites of commercial possibility and social aspiration — were obvious: the institutional centers of metropolitan natural history based in Kew and Bloomsbury. Less transparent but equally material were the cumulative structures of fluvial exploration through which, as we know, northern South America had been accessed since the late sixteenth century. Victorians were self-conscious about their Elizabethan inheritance, and much as Hakluyt had looked to King Arthur and Owen Madoc for legitimating imperial precedent, mid-nineteenth-century British expansionists found their glorious tradition in Ralegh and in Hakluyt himself, both of whom inspired significant institutional centers and whose works were reissued in new and influential editions.[45]

The English, along with the Dutch, French, and Irish, were shut out of the Amazon by Portugal from the 1630s until the opening of Brazilian ports to friendly foreign vessels in 1808. Deferral, though, as the clamor surrounding Humboldt's pioneering voyage along the Orinoco and Rio Negro in 1799–1804 made clear, only stimulated appetites. Sixteenth-century American expeditions were rediscovered in the midst of the imperial vogue for travel writing, and seized upon as invitations rather than mere precedents. From 1808 on, Amazonian rivers were

flooded with foreign entrepreneurs, spies, and scientists — with most individuals playing multiple roles. Bates and Wallace followed trails established not only by fellow collectors, but also by the repeated attempts of
British naval expeditions to map a transcontinental link between the
Atlantic and Pacific via the Amazon and Andes, and by the overwhelming domination of Amazonian commerce by British financial institutions.[46] Moreover, they were also traveling in the wake of a substantial
Portuguese tradition of scientific exploration inaugurated by Jesuits
such as Padre João Daniel and given major impulse by the celebrated
nine-year expedition of Alexandre Rodrigues Ferreira.[47] Writing in the
RGS house journal following Bates' death, William L. Distant, an old
friend and a fellow entomologist, clearly identified this cumulative
aspect:

> Not only did [Bates'] expedition effect a history of the natural
> treasures of this interesting zoological province, but it also stimu-
> lated the zeal of many private and wealthy collectors, who subse-
> quently promoted and assisted other zoological enterprises.[48]

William Chandless' RGS surveys of navigable tributaries took place
soon after Bates' return, as did Brown and Lidstone's detailed report for
the Amazon Steam Navigation Company on the potential of territory
ceded to the British firm by the Brazilian state.[49] It was through such
rapidly proliferating networks that the hospitality trails of sympathetic
European merchants and officials came into being. Indeed, the prior
existence of logistical support had been one of the factors determining
Bates' choice of the Amazon as a collecting site.[50]

We should not ignore the extent to which apparently benign field
activities — collecting, connecting, and circulating rare and exotic species, filling orders from metropolitan savants, communicating systematic observations on botany, zoology, physical geography, linguistics,
ethnology, and sociology to interested professionals — were often indistinguishable from the more patently instrumental projects of botanical
espionage and transplantation also undertaken through state channels.[51]
Such overlapping projects were of prime importance in configuring the
region, and they were dependent on decisive micropolitics. We have
seen that natural historical practice was overdetermined by a range of
contingencies and orientations — biographical, political, philosophical.
Critically, we must also acknowledge that the politics of professionalization in the metropolitan sciences that propelled Bates across the Atlantic

were themselves predicated on disciplinary regimes imposed by commercial and aesthetic codes for the collecting of nature then developing
in Europe. This is one reason why the natural history collection is of
such interest. Tied more tenaciously to traveling scientific practice than
even the published narratives, and equally critical to his career, Bates'
vast collection was a key site for the elaboration of identity — both his
own and that of the Amazon. Distant, writing in 1892, makes the point
most succinctly:

> The collections were unrivalled, and one can still hear echoes
> . . . of the intense interest with which Bates' consignments were
> anticipated. The banks of the great river were at last telling the
> tale of their inhabitants to the zoologists of Europe, for the
> collections were widely circulated.[52]

The collection was a principal locus of anxiety. Marooned in the
field with few reference books and incomplete knowledge of the most
recent work in systematics, naturalists (no matter how skilled) were often unable to make the fine judgments that enabled species to be described, classified, and slotted into a Linnaean grid.[53] Instead, they
supplied the metropolitan expert who, like a bourgeois Adam in his
paneled library, simultaneously named and brought the natural world
into being, occasionally acknowledging the collector with a Latinate
flourish.[54] Yet, it was people with the experience of travel behind
them — Huxley, Hooker, Darwin, Wallace, and Bates — who were most
intimately associated with the Darwinian revolution, and Bates was
quite explicit in his belief that this apparent paradox was governed by a
causal relationship. In an 1862 letter to Darwin, he notes that his old
friend Edwin Brown of Burton-on-Trent

> is amassing material (specimens) at a very great expense. He
> has never traveled: this is a great deficiency for the relations of
> species to closely allied species & varieties cannot, I think, be
> thoroughly understood without personal observation in differ-
> ent countries.[55]

Bates later referred to Brown's kind of naturalist as a "species grub-
ber" to be "ranked with collectors of postage stamps & crockery," and
there were important distinctions being shored up by this disdain.[56] Not
only did he wish to separate those who traveled from those who stayed
at home, but also, and more enduringly, he was dividing what he saw as

the inconsequential journeymen who collected without reflection from the scientists whose theorizings imbued their collecting activity with real meaning.

In this aspiration toward the larger questions, both the ideas and style of inquiry developed in Humboldt's *Personal Narrative* are quite explicit.[57] Humboldt's Kantian distinction between "a true history of nature and a mere description of nature" (the latter, in his view, being symptomatic of Linnaean natural history) involved the application of a rigorous and technologically bolstered empiricism.[58] He traveled with the declared intent of confronting natural phenomena in all their vital complexity and affective detail and precisely to transcend dependence on the lifeless extractions of the herbarium and cabinet. A true natural history would be revealed only through a study of the inter-relationship of all of nature's aspects in a grand synthetic enterprise. Conspicuous among these relationships were personal emotional and aesthetic responses: legitimate, valued data that, in this age of the sublime, introduced a Romantic variant of a familiar (environmental) determinism in which an empathetic emotional response could indicate the effect of particular types of natural environment on human society. There is, then, considerable friction between the pulls of empiricism and Romanticism, and we find the mutual indispensability of reason and aesthetics provoking perspectives at odds with disciplinary compartmentalization. Malcolm Nicolson has put it nicely: "The mathematical precision of the stars' orbits," he writes, "was just as valid a topic for study as their sparkle and its associated delights."[59] By the time the Darwinians had finished digesting Humboldt most of the sparkle had fizzled out. But this does not mean that Bates' occasionally anodyne prose should be read as a detached stylistic analogue of a narrowly investigative empiricism. Feelings still mattered. As did Beauty and Truth. A collection of quality and elegance, and the rare and delicate creatures of which it was composed, was a vessel deep enough and wide enough to hold all these absolutes, and more besides.

Bates' criticism of Brown expressed the simmering antagonism between a resurgent English "natural" natural history that drew on native authorities (John Ray in particular) and what he and other Humboldtian Darwinians concurred was a listlessly mechanical classificatory impulse descended from Linnaeus.[60] Linnaean taxonomy had transformed both the plant and animal sciences, introducing an absorbing focus on the minutiae of taxonomic organization. The natural historical modes of representation through which methodological imperatives came to be expressed worked to flatten the specificities of geographical, cultural, and historical location in a regime of recontextualization and distinction.[61] Darwin and his circle self-consciously distinguished themselves from this segmenting optic by the development of a theory of origins the force of which was understood as issuing from its holism. Nonetheless, it was systematics that underwrote evolutionary theorizing, and the theoretical urge was constantly in tension with the demands of laborious taxonomy.[62] Moreover, this routinized practice had its own financial and aesthetic charms. There is a false note in Bates' contempt for the mere collector, with its denial of his own seduction by the appeals of classification.

The assembly of a private collection was one of Bates' principal goals in traveling to Pará. An impressive natural history cabinet filled with rarities was a recognized form of capital in the appropriate circuit, with significant exchange value and an indispensable prestige function that could catapult its owner into the ranks of the learned.[63] But the question posed by Bates' comment on Brown was that of the collection's immediate purpose, and, in this, it is clear that notwithstanding the actualities of his situation, Bates saw himself as the heir of Humboldt, rather than of the journeymen Banksian collectors. Indeed, it is as an instance of a new social actor — perhaps Humboldt's most significant invention — that he steps onto the historical stage: the post-Linnaean (post-Banksian) explorer-scientist, a subject with many counterparts in colonial service.[64]

It is through his work in refashioning and overcoming the undervalued figure of the natural history collector that Bates maps his scientific and social aspirations and opens the routes through which his Amazons will travel. Back from the field, he haltingly forged relationships with senior scientific figures. In particular, as his correspondence clearly shows, both Darwin and Joseph Hooker acted toward him as solicitous and sensitive mentors. He, in turn, armed with the authority of travel, reciprocated with perceptive insight into the relationship between tropical entomology and natural selection, providing apparently endless data tapped by Darwin through precise and persistent questioning. With Bates unable to find work among the very limited opportunities then available in London professional science, it was Darwin who suggested he write *The Naturalist*, arranged introductions, advised him on contract negotiations with John Murray (London's leading publisher of travel books), nursed him through periods of despondency, encouraged his theoretical development, and guided him across the inhospitable terrain of the capital's scientific establishment. Through Darwin, Bates established his connection with Hooker, a powerful scientific patron who, in late 1865, succeeded his father as director of the Royal Botanic Gardens at Kew.

In casting his lot with the Darwinians, Bates inevitably attracted hostility from their opponents, especially among the systematists at the British Museum, where his job applications were rejected and his claims about the number of new species contained in his collection were held up to ridicule. In a series of paternal letters, Hooker coached him on the mores of the scholarly upper class, explicitly situating his comments in terms of Bates' future career prospects. "It is," he advised, "extremely difficult to *establish a footing* in London scientific society: it is all along of [*sic*] the law of the struggle for life! You are instinctively regarded as an interloper, and it must be so in the nature of things. Do, I entreat you, smile at their sneers."[65] Finally, of his new set, it was Murray who convinced the RGS to hire as their senior administrator the young entomologist with no executive experience.[66] It was an apt decision made possible by the persistence of amateurism in British science: to organize their insect collection, the trustees of the British Museum had appointed a well-connected poet.[67]

As Distant pointed out, it was through the collection that "the banks of the great river were at last telling the tale of their inhabitants." Removed from their "wild" context and resituated in collections physically organized to express hierarchical principles, natural history specimens became narrativized as tactile metonyms, not only for a generalized natural world, but, more specifically, for the region. The collection marked region within an encompassing story of imperial destiny and masculine daring. Allied to the travel narratives of prominent collectors, the contextual particularity of provenance became a critical supplement by which the identity of the specimen could be produced.[68] Part of Stevens' job as agent was to breathe life into these dead insects with both history and the associative power of the local, and one of his tactics was to circulate selections from Bates' letters and essays from the Amazon, adding biographical substance to both the author and the non-humans who were his victims and allies.

Stevens and Bates collaborated to exploit the plasticity of tropical nature by drawing on and raising the nascent symbolic capital of Amazonia. The agent's chummy note to *Zoologist* readers that introduced the first extract from Bates' correspondence gives some insight into his sophisticated management of the gentlemanly codes smoothing the paths of commerce:

> Thinking some of the readers of the 'Zoologist' who are ac-
> quainted with Mr. H. W. Bates would like to hear how he is
> getting on in his rambles of South America . . . I have the plea-
> sure of sending extracts from some of his letters to me; and
> notwithstanding the many hardships he has undergone his
> health continues most excellent, the climate being fortunately
> very delightful and healthy. Among the many charming things
> now received are several specimens of the remarkable and
> lovely Hectera Esmeralda, and an extraordinary number of
> beautiful species of Erycinidæ, many quite new, and others only
> known by the figures of Cramer and Stoll.[69]

Bates' first letter follows immediately, and Stevens, with a canny eye to the authenticity of the primitive, edited it to begin: "I get on very well with the Indians."

A great deal of Bates' activity was driven by demand. He conferred with Stevens over the preferences of individual savants, and carefully chose specimens to whet their appetites and induce them into signing on as subscribers. Despite his expertise and Stevens' supplies of taxonomic monographs, however, Bates' letters reveal that he frequently had only an approximate idea of what it was that he was shipping.[70] Novelty was not a negotiable character, but neither was it readily apparent. Reveal-ingly—as an insight into the historicized and ideological underpinnings of foundational scientific activity—the selection criteria Bates was forced to apply in lieu of precise inventory were almost entirely aes-thetic, based on the attractiveness and size of the organism. This was shrewd, if necessary, practice. Metropolitan demand was based as much on taste as on gaps in the systematic grid.[71] Given the latitude presented by the vast spaces existing in biological taxonomies, buyers wanted their novelties to satisfy as both aesthetic objects *and* natural historical icons.

A typical passage from Bates' letters in the *Zoologist*—exotic and anecdotal—ties identifiable specimens to a particular collecting practice, offering insight into the daily life of the field scientist abroad while re-vealing how the inclinations of metropolitan savants set the terms for his spatial practice, with his response to their needs determining his work rhythm.[72] On shipping a consignment of "the beautiful Sapphira, which you wished for more particularly," he cautioned Stevens:

> I hope what I send will satisfy you. . . . Do not think it an abundant species because I now send you so many; it is because I devoted myself *one month* to them, working six days a-week with a youth hired to assist me, both of us with net-poles 12 feet long.[73]

Metropolitan demand for a particular item also often dictated Bates' destination. Once there, he might find himself filling orders for items of distractingly peripheral, though symptomatic interest — the human hair referred to earlier or precise matches of Indian skin tone, for example. In this way, the purity of his science became subject to diverse corruptions, of which he himself was only too aware. No matter how far his wanderings took him from the metropolitan hearth, he never managed to shake off his dependence on the lifeline of the imperial-scientific network, nor make the leap of faith into that life of "liberty and independence" about which he had written so elatedly to Frederick. He demurred, fighting to carve out areas of autonomy by prioritizing the search for insects and carefully tending to his private stock, selling only duplicates and keeping as full a set as possible at his side for reference.[74]

Even more than the celebrated butterfly mimics, it was the beetles of Ega that guaranteed Bates' fame among his entomologist peers. His astonishing haul from that site alone included 3,000 species new to Europeans. This was the climactic event that transformed the obscure naturalist and fulfilled the promise of travel. It shows the collection to be a site where the rich particularity of the local was simultaneously evoked and unmoored and a regional identity reinforced. Bates and Stevens' textual framings marked the biological exuberance captured in Ega as both local and transcendent, placed yet symptomatic. In contrast to now-standard arguments about the stripping of context and social meaning (i.e., culture and locality) from organisms in their incorporation in the circuits and projects of metropolitan science, it is clear that systematics here involved considerably more than a practice of decontextualization.[75] The extraction of insects from the forest and their reinvention as specimens in the collection demanded persistent, manufactured traces of locality as key components of value at every point. At the same time, scientific practice participated actively in a narrativizing of geography.

It is as his day closes and the tropical night shutters down that we meet this naturalist on the Amazon. When we read through his letters and notebooks today, we find him hunched over a cluttered table in an empty room on the outskirts of an isolated forest settlement, ceaselessly numbering species by the smoky glow of his oil lamp—totaling and bracketing, calculating and parsing, until the fine balance between time devoted to other people's requirements in order to support his personal project and that tenacious project itself is lost, and the activity becomes its singular justification. His status, his identity as traveler, explorer, and, most important, scientist, becomes inseparable from the numbers. And, when he finally publishes *The Naturalist*, the first data he presents, on the second page of the preface, are a species count, the bald enumeration of his outrageously massive collection:

Mammals 52

Birds........................... 360

Reptiles........................ 140

Fishes 120

Insects..................... 14,000

Mollusks........................ 35

Zoophytes 5
_____

14,712[76]

The theatricality of this rather Conradian image of Bates—deep in the jungle fastness, isolation nibbling at his rationality, forsaken at the distant terminus of a precarious but confining imperial network—should not distract from the point at issue: Bates' collection had a heavy load to bear. It explicitly signaled the abundance of Amazonian biology. But it also wracked his already frail constitution and—in the tales of hardship and tribulation—collapsed into itself that commonplace bifurcation between the ecstatic profusion of tropical nature and its pervasive menace. Moreover, although his collection was the emblem of his social and professional aspiration, in the act of assembling it he was irreducibly marked (once again) as plebeian. It is in this light, as much as in terms of his hopes about employment and the aggressive contemporary contest to define science, that we should understand his distressed reaction when John Gray, the keeper of the Department of Zoology at the British Museum, raised demeaning, calculated queries about the material he had brought back from his travels.

Unlike Conrad's incarnation of the colonial nightmare, Bates made it home to the "inanities of 'society'" that his friend, the banker and essayist Edward Clodd, tells us he loathed.[77] Not only was a new Bates, the translator of butterflies and beetles, making his appearance in London. With him came the Amazons—where an inexperienced Leicester naturalist could find nearly 15,000 species, "no less than 8000 . . . *new to science*," and an emerging site of unrestrained hyperbole.[78]

IMPUNITY AND IMPURITIES

> I should have liked a sympathizing companion better than being alone, but that in this barbarous country is not to be had. I have got a half-wild coloured youth, who is an expert entomologist, and have clothed him with the intention of taking him with me as assistant: if he does not give me the slip he will be a valuable help to me.
>
> —Bates to Stevens, Pará, August 30, 1849

Metropolitan science—its theorizings, its literatures, its spectacular collections, its popular showcases—relied on an insistent stream of material, much of which flowed through still embryonic channels originating in distant territories.[79] As we have seen, commerce and aesthetics combined to influence the shape of its production in fundamental ways. Bates' struggle to control a space within the imperial-scientific networks— his dogged attempts to carve out autonomy through on-site taxonomy— can be interpreted as an effort to capture more and more of the analytical activities associated with particular prestigious nodes. This was critical to his destabilization of the hierarchy of professionalizing science. We can see him striving to insert himself at what were structured as progressively higher levels, where advancing status corresponded to the increasingly manipulated character of the data being handled.

Although it was with deep misgivings that Bates enfolded himself in the embrace of the metropolitan species grubbers, it was perhaps even more unsettling to be caught in the bonds of dependency that tied him to his Amazonian porters, guides, cooks, canoeists, pilots, nurses, hunters, collectors, protectors, translators, advisors, informants, companions, hosts, and local experts like Vicenti, a "dreadfully independent and shrewd" character, who, nonetheless, "is an excellent assistant to us":

> [H]e is better acquainted with the names and properties of plants and trees than any man in Pará, and is a glorious fellow to get wasps'-nests, and to dig out the holes of monstrous spiders.[80]

Bates' on-the-ground interaction with Vicenti and the other rural Amazonians with whom he worked offers one more way to think about the making of the region. There were, we know, commercial and institutional imperatives shaping his traveling practice, and we have already seen enough of the materialities of exploration to realize that this story is not entirely about an Anglophone siting of Amazonia. But what happened to Bates' natural science in the moment of encounter with Amazonians and this hyperbolic nature? What mimetics and hybridities ensued from the field politics of intersubjectivity?[81]

European travelers had complained of labor shortages in the Amazon well before the Cabanagem. But Bates' ability to travel was wholly predicated on the availability of people prepared to fulfill the overlapping functions of crew member, porter, and guide. Even when he closely follows the emerging hospitality trails of European assistance and local political authority, moving along a network of planters, merchants, and municipal officials assembled through letters of introduction arranged in London, Pará, and Santarém, his progress can be held up for days or weeks or even entirely halted by the inability to secure assistance.[82] Despite their own divisions, there are times when elites and subalterns appear to conspire in obstructing him. Considerably delayed in making a planned trip to the upper Tapajós in 1852, he finally sails in June, a season of treacherous tides and unpredictable storms:

> In arranging my voyage, I found the usual difficulty in finding men. Indians only understand the management of canoes; and these are so few in number in comparison to the demand for them, that they are not to be found. The authorities only can

assist a stranger, but these parties in Santarém are not at all obliging, and I was compelled to hire two mulattoes, — one, a coarse specimen from the South of Brazil, the other, a harmless young fellow of very little use to me. The bigger one proved a great annoyance. I soon found that he understood less of navigation than myself; but he was insolent, and would have his own way. Our first day's voyage was very inauspicious. We weighed anchor at Santarém at 8, A.M., after a good deal of trouble with the police officers, who would not let this fellow go until I had paid his debts.[83]

They arrived in Aveyros after running aground and coming close to death. Bates at once dismissed the two men and used his prior acquaintance with the town authorities to secure the Indian crewmen on whom he placed such value. Within days, he was off again, but in his next letter he tells a familiar, if ironic, tale:

Altogether [this voyage on the Tapajós] has been the most labourious excursion I have made. . . . The two Indians I obtained with great difficulty of the Commandant of Aveyros, gave me constant trouble and anxiety, — two lazy, insolent young lads, who at last, when I wished to ascend the river to Curé, refused to accompany me any further.[84]

This is one native response to the work of imperial science. It can force the naturalist to surrender zoological specimens that his hungry boatmen would rather eat. It can leave him staring wistfully landward as impatient oarsmen whisk him away from a rich collecting site. It can take him on interminable diversions as his employees ferry relatives and friends between distant riverine settlements. It can see to it that the store of cane liquor he brings along as a preservative is hijacked for more democratic ends.[85] It can render valued objects worthless — an alligator's head with its teeth pilloried for "charms," in one instance.[86] And it can at times create a tenseness that hovers over these travels like a sickly pall to burst into a sudden shower of violence — as when the botanist Richard Spruce narrowly thwarts a murder plot by his four Indian companions.[87]

Explorer-scientists were vulnerable and dependent, a resource as well as a burden. The lack of direct coercive sanctions available to the naturalists, their acute physical vulnerability on sparsely inhabited, poorly mapped, and unpredictable rivers, and the generalized labor shortage with which foreign travelers were confronted, all gave local workers unusual relative strength. They were often in the gratifying position of being able to demand payment in advance for a journey and then, on receipt of the money, to abscond or, on occasion, to spend it and then win more before setting out.

Even though a European traveler was more or less entirely invested with the protective prestige of the Amazonian elite, such social relations were rather different from those that actually obtained between native labor and the local or provincial authorities. Punitive unpaid forced expedition, conscription into the abusive *Corpo de Trabalhadores*, aggressive press-ganging for provincial militias, routine and sadistic brutality—the intensified state regulation of Indian and *ribeirinho* labor imposed following the suppression of the Cabanagem radically changed conditions in the interior by extending and deepening racialized forms of control that had previously been limited to the area around Belém.[88] While never succeeding in ignoring these disagreeable goings-on, the responses of travelers varied considerably. Some, the North American Edwards, for example, endorsed such arrangements as normalizing an otherwise impossible transport situation.[89] For Bates, the situation was more problematic, and at times the post-Cabanagem upheavals seem to echo the industrial revolution transfiguring the rolling Midlands landscape he had only recently scoured for his first butterfly specimens.

In similar ways but often in contradiction to the demands of metropolitan buyers, native involvement in the naturalists' progress strongly influenced these explorers' spatial practices by restricting where they were able to travel, how long they would remain in a particular location, and, frequently, the extent of their investigations once they were settled. In addition, more effectively even than topographical obstacles, the desertions of crew members and servants, or their refusal to enter areas occupied by hostile, undefeated Indian groups, would—just as much as the resilience of those groups themselves—temporarily close off whole sections of Amazonia to scientific enterprise.[90]

In general, though, positive support was as frequent as obstruction and as readily forthcoming from rural Indians and ribeirinhos as from members of the elite. The daily logistical assistance given to the visiting naturalists—the sheltering, canoeing, portering, hunting, and fishing that enabled travel—was critical to their success. So, too, was the contribution of the *regatões*, the itinerant river traders who carried Bates' collections unescorted, without incident, and often without charge to Pará for shipment to England. Just as the pliability of the relations between Bates and the people who performed many of these services offered room for maneuver on the part of the latter, so for some, this same space, and the favorable wages and novel conditions Bates was forced to offer, made such work inviting.[91]

Less mundane, though, were the activities of those individuals who worked for him as collectors. Many of these supplied specimens on approval, and his arrival in a village prompted a procession of hunters, young and old, male and female, to emerge from the forest bearing animals for sale. Some helped by training him in specific technologies: the use of blowpipes for killing birds perched high in the forest canopy, for example. Boys accompanied him into hunting grounds, silently indicating animals that he would attempt to shoot and they retrieve in seemingly impenetrable undergrowth. Men allowed him to tag along on hunting trips. Other people — like Vicenti — established more formalized, less transient relationships as assistants. Bates' 1851 description of his first visit to Ega is helpful here:

> I worked very hard for Coleoptera in Ega from the 1st of January to the 20th of March, being the showery and sunny season, before the constant rains set in. Whenever I heard of beetles seen at a distance, I would get a boat and go many miles after them, and employed a man (the only one disposed for such work in the whole village) with his family, who worked in some clearing in the forest, to hunt for me. Every day he brought me from ten to twenty Coleoptera, and thus I got some of my best things: so that I think I looked Ega pretty well, and the results may be taken as representing the products of the Upper Amazons.[92]

Relationships of this type throw questions of authorship into sharp relief,[93] and examples from other imperial contexts are not hard to find.[94] Take Albert Howard, a sensitive colonial official impressed by the indigenous agriculture he had witnessed in India, who returned to England to found the European organic farming movement.[95] Or there is that on which Mary Pratt muses when she wonders if Humboldt's native guides communicated "their own knowledge of the ecosystem and their reverence for it" during the ascent of Chimborazo that led to the influential planar zonation of the Andes depicted in the *Essai sur la géographie des*

Turtle-fishing and adventure with Alligator.

plantes (1807). As Pratt points out, this was an indigenous mental topography that was to reappear in John Murra's influential "verticality
thesis" of Andean resource management and spatio-social organization.[96]

Scientific practice turns out to be a conjunctural negotiation of
emergent and relational knowledges. Amazonians' understandings of
the forest mediated by their assessments of the institutional resources
and priorities of the visitor enter into fluid dialogue with Bates' own
conflicted allegiance to natural historical systematics as mediated by all
the complications stirred up in his Amazon experience. This needs un-
derlining: at stake is the making of spatial categories, metropolitan natural science, differentiated subjects, and local materiality. Although
Bates' training was ever toward the abstraction of the general from the
specific, these field interactions constantly pulled him back to locality,
and again, we see the critical importance of particularity.

Not surprisingly, Bates understood his science as being of a different order of rationality from what is now often called indigenous
knowledge. Although his collecting relied on local expertise and his future career rested on the ability of informants to trap large numbers of
diverse organisms, he was confused by any sign of native familiarity
with the science of physiological process.[97] Yet, this knowledge hierarchy was difficult to sustain. The assignment of local people's ingenuity

in the manipulation of plant materials (by which he was enduringly fascinated) to a category prior to science was undermined by the high status of the instrumental imperial science of economic botany. Applied local knowledge formed an intellectual resource of which he was fully aware and a pool of commercial data to which he was directed by metropolitan demand.[98] Yet it was methodologically treacherous.

All too often, and particularly when working with botanical specimens, Bates was forced to suspend the normal rules by which objects collected in their habitat are situated in taxonomic relationships. The standard procedure did not apply. Rather than reinventing a natural object as a cultural artifact, Bates started out with the discovery of a cultural object — a plant derivative, perhaps a medicine or a household implement — and then, through fieldwork, tried to track back to reconstruct its natural form. Only in this way could he break down the specimen into the definitive morphological elements through which it would reveal its secrets. This procedure greatly increased his dependency on local informants:

> The difficulty is not in collecting together plenty of different kinds of balsams, resins, or medicinal roots and barks (really or so reported), the real difficulty is in identifying these separate objects with the tree which produces them, and acquiring a flowering specimen of it. This is much aggravated by the loose terminology of the Indians who give the same name to very different things.[99]

It is only after the plant had been reassembled that a species became available to taxonomy. And, only then, in the act of being successfully catalogued, did it become loosened from its relationship to local practice.

Bates knew his Spix and Martius. But even these venerated predecessors encountered only a tiny portion of the novelty of the Amazon valley.[100] Hired informants and field assistants not only selected many of the species for inclusion in his collection, but also provided much of the data that enabled identification. Their descriptions of local ecologies and their namings of individual species — often in sets with implicit and persuasive typological affinities — structured a dialogic field of interleaving taxonomies.[101] Reliant on local familiarity with the properties of individual species, the naturalist, restricted by classificatory lacunae, had little alternative but to begin work by recording vernacular names, traits, and meanings (assigned by local people according to both their own priorities and their strategic understandings of the scientist's needs). One effect of this procedure is to illustrate the Linnaean-derived dependence of biological systematics on morphological distinction. Another is to highlight the spatial and conjunctural contingency of classification: if the plant is not significant to Amazonians there at that moment, it might well not appear in the record. Still another is to draw the natural historian into the logics of immanent properties and alternative taxonomies, ones that may or may not correspond to phenotypic characters held as significant elsewhere.

Local narratives of nature articulated with the Darwinian predisposition to Humboldtian holism, insinuating themselves into the space created by disputes over the methodology of biological systematics and the contested status of systematics in the project of scientific natural history. And these narratives underwrote the situated local knowledge of the traveling naturalist. Aside from economic botany, we see this in a less instrumental but perhaps more formative mode as Bates depends on forest people to indicate and explain weather changes, the intricacies of rivers and tides, the habits and ecology of particular animals and plants, and the histories of land use that enable him, for example, to distinguish between *capoeira* (regenerating agricultural fields) and long untouched areas of vegetation. Piece by piece, he incorporates native descriptions of forest structure, fluvial dynamics, and seasonality, translating these into a discursive patchwork in which technical language and racialized determinisms sit awkwardly with the collapsing of ethnographic distance that comes with his assimilation into the rhythm of daily activity. In a typical passage of this type in which he describes events in Ega, Bates reproduces local narratives that bring together seasonal activities, climate, faunal distribution, and fluctuating livelihoods, legitimating his account through the use of a native terminology that represents the authority of reported speech. Albeit through its rearticulation, it is native experience and explanation that authorize scientific discourse. Bates offers a bricolage of ethnology, physical geography, ecological zoology, and political economy, proposing a synthetic vision of Amazonian life at odds in both tone and focus with the systematist's optic:

> The fine season begins with a few days of brilliant weather —
> furious hot sun, with passing clouds. Idle men and women,
> tired of the dulness and confinement of the flood season, begin

to report, on returning from their morning bath, the cessation of the flow: *as aguas estão paradas*, "the waters have stopped." The muddy streets, in a few days, dry up; groups of young fellows are now seen seated on the shady sides of the cottages, making arrows and knitting fishing-nets with tucúm twine; others are busy patching up and caulking their canoes, large and small: in fact, preparations are made on all sides for the much-longed-for "verão" or summer, and the "migration" as it is called, of fish and turtle; that is, their descent from the inaccessible pools in the forest to the main river. . . . The fall continues to the middle of October, with the interruption of a partial rise called "repiquet," of a few inches in the midst of very dry weather in September, caused by the swollen contribution of some large affluent higher up the river. The amount of subsidence also varies considerably, but it is never so great as to interrupt navigation by large vessels. The greater it is the more abundant is the season. Every one is prosperous when the waters are low; the shallow bays and pools being then crowded with the concentrated population of fish and turtle. All the people, men, women, and children, leave the villages, and spend the few weeks of glorious weather rambling over the vast undulating expanses of sand in the middle of the Solimoens, fishing, hunting, collecting eggs of turtles and plovers, and thoroughly enjoying themselves. The inhabitants pray always for a "vasante grande" or great ebb.[102]

It is in the "intersubjective space of ethnographic encounters"[103] that we find explanations for the specific logic of practice. Bates, like so many fieldworkers before and since, masks his inhabiting of this intimate space — denying its potency by asserting his mastery within it. But its effects on him and his science are far-reaching. By the time he sits down to write the substantive penultimate chapter of *The Naturalist*, his vision is of a contextualized, ecological taxonomy that reflects the mediation of metropolitan scientific dispute by Amazonian encounter. And he is able to advance his claim to professional stature based not just on the power of numbers, as he has in the preface, but on a theoretically confident reading of his empirical achievement:

As may have been gathered from the remarks already made, the neighbourhood of Ega was a fine field for a Natural History collector. With the exception of what could be learned from the

few specimens brought home, after transient visits, by Spix and
Martius and the Count de Castelnau, whose acquisitions have
been deposited in the public museums of Munich and Paris,
very little was known in Europe of the animal tenants of the
region; the collections that I had the opportunity of making and
sending home attracted, therefore, considerable attention. . . .
The discovery of new species, however, forms but a small item
in the interest belonging to the study of the living creation. The
structure, habits, instincts, and geographical distribution of
some of the oldest-known forms supply inexhaustible materials
for reflection. The few remarks I have to make on the animals
of Ega will relate to the mammals, birds, and insects, and will
sometimes apply to the productions of the whole Upper Amazons region.[104]

Bates' was a self-consciously mobile science depending, as he put it,
on "personal observation in different countries." His travel, though,
was always fraught with danger, no less intellectual than physical and
moral, and turned out to be a persistent site of excess and corruption.
The point here is not only the authorizing ethnological invocation of the
"personal" in the presence of difference, to which I have already drawn
attention. There is also weight to that modest word "observation," with
its claims to independence and its assumption of the prior configuration
of nature and space, of an Amazons, like its butterflies, awaiting the
defining taxonomic eye.

"Bates of the Amazons"

Back in England, Bates eventually found his niche as assistant secretary
of the Royal Geographical Society. Perhaps his most important duty,
and the one for which his obituary writers praised his accomplishments
above all else, was sympathetically to advise prospective travelers
and edit their communiqués for publication in one of the Society's two
periodicals.[105]

There is an unmistakable whiff of stiff-necked glamour hanging
around the pages of the *Proceedings* and *Journal* of the RGS in this
period, and, reading them now, we get a sense of the expansive energy,
of the dynamism and planetary reach of this rapidly coalescing center

c. 1892

that had inherited the Banksian mantle as "Britain's quasi-official directorate of exploration."[106] Bates played a backroom role as a modernizer at the RGS, promoting Darwinism whenever possible and pushing for the institutionalization of geography as an academic discipline.[107] Yet it was the aura of the Amazons he had done so much to create that guaranteed his fame, and his obituaries unanimously recalled this defining episode of his life and the proprietorial nickname by which he was affectionately known: "Bates of the Amazons."

In an extensive obituary in *The Fortnightly Review*, the novelist Grant Allen recalled an evening at Edward Clodd's North London home "when Bates broke his wonted reserve in a rare fit of communicativeness." Allen describes the old man as speaking with "child-like simplicity" and compares his account to one of "religious martyrdom":

> Bates told us with hushed breath how on that expedition he had at times almost starved to death; how he had worked with slaves like a slave for his daily rations of coarse food; how he had faced perils more appalling than death; and how he had risked and sometimes lost, everything he possessed on earth with a devotion that brought tears to the eyes of grown men who heard him.

As they rose to leave, these men, who included the writer Samuel Butler and the Africanist explorer Paul du Chaillu, expressed the same regret: "Oh, if we had only had a phonograph to take that all down — accent, intonation, and everything — exactly as he spoke it!"[108]

It is a wonderful and complicated image. The London elect at a moment of ascendancy. Patronage, science, exploration, and literature gathered to hear tales of the great river. It is a site of region-making that we can now barely imagine: a point where materiality and discourse come together in the most ordinary of ways at a moment when discovery and empire are still the business of the day, and in a place where all that effort — the sweeping out of the workshop, the part-time studying, the endless debating of Malthus and Lyell, the years of note-taking and drawing, the perpetual translation, the preserving and packaging, the dread and the longing — dissolves in the landscape of accomplishment. It is a glimpse into a domesticity in which all those anxious practices that I have argued are so important to the making of Amazonia in this time of rediscovery are finally, collectively erased.

Or are they?

This too is a colonial situation. Like those Amazonian trails Bates knew so well, it is a space of encounter and creation, defined in this instance by an unmarked imperial habitus. These men are also *there*, in place, at this historic moment in which a region is made in storytelling, made real through the authenticity and authority of experience.

And the Amazon that Bates conjures! The stories that he tells! We can only guess at their specificities, but we know their contours: limitless nature, incredible hardship, broken health, intimate comradeship, an impossible freedom. But, even in this circle of communion, the anxieties return; the politics of class and the identifications of race slip back in. What is it to which these men of substance are compelled to draw attention in the midst of all this enchantment? It is Bates' accent, his intonation, his provincial origins, his childlike lack of cosmopolitanism despite his heroic travels. It is, though Allen does not say it in so many words, the illiterate wife and the many children who never make it into the professional classes. It is a terrible anticlimax, but it confirms the rationality of anxiety.

Several of the notebooks Bates kept while on the Amazon are now in the manuscript collection of the Entomology Library of the British Museum of Natural History in South Kensington. They are simple exercise books filled with delicate watercolors of butterflies and beetles, miniatures of such clarity that they seem hardly faded despite the distance traveled. In a careful, precise hand, Bates has catalogued his collecting and with it those pervasive instabilities — "some mistake here. . . . I think I have ticketed the wrong specimen, the insect is *not* Pleuracanthus."[109]

6

THE DREAMLIFE OF ECOLOGY
South Pará, 1999

The Bleeding Heart of Ana Almeida da Silva — Materialities of the
Obvious — An Old Friend — The Synergies of Extraction and the
Economy of Terror — "A Template Awaiting Application" —
Faustian Politics — A Tree That Travels (and Transforms) —
Affinities and Contingencies — The Monarch of Mahogany — The
Political and Juridical Economies of Taxonomy — A Species of
Elegance and Charisma — Rhythms and Moods of the Research
Habitus — Imprecision Is Not the Point — Managing the
Extravagant Density of Complicating Presences — Remarkable
Productivity of Scientific Practice — Moacyr Who Haunts the
FMP — To Try to Mend a Bleeding Heart

I took this photo at Ana's *sítio* — her house and farm — a three-room,
palm-thatched, adobe house off a red-dirt road in the south of Pará.

At the front gate, Ana has hung a sign, an announcement, an affirmation, and — although you need to know her a little to realize this — a
challenge. In big, handwritten lettering, it reads: *SONHO MEU* (My
Dream). Ana's sítio glows with the beauty of the cared-for, and the photo
shows a field of healthy pineapple under a grove of shiny *babassu* palms
that recede into the distance. But scanning right to left, the eye suddenly
catches something in the foreground, something jarring that takes a moment to decipher: a bleeding heart, a rock, shoved hard into the sheared-
off stump of a tree and drenched in red paint. The Bleeding Heart of Ana
Almeida da Silva, beauty and pain in the dreamlife of ecology.

MATERIALITIES OF THE OBVIOUS

The southeast quadrant of the giant state of Pará lives on in infamy.
Though the long days and nights of land-driven violence are largely

passed, the towns of the interior south of Belém still resonate in re-gional consciousness like names recited at a graveside.[1] Mention to cos-mopolitans in the capital that you are heading down to Redenção or to the logging citadel of Paragominas, and conversation at once shifts to anecdotes of intimidation and emigration.

On the long bus ride south through landscapes of dried-out, rolling pasture, I scan a provincial newspaper filled with lurid stories of the recent discovery of cocaine processing labs deep in the jungle, ironies of a chimeric modernization. This is the unfulfilled promise of transition from predatory extraction to productive capitalism, ambiguously sig-naled by the chaotic state capture of the informal mining sector, be-trayed by the transnational economy of drugs and clandestine slave la-bor camps that swept in to fill the gap.[2] Drugs in the Amazon provide the occasion for a national moral panic, anxiety about U.S. regional ambition, and opportunities for state arbitrariness, militarization, and the late-night road blocks and baggage searches that repeatedly inter-rupt highway travel. In popular discourse, though, drugs just add sur-plus to the excess of *o sul do Pará*, the south of Pará, where the most familiar folk figure is the hired gun, the *pistoleiro*.

This is a world that lends itself too easily to invocations of the frontier. In the barely thirty years since Redenção was founded by ranchers, loggers, and colonists, it has come to mark not only the boundary of forest and savanna, but a coterminous border of social difference.[3] Researchers and journalists have followed horse-riding cowboys tending herds of zebu cattle; they have watched mining camps spring up on no more than the whisper of a gold strike;[4] they have seen roads of uncertain destination head off into forbidding terrain; they have walked dusty streets in the shadow of prostitutes, gunmen, and painted Indians; they have recognized the law in a posse; and they have *known* they were in the Wild Wild West.

One hundred years later and a few thousand miles south, this is Frederick Jackson Turner's frontier stripped of manifest destiny.[5] For many of today's commentators, both within and outside Brazil, the naturalized trope of the Amazon frontier signifies a negative dialectic, the violation of noble savage and pristine nature by a degenerate, downwardly spiraling Civilization.[6] That the frontier—implying linear spatialities, discrete social systems, and the inevitability of incorporation— is a rather unhelpful metaphor with which to make sense of contemporary regional complexities is perhaps beside the point.[7] More important is its assumption of an irresistible historical trajectory: a tragic narrative of resolutely non-Messianic time that traces the inexorable corruption of Edenic nature and its indigenous stewards.[8]

The absoluteness of the frontier metaphor also contains an appeal to a politics of protection, one liberal response to Turnerian triumphalism. Anthropologists of the region, still struggling with the legacies of Julian Steward and Claude Lévi-Strauss, have long been familiar with this type of premature nostalgia and its expression in the idiom of salvage.[9] Such notions may be out of fashion in a discipline that now favors processual and open-ended reworkings of the culture concept, but they have emerged reinvigorated in popular discourse preoccupied with the metanarratives of globalization. Natural scientists, for their part, have been largely untroubled by the naturalization of culture as endangered and the associated conflation of environmental and social agendas that continues to drive much green activism.[10] Instead, they have effectively participated in the figuring of the social upheaval in Amazonia since the 1960s as an environmental crisis, one that enables their casting as both archivists of a disappearing world and its defenders, successfully fomenting a public rhetoric that generates political urgency around their work. In contrast, anthropologists, floundering in the attempt to communicate broadly a nuanced notion of culture, have been disabled by the sheer obviousness of the notions we seek to displace.[11]

The south of Pará is branded with the emphatic materiality of the obvious. For one thing, it is entirely too obvious that this is a frontier, and it is similarly obvious that there is urgent salvage work to be undertaken here. "You know," a longtime resident informed me helpfully, "this *used* to be part of Amazonia." And, for environmentalists, the area offers a chilling glimpse of the hellfire already licking at the edges of what is left of the region.

Watching the unexpectedly domesticated landscapes slide by the spattered window of the overnight bus, I felt the view haunted by specters of comparison: the neatly whitewashed ranch houses, the low exposed hills, the empowering aesthetic of prospect enabled by the clearcut, all was immediately reminiscent of the colonial-era paintings of coffee estates hanging in the Museu de Belas Artes in Rio de Janeiro.[12] This is an aspirational landscape, a landscape that people I know in Amapá, way up on the other side of the Amazon River, would enthusiastically call *linda* and *limpa* and *bonitinha, né?* breathing deeply their relief from the claustrophobic indeterminacies of the forest gloom. Yet, this must also be an ugly landscape, a despoiled landscape of the not-there — a landscape produced through an overdetermining narrative that my fieldnotes confirm: massively cleared and charred, choked with thorny scrub and sprouting babassu palms, interrupted here and there by statuesque forest remnants, exuberant yellow-flowered *ipê* and full-crowned Brazil nut trees, pitiful memorials, living dead.[13]

We know the obvious as a form of Gramscian common sense, discursive practice that reiteratively constitutes subjectivity.[14] If the traveling social scientist, trained to resist the allures of environmentalist dreamworlds, is disoriented by the specter of an absent forest long gone, how much more visceral must be this encounter for Amazonianist ecologists, heirs to that rich lineage of natural historical thinking that produces this region as the heritage site of planetary biodiversity?

FAZENDINHA

Paul had driven the white Ford pickup in from Fazendinha and was waiting at the bus station as promised. Trained in the same graduate school, we had known each other for years but crossed paths with less frequency as our interests diverged, and I had found my way through the social sciences and he had realized that the roomiest space for a modern-day naturalist was under the sign of ecology.

It was working in the Amazon that drew us together. This present reunion rehearsed another, several years earlier, when Paul, less of a novice in Pará than myself, had met my plane from New York at the airport in Belém and helped with my critical initial negotiation of that disarming city. Over long beers in a backstreet bar, he mapped for me the politics of the local conservation community, and we commiserated with each other in what I now know to be standard pandisciplinary rituals around fieldwork anxiety.

It turned out that Paul and I were inspired by similar, and perhaps peculiarly Amazonian, paradoxes. We had both stumbled across something we felt to be of tremendous importance, yet of which almost nothing was known in the scholarly worlds in which we moved. I had encountered the anthropogenic streams of Igarapé Guariba. Paul was becoming involved with bigleaf mahogany (*Swietenia macrophylla*), the most valuable tropical timber species in the world, the most rapidly disappearing, and, in relation to its considerable socioeconomic significance, a tree still poorly known in its habitat.[15] The life history of Amazonian mahogany, he told me, was almost unknown because, once located, trees were never left standing long enough to study. Soon after, in a moment of prescient symmetry, we found ourselves at the busy bus station, gesturing good-byes as he embarked on his first exploratory trip to the south.

As you might expect, mahogany of any significant size is hard to come by in the south of Pará these days. And, even though ranching and the massive state support given to corporate colonization is widely acknowledged to have provided the dynamic for much forest conversion in the 1970s and 1980s, relatively little attention has been paid to the tight political, economic, and personal connections that facilitated the synergistic collaboration of cattle and timber money.[16] Ranchers did not just slash and burn. They worked closely with loggers who sent in their spotters to locate mahogany — its distinctive crown clearly visible from low-flying planes. Indeed, while it was the construction of the road our buses took — the BR-316 from Belém to Brasília — that created the conditions for the radical transformation of the area's landscape and the rapid extraction of its most valuable trees, it was the aggressive coalition of loggers and ranchers chasing state subsidies along advancing transport corridors that kept the swiftly multiplying local sawmills working day and night.[17] As Paul wrote after a visit to Pará in 1995:

> The scale and rate of this process can only be appreciated from the air: little forest remains 50–100 km either side of any significant road, and enormous swathes of newly felled forests, commonly cut in geometrically regular shapes covering many thousands of hectares, await dry season burns and broadcast seeding for pasture formation. Undisturbed forest is rare—if it exists at all—east of the Kayapó and Cateté Indigenous Areas, and even on those reserves mahogany extraction in the late 1980s and early 1990s left a vast network of forest roads and skidtrails. The east-west corridor bisecting these two reserves, along the BR-279 from Xinguara to São Felix, has been essentially cleared of forest. Ranch and colonist expansion is currently directed north from Tucumã and São Felix, following logging roads that penetrate Indigenous Areas three to four hundred kilometers distant.

By 1995, there were only two potential locations of forest stands of mahogany remaining in south Pará.[18] One, as suggested here, was within the Kayapó Indigenous Area, where significant remnant mahogany populations had survived the extensive cutting that took place just prior to the 1992 federal moratorium on the logging of Indian territories (a gesture to the UNCED Conference in Rio).[19] The other was on land held privately by ranchers and timber merchants who were keeping their standing stock as a form of equity. However, with the growing militancy of the Movimento dos Trabalhadores Rurais Sem Terra (MST), the landless workers' organization, this strategy was becoming more risky.[20] Its most brutal possibilities were seen in April 1996 at Eldorado de Carajás, just a few hours north of Redenção, when nineteen *posseiros* (land occupiers) were massacred by military police (ten executed point-blank with bullets in the head or neck, others hacked with machetes). As a further discouragement to invasion—a pre-emptive move to lower the value of their land—many landowners, then as now, were hurrying to cash in their remaining mahogany, which, by the early 1990s could generate up to U.S. $700 per cubic meter.[21] By this time, however, IBAMA—the understaffed and often ineffectual Brazilian federal environmental agency—had begun requiring logging companies to set aside a portion of their land for mahogany management and conservation. For a relatively minor inconvenience, the payoff could be substantial, with the IBAMA imprimatur leading directly to increased export quotas and relaxed federal scrutiny.

Driving north from Redenção, it takes about forty-five minutes to reach Fazendinha and its strip of whitewashed storefronts that break the potholed monotony of PA-150. Fazendinha is a company town built around a sawmill that stands apart, set above the low-grade worker housing stretching back on either side of the highway. This town was built by mahogany and owned by Fazendinha Madeiras S/A (FAMASA), a local timber company whose fortunes, like those of its diminishing number of employees, is on the wane now that *madeira de lei*, first-grade timber, and the cash it brings are harder to find.

The day Paul arrived, Umberto Fischer, the owner of FAMASA, had his sawmill manager take him out for the first time to the Projeto de Manejo, the Fazendinha Management Project (FMP). They followed the unpaved road as it veered west across the flattened landscapes. They crossed ranches, stopping to swing open and close the heavy wooden gates, throwing up blankets of red dust as they hurtled past the men repairing miles of wire fencing on these blindingly hot days. Then, one more gate, and they left the glare of pasture behind. Pitching along the dried and rutted mud tracks, suddenly hemmed in all around by the humid crush of broad-leaved trees, palms, and the fragrance of vines.

The FMP was FAMASA's IBAMA-mandated set-aside, a 4,400-hectare rectangle, a forest island in a sea of pasture. In mid-1995, when Paul showed up, IBAMA and FAMASA had already bulldozed a grid of roads that divided the Project into 12 metric tracts or *talhões*, each a more or less 1-kilometer slice off the top of the area's 3-kilometer width. These units had been subdivided in turn by narrow trails hand-cut at 200-meter intervals, every 350-hectare talhão therefore being divided into 16 equal 22-hectare sections.[22] Inside the 12 talhões, IBAMA had instructed FAMASA to nail aluminum tags to selected mahogany "seed trees" (*matrizes*), and the logging team was directed to spare a selection when it came through the area in subsequent years.

Gridded and mapped since 1992, the Project was, in Paul's phrase, "a template awaiting application." But it was also what he would often describe as a "beat-up" forest, and one indelibly marked by the historical specificities of location. Of the 815 mahogany trees in talhões 1 through 6 recorded by the FAMASA team during demarcation, 640 had been logged by the time Paul arrived. These, of course, included nearly all the large individuals.[23]

Guided by IBAMA, FAMASA had made a significant investment here. As well as the initial disciplining of the site, they set up a small number of 0.5-hectare experimental plots in which they removed all of the understory, creating an airy park-like ambience. They maintained a permanent crew of four men on hand to keep the trails clean and prevent human invasion, and the general sense was that management goals were being met through the simple preservation of the 175 surviving mahogany seed trees.

An interesting narrative of contingency was about to unfold. Although we might expect Umberto, the owner of FAMASA, to feel content with this arrangement—low investment, minimal overheads, relatively high returns—his treatment of the North American visitor was exceptional. Along with his manager and resident agronomist, Umberto gave Paul a tour of the sawmill and associated nursery, and then, as we know, he sent him out over the rough dirt tracks that led to the Project.

That this convergence was based on more than formal politeness would quickly become clear. A room in Umberto's ranch house was soon serving as Paul's base off-site, and Umberto himself became the active sponsor of the Project's redesign. For the first five months of operation, it was his logistical support that enabled Paul to assemble a small team of workers and start building a functional camp. On a weekly basis, Umberto trucked in quantities of food and water (for consumption, and also to maintain a seedling nursery), and he went to the not inconsiderable trouble and expense of having the roads out to the camp graveled so they would be passable through the rainy season.

Of course, there were compensations. Within a short time, the FMP had become an established research site, backed by some prestigious U.S. institutions and worked by a range of North American and Brazilian biologists. And, not long after, the BBC dropped in to film a segment in which the sawmill operator represented responsible mahogany management in the midst of regional disaster.

Yet, given the widespread ambivalence of the Amazonian timber industry toward the ecological imaginaries of foreign researchers, the level of Umberto's commitment requires further explanation. With commercial stocks of madeira de lei virtually extinguished in the south of Pará, the strategies available to the calculating logger are limited. One obvious response is to move out to new areas of extraction—a standard solution to shortage that is currently sending cutting crews and small-scale sawmills west toward Acre. Another — a familiar trajectory once export markets have been secured, although one with a checkered history in the region — is to experiment with the transfer of valuable species to plantation culture.[24] With additional land deep in the southwest of Pará, and a 350-hectare plantation and nursery adjacent to the Fazendinha sawmill, Umberto was already covering his angles.

Paul's alliance with Umberto emerged from some hard thinking. As one of a group of mostly Brazilian conservation-oriented ecologists working out of IMAZON, a Belém-based non-governmental organization (NGO), his practice was based on dialogue with the very actors who had traditionally been cast as the demonic figures in the Amazonian passion play. As with others in the group, Paul framed his research as an appeal to the instrumentalism of the regional logging industry.[25] Although such Faustian politics are troubling to environmental absolutists, in this respect, at least, the IMAZON team was working within a well-established lineage. As Yrjö Haila has pointed out, ecology has long been a worldly science. Indeed, "nearly every ecologist active at the turn of the [twentieth] century was involved in solving practical problems in such diverse fields as agriculture, forestry, fisheries, demography and life insurance statistics."[26] Despite his own emotional investments, Paul publicly distanced himself from activists campaigning for a logging moratorium, and he took a tactically agnostic position on the acrimonious disputes between extraction and conservation advocates over the listing of mahogany under Appendix II of the Convention on International Trade in Endangered Species (CITES).[27] Despite his personal commitments, his public self-fashioning — expressed in proposals, field reports, and presentations — was as the modest technocrat, disinterestedly producing the facts necessary for an apolitical adjudication.[28]

It was the loggers, Paul argued, who had most to gain from the life-history data on phenology, pollination, seed dispersal, and seedling response to manipulation that he was collecting. Despite the radical short-termism of their practice, they were, he pointed out, the only significant regional actors with both a stake in protecting long-term forest cover and the capacity to do so.[29] Twenty years after the ferocious clearances of south Pará — in which mahogany stems as slender as 30 centimeter diameter breast height (dbh) or less were taken — there was still no possibility of a profitable second cut. Moreover, the standard trajectory was to wholesale conversion to pasture, burning the now sought-after *ma-*

deira branca, the second-quality timber, along with material of no commercial value.[30] Conveniently located high-value timber no longer existed in quantity, and the lower-grade woods were being brought in from considerable distances.

It was, then, a favorable conjuncture for strategic alliance. By providing the basic data that would enable some fairly simple changes to the timing and intensity of harvesting — synchronizing extraction with seed production and seedling growth, for example — Paul offered Umberto the prospect of shifting mahogany logging onto a cyclical regime structured around elements of longer-term, albeit lower-intensity, productivity. In the context of international pressure for a ban on mahogany logging, this was a proposition worth entertaining — at least until it impinged on normal business practice.

Despite the palpable sense of gathering crisis, both ecologist and logger knew that the exhaustion of bigleaf mahogany remained spatially restricted. Although they were fairly safe in predicting the tree eventually becoming so rare at valuable sizes as to be commercially extinct outside plantations, not only was that not yet the case, but improved transport infrastructure and enhanced industry mobility meant that loggers' fields of activity were fully expandable across this adaptable species' entire range.[31] Moreover, as Paul and his colleagues knew, their appeal to an economic rationality mediated by an ethic of sustainability and a notion of evenly unfolding time was of limited force in a world of prolonged primitive accumulation, quite particular cultural and political-economic logics, and perpetual crisis. For one thing, as we have seen, while struggles over land ownership, occupation, and life itself remained so volatile and fluid in Amazonia, neither ranchers, loggers, nor poor colonists were much inclined to think in terms of forest-based futures.

There is, though, little naïveté here. Compared to an earlier age of applied ecological research in the Amazon (when experts blithely encouraged farmers to adopt impossibly high-input agricultural practices as a means of stabilizing "frontier expansion"),[32] contemporary natural scientists and their interlocutors operate in a world of decided realpolitik, forging collaborations where they may. Much of this pragmatism is enforced by the politics of negotiating multiple publics. For Paul and Umberto, mahogany is possessed of a transformative translocality. This is a tree that travels, a tree that creates anew those with whom it comes into contact, and that does so through its — and thus their —

interpellation in a set of debates that can be lively to the point of violence. Thanks to mahogany, it is around the FMP that diverse and overlapping sets of human actors get drawn together: officials of IBAMA and the U.S. Forest Service, NGO activists, timber industry advocates, journalists, academic researchers, and multiply positioned residents of south Pará. Their exchanges are shot through with the crisis-driven rhetorics of biodiversity and habitat conservation, the combative confidence of the neoliberal assertion of entrepreneurial rights, and the authoritative expansion of natural scientific expertise into the realm of social policy.[33]

Mahogany is a species of many parts, and one of Paul's tasks is to ensure that the fetishized aura of its wood is displaced by the (differently fetishized) integrity of its tree-ness. Out of a particularly crushing and disabling anonymity—the absence even of a convincing life history—the FMP aims to produce a cosmopolitan tree with a localized meaning and specificity, a richly situated yet mobile identity. Deep in the interstices of instrumentalism, holding it all together in fact, it turns out that this Project is an affective work of creation: for Paul, a collaboration built on affinities both human and non-human; for Umberto, a moment of curiosity, and, perhaps, in a haphazard way, of redemption.

These, though, are alliances born and raised in contingency. By the time I arrived in Redenção in July 1999, Umberto's stormy relationship with his ex-wife had degenerated into wrangling over filial inheritance. The FMP became just one of several parcels seized on by impatient daughters, and—over Umberto's ineffectual objections—immediately sold to Coutinho, a much larger regional lumber concern. Paul, unceremoniously, had been given one more year to wrap up and leave. Unless, that is, he could come up with U.S. $1.7 million and exercise his option to purchase the Project.

WOOD OF WOODS

Mahogany is no longer what it was in the early 1900s, when Allan Carman, "biographer to His Majesty," wrote the *Monarch of Mahogany Visits Schmieg-Hungate & Kotzian*.[34] Schmieg-Hungate & Kotzian were an Upper East Side Manhattan furniture-maker, and this royal tour begins with a grainy photo of the Monarch's arrival in New York: a very large log lowered on a very muddy dockside, heavy metal hooks

The arrival of the Monarch of Mahogany at New York

in each end, an anonymous man in hat and black gloves looking impassively on.

What now seems a rather desultory image takes us to a time and place in which the extraordinary reach and persuasiveness of capital was a cause for confidence rather than anxiety. The Monarch, Carman writes, is now over 300 years old. He was raised in the forests of Cuba, and has been located with only the greatest difficulty. He must be "induced" to leave his homeland. He must be informed that "suitable arrangements [will] be made for his comfort," that the most up-to-date facilities have been prepared, that the finest craftsmen await him, and, rather ominously, that "a most interesting program of usefulness [has been] outlined."[35] For Carman, Schmieg-Hungate, and their Manhattan clients, the Monarch's life is just beginning. All that went before — those stately centuries — was mere preparation. In a truly modern inversion of the environmental narratives with which we are now so familiar, fulfillment and self-realization lie in the bourgeois transformations of the commodity form: a reproduction Chippendale armchair, a tripod table, and a "lovely" period commode, each purchase verified by a certificate of authenticity and the evidential tactility of that image of arrival on a rainy New York morning.

In his arch attempt to manufacture biography, Carman parodies the localizing strategies of the metropolitan agents who handled specimen sales for the traveling Victorian naturalists. Unlike the butterflies and beetles of the mid-nineteenth-century collection—whose aesthetic appeal was closely correlated with their structural integrity—mahogany's apotheosis relied on its radical physical transformation through milling, turning, carving, staining, filling, and polishing. Though the species certainly also had a scientific career of its own, its primary induction into the metropole was via circuits of exchange quite distinct from those inhabited by the biological specimen. Thus, in addition to the exoticism of the king's provenance, Carman takes pains to draw attention to the exceptional quality of the craftsmanship through which the Monarch was to be domesticated and in so doing, he marks a critical source of value.

Although singled out for its resilience and workability much earlier, mahogany had been a dominant presence in European markets since only the mid-eighteenth century.[36] Its buoyancy and reluctance to splinter on impact had made it an early choice for naval and transoceanic shipping, yet it was later, during what the British commercial histories call mahogany's "golden age," that the wood became so highly prized. The century from 1715 saw the displacement of native oak and walnut in furniture- and cabinet-making as mahogany's great tensile strength enabled lighter and more delicate innovation, and the distinctive styles of the period—Chippendale, Adam, Hepplewhite, and Sheraton— emerged out of the technological breakthrough of the new material. This British presence in both furniture and shipbuilding became decisive, enabling Britain to regulate the expanding world markets in a resource it had claimed from as early as the 1588 defeat of the Spanish Armada. Unsurprisingly, given his opportunistic talents, it was Walter Ralegh who had brought one of the first shipments to Europe on his return from Trinidad in 1596.

It was only in the first decades of the twentieth century that U.S. buyers, capitalizing on their proximity to the source, succeeded in capturing the bulk of the trade. By the 1960s, over 90 percent of American mahogany was passing through U.S. ports. In the meantime, both supplies and demand were becoming erratic as standing stocks depleted. The popularity of the wood declined with escalating costs, changes in taste, and the undermining of its reputation through the passing off of lower-grade substitutions.

In their efforts to maintain their share of the high-end market, U.S. timber companies — operating in a strongly vertically integrated industry — worked on two fronts. Through their trade organization, the Mahogany Association, they repeatedly lobbied to restrict use of the name "mahogany" to specific taxonomic groups. With the Caribbean species now commercially extinct, and, of the three American species, only *Swietenia macrophylla* retaining economic significance, this should have been fairly straightforward. But the cachet of mahogany was such that it was necessary to distinguish these "true" American species (and a few, principally African, allied members of the Meliaceae family) from other, often botanically unrelated, hardwoods sold as what we might call hyphenated mahoganies (Burma mahogany, Borneo mahogany, etc.).[37] Competition over the politics of market transparency between divergent taxonomies (variously derived from trade custom and practice, properties of the timber, and botanical definition) thus produced some inconclusive wrangling lasting from the 1920s through to congressional hearings in 1963.[38]

Alongside this legislative agenda, the industry demonstrated a facility for conjuring a potent mahogany imaginary. In a series of publications that span the first half of the century, the tree and its timber are skillfully placed center stage in a narrative of tropical empire that enhances the accomplishment of the purchaser of drawing-room furniture. Deep in the intimacy of the home, resplendent from the knife, the feminized king is offered explicitly as a material testimony to the subjection of colonial nature.[39]

Whether or not consumers invested in its penny-novel plotting of provenance, the industry had a story to sell. "Mahogany hunting," wrote William Payson in 1926, "is almost as much of an adventure as big game hunting":

> The work of finding and felling the trees in their native jungles and of shipping the logs to the world's markets is still an enterprise scarcely less primitive than in the days when the mariners of Cortez and Raleigh first came upon this sovereign timber three hundred years ago in the wilds of tropical America.[40]

The outsize plates in Payson's book detail the perils of the jungle logging expedition, dramatically placing pith-helmeted European timber

*This lovely commode is an original design in the style
of the creators of furniture fashions of the late eighteenth
and early nineteenth centuries. Like the other pieces
shown, it can be fashioned from the wood of the famous
log and suitably used for hallway, living
or dining rooms*

merchants — as if in postcards home — among bare-chested natives, towering trees, and enormous logpiles. The images show a modernized industry with rail links, customs posts, and heavy equipment. But though
proud of colonial accomplishments, Payson cautions the reader against
these signs of contemporaneity:

> One of the main reasons why the colour and romance of mahog-
> any logging still survive wherever it is undertaken and why the

adventure is still primitive and frequently even dangerous, lies in the fact that what might be termed the mahogany frontier has steadily receded, ever necessitating a deeper penetration into the bush on the part of the mahogany hunter. As the timber near the coasts and navigable rivers has gradually been cut away new trails have had to be blazed further and further into the tropical forests. The work thus constantly requires pioneer effort.[41]

Still a charismatic species, mahogany is today a key emblem for environmental mobilization. But it is clear that the tree and its timber have long been implicated in other types of world-making enterprises. Mahogany was there so often in those formative spaces of metropolitan history, holding things together and keeping them afloat: the piety of the early New World cathedrals, the capture and breakup of the Spanish Armada, the grandeur of Philip II's Escorial, the elegance of Chippendale, the swiftness of the PT attack boats in the Second World War. The species' particular symbolic capital is deeply tied to the successful discursive work of the logging and furniture industries, to the stories that confer distinction and value and that—acknowledged or not—continue to underwrite the affect the tree commands. This is yet one more entanglement of conservation with the realpolitik of nature; one more site at which the unfolding histories of environmental governance condense and converge; one more ground prepared for pragmatic alliance.[42]

IMAGINE THAT YOU ARE WALKING THROUGH A FOREST

Imagine that you are walking through a forest of interarticulated branches. Some are covered with ice or snow, and the sun melts their touching tips to reveal space between. Some are so thickly brambled they seem solid; others are oddly angular in nature, like esplanaded trees.

Some of the trees are wild, some have been cultivated. Some are old and gnarled, and some are tiny shoots; some of the old ones are nearly dead, others show green leaves. . . .

Your job is to describe this forest. You may write a basic manual of forestry, or paint a landscape, compose an opera, or improve the maps used throughout. What will your product look like? Who will use it?

—Geoffrey Bowker and Susan Leigh Star[43]

By July, the mahogany fruits are falling in Fazendinha. Large, pendulous, pear-shaped, and woody, they burst open like stars and the long, elegant seeds break free and spin, scattering downwind, burying themselves in the forest floor.

Monday to Saturday at this time of year, Paul and his field crew — Luiz, Jaime, Ana, Paulo, Gato, and Mandioca — leave camp early, when the wet of the morning still makes you shiver, and drive the pickup out to one of the talhões. Paul has allocated tasks the night before in conversation with Luiz or Jaime, and all is subdued and businesslike.

After three years of concentrated activity, this is going to be a short field season for Paul. A fourth year's data is something of a coup, providing an exceptional longitudinal depth to what is already, with over 600 subject trees, the largest study of neotropical mahogany in progress. Armed with maps that locate each tree in the talhão, the crew sets about recording growth increments, fruit and seed production, mortality, and phenological behavior (the timing of leaf-flush and reproductive activity). Although this is the central piece of the Project, there are numerous supplementary studies in place, some of which involve researchers with other specializations: comparative treatment plots manipulating light, moisture, and nutrients to simulate specific types of disturbance; ongoing measures of climate and water table; regular monitoring of the effects of pests and vines; and detailed investigation of both pollination mechanisms and population genetics.

Not only year on year, but day by day and hour by hour, this field recording of growth and reproduction is profoundly repetitive work. Efforts are concentrated in talhões 1–6, with the most comprehensive data collected in 2, 3, and 4. All live mahogany trees in these 1,100 hectares have been mapped using a compass, clinometer, distance tape, and machete. All stumps and dead stems also — standing and fallen — and all the streams too. Imagine the labor involved.

Unsurprisingly, the map is the foundational technology of the Project, an artifact that bears a double burden of visibility, structuring the meaning of this forest both here, as we trudge along these many miles of trails, and there, as Paul hawks the FMP around offices and seminar rooms, searching now for backers and buyers. Without the map, this forest could neither leave Pará (at least not in one piece!) nor stay here — and its prospects of avoiding the logger's saw would be slim indeed.

Even with the map, though, the gap between ways of knowing (between the forest and the data table) is often too wide and obstructed for easy translation.[44] As we clumsily negotiate these abundantly overgrown trails, our enforced dependence on this elaborate, GIS-rich, multicolored image of keyed and differentiated objects-in-space points to a quirky paradox in the mimetics of cartography. The inability of a map to offer anything more than traces of an archaic landscape demands an awareness of the agency of the non-human — something already appreciated by experienced forest-walkers exasperatingly unable to locate a registered but obstinate tree on a numbered path. Mahogany likes to grow apart, at low densities, spread wide across the landscape. The trees enforce a lot of walking, and a lot of map-reading in vegetation thickly matted with bamboo and sawgrass, growing back straggly and almost impenetrable after logging and fire. There are no hill tops, no open fields, no prospect. Moreover, everything moves in a forest, although you need a static scale to make this apparent. "Trees," Paul tells me as we struggle on, "are very active creatures." And, imperceptibly but decisively, so are vines, herbaceous understory, streambanks, and decomposers.

July days follow a similar pattern. We are here to measure. The map leads from mahogany to mahogany, orienting us to the trails. At each tree, a tableau vivant forms: Jaime and Luiz circle the stem with the steel measuring tape and read off at three heights: 160 centimeters, 130 centimeters (dbh), and 100 centimeters. Paulo and Paul stand to the side, peering up through binoculars, counting fruit capsules and making a judgment as to the tree's phenological status.[45] The others — Mandioca and Gato — are bent over, scratching in the leaf litter with their machetes, searching for fallen fruit capsule pericarps and seeds, or else ahead on the trail, locating and reopening our route. Ana — yes, the same Ana of the Bleeding Heart — sitting or leaning on a stump, takes it all down on her clipboard. By the end of the day, upwards of seventy-five trees have been recorded like this and close to 25 kilometers of forest walked.

This year's measurements serve to verify those of the previous year. As she enters the new data, Ana compares them with the old, checking for anomalies and occasionally revising the earlier figures to bring them into line. The smaller trees are easier and measurements more accurate. The few big trees still here require makeshift wooden scaffolds and much leaning and reaching across tall buttresses. Many of them have uneven, callused trunks on which the measure refuses to lie flat, or vines

that may or may not get hacked away. Very quickly I become fascinated by the infiltration of imprecision and the arbitrariness of numerical coding. Struggling along in this difficult terrain, the moods of the team members shift with hunger and thirst, the intimate pleasures of conversation and shared forest fruits, the increasing tiredness and boredom, and, often, a final, spirited sprint to the finish. As moods vary, so does attention to detail. I assiduously note the subtle and not-so-subtle ways in which the softnesses of biological contours become bludgeoned into integers. Yet this analytic soon seems far too obvious. And unhelpful, as the last thing I want is to present this impressive Project as an untrustworthy product of an anomalous "bad science."

Nevertheless, an important politics is held in the gap between the utopia of methodological purity and the awkward realities of field practice, a politics that can be found well beyond the FMP. There are, for instance, the irresistible imperatives to data precision, underwritten by anxieties about the relatively low scientific status of ecology.[46] One important example in the context of project design is experimental replication.[47] Although a primary disciplinary necessity, replication, Paul explains to me, is often "silly" in a field of this type. This, of course, does not mean he considers it valueless. In fact, he puts tremendous energy into its pursuit. For the sake of replication, he works at three separate sites in south Pará in addition to Fazendinha, tracks the seasonal migrations of deepsoil water across two slopes rather than one, and carries out inventories at four paired top- and bottomslope plots, creating the annual task of measuring an additional 2,500 trees. The difficulty lies in both the inability of replication to absorb variability effectively, and in the porosity of surveillance and control. It is not that replications are unnecessary, but that they are inadequate. They are demanded by an appreciation of the extraordinary heterogeneity of this landscape, yet this same variability produces two significant problems. In the first place, there seems to be no way of truly establishing the identity between distinct experimental units; and, in the second, the basis on which the specific number of replicates is determined involves a decided arbitrariness — and is often dictated by the everyday logic of logistical imperative.[48] Nevertheless, precision's powerful rhetoric arbitrates the Project's legitimacy, and methodology provides the key focus of the critical interrogation to which the professional review process subjects Paul's reports and papers.[49]

One morning, we are all standing under the shimmering silver crown of a tall mahogany tree, swatting at deerflies as we wait for the measurements to be completed. Pointing to a nearby *garra branca* (a larger but less valuable species than mahogany), Paul muses out loud that you often find these trees growing close to mahogany. He doesn't know why — maybe they like similar growing conditions? After a moment's quiet, Luiz responds. It's true: when the *explorador*, the spotter on a logging team, sees garra branca, he gets excited. He knows there'll be mahogany nearby. Similarly, Luiz continues, confirming an upslope-downslope distribution pattern that Paul is keen to demonstrate, the explorador will look for mahogany by following a stream, but he knows he won't find any until the channel narrows and he reaches the top of the watershed.

Luiz has four years' experience working with logging teams in this area, accompanying the spotters in their hunt for the R $3 paid for each tree found.[50] Out in the forest at four in the morning, marking trees, bulldozing trails, dragging out the trunks with heavy equipment until ten at night all through the dry season. A non-stop, ear-splitting whorl of engines and chainsaws. Luiz learned a lot about natural history here in those four years with the loggers and he gained an ability to read the marks of prior political economy in the landscape, a sharp narrative eye that turns a slash in a tree trunk into the *maldade*, the malice, of the passing explorador. If the FMP folds, the chances are he will utilize his expertise again in the same line of work. This, of course, is an irony lost on no one. Others on the team have done their share of logging, and Jaime smiles wryly: "First I was cutting the forest, now I'm saving it."

Paul is respectful of the team's forest knowledge, and, he tells me, his understanding of the landscape and floral ecology in this place has come about through "a joint learning and teaching venture with them." Yet, he also tells me, these people are relatively new to this landscape. Although in the early days his dependency on them was thoroughgoing, now it is more a case of logistics and labor. They are colonists and immigrants in south Pará, fieldworkers whose situated botanical experience does not compare with that of the Dayaks with whom he worked years before in Southeast Asia. These Brazilians' awareness of ecological relationships, he tells me, is uneven and limited. Jaime agrees, and when I ask him if he knows the forest well, he says he knows this part of it pretty well. Born and raised outside the nearby town of Conceição do Araguaia,[51] he is not merely being self-effacing: he knows this forest well enough to understand the significance of location and the indeterminacies of ecological heterogeneity.

Although heterogeneity presents challenges for a scientific method that arrogates the right to generalize heroically from the particular, spatial restriction in itself is not confounding to a research practice that operates on a principle of synecdoche. By necessity, the FMP will have something—however hedged by caveat—to say about the region. And it is therefore not parochialism that limits the scientific relevance of Luiz's observations. This is a problem of translation and rhetoric. His is information but not data, and—although what counts as data is always dependent on the community and moment in which those data are being circulated—it is on such distinctions that methodological practice reproduces and justifies itself.

Luiz and Paul were demonstrating something important about the way methodology arbitrates multiple knowledges. Out in the forest, method emerges as a complicated sorting procedure with a simple, but crucial, goal: the manufacturing of objects that can convince as data. It is a process through which the hierarchies of knowledge relevance are established and in which the descriptive is distinguished from the analytic, the anecdotal from the systematic, the mythic from the factual, the information from the data. As such, it is the inescapable ground on which the credibility of ecology as a science must be tested. Yet, equally, performed in this particular natural-cultural world where the main characteristics are instability and excess, methodological purity is the one test that a field science can only fail. What practice produces, rhetoric must be dedicated to erasing.

However necessary the analogy, the forest is not very much like a laboratory. In fact, it is only through some very specific exclusions that it is able to function as a site for data generation at all. It goes without saying that the forest emerging in conventional natural scientific rhetoric is one in which the collaborations of humans and the obstinacies of non-humans that are so fundamental to the practice of field experimentation are absent. But, given that this is a forest designed to save the forest, there is a certain logic to these exclusions. The FMP that circulates as an intervention in debates on the future life of mahogany relies on the purity of nature for its work in the public language of policy discourse—as a scientific research site and in the form of data.[52] Yet, this clinical identity through which arguments over the regulation and management of species are waged is, in practice, only a supplement to the affective meanings of mahogany. Once more pointing to both the ambivalence and the excess from which data are produced, it turns out that rather than effacing mahogany's romance, the FMP relies on it, using this tree's historical charisma to generate justification, funding, and attention from loggers and environmentalists alike.

COMPLICITIES

Paul's research reflects long-standing disciplinary struggles to make sense of the natural world while not losing sight of the conservationist impulse to intervene in it. Committed to describing the functional inter-relationships of a relatively coherent natural system, he is forced to devote considerable energy to managing the extravagant density of complicating presences. In Fazendinha, as we have already seen, some complications find their way back in.

As well as struggling against the everyday corruptions of the human and the intractability of the non-human, Paul and his IMAZON colleagues are attentive to the profoundly anthropogenic character of their research sites in south Pará. In other words, although they milk the duality in their political sacralizing of the forest, they also appreciate the shifting artificiality of the nature-culture divide. I remain skeptical about the hunt for natural processes in which they are ultimately involved, with its peeling away of the accreted layers of culture in a search for the essential. Yet Paul and I call a truce somewhere in the region of a critical realist approach to the non-human. Similarly caught in webs of affect and uncertainty, I concede a limited, strategic version of his claim for those things—relatively autonomous in their biophysicality—that he calls nature.

Something else that occupies our conversation is the apparent convergence over recent decades between theoretical developments in ecology and the social sciences. The rise of non-equilibrium ecology, influenced by chaos theory and emphasizing landscape heterogeneity and the contingency of disturbance, seems to map readily onto parallel moves in the human sciences to resist totalizing narratives by valorizing the heterogeneous and the paradoxical.[53] Paul traces his own deconstructive lineage through the Yale School of Forestry, where his training brought him into conversation with David M. Smith, a key figure in the elaboration of a natural historical approach to silviculture, and with Herbert Bormann, whose partnership with Gene Likens produced the seminal Hubbard Brook Ecosystem Study of the 1960s and 1970s.[54]

As might be expected from distinguished faculty in a school founded by Aldo Leopold, both of these scholars promoted the role of basic research in the context of a managerial approach to nature. Both also drew on a U.S. tradition of the working forester with an intimate knowledge of trees as both individuals and species, and both developed practices self-consciously sensitive to immanent patterns in natural systems.[55] In its allegiance to ideas of succession and homeostasis, the Hubbard Brook project was more conservative than the research that geographers and anthropologists now champion as pointing to the obsolescence of the ecological models utilized by social scientists.[56] Yet Bormann and Likens did depart from the abstractly technicist orthodoxy of systems analysis promoted by H. T. Odum, emphasizing instead forest history (that included human history), ecological complexity, disturbance, and temporal and spatial patchiness. They envisioned their New England watershed as an unevenly processual "shifting mosaic."[57] In addition, they recast the emerging research archetype of long-term, large-scale "big science" by stressing multidisciplinarity, hands-on empirical labor, and non-hierarchical working relations.[58]

The transposition of this research model from temperate to tropical systems raised significant theoretical and logistical dilemmas. Tropical forests have far longer growing seasons, considerably greater diversity in plant and animal populations, more intricately co-evolved reproductive biologies, and population structures of a different order of complexity from their temperate analogs. Even basic mechanical techniques, such as those for calculating the age of trees, were found to be ineffective.

Equally challenging were the frequently opaque institutional and personnel arrangements that emerged in the process of undertaking what could be highly capitalized research projects around obscure agendas in the developing world. In Fazendinha, for example, Paul finds himself not simply the employer of his crew, but their *patrão*, a regionally conventional figure binding the Project together through intimate and reciprocal patronage relationships. The assumed transparency of cash-based exchange thickens into the sticky soup of mutual but differential duties, obligations, and rights. Over the years, the pool of FMP workers has narrowed to the members of one extended family, so that Paul now confers with Ana about the potential impacts of seasonal layoffs on particular relatives and the best way to ensure that her brother-in-law uses his salary to benefit his wife and children. It means, for example, that Paul is pulled into the logic of some highly particular Amazonian social relations, advancing salary on credit to his most senior workers with paternalist provisos that specific monies be used for specific domestic purchases, such as a chainsaw, a plot of land, or construction materials. In this way, Paul finds himself responsible for a large number of connected people who are not his direct employees, and decisions about the Project's future and its labor capacity become significantly freighted.

There are, then, closely related methodological and social conundra here. At first sight, forest ecologists might appear to be involved in an endeavor that, however oriented to heterogeneity, is ultimately and inevitably a restrictive procedure of simplification. However, when we consider ecological practice in a more inclusive sense — to encompass the writing of research papers, the demarcation and construction of field sites, the employment of assistants, the coordination of collaborators, the elaboration of patron-client networks, the circulation of technologies, the consultation in local political process, and so on — it becomes clear that such traveling projects are highly productive of all kinds of new and altered social and discursive relations.

One obvious way in which such productivity occurs is as ecologists write places in the act of narrating nature.[59] By describing a stripped-down, geographically situated space in which the social is excised from a world of nature, natural scientists working in Amazonia have brought places into existence as the imagined sites of functional natural processes.[60] Moreover, through the conventional scaling-up of the specificities of the site, such places, in turn, have come to represent larger landscapes, and, not infrequently, the entire region. In relation to the work of cultural ecologists — those anthropologists working in the tradition of Julian Steward — the significance of such representations of Amazonia, in which the consequential ecological distinction has been between *várzea* (fertile floodplain) and *terra firme* (nutrient-poor upland forest), cannot be overstated. In contrast, a non-equilibrium focus on patchiness has helped bolster pre-existing fine-grained analyses of ecological heterogeneity.[61] In the social sciences, however, as Eduardo Viveiros de Castro points out, such shifts can lead, without contradiction, merely to a more differentiated ecological determinism.[62]

In the south of Pará, the field site itself is already explicitly humanized through histories of logging and fire. Distinctions between nature and culture on the ground are therefore less secure, the contamination of data is more profound, and the narration is of a damaged landscape, a suitable case for salvage. Paul argues in response that he is working in a "management unit," not a forest. I understand this as a zone of regulation, a revisioning of nature that effectively converges with the policy nexus through which environmental politics becomes a key location of transregional governmentality.[63]

Such ecological narratives are central to understanding how it is that Amazonia continues to be so strongly associated with particular natures. But socio-spatial relations are made in ways additional to writing. Unexpected combinations arise through the coming together of human and non-human histories and practice in the effort to create and maintain the FMP. In fact, too much is made here for one narration: conjunctural political alliances, new lives for the Wood of Woods, houses and chainsaws for Luiz and Jaime, a bleeding heart for Ana Almeida, a place on a map, a reconfigured locality. New experiences, possibilities, and dilemmas for us all.

MOACYR

Ana, who never seemed afraid of anything, told me she was scared to death when she took this job in the forest. Like any Amazonian I ever met, she didn't want to be stuck out in the woods, a sitting target for who-knows-what wild beasts of the imagination. She didn't much want to leave her three young children home in the *colônia* all week with her mother. She didn't want to be the only woman out here with a work crew of men. She also wasn't crazy about cooking and cleaning or about hanging around the whole day with no company but the radio and no means of transport out of here except a bicycle.

But her sister walked out after the first week for a job in town, so the position came open and Ana needed the money. And, after a short while she realized this life had its pleasures. When we first met and I couldn't help admiring the perfection of her sítio and the orderliness of the camp, she told me without hesitation that all of it—the Project, her house, her garden—was due to Moacyr.

As Paul is the first to say, Moacyr built the FMP, working through the long rainy seasons under terrible conditions, setting up experiments, improvising technologies from plastic tubing and wooden stakes, molding a team, drawing on his fifteen years' experience as a field assistant for visiting U.S. and Brazilian scientists. And it is Moacyr who continues to haunt the FMP, his name spoken twenty times a day as we pass the trees he marked, read the maps he drew, follow the trails he cut, or shower with the comically ingenious gravity-piped water system he invented. Moacyr. I had been hearing about him for years: a phenomenon, a research assistant who designed experiments and managed projects, who understood the logic of science, who could motivate a work crew like no one else, whose storytelling could enthrall a room, whose physical endurance knew no bounds.

One night, I stayed at Ana's sítio. We had finished eating and were sitting outside in the warm darkness. The children were asleep and we talked quietly, the oil lamp throwing shadows across her garden, glinting on the red of her bleeding heart. Ana fetched an album and slowly thumbed through her photos of the two of them together, laughing at her outfits and his gravitas. Moacyr was strong and wiry, older, more contained. Ana looked happy and excited, full of expectation.

I took another long bus journey, this time to Paragominas. Moacyr and I met that first evening, found a café nearby, and sat drinking Cokes. Ana had warned me about his charm, and she was right. He told me how his life had been tied to the history of this small town, somewhere that, along with Redenção and a few other centers, had been the very eye of the storm that swept through eastern Amazonia in the 1980s. Back then, when the sul do Pará was still reeling from the opening of the BR-316, Moacyr would go into the forest to cut timber by hand and bring back logs to the sawmills for which Paragominas was becoming famous. It was during those years that he came to know timber, establishing that familiarity the scientists were now trying to recover.

The next morning, Moacyr found a couple of bikes and we rode up the dusty red hill and out of town in the full sun to Fazenda Maria. Some critical research had been carried out at this site in the early 1990s, demonstrating (against the entrenched orthodoxy of shallow roots and a tightly closed nutrient system) that Amazonian trees and pasture grasses can have deep tap roots reaching down to the water table.[64] The site is mostly a relic now and the camp lies abandoned, mildewed photos pinned behind plastic sheeting: clowning researchers, arms entwined. The shafts that made this place famous are still here and still studded with electronic monitoring equipment, the exposed roots visible in the darkening depths where giant toads now sit, trapped and helpless.

Moacyr and I were meeting at a difficult moment in his life, and the account he gave me of his career reflected that. When researchers first arrive, he said, they have little idea of what it means to work in the Amazon. Their language skills are often poor, their ability to walk in the forest doubtful, they know the soils and plants only from books, they don't understand how to negotiate social relations. Such experts rely on people like himself to leaven their *teoria* with *prática*: to interpret their initially garbled Portuguese, to guide them through the materiality of the forest, to translate their tidy blueprints into functional experiments, to mediate their relations with the work crew, to steer a course through the opacity of Amazonian difference.

There are a number of standard experiments Moacyr can put in place independently — biomass and productivity measures, for example. Otherwise, he works through the specific problem, trying to determine as precisely as possible what is wanted and thinking up an appropriate experimental design. If the researcher comes with clearly drawn diagrams, so much the better; Moacyr can just go ahead and prepare the plot or build the necessary structures.

But from the first day the irony begins to unfold. The more successfully he teaches, the faster the visiting scientist learns to be independent. Within a couple of years, the project is established, the team is trained, the area mapped, the replicates in place, and everything has settled into a secure routine. Once indispensable, his skills are no longer needed. And his price, which has risen steadily over the years, is too high.

There was no more of this work available for Moacyr, and he no longer put his faith in science. He seemed to have outgrown the expected relationship, chafing at the imposition of discipline and testing the limits of his mediating role, exploring his charisma. He suspected that experienced researchers preferred to work with other, more deferential assistants and that they were advising their junior colleagues to do the same.[65]

When we met, Moacyr had left the FMP and Ana, and he had no money to get back to Redenção. Paul, who lists Moacyr as co-author on all Project publications, but who was exhausted by the struggle of wills, had no more work for him. Moacyr told me he had had enough of working with foreigners. He looked back on his fifteen years with the research community and bemoaned his failure to get the formal training that would allow him to demand a salary proportionate to his skills. If he only had a degree, if he was an *Engenheiro Florestal*. . . . Instead, he was adrift, kicking his heels and conjuring schemes to extract cash from the ever-more-distant forest. My visit only seemed to deepen his isolation. Had I seen the pineapple he'd planted in Ana's sítio? he wondered. Was the *cajú* fruiting yet?

BEYOND (A TOWN CALLED) REDEMPTION

> I knew they were pheasants, although since dreams usually transform things, they had long tails covered with iridescent eyelike spots similar to those of peacocks or rare birds of para-

dise. . . . In the brilliant sunshine they made the most splendid pile imaginable, and there were so many of them there was hardly room for the steersman and the rowers. Then we glided over calm waters and I was already making a mental list of the names of friends with whom I meant to share these treasures.

— Goethe[66]

As memories fade into the past, they often become dreamlike, anchored only by embodied, deeply embedded details. Dreams likewise gain the materiality of memory, blurring our sense of the real, haunting our days, and driving us on.

Goethe's iridescent vision is a yearning for a rarer, more dazzling, less mediated, more intimate, and fuller nature, simultaneously wild and tame, autonomous but domestic. Yet, it is also a modern fable: the peacock-pheasants in his splendid pile are dead, killed by "natives" for his pleasure. Such profoundly historicized environmental narratives — still colored with Romanticism — now travel that highly charged stretch of the oneiric that runs between Utopia and Apocalypse, a track along which dreams and nightmares meld and morph, feeding each other in co-dependency, afflicting politics with the exigency of crisis.[67]

The scientific dreamlife of ecology eschews ambivalence for the security of teleology, a meditation in a sacred forest free from the gloom of moral ambiguity. Yet, no one who knows the first thing about the culture and practice of this field science even slightly believes such public fantasies — least of all, of course, those contemporary naturalists whose daily task is the management of natural-cultural excess. Conducted under the sign of methodological purity, however, ecology necessarily reproduces its own fictions. As a knowing aspect of a pragmatic realpolitik, this paradox is at least functional. But it should not obscure all those ways in which scientific practice remakes people and places, bringing them face to face in new and transformative ways.

The FMP has created more than Ana's bleeding heart. But by ignoring that experience and the dreams to which *it* points, traveling science condemns itself to bringing into being an Amazonia that is potent, deeply troubling, and already familiar: a site for salvage and the redemption of the modern.

As Ralegh, Bates, and Paul could all attest, there is, though, a realm of affect and encounter which breaches the divide between the human and natural sciences. Paul, a level-headed romantic who thinks of himself as a natural historian, understands this well. In the margins of his scholarly production he is compiling his most satisfying work: a field guide to the trees of the FMP. It is an important contribution. In some ways the opposite of normal science, it limits its claims to what the trees make possible. If their range is restricted, so is the guide. Such handbooks are almost non-existent for the Amazon.[68] Perhaps the task is just too daunting.

Like Henry Bates in the final pages of *The Naturalist*, Paul is exploring the possibilities of his science from a place saturated with the instabilities of the field. Each of his trees comes to life with a situated identity and a sociality. He begins his description of *farinha seca*, *Licania* sp., a Chrysobalanaceae, by telling us about *farinha*, "coarse manioc flour that is the true staple of the Amazonian diet, eaten 'seca' — dry — by the handful or heaped on top of rice and beans." This tree, however, is certainly not edible, its name instead an ironic play on the word *seca*, which, when used in relation to a container of food or drink, means empty or finished. Like that of Vicente Chermont de Miranda, Paul's dialogic natural historical glossary is a mark of familiarity with both trees and people, an intimacy: "If you swipe [the tree's] lower stem with a machete a cloud of fine bark-dust bursts into the air, and with some imagination you might think of tossed farinha and feel hunger pangs a great distance from the nearest meal."

Taperebá, a tree that produces a much-prized regional fruit, presents a mystery the solution to which enrolls multiple actors: "Why is it that this species . . . is so vastly distributed across the neotropics? Taperebá is a tree that moves about the landscape easily — not only people savor its fruit — and is probably an opportunistic colonizer for which 'ideal' regeneration conditions are quite broadly defined." *Cupania scrobiculata*, a Sapindaceae, had no local name. "We named this tree ourselves from its generic moniker, which is odd considering how common it is, especially in upper-slope sandy clays. Providing people neither goods nor services, cupania never needed a local name before."

There is a seed of possibility here. Despite all the asymmetries of continents, knowledges, disciplines, and locations, there is affinity emergent in misrecognition and forced accommodation. With the domain of environmental politics so circumscribed by emergency, where else but in the lived intimacies of such practices can the recuperation of the wide worlds of a bleeding heart begin?

7

FLUVIAL INTIMACIES
Amapá, 1995–1996

The Language of Water — Intimate Places — The White House, A
Haunting — The Vila as Chronotope — Sônia and Miguelinho — A
Perverse Irruption and a Lurid Moment — The Mote in the
Association's Eye — Life and Debt — Yes, It Still Looks Like
Aviamento — The Cantina — Tainted with the History of Its Own
Birth — Açaí Is Delicious! — Hard Times in Macapá — Fear of a
Free Market — A Terrible Responsibility — The Fractures through
Which She Sails — Tough, Dangerous Work — Recursive
Performance of Public Surveillance — "Even Beasts Feel Love" —
Eliana

There is a moment early on in his strange and beautiful book, *Water
and Dreams*, when Gaston Bachelard tells us that "the language of water" is not metaphorical. This seemingly obscure point is later developed in a discussion of the mimetic inadequacies of onomatopoeia, and
it shows Bachelard reaching to convey the profound unity that ties people and water, indissolubly. His starting point is autobiographical. "I
was born in a section of Champagne noted for its streams," he confides:

> The most beautiful of retreats for me would be down in a val-
> ley, beside running water, in the scanty shade of the willows
> and water-willows. And when October came with its fogs on
> the river. . . .
>
> I still take great pleasure in following a stream, in walking
> along the banks in the right direction, the way the water flows
> and leads life elsewhere.[1]

As he writes, Bachelard is in the midst of his multivolume meditation on the elements, the "hormones of the imagination," as he calls
them. He has already caused quite a commotion with *The Psychoanal-
ysis of Fire* (1938), but there is something too personal about water: it

confounds him, prevents him from achieving the rigor that would allow the invocation of the psychoanalytic. Instead, he describes his essay simply as a study in literary aesthetics.

But in this he is altogether too modest. The book is unexpected and creative. And its most telling insight, that in water people find "*a type of intimacy*," and that "already, in his inmost recesses, the human being shares the destiny of water," translates across continents, contexts, and disciplines.[2]

Bachelard has a wonderful way of explaining this. He argues that "the language of waters is a direct poetic reality; that rivers and streams *provide the sound* for mute country landscapes, and do it with a strange fidelity; that murmuring waters teach birds and men to sing, speak, recount; and that there is, in short, a continuity between the speech of water and the speech of man."[3]

I love this idea of the speech of water. Its animism summons entirely different traditions of thought and instantly enlivens the narrow materialism of Euro-American academia, a tide to wash away parochial convention. Its enlivening of nature carries me back to Igarapé Guariba, to what people there call the *rio-mar*, the river-sea, and in which live all kinds of worlds, all types of beings, and all manner of intimacies.

Bachelard's method for unfolding these poetics is, appropriately, through poetics — a rich and idiosyncratic study of image and imagination. In this final chapter, I want to approach the same end in an entirely different way: through an account of rivers, trade, and the grounded prosaics of everyday political economy in Igarapé Guariba. Bachelard's work is the invitation and inspiration. Yet where he holds water in view, up to the light, sharply examining its facets and ungraspable fluidities, I meet it seeping through at the margins, always there, always in motion, always in mind, and — as if to demonstrate Wittgenstein's observation that "the aspect of things that are most important for us are hidden because of their simplicity and familiarity"[4] — nearly always invisible.

INTIMATE PLACES

It is by transgressing the conventions of human space that rivers reveal the poverty of scalar categories. They are, as Bruno Latour has written of railroad tracks, "local at all points," while being definitively, unstoppably translocal.[5] Well, not entirely unstoppable, of course, as dam-building and other engineering have shown only too plainly. But always *immanently* translocal—if not saturated with nostalgia for other geographies, then brimming with the promise and the possibility of Bachelard's elsewhere.

Not even locality is contained within spatial borders though. As people journey along these Amazon rivers, they take places with them in their embodied and imaginative practices.[6] But, as everyone knows, locality also has its spatial correlate, and even imaginary places usually have a physical location, the anchor and first mark of placefulness.[7] Lines of demarcation may be tenuous, permeable, and rapidly dismantled and reconstituted, but they nonetheless confer a kind of fixity. Places seem to need boundaries and to make sense in terms of insides and outsides, even if these are permanently in the being-made and even if we have trouble knowing exactly where they are at any given moment. And rivers? Rivers themselves are both guardians and betrayers of places. And, what's more, despite often being themselves the borders that make places, they are places too, as mobile as can be. Nevertheless, it makes no sense for this Amazonian natural history to follow Bachelard in opposing water to landscape. We have been wading in *terra anfíbia*, an amphibious world of mobile porosities where land and water become each other, and where humans and non-humans are made and unmade by those same sediments that bring histories and natures flooding into the immediacy of the now.[8]

Bachelard tunes out the dissonances of power and politics from his murmuring waters. He prefers an easy nostalgia, one that fills his present with the pleasurable romance of the pastoral. But the type of intimacy in which he lingers is more than mere proximity. It is also the mark of a lived relationship between humans and nature, an expression of biography—of the politics tied up in the lives of both people and landscapes. Different natures and histories produce a wide range of mediations of experience, varied and differential structures of feeling, and complex and constitutive intimacies.[9] Such intimacies are sites where the politics of space are practiced: where places, regions, and localities get worked through, made, and grounded, literally.

In a series of provocative essays, Alphonso Lingis takes us to intimacies quite unlike Bachelard's comforting ruralities.[10] Although similarly at the edge of the inexpressible and pushing against rationalist analyses and cultural logics, this is a dangerous space of desire, claustrophobic even when most at ease. Lingis is not party to the conservatism that ties place, rootedness, and the intimate, and instead strives for that fleeting communion in which intimacy burns in anonymous coupling. Despite their expression in the idiom of individual experience, these intimacies are always compromised by contexts and events, are never exterior to power. They emerge through a reflexive ethnography of encounter, and in this respect as well as in his refusal to romanticize locatedness, Lingis opens up intimacy as a broad and differentiated realm of affective sociality, a realm characterized by embodiment and relationality.

Where Bachelard points to the intimacies of proximity that tie human and non-human, Lingis helps me find intimacies in the dynamic and disruptive, in the asymmetrical politics through which place, economy, and history are made in Igarapé Guariba. And, in another way, so does Doreen Massey. In a critical formulation, Massey writes about places as meeting points of social relations, as the outcomes of difference and inequality that also produce difference and inequality. And she points to the things people — all of us — do to bring places to life and to make them as much as possible the way we want them: those things we do physically with hands and machines, and the things we do with our imagination and our talk. The things we do with affect and the things we do with labor.

Social spatialities are simultaneously contingent yet located. Bringing together space and time, Massey describes places as "particular moments" in intersecting, spatialized social relations, some of which are "contained within the place; others [of which] stretch beyond it, tying any particular locality into wider relations and processes in which other places are implicated too."[11] Such translocal places are relational, involved in the complex articulations of effective geographies, tying humans and non-humans across time and space.[12] Such places are formed in the complicities of human and non-human agency — and such complicities are further entangled through the work of place-making.

Places are never stable, and space is never empty. Both are always active, always being made, always in process and in practice. Place and space are always in that flow of becoming, caught — and it's as if Deleuze and Guattari were thinking of Igarapé Guariba when they imagined the metaphor — in "a stream without beginning or end that undermines its banks."[13] There is no point of stasis: people are in motion, the tide turns, the banks crumble. Shifting historical sedimentations form the unreliable ground on which lives are made.

"The world," Foucault writes, "is a profusion of entangled events."[14]

Throughout this book I have resisted the impulse to purify these con-junctural assemblages and instead have written across and between the consequential analytical divides that partition local and global, past and present, materiality and meaning-making, affect and rationality, human and non-human.[15] In this Amazonian natural history an analytics of en-tanglement has found its ground in the complex co-constitutions of inti-macy. And here, back in Igarapé Guariba, those situated, differentiated practices of intimacy are fluvial: intimacies of lives that inhabit rivers and of rivers that inhabit lives.

The White House

My fieldwork in the Amazon estuary has always involved traveling with traders on the region's rivers. In fact, those have often been my favorite moments, the times I've felt most at home. Huddled up on the roof of a small boat as it putters slowly between ports, a little shivery as the sun comes up on the unbroken brown plain of this river-sea, chatting with friends and new acquaintances, sharing crackers and sometimes hot sweet coffee — each of these journeys is a space outside, suspended in the freedom and tension of expectation and mobility. Traveling taught me to think of the trading networks that unfold along these Amazonian rivers as embodied practices, meaningful relationships assembled and followed by the people who depend on them, a way that Amazonians take a place out into the world beyond the mouth of a river.

And it has often been at river mouths that the politics of rivers have played out here. Prior to the twentieth century, they formed defensible points of military strategy in the many struggles that wrenched at the region: those between native and European, those among the would-be colonial powers (English, Irish, Dutch, Spanish, Portuguese, French), and those that pitted slave and Indian against Liberal forces during and after the Cabanagem. Unsurprisingly, river mouths can still figure as strategic outposts, now as sites where *patrões* impose transport barriers and establish their own fiscalization, acting simultaneously as monopso-nists with depots for the reception of farm and forest produce, and as monopolists with stores for the sale of household goods. Beyond the river mouth (or the impassable rapids or falls) often lies another coun-try, a private domain.

Igarapé Guariba was like that. Viega's house standing at the mouth of the river, raised on a bluff with a view across the mouth-bay, white-painted, tile-roofed — the only tile-roofed building in this village of twenty-five houses just off the Amazon River on the floodplain of Amapá. Next to it stood a warehouse and attached to that a store. This was once the *vila*, the economic center, a river mouth complex of buildings where Old Man Viega's *fregueses*, his clients — the people who worked the land along this river and in return owed the landlord their labor and their income, just about everybody, in fact — came to exchange their produce for merchandise.

Most of the other structures in the vila have disappeared with time, but the house is still standing, the worn white paint clinging to the wooden boards beneath. The Old Man himself is now long gone, his heart giving out soon after his fregueses succeeded in forcing him off the river. These were dramatic events that took place almost twenty years ago now. But they were struggles, I've realized, that have never really ended. And in the run-down white house at the river's mouth they have their site of oneiric condensation. That house is now a haunting, with all the dangers, transgressions, and seductions that brings. Because, despite everything that has happened, despite the changing of regime and the entry of a new order, there are still Viegas living there, plying the river, muddying its already turbid waters.

EXILE AND RETURN

Raimundo Viega, the Old Man, the patrão, came to Igarapé Guariba for the timber. The late 1950s were a propitious time for entrepreneurial Amazonians. With newly aggressive state and federal policy directed at territorial integration, the first major road was constructed to the north of the country (the Belém–Brasília highway, 1956–60), and a rudimentary development infrastructure put in place via the Amazon Credit Bank and the Superintendência do Plano de Valorização Econômica da Amazônia — early intimations of what was to become a fearsomely opaque bureaucracy.[16]

Viega had other commodities in mind — animal skins, oilseeds, bananas, watermelon, cattle — but it was the timber that drew him out along the Canal do Norte, the northern channel of the Amazon estuary. And, as we might expect, one of his first projects in Igarapé Guariba was the sawmill.

It was a simple setup: just one circular saw powered by a gasoline-fired generator. It was so simple, in fact, that it limited him to trees of less than 48 inches in diameter, and, because of the poor quality of the cut, restricted his sales to the domestic market. Like most operators in the interior, he was also unable to "peel" trunks large enough to exploit the lucrative veneer and plywood markets. He cut *cedro, andiroba, aç-acu,* and *muritinga,* separating out the larger pieces and the high-quality woods and sending them off to Macapá for processing, or else bartering them on consignment to river traders. Such practices gave him ample capacity, and despite buying all the wood he could from his fregueses in Igarapé Guariba, he was still able to take in greater quantities from outside.

Viewed from the city, the Old Man's operation looked like any one of the hundreds of inefficient, shoestring operations that sprang up at the time.[17] Octávio told me it was a *"brinquedo,"* a joke, a toy. But in Igarapé Guariba, even today, that river mouth complex with its large white house remains a powerful mnemonic, what Mikhail Bakhtin called a chronotope, a temporal-topographic metonym that condenses time and space into place.[18] Again and again, the structures of the vila become real in conversation, organizing narrative, paradoxically referencing both the positive attribute of great *movimento* (liveliness and activity) and the darker memories of what is understood as *escravidão* (slavery). The sawmill, the store, the warehouse, the boatyard, the white, tile-roofed house: they now act, in Bakhtin's memorable phrasing, as "places where the knots of narrative are tied and untied. . . . [Places that] make narrative events concrete, make them take on flesh, cause blood to flow in their veins."[19] And even more than this. For all kinds of people who lived in Igarapé Guariba in those days, these remain sites of such energy that events occurring elsewhere "appear as mere dry information and communicated facts."[20]

When things fell apart for Viega, they did so catastrophically. He lost the upstream land in a legal action brought by his own fregueses, and he soon faced open competition on the river from the boat-owning Macedos, one of the families whose futures he felt himself to have assumed in trust. The pleasure he drew from the modernization of his community drained away. His affection for the place turned sour and the heart condition that had killed his four brothers began to plague him. He holed up in his house in Macapá, physically withdrawing from the interior. He took regular trips across the estuary to Belém to visit his doctor. Direct supervision of the store and warehouse business lapsed. Soon, the manager disappeared with the takings somewhere out in the open expanse of the Amazon rio-mar.

After Raimundo's death in 1983, Igarapé Guariba and the other properties went to his children. Within a few months, they had reneged on what residents say was the Old Man's promise to let them stay where they were and had sold the north bank of the river, the side opposite the vila, to an absentee landlord in Brasília.

The new landowner was an air force colonel[21] who immediately petitioned the federal environmental agency IBAMA for authorization to cut the *açaí* groves that dominated the forest opposite the vila. The groves were the product of more than twenty years of farmer management for the rich palm-fruit that forms a central part of people's diet in these estuarine communities. But the Colonel had other interests. With technical advice from IBAMA, he implemented a project for the "sustainable extraction" of açaí palm-heart, a product derived from the growing meristem, and most commonly harvested by killing the tree.

The Colonel's açaí was shipped to a canning factory upstream on the Amazon toward Macapá. Even though this was a sad, part-time operation suffering from the disappearance of the açaí groves under harvest pressure and the diminishing size of the extracted hearts, the palm-heart industry itself was still highly profitable for well-capitalized landowners and entrepreneurs.[22] In recent years, however, there has been a boom in fruit prices as urban consumption of the thick liquid made from the purple berries has rocketed, and açaí itself has come to claim an ever-greater share of rural incomes. Logically enough, these shifts have been accompanied by the emergence of a powerful anti-palm-heart discourse in many rural communities. One result of this is that the work of the traveling buyers who tour the estuary encouraging farmers to sell their standing stock for ready cash has become increasingly difficult, and they now often settle for the unwanted stems removed during annual thinnings. The açaí palm has become intensely politicized, embedded in rhetorics of class and political economy, and an ambiguous symbol of conflicts between "local" and "global" economies. In Igarapé Guariba, palm-heart is associated with rich land-grabbers. People there identify it as a luxury food, selling overseas for preposterous prices. *Vinho de açaí*, by contrast, the purple "wine," is emblematic of an honest, simple life.

IBAMA's contribution to the Colonel's project was primarily aesthetic. In a familiar story, the land was divided into uniform, rectangular lots separated by narrow trails. Aluminum plaques were tacked to the trees at the front, and square boards decorated with the IBAMA logo stuck into the bank of the river at suitable intervals. The Colonel sent in four workers (employed at piece-rates) and a manager to whom he gave a leaky old boat. Ivan, the manager, built a simple wooden house to which he attached a sign that read "IBAMA: Palm-Heart Project Manager." Then all five started cutting trees so enthusiastically that within a few years there was not even enough açaí to feed themselves.

Everybody else — "the community" — had long before taken their belongings, given up their gardens, and moved across the river to what remained of the Viega family's land. The indemnification finally agreed on by the Old Man's heirs had cost these siblings all the profit from the land sale — despite its inadequacy in the minds of the displaced — and had sedimented the increasing bitterness on all sides.

Although the Viega children will not say this, all the residents of Igarapé Guariba agree that everything went to pieces after the heirs got the land. For a few years the vila at the river's mouth was entirely silent. Then, one morning in mid-1989, Miguelinho, the Old Man's grandson, arrived with his wife, Sônia, at the entrance to the boarded-up store. "We arrived on the 29th of July 1989," Sônia told me, taking in the tidy, well-stocked room with a sweep of her arm. "We opened the doors. There was nothing. Just empty shelves and spent gun cartridges. Just a whole bunch of old stuff."

Miguelinho was already drinking heavily by the time he came back to Igarapé Guariba. People out here knew him well from Macapá, and from his reputation for sudden and unpredictable violence. I was fascinated by the Viegas' big white house that everyone watched, silently, as we went by on the river. When I finally passed through its doors, I stayed for hours, engaged in a long, long conversation that took me deep into another Igarapé Guariba, a different history and a different sensibility. It was late at night, and we were still sitting in the flaring shadows of Miguelinho and Sônia's ramshackle front room. We had been talking about Miguelinho's grandfather and his memories of the river, and the talk had become noticeably tense. Miguelinho had just dug out one of the court documents that the Old Man had served on Tomé during the dispute that led to the patrão's departure. Abruptly, Miguelinho broke off: Didn't I know? He had been listening to news radio earlier that evening, and the Cubans were shooting down American planes. Suddenly he was right in my face. How did I feel about that, he was shouting, CIA liar that I was? And what the hell was I doing on his grandpa's land anyway?

Necessarily, it was Sônia who ran their household. At first, they nearly didn't make it, she told me. Miguelinho was a liability. Even though he had grown up in Igarapé Guariba and had been in school here with José Macedo and his brothers—the new leaders of what had then been his grandfather's world—he kept picking fights with everyone, boasting about his rich family. Then he shot and nearly killed a man over a drink, and the couple had to face down a boycott. For a while, the community closed ranks and no one would trade with them. While Miguelinho drank and ranted, Sônia would pick up their four children, often in the middle of the night, load their sputtery 10HP boat, and go to work alone, up and down the neighboring rivers, trading with anyone who would do business with her. Burdened with the family name and an unpredictable husband, her one strategy—exasperating to the upstream leaders in Igarapé Guariba—was to undercut her competitors, shaving her profit margins and pushing her boat to the edge of disaster, gradually building up her trade in the same fish, bananas, and açaí through which the Macedos sought to overcome the history that she so materially reinstated.

The sawmill and the store sat next to each other at the mouth of the river and were the persisting emotional core of the community. In the vila, Viega had built a school, a small chapel, a workshop where manioc flour was processed, and a few houses for the mill-workers. And he had brought in part-time electric light in a gesture that iconicized his project of paternalist modernity. But by the time Miguelinho, his grandson, returned to Igarapé Guariba, the school and chapel had slid off the crumbling bank into the expanding river, the lights had long since dimmed, and the forest was growing back around the houses.

The arrival of these new Viegas was a sudden and perverse irruption, a revival of all the contradictory fears and longings, the experience of movimento and escravidão, that had so agitated the river's banks in the past decades. Suddenly, the memories of that time took on flesh once more, and, in what seemed to the Macedo family the most calculated and insidious affront, Sônia at once opened a *cantina*, an all-hours bar, in her front room, enticing the men who lived on the nearby stream to come sell their produce, to exchange it for liquor and for Miguelinho's rowdy company, to lounge around the pool table, schmaltzy dance music blaring out across the deserted river.

These were days of tremendous anxiety in Igarapé Guariba. Having moved across stream and surrendered their açaí to the palm-heart project, residents now found themselves facing new crises. The Viega heirs who still owned land on the Rio Preto began sending in workers to cut palm-heart in Guariba itself. This was the beginning of a dispute that was finally resolved in 1993, when the Macedos led groups of men in the formal demarcation of community land. For a time, though, the atmosphere of violence was palpable. The Macedos talk about threats and insecurities. Dona Rita Viega, the Old Man's widow, now living in Macapá, describes buffalo hacked with machetes and left to rot, fetid, by the river. The formation of the Residents' Association that united the ex-fregueses was decisive. Lene Viega, daughter of the landlord, tells me that everything changed when the Association—a pawn of the Rural Workers' Union, she says—forced itself into their world. The memory of this breach in the social contract that came with the entry of these hostile outsiders is, more than any other, what provokes her acrimony. When the map was redrawn, finally, in a court of law, the Viegas were left with nothing but their upstream cattle ranch.

Yet, why is it that there are no truly new beginnings? Why must everything be always tainted with the histories of its own birth? There was to be no getting rid of that corrosive mote in the Association's eye, that persistent, alternative, negative modernity. Although the land on which Sônia, Miguelinho, the store, and the cantina were on now belonged to the Association, they were nonetheless there. And they had no intention of going away.

FEELING DEBT

> *Nestor Viega:* In those days everyone had a patrão. . . . Let me explain this in a way you'll understand. You're working for a university: someone tells you what to do; you tell someone else what to do. They tell you to go and do this research; you tell them to read your research. This is exactly the form business takes in the interior.
>
> *Hugh:* But it's not the same, because in my line of work. . . .
>
> *Nestor:* Look, it's cultural. It's no different at all if you take the trouble to analyze it head-on. If you analyze it, you'll see that it's fundamentally similar. What I'm explaining to you is a hier-

archy — okay? Isn't it obvious that you have the soldier, the sergeant, the colonel, the general? Business is the same. Business in the interior is exactly the way I'm explaining it to you. The guy who supplied us out here, for example, we had to go and find him in Belém, his name was Mário Alves. He sold to *papai*, papai sold to the *caboclo*, the caboclo sold back to papai, papai sold to Mário Alves. . . . What I'm saying is that this type of business was a society . . . it was a family thing.

It was not simply the corruptions of history that exasperated José Macedo and his brothers. It was, more irksomely, their own inability to escape its bounds. I was never quite convinced that even without Sônia and Miguelinho's presence on the river, José's consciousness of bad faith, his sense that present politics were patterned by a past he despised, could have been easily disavowed. There was too much overlapping practice. In this small place, they were all caught too deeply in the particular translocal intimacies of Amazonian river trade.

Consider debt, for example. Indebtedness is a potent means of social control in Amazonia and has long been a defining feature of *aviamento*, the intricate system of credit relations that emerged during the nineteenth-century rubber boom and involved large numbers of intermediary merchants moving capital (in the form of a variety of transformable goods) from places like Liverpool to other places like Igarapé Guariba, and back again.[23] Despite many theorists' consignment of it to the dustbin of pre-capitalism, aviamento persists, transfigured, throughout the region.[24] And, in its characteristic personalization of economic transaction, aviamento ensures that Amazonian indebtedness is shot through with ambivalence. Inseparable from the coercive character of debt is an interdependence that can offer security to people working in isolated areas with few direct social relationships other than the periodic visits of traveling traders.[25] It smacks of compulsion, yet, as we have seen in Chapter 3, the everyday hegemony of the patrão is self-consciously authorized through the intimacy of personal association. In this way debt becomes one more terrain in which contemporary politics uneasily cohabits the past.

Back in the days when Miguelinho was still a schoolboy and the vila was the economic heart of his grandpa's community, each household had its own notebook in which the store clerk kept a running transactional account. The book entries were coupons, replacements for money and accepted only in Viega's store. They were the means of controlling exchange that represented the accumulating debt of the fregueses — in the red from the moment they received the goods with which to build their first house. Benedito Macedo, José's father and an old man himself now, laughs as he tells me how he likes to think of all that uncollected debt totaled neatly but pointlessly in those columns when Raimundo died. But then, changing register, he points out that, unlike other families who allowed Viega to keep their books in his store, the Macedos insisted on holding theirs at home so they would always know the state of their finances.

Members of the Viega family — Miguelinho, Sônia, and the wealthier relatives now living in Macapá — today unanimously diminish the coercive significance of historical debt, emphasizing instead the virtues of paternalism and the positive lubricating role of patrão-dependent credit networks in easing the flow of goods. Seu Benedito, in contrast, talks about the success of his family in managing the pitfalls of cash-poverty through those times: never taking more goods than they knew their resources could cover, always frugal and conservative, always within their narrow means, refusing to succumb to the temptations of cane liquor, positioning themselves for the hour independence would be within their grasp. As a negative exemplar, Seu Benedito describes his old friend Pedro Preto, drinking away his hard labor and now living hand-to-mouth, without even fishing nets of his own.

But, inevitably, debt is ambiguous even for the Macedos. José Macedo is a hard-working man with a large family who worries continuously about the future of Igarapé Guariba. When he and his father look at Sônia, they see a moral continuity with the old patrão in her erosion of community integrity, most shamefully in the seductive use of cane liquor to enforce relations of indebtedness. Yet they, too, run a small front-porch store, and they, too, sell alcohol, though almost clandestinely and only for consumption off-premises. Moreover, their public discourse echoes the one Nestor Viega and his siblings attribute to their papai: to advance merchandise on credit is to help neighbors through the bad times. There is some agile reconciling afoot. Sônia's credit is a destructive force in the community; theirs is a cohering mutual aid.

For most families in Igarapé Guariba today, as in the time of Viega, a degree of indebtedness is a necessary part of life and an expression of a dependency that is likely to cease only with the social relationship of which it is part — with death or other disaster. Many people now spread their debt and proliferate their dependencies, building independent clientalist relations with merchants (and politicians) in Macapá in a way that was impossible while the monopoly on credit was held by Old Man Viega.

The Macedos do the same, but their networks replicate the hierarchies forged by Raimundo Viega in a manner distinct from that of their own neighbor-fregueses in Igarapé Guariba. For the other families in this community, debt relations are a creative practice through which they can sustain economic and social alternatives outside the structures imposed by the Macedos. For the Macedos themselves, the resources captured through patronage relations are what enable them to maintain their local authority in Igarapé Guariba. It is all about rivers again. All about maneuver and negotiation in a space that is simultaneously compressed by the geographic logic of the riverine community and exploded by the expansiveness of fluvial travel.

Açaí

The intimate, politics-saturated relations through which debt is realized in Igarapé Guariba are just part of a series, an extensive set of traveling iterations. Those boats on which I huddled in the early morning sunshine were most often making the four-hour trip along the Amazon to Macapá. And, for six months of the year, they'd be laden down with açaí, the most valuable forest commodity available. The açaí trade brings together those things I am trying to make sense of here: Amazon rivers, the politics of space, and the work of historical intimacies. I want to follow it to and from Igarapé Guariba, and back and forth between the Viegas and Macedos. But we should begin in Macapá.

The streets close to the docks in Macapá are lined with small stores selling general goods to people from the interior. The shopowners who trade there generally act as patrões to a number of rural fregueses, advancing goods on monthly credit, "discounting" their merchandise against forest products brought in on the boats. Although the relationships are most commonly expressed in the vocabulary of clientalism (patrão and freguês), these are the persisting structures of aviamento, and the storekeepers act as minor *aviadores*, their clients as *aviados*. In turn, these patrões become fregueses in relation to the larger urban wholesalers who stock their stores, and, when they get back to the interior, the fregueses (such as José Macedo) who visit the stores in Macapá may become patrões to the local collectors who supply them with forest products such as açaí. Nestor Viega explained it for me:

> You have the guy who's in charge down here. That's how it starts. Then he has his patrão. Just as he's the patrão here, he has another one over there, and the other one has another one still. It's a scale, you understand? So, for example, he goes to his patrão . . . well, papai didn't actually have to go to Belém, he'd send a letter: "Look, I need such-and-such goods, I'm going to send you such-and-such in return: bananas, rubber, etc. and I need such-and-such. I'm paying the bill, so you send me some more stuff." What he meant was, "I'm going to use your goods. I'm going to supply my freguês. My freguês is going to pay me. I'll pay you. The guy over here's going to pay what's-his-name over there, and so on.

Of course, it requires a certain cultural capital to create effective clientalist relationships in the first place. Not just anyone can do it, and the ability to do so both marks and generates prestige. One afternoon in Guariba, I found myself in the middle of an argument. My friend Dora's father in Macapá had just decorated their house for his youngest daughter's *quinze anos* party with 800 balloons. Dora's husband was scathing: "Tio Paulo's a fool throwing away all his savings on this," he was shouting as I walked in. But Dora had a stronger grasp of cultural economy: "It didn't cost him one *centavo*," she snapped back, quick as a whip. "He got it all on credit."

Tio Paulo, in fact, was well known in Macapá. Nowadays, he is more or less retired. But he had done many kinds of work over the years and for a while had even tried his hand as an açaí distributor. But that wasn't the kind of work that suited him, getting up at all hours to hang round the docks and bully incoming traders into selling him their fruit. Instead, he would periodically supplement his pension by sailing off to stay with his two daughters in Igarapé Guariba, working on the boats, earning a pittance, but bringing back fish to sell to his relatives and açaí for the dockside buyer—"*tirando o boi*," making ends meet, as Benedito Macedo, José's father and Paulo's longtime friend, put it.

Distributing açaí could have been a lucrative line of work. Minor fortunes have been made since the industry took off in the past few years, and conversations with people in the trade suggest there are about 25,000 people in Macapá and the surrounding floodplain earning their living from it for at least part of the year.[26]

Açaí is the fruit of the *açaizeiro*, a slender, graceful palm that can always be found growing around houses on the estuarine floodplain. Traveling on the rivers, you spot the distinctive trees first and then the wooden houses tucked away underneath. Farmers manage açaí in a complex and sophisticated manner, thinning its multiple clumps, removing senescent individuals, building up the soil to prevent waterlogging, manipulating the crown architecture, clearing around the base to remove competitors and make sure there are no hidden animals to surprise children and teenagers shimmying up to harvest the fruit.[27] After three or four years, the palm begins producing heavy bunches of dark, grape-sized fruit with a thin pulp surrounding a fibrous seed. After about eight years it reaches a peak, continuing to bear fruit for a further ten.

Rosiane (left) and Braga strike a pose as they prepare the evening's açaí.

People in the interior soak and mash the fruit, and mix it with river water to make a purple liquid. This used to be an afternoon task for women and girls, who worked it through sieves by hand. Now, many households have a wooden, hand-powered juicer, and men and teenage boys take turns working the soaked fruit. When it comes time to eat, everyone thickens their bowl with manioc meal or — if more middle-class and living in the city — often with tapioca, eating the result either with or without sugar.[28]

Açaí is a definitively rural food and, while in season, an indispensable part of the day's largest meal, served alongside fresh fried fish, salty boiled shrimp, or forest game. Yet, it has been the estuarine cities of Belém and Macapá that have driven the recent market. As people have left the often chaotic countryside for the service-deficient, violent, but alluring peri-urban slums that ring the more affluent centers, they have brought their taste for açaí with them and they've sparked shifts in the diet of an urban middle-class prone to ruralist nostalgia.[29] By midday on almost every streetcorner in Macapá, you see a 5-foot pole with a 6-inch rectangular red metal flag — the sign that the açaí seller is ready to begin the lunchtime trade.

I never met a retailer in Macapá reluctant to tell the hard-luck story of declining profits and intensifying competition. Just a couple of years ago, it seems, you might go three or four blocks before finding a stall, but now they're everywhere. Back then, a seller might juice four sacks of fruit a day.[30] Now he or she has to settle for one and a half. At the same time, high demand and the marketing stranglehold of the big suppliers have pushed up the price, and low-income urban workers might drink açaí only every few days at best.

To capture local trade the retailers sell to their customers on credit, but then they have to deal with lack of cash and the headaches at the end of the month when the time to call in debts comes round. The competition is killing them. In Macapá they all agreed that this was a function of the combination of two factors: the sudden deep freeze into which the job market had been plunged by President Fernando Henrique Cardoso's 1994 *Plano Real* currency stabilization, and the rapid influx of work-hungry people from the interior and the northeast of Brazil in response to the empty promise of Macapá's *zona franca*, the free-trade area legislated in the early 1990s.[31]

Most açaí businesses are set up through suppliers, capitalized entrepreneurs who arrange contracts with both urban retailers and rural transporters, and who exercise considerable control over the market. The suppliers collect fruit from the boats as it comes in from the interior, and they distribute it in town. They could be called *atravessadores*, those who pass something on, middlemen, but they balk at the term, reserving it for the smaller operators they see scavenging the docks and disrupting business through gangster tactics — pressuring the boatmen and showing no concern for long-term trading conditions. These larger-scale suppliers see themselves rather differently and prefer the more polished term *fornecedores*. They are the açaí elite who foster paternalist relations with rural suppliers and urban retailers — helping them through difficult times, disciplining them by manipulating pricing and restricting supply, maneuvering to marginalize their atravessador rivals.

The supplier who takes most of the Macedo brothers' açaí is Jacaré, an easy-going, unaffected man in his mid-50s, who never touches açaí himself: "It's a drug," he says, only half-joking. "Look at my son, he's addicted!" Jacaré has bought açaí from José Macedo for nine years now, and it was José who gave me his phone number and told me to look him up next time I was in Macapá.

Jacaré's strongly vertically integrated operation accounts for 10 percent of the thousand sacks of açaí that enter the city daily from the interior of Amapá, and he distributes to fregueses beyond Macapá in towns all around the state. He sets people up as retailers on either a profit-sharing or a rental basis. And any agreement with him includes a commitment to buy his fruit.

Despite the small margins and the discourse of dissatisfaction, it is clear why so many people are entering the retail end of the trade.[32] With the national minimum wage set at R $112 a month for those able to find work, açaí is a compellingly dynamic and relatively accessible sector of the regional economy. Yet, access always depends on some form of capital: a potential retailer needs both cash and the cultural capital earned through participation in networks of patronage and alliance, the type of business that Nestor Viega acutely calls "a family thing."

Açaí is both seasonal and perishable. In Igarapé Guariba and along the Amapá floodplain, the harvest lasts from January to June. At other times, the Macapá retailers are supplied from Belém. Despite this, there is still a between-harvest period when demand is high and supply low. In these few weeks at either end of the season, dockside prices in Macapá can reach extravagant heights.[33] This is the moment when rural suppliers like the Macedos stand to make a significant profit. But they have to weigh this temptation against the potential losses in the middle of the season when atravessadores can beat them down as far as they like, and prices drop so low that boat owners throw sacks of fruit overboard rather than waste fuel carrying it back to the rivers. The existing solution to this dilemma is for the rural supplier to contract with the fornecedores—an arrangement, like that between contractor and retailer, that draws on and may create enduring social networks and cultural ties.

To guarantee delivery to his urban retailers, Jacaré sets quotas with the Macedo brothers and his other rural suppliers through a rolling-over, two-month, fixed-price contract. José Macedo and the other boat owners accept that the price at the beginning of the harvest, when fruit is in short supply and dockside prices are high, will be lower than if they sell independently to the atravessadores. But they also know that later on, when the market is glutted, they will have a guaranteed buyer at a subsidized price.

Such contracts discipline the rural suppliers at the same time as they squeeze the atravessadores who normally operate without contracts, taking from the boats on consignment, and selling on the quayside to independent retailers. At either end of the harvest, when supplies are low and prices high, and in an echo of Old Man Viega's attempt to establish monopsony on the river, Jacaré works to intimidate a rural supplier like José from dealing with the atravessadores. José is always under pressure from his own fregueses back in Igarapé Guariba to achieve the highest dockside prices available. But he knows that if he shortchanges Jacaré at this time of year by selling outside the contract and only providing a portion of the promised sacks, the supplier will quickly find out—and that he's liable to respond by refusing to renew the contract for the following season. In the mid-season glut, however, when the boats are laden and the quayside atravessadores are aggressively beating down the price until the rural collectors are close to despair, Jacaré, in a move characteristic of the Amazonian patrão will at times buy the worthless excess fruit from his contractees and absorb the loss.

The post-harvest quietus marks a period of considerable uncertainty for José and the other boat owners of Igarapé Guariba. This is when they search for the contracts that will protect them from the free market at the dockside for another season. A deal with Jacaré on its own will neither keep them in business nor satisfy their fregueses, and they scramble to compete for other arrangements. Not counting the Colonel's vessel, there are three motorized boats in Guariba: two, the *Star of Guariba* and the *United We Conquer* belong to José and his brothers. The other is Sônia's *Immaculate Conception*.

SOCIAL WORK

José Macedo and his brothers fret unceasingly about their ability to lead the community. Their work is development and modernization, the work of place-making. And here, right now, açaí is king — even though it brings to the fore some painful contradictions.

During the açaí season, each boat makes at least two trips a week to Macapá. They leave with the tide to save fuel, but they start off by making a tour of the river to collect fruit. The Macedo brothers pick up sacks according to a controversial quota they allocate at the start of the season. The quota fixed in Igarapé Guariba is directly derived from that set by Jacaré. Indeed, the brothers calculate it from their contracts — the winning of which is the mark of their commitment to community progress and the justification of their leadership. It is, they make clear to me, a terrible responsibility.

José and his brothers allocate quotas by family size: the larger the family the more sacks they allow per voyage. But it is a system with ample room for arbitrariness and patronage, and the quota is a constant source of friction. A persistent theme of conversation in Guariba is how much better things could be if the Macedo brothers would "liberate the quota." Instead of the two, or sometimes three, sacks allowed, collectors say they could harvest eight or even ten. This may be true, but it is also just talk.[34] Everybody here understands the political economy of açaí and the rationale of the contract. Everyone knows how the market crashes in the middle of the season and that the quota is only part of the problem.

For one thing, there are strategies for circumventing it. Some people who live near the mouth of the river strike deals with traders who cast anchor out in the rio-mar toward the end of the season. They load their canoes with sacks and paddle out into the Amazon to complete the sale. Others use kin networks to pass fruit to boat-owning relatives on neighboring rivers. Such tactics are keenly reminiscent of the old-time traders who used to travel the river at night to escape Old Man Viega's polic-

ing. For the Macedo brothers—even as they were for Viega—such activities are destructive of community cohesion. After all, it is through
the distributed profits of the açaí trade that modernity is arriving in
Igarapé Guariba. But many of their fregûes-comrades dismiss such rhetoric. The real issue for them is not how much the Macedos can sell, but
how much and at what price they buy. Implicit is a critique of the contradiction between the egalitarian discourse of community and the conspicuous improvements in the material life of the Macedos themselves
since the boom began and they started accumulating gas-fired fridges,
oil-powered chainsaws, and the big, soft couches from which to watch
their new battery-operated TV sets.

It was a long time before I found out that no matter what Jacaré or
the atravessadores are paying in Macapá, the Macedo brothers buy açaí
in Igarapé Guariba for 40 percent less. When I first heard this, wrapped
up as I was in the heroics of the exodus from the other bank and the
expulsion of the old regime, I was stunned. But I confirmed it straight-
away with José. If Jacaré is giving them R $20 a sack, they pay the
fregûes R $12. If Jacaré is offering R $16, they buy for R $9.[35] But what
about this unified community I heard so much about, marching forward
together, out from the dark days of Old Man Viega's slavery?

José is a sincere man, someone who fought long and hard in church
organizations and rural workers' unions for the rights and dignities of
rural Amazonians, not only for the removal of the one Old Man from
this river. He doesn't need me to point out the contradictions. Any de-
fensiveness he might feel talking about these prices soon dissipates in
the enumeration of the responsibilities and expenses of running a boat
and in the conviction that boats are the indispensable vehicles of community progress, that a riverine community *must* support the boats that
hold it in the world and the boat owners who take this charge upon
themselves. The stresses of cultivating and maintaining the social networks that enable the contracts and create other future possibilities are
near-overwhelming. There's no time to stand still. And he continues by
pointing to the daily solidarities of his regime: we rarely refuse to carry
people upstream on expeditions to hunt, fish, farm, and harvest açaí.
Nor do we charge freight when we take their produce into Macapá and
bring their shopping home. And neither—like Gordão in Carapanatuba
and all those guys in Bailique—are we making people pay R $5 or
R $10 for the trip into town, even though sometimes the boat is so

overloaded you think it will never make it (and who knows how much gasoline is being wasted).

But somehow this logic doesn't mend the fractures through which Sônia sails. She has another system and offers another vision of life on the river. She works to demand, avoiding the symbolic contamination of the hated quota. In her discursive ordering of the trade, she is transporting fruit without constraint at the behest of the collectors. On the day before her voyage, she tours her clients' houses and drops off sacks, stopping just long enough to negotiate quantity. How much can they give her? She'll take all they've got. Then, at the hour of sailing, she might make more visits just in case someone has a little extra to sell. She sets her price by marginally but significantly trumping the Macedos. If they give R $12, she pays R $14. If they pay R $9, she gives R $11. Like them, she too discounts açaí against orders for household goods she fills on credit with her patrões in the stores that line the dock in Macapá. But whereas they scrupulously charge their clients the same retail price they pay in town, back in Igarapé Guariba, Sônia sells this merchandise at large mark-ups directly across the counter in her store in the tile-roofed house at the river's mouth, reclaiming the profit she has lost in attracting custom, reviving the ghost of her husband's grandfather.

What really infuriates the Macedos and invigorates politics in Igarapé Guariba as a soap-opera feud between two powerful families is the way Sônia and Miguelinho trade açaí for shots of cane liquor at their bar the whole day long, until the cash-poor caboclo is too drunk to buy any more and has to be carried down to his canoe and floated off back to his family. For José Macedo, such corrupting practices and public humiliation exemplify the continuity between past escravidão and contemporary disunity, a holdover personified by these last of the parasitic Viegas.

There are other disappointments and betrayals. For José, it is ingratitude and lack of vision that drive his neighbors to sell açaí marked for him to Sônia. Sometimes he arrives as scheduled at the house of an Association member to be told that the man did not harvest açaí that day. Yet later, in dismay, he learns that Sônia is traveling the same night with a full shipment that includes açaí from that very house. Arriving in Macapá half-empty, José shares the sacks out evenly among his disgruntled buyers, excusing the shortfall, promising it is not going to happen again, feeling the next year's contracts sliding through his fingers.

On the days before they head into Macapá, the Macedo brothers organize trips to an upstream area of forest that was divided into large family-owned lots following Viega's departure. Small groups of invited men, the occasional woman, and a smattering of teenage boys arrive at Seu Benedito's house with the first tide and tie their canoes to the back of the boat. They sit on the porch in the dark, smoking and talking softly, pouring coffee from Seu Benedito's thermos, slapping at mosquitoes and long-legged *muriçocas*.

It takes an hour to get upstream. When the boat moors, everyone separates into twos or threes and paddles out to an area of their own land where they expect to find ripe açaí. Collecting takes most of the day. Someone spots a tree laden with dark fruit. They climb the smooth trunk, feet gripping a twisted sack or palm-frond for purchase, cut the heavy bunch with their machete, and bring it carefully down, trying not to lose too much on the way. Back on the ground, one or two people strip the fruit from its woody stalks and fill sacks provided by the boat owners. It is rough, dangerous work, hard on hands and feet, made worse by the relentless insects.

The emphasis is on speed and volume. On a good day — if it does not rain, if no one gets injured, if there are big bunches and short trees — two people might collect four sacks, each holding the fruit from seven or eight bunches. But to do that, collectors have to cut corners, boosting quantity by throwing in unripe, green fruit, tipping in the dust from the flattened sack on which the berries were stripped, ignoring stalk and leaves that find their way into the sack, not worrying if the seeds are wet.

Back on the boat, the sacks are in the hold. While everyone else sits on the roof in the late afternoon sunshine, talking and finishing their work, José and one of his brothers spend the return trip below, emptying and refilling each sack, carefully checking the contents and sifting out a portion of the debris and impurities. Arriving that night at the crowded dock in Macapá, José delivers his cargo to Jacaré's agent, who caps the transaction by emptying the sacks and transferring the fruit to new ones, again checking the contents for debris and impurities, continuing the ongoing, recursive performance of public surveillance.

Sônia will leave Miguelinho for good one day. At least that is what Miguelinho's sister Eliana tells me at four in the morning as we sit bundled up together on the waterline at the back of a battered launch,

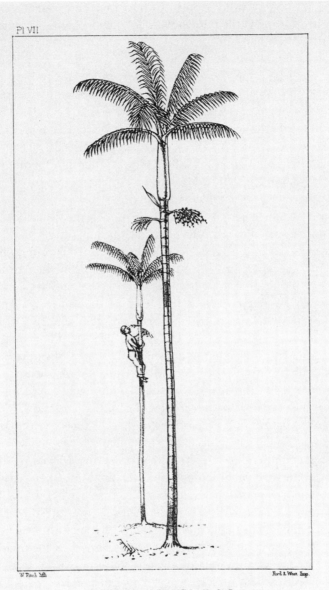

Pl VII

W Finch lith.   Ford & West Imp.

EUTERPE OLERACEA   Ht 60 Ft

watching the foamy wake ripple out into the forest darkness. We are heading to Macapá loaded down with açaí, and Eliana is going back to start her day as a maid in the city.

Sônia is "uma grande mulher," a great women, says Eliana, and one day she'll take the *Immaculate Conception* and the kids and start up on her own as a *regatão*, a trader sailing between the islands off Macapá. She might as well. She couldn't work any harder: "She's left many times even though she's scared of him," Eliana whispers hoarsely above the wake. "But, you know, the man wants to die. That's why he drinks like that. He knows it's killing him." When I'm talking to Sônia, though, it is so much more confused: "Even beasts feel love," she says, with an assertive mix of pride and despair.

However much people might chafe under the Macedos' regime, Sônia and Miguelinho can offer a social life but little social network. Located on Association land but not situated in the community, their cantina may be an alluringly utopic space for local men tired of the austerity of life on this river, but it is an insecure enclave. José and his brothers can never compete at this level of desire, so they plot constantly to remove Sônia and Miguelinho from the land, to visit on them the fate of the grandfather. For these Macedos, the tile-roofed cantina is an ongoing transgression, an anti-modern sphere of unpredictability: men get drunk and talk too loud about quotas and prices, sometimes they go so far as to threaten their leaders with machetes, too often they squander their families' money in binges of self-destruction.

Despite Miguelinho's perorations on his relatives' wealth and influence, he and Sônia have only paltry patronage on which to draw. Indeed, Miguelinho's bluster merely reinforces the Macedos' ability to marshal progressive rhetoric and implicate these forsaken Viegas in an historic project of parasitic landlordism. To their well-connected professional family in Macapá, such poor relations are an embarrassment. That chilly dawn as we talked on the boat, Eliana really was in a hurry to get back to town and begin her day in the houses of the middle class.

Just like her wealthy relatives whose bitterness now feeds itself in exile, Eliana loves Igarapé Guariba. "You can breathe there," she tells me, "it's not polluted like the city." When she can, she comes out on a Saturday and stays with Sônia in what is left of the vila. She works on the boat, goes fishing, swims in the river, and helps out with the children. The rest of the time she is in the bar, entertaining her elderly boyfriend, José's father, Seu Benedito Macedo.

Benedito's wife, Nazaré, died four years ago but, nonetheless, his sons disapprove of Eliana. For one thing, she is a Viega. But the old man doesn't seem to care. When he gets word that Eliana has arrived, he finds his wide-brimmed hat, takes his shiny green canoe, and paddles downstream, past the school where his grandchildren learn by rote, past the boarded-up health post, past José's shiny new satellite dish, past every one of his neighbors' houses, smoothly paddling as if drawn by invisible strings to the spirited music that floats to meet him from the open door of the old white house.

NOTES

CHAPTER 1

1. The best general introduction to this period can be found in Susanna B. Hecht and Alexander Cockburn, *The Fate of the Forest: Developers, Destroyers and Defenders of the Amazon* (London: Penguin, 1989).

2. Walter Benjamin, *One-Way Street, and Other Writings*, trans. Edmund Jephcott and Kingsley Shorter (London: New Left Books, 1979), 50; emphasis added. Benjamin continues with an apposite tropicalist metaphor, describing a text as a "road cut through the interior jungle forever closing behind it." For a more formalist reading of landscape as text, see James S. Duncan, *The City as Text: The Politics of Landscape Interpretation in the Kandyan Kingdom* (Cambridge: Cambridge University Press, 1990).

3. For a review of this literature, see Hugh Raffles and Antoinette M.A.G. WinklerPrins, "Anthropogenic Fluvial Landscape Transformation in the Amazon Basin," manuscript.

4. See, for important discussions, Stephen Greenblatt, *Marvelous Possessions: The Wonder of the New World* (Chicago: University of Chicago Press, 1991); Peter Hulme, *Colonial Encounters: Europe and the Native Caribbean, 1492–1797* (London: Routledge, 1992); and Anthony Pagden, *European Encounters with the New World: From Renaissance to Romanticism* (New Haven: Yale University Press, 1993). My use of the term *early modern* here and elsewhere in this book should not be taken as endorsement of a teleological periodization of a uniform European modernity. For effective polemical attention to this question, see Lorraine Daston, "The Nature of Nature in Early Modern Europe," *Configurations* 6, no. 2 (1998): 149–72.

5. "The true method of making things present is to represent them in our space (not to represent ourselves in their space). . . . Thus represented, the things allow no mediating construction from out of 'large contexts.' The same method applies in essence, to the consideration of great things from the past — the cathedral at Chartres, the temple of Paestum — when, that is, a favorable prospect presents itself: the method of receiving the things into our space. We don't displace our being into theirs; they step into our life." Walter Benjamin, *The Arcades Project*, trans. Howard Eiland and Kevin McLaughlin (Cambridge, Mass.: Belknap Press of Harvard University Press, 1999), 206.

6. Dipesh Chakrabarty, *Provincializing Europe: Postcolonial Thought and Historical Difference* (Princeton: Princeton University Press, 2000), makes this point in terms of "the plurality that inheres in the 'now,' the lack of totality, the constant fragmentariness, that constitutes one's present" (243). This argument can be considerably strengthened by the application of a more developed notion of space, one that pays attention to the plurality of *spatial* moments in the "now." For important contributions along these lines, see the work of Doreen

Massey, who has long argued that space can be understood as "a configuration of a multiplicity of histories all in the process of being made." Doreen Massey, "Travelling Thoughts," in *Without Guarantees: In Honour of Stuart Hall*, ed. Paul Gilroy, Lawrence Grossberg, and Angela McRobbie (London: Verso, 2000), 225–32, 229. For a sustained project that unsettles and ties time and place through the contingency of memory and biography, see the luminous work of W. G. Sebald, particularly his novel *Austerlitz* (New York: Random House, 2001).

7. Amazonia seems to be a particularly unreliable region. In one register, a deeply irresistible *mythos*, it stands as the most palpable of geographical entities. Yet just try to draw a map! The biologist's *Hylæa* refuses to correspond to the hydrologist's basin (a popular but difficult unit in a world of such prodigiously mobile floodplains). And neither is coterminous with the regions mapped by politicians: neither that of the burgeoning pan-regional indigenous movement nor the one codified in the 1978 Amazon Cooperation Treaty — a pact that crosses watersheds to tie together eight nations, including Guyana and Suriname but not French Guyana. Considering these incongruencies from Amapá is particularly appropriate. Universally considered part of the regional hydrological unit, Amapá is "riddled by river systems draining into either the Amazon or the Atlantic and therefore simultaneously part and not part of the Amazon basin"; see David Cleary, "Towards an Environmental History of the Amazon: From Prehistory to the Nineteenth Century," *Latin American Research Review* 36, no. 2 (2001): 65–96, 66. Also Alcida Rita Ramos, "The Indigenous Movement in Brazil: A Quarter Century of Ups and Downs," *Cultural Survival Quarterly* 21, no. 2 (1997): 50–53. Such variety and simultaneity point to the instrumentalism of cartography, each region embodying both functional logic and political project. They also indicate that regions are made in the face of alternative possibilities for conceiving of space and territory. On places as "particular moments," see Doreen Massey, *Space, Place, and Gender* (Minneapolis: University of Minnesota Press, 1994), 120. For important accounts of Amazonian region-making that emphasize representational practice, see Neide Gondim, *A invenção da Amazônia* (São Paulo: Marco Zero, 1994); Pedro Maligo, *Land of Metaphorical Desires: The Representation of Amazonia in Brazilian Literature* (New York: Peter Lang, 1998); and Candace Slater, *Entangled Edens: Visions of the Amazon* (Berkeley: University of California Press, 2002).

8. Ann Stoler, in a sustained project concerned with the discursive practices of various colonialisms, has examined intimacy as a realm of biopolitics and government, analyzing how "intimate matters and narratives about them figured in defining the racial coordinates and social discriminations of empire." Ann Laura Stoler, "Tense and Tender Ties: Intimacies of Empire in North American History and (Post) Colonial Studies," *Journal of American History* 88, no. 3 (2001): 829–65, 830; see also idem, *Capitalism and Confrontation in Sumatra's Plantation Belt, 1870–1979* (New Haven: Yale University Press, 1985); idem, *Race and the Eduction of Desire: Foucault's History of Sexuality and the Colonial Order of Things* (Durham: Duke University Press, 1995); idem, *Carnal Knowledge and Imperial Power: Race and the Intimate in Colonial Rule* (Berke-

ley: University of California Press, 2002). Lauren Berlant and the authors of the papers collected in an important Special Issue of *Critical Inquiry* have helpfully explored intimacies in terms of the ways "attachments make worlds and world-changing fantasies" (Lauren Berlant, ed., "Special Issue: Intimacy," *Critical Inquiry* 24, no. 2 [Winter 1998]: 288). Also effective, as I discuss in Chapter 7, are the interventions of Alphonso Lingis: see *Abuses* (Berkeley: University of California Press, 1994) and *Dangerous Emotions* (Berkeley: University of California Press, 2000). For a productive intervention that interrogates "intimacy" by situating multiple valences of affect in critical relation to kinship, see Elizabeth A. Povinelli, "Notes on Gridlock: Genealogy, Intimacy, Sexuality," *Public Culture*, forthcoming.

9. Two additional conceptions of "natural history" that have influenced this study in quite different ways should be mentioned. The first refuses the cultural and the social, adopting a radically reductionist (although affect-laden) molecular conception of nature. See Edward O. Wilson, *The Diversity of Life* (Cambridge, Mass.: Belknap Press of Harvard University Press, 1992). For a second, more complex conception that proposes "natural history" (*Naturgeschichte*) as a critical methodology through which to explode the "prehistoric" ontology of modernity, see Benjamin, *The Arcades Project*, and the detailed exegesis by Susan Buck-Morss, *The Dialectics of Seeing: Walter Benjamin and the Arcades Project* (Cambridge, Mass.: MIT Press, 1989), 55–80, 160–61. My own project might well be seen as a "natural history of the present" (a formulation I owe to Donald Moore), drawing as it does on a genealogical method of historical analysis—albeit one that emphasizes traces and simultaneities as readily as rupture. See Michel Foucault, "Nietzsche, Genealogy, History," in *Language, Counter-Memory, Practice: Selected Essays and Interviews*, ed. Donald F. Bouchard, trans. Donald F. Bouchard and Sherry Simon (Ithaca: Cornell University Press, 1980), 139–64. My project has gained greatly from and remains complementary to the now established bodies of research in environmental history and historical ecology. However, I am less concerned with these particular notions of nature (environment, ecology), and instead aim to resist a priori definitions or restrictions of domain. Rather, I emphasize the dynamic spatial and temporal co-constitution of natural-cultural materiality in terms that remain grounded and specified but that are also as full and relational as possible.

10. These sparks were first fired for me by the peculiar symmetry between Bruno Latour's *We Have Never Been Modern*, trans. Catherine Porter (Cambridge, Mass.: Harvard University Press, 1993) and Lorraine Daston and Katherine Park's *Wonders and the Order of Nature, 1150–1750* (New York: Zone Books, 1998). Also, memorably, by a visit to the Museum of Jurassic Technology in Los Angeles, a catalytic afternoon for which I have to thank my perceptive friends Bill Maurer and Tom Boellstorff. For recent, helpful accounts of a post-"settlement" nature, see, *inter alia*, Donna J. Haraway, *Modest Witness@ Second Millennium. FemaleMan© Meets OncoMouse™: Feminism and Technoscience* (New York: Routledge, 1997); David Demerritt, "The Nature of Metaphors in Cultural Geography and Environmental History," *Progress in Human*

Geography 18, no. 2 (1994): 163–85; Bruce Braun and Noel Castree, eds., *Remaking Reality: Nature at the Millennium* (New York: Routledge, 1998); Philippe Descola and Gísli Pálsson, eds., *Nature and Society: Anthropological Perspectives* (New York: Routledge, 1996); and Donald Moore, Anand Pandian, and Jake Kosek, eds., *Race, Nature, and the Politics of Difference* (Durham: Duke University Press, forthcoming). On early modern natural history, see, within a growing literature, Paula Findlen, *Possessing Nature: Museums, Collecting, and Scientific Culture in Early Modern Italy* (Berkeley: University of California Press, 1994); Scott Atran, *Cognitive Foundations of Natural History: Towards an Understanding of Science* (Cambridge: Cambridge University Press, 1989); Karen Reeds, "Renaissance Humanism and Botany," *Annals of Science* 33 (1976): 519–42; Allen J. Grieco, "The Social Politics of Pre-Linnean Botanical Classification," *I Tatti Studies: Essays in the Renaissance* 4 (1991): 131–49; Daston, "The Nature of Nature"; Nicholas Jardine, James A. Secord, and Emma C. Spary, eds., *Cultures of Natural History* (Cambridge: Cambridge University Press, 1996); Antonello Gerbi, *Nature in the New World: From Christopher Columbus to Gonzalo Fernández de Oviedo*, trans. Jeremy Moyle (Pittsburgh: University of Pittsburgh Press, 1985); Keith Thomas, *Man and the Natural World: A History of the Modern Sensibility* (New York: Pantheon, 1983); and Clarence J. Glacken, *Traces on the Rhodian Shore: Nature and Culture in Western Thought from Ancient Times to the End of the Eighteenth Century* (Berkeley: University of California Press, 1967). On collecting in this period, see Findlen, "Possessing Nature;" Krzysztof Pomian, *Collectors and Curiosities: Paris and Venice, 1500–1800* (Cambridge: Polity, 1990); Oliver Impey and Arthur MacGregor, eds., *The Origins of Museums: The Cabinet of Curiosities in Sixteenth- and Seventeenth-Century Europe* (New York: Clarendon Press, 1985); Horst Bredekamp, *The Lure of Antiquity and the Cult of the Machine: The Kunstkammer and the Evolution of Nature, Art and Technology*, trans. Allison Brown (Princeton: Markus Wiener Publishers, 1995); and Pamela H. Smith and Paula Findlen, eds., *Merchants and Marvels: Commerce, Science, and Art in Early Modern Europe* (New York: Routledge, 2001).

11. Mary Poovey, *A History of the Modern Fact: Problems of Knowledge in the Sciences of Wealth and Society* (Chicago: University of Chicago Press, 1998), 9. Also, Lorraine Daston, "Baconian Facts, Academic Civility, and the Prehistory of Objectivity," *Annals of Scholarship* 8, nos. 3–4 (1991): 337–64.

12. Daston and Park, *Wonders*, 159.

13. Benjamin, *The Arcades Project*, 205.

14. Ibid., 206.

15. Walter Benjamin, *Illuminations*, ed. Hannah Arendt, trans. Harry Zohn (New York: Fontana, 1973), 60.

16. "The fundamental level of ideology . . . is not of an illusion masking the real state of things, but that of an (unconscious) fantasy structuring our social reality itself." Slavoj Žižek, *The Sublime Object of Ideology* (London: Verso, 1989), 33. For helpful and concrete discussion, see Bill Maurer, "Uncanny Exchanges: The Possibilities and Failures of 'Making Change' with Alter-

native Monetary Forms," *Environment and Planning 'D': Society and Space*, forthcoming.

CHAPTER 2

1. Mao Zedong, "Where Do Correct Ideas Come From?" in *Selected Readings from the Works of Mao Tsetung* (Beijing: Foreign Languages Press, 1971), 502–4, 502. Mao's use of the term "correct" may perhaps best be placed "under erasure" — that is, recognized here, to adapt Stuart Hall's gloss on Derrida, as "an idea which cannot be thought in the old way, but without which certain key questions cannot be thought at all." Stuart Hall, "Introduction: Who Needs Identity?" in *Questions of Identity*, ed. Stuart Hall and Paul Du Gay (Thousand Oaks, Calif.: Sage, 1996), 1–17, 2.

2. Alfred Russel Wallace, *A Narrative of Travels on the Amazon and Rio Negro, with an Account of the Native Tribes, and Observations on the Climate, Geology, and Natural History of the Amazon Valley* (London: Reeve, 1853). Page references are from the pocket reprint edition of 1911 published in London by Ward Lock.

3. Darwin to Bates, December 3, 1861, in Robert M. Stecher, "The Darwin–Bates Letters: Correspondence Between Two Nineteenth-Century Travellers and Naturalists," *Annals of Science* 25, no. 1 (1969): 1–47, and 25, no. 2 (1969): 95–125: [letter 14], 20. Under economic and career advancement pressures to travel again, Wallace finally made his name in Southeast Asia, returning to England to write his great *The Malay Archipelago: The Land of the Orang-Utan, and the Bird of Paradise. A Narrative of Travel, with Studies of Man and Nature* (New York: Harper and Brothers, 1869).

4. All Wallace's and Darwin's biographers discuss the muted rivalry over the theory of natural selection. Wallace, it seems clear, was unwilling to force a confrontation over the issue. This is generally explained by reference to his unassuming personality. But it is also apparent that Wallace was a man cursed with the gift of plain speaking and was quite willing to court controversy where principles he considered important were at stake — as, for instance, in his highly public wager with John Hampden over the flatness of the earth in 1870 and his testimony as a defense witness at the celebrated London trial of the North American spirit medium Henry Slade in 1876. Neither of these episodes improved his stock with scientific luminaries like Joseph Hooker. With regard to natural selection, it seems likely that personal diffidence was bolstered by a realistic appraisal of his chances of emerging unscathed from a confrontation with Darwin and his powerful sponsors, as well as by an assessment of the damage that such a dispute would inflict on the difficult project of popularizing heretical ideas on evolution. Nevertheless, Wallace's irregular views on spiritism and vaccination, his outspoken socialist politics, and his prickly inability to negotiate the social quagmire of scientific patronage all contributed to a chronic inability to land a scientific post. There is as yet no major biography of Wallace. For useful material, see Amabel Williams-Ellis, *Darwin's Moon: A Biography of*

Alfred Russel Wallace (London: Blackie, 1966); Harry Clements, *Alfred Russel Wallace: Biologist and Social Reformer* (London: Hutchinson, 1983); and Wilma George, *Biologist Philosopher: A Study of the Life and Writings of Alfred Russel Wallace* (London: Abelard-Schuman, 1964). Consistently interesting is Wallace's detailed and readable *My Life: A Record of Events and Opinions*, 2 vols. (New York: Dodd, Mead, 1905).

5. See Ralph Colp Jr., " 'I Will Gladly Do My Best.' How Charles Darwin Obtained a Civil List Pension for Alfred Russel Wallace," *Isis* 83 (1992): 3–26; Wallace, *My Life*, II, 394–95; and Stecher, "The Darwin-Bates Letters," [letters 97–99], 123–24.

6. Wallace, *Travels*, 37.

7. Henry Walter Bates, *The Naturalist on the River Amazons: A Record of Adventures, Habits of Animals, Sketches of Brazilian and Indian Life, and Aspects of Nature under the Equator, during Eleven Years of Travel*, unabridged ed. (London: John Murray, 1892), 58.

8. Ignácio Baptista de Moura, *De Belém a São João do Araguaia, Vale do Rio Tocantins* (Belém: Fundação Cultural do Pará Tancredo Neves/Secretaria de Estado da Cultura, 1989 [1910]). As I discuss in Chapter 5, Bates and Wallace were also drawn to egalitarian politics. However, in Brazil, their radicalism was undercut by colonial allegiances.

9. Eladio Lobato, *Caminho de canoa pequena: História do município de Igarapé-Miri*, 2nd ed. (Belém: Imprensa Oficial, 1985), 64–70. Moura, *De Belém a São João do Araguaia*, 41, also draws attention to the lack of wage labor in the Amazon as a contributory factor in this decline.

10. Manoel Buarque, *Tocantins e Araguaya* (Belém: Imprensa Oficial do Estado do Pará, 1919).

11. Ibid., 4. *Negro*, which I have translated as "nigger," was also a standard synonym for "slave."

12. See S. D. Anderson, "Engenhos na várzea: uma analise do declinio de uma sistema de produção tradicional na Amazônia," in *Amazônia: A fronteira agrícola 20 anos depois*, org. Philippe Lenna and Adelia Engracia de Oliveira (Belém: Museu Paraense Emílio Goeldi/ORSTOM, 1991), 114–26.

13. Buarque, *Tocantins e Araguaya*, 4.

14. I take this phrase from Líbero Luxardo, *Marajó: Terra anfíbia* (Belém: Grafisa, 1977).

15. Márcio Souza, *Mad Maria*, trans. Thomas Colchie (New York: Avon Books, 1985); Henry M. Tomlinson, *The Sea and the Jungle* (London: Duckworth, 1912); Werner Herzog, *Fitzcarraldo* (1982); Les Blank, *Burden of Dreams* (1982).

16. Buarque, *Tocantins e Araguaya*, 4.

17. Lobato, *Caminho de canoa pequena*, 132–33.

18. Leopold H. Myers, *The Clio* (London: Robin Clark, 1990), 93.

19. Ibid., 133.

20. Ibid., 126–27.

21. Others went to the towns of Sant'Ana do Mutuacá (which became Vila Nova de Mazagão), Sant'Ana do Cajary, and the now-extinct Vila Vistosa de

Madre de Deus, all in today's Amapá. See João da Palma Muniz, "Limites municipais do estado do Pará," *Annaes da bibliotheca e archivo publico do Pará,* tomo IX (Belém: Imprensa de Alfredo Augusto Silva, 1916), 383–515; Maria de Fátima P. da Silva, *Assunto: Vila de Mazagão Velho,* mimeograph (Macapá: Universidade Federal do Amapá, 1992); and Roberta Marx Delson, *New Towns for Colonial Brazil* (Ann Arbor: UMI, 1979).

22. For a more detailed discussion of aviamento, see Chapter 7 below. For descriptions of aviamento during the rubber period, see, *inter alia,* Arthur Cézar Ferreira Reis, *O seringal e o seringueiro,* documentário da vida rural, no. 5 (Rio de Janeiro: Ministério da Agricultura, 1953); Roberto Santos, *História Econômica da Amazônia (1800–1920)* (São Paulo: T. A. Queiroz, 1980); Barbara Weinstein, *The Amazon Rubber Boom, 1850–1920* (Stanford: Stanford University Press, 1983).

23. Lobato, *Caminho de canoa pequena,* 127.

24. Ibid., 133.

25. Ibid., 126–27.

26. D. G. McGrath, F. de Castro, C. Futemma, B. D. do Amaral, and J. Calabria, "Fisheries and the Evolution of Resource Management on the Lower Amazon Floodplain," *Human Ecology* 21, no. 2 (1993): 167–95; Janete Gentil, "A juta na agricultura de várzea na área de Santarém-Médio Amazonas," *Boletim do Museu Paraense Emílio Goeldi: Série Antropologia* 4, no. 2 (1988): 118–99.

27. João Murça Pires and Ghillean T. Prance, "The Vegetation Types of the Brazilian Amazon," in *Key Environments: Amazonia,* ed. Ghillean T. Prance and Thomas E. Lovejoy (London: Pergamon, 1985), 109–45. These authors closely follow the earlier definitive typology of Prance, "Notes on the Typology of Amazonia III. The Terminology of Amazonian Forest Types Subject to Inundation," *Brittonia* 31, no. 1 (1979): 26–38. For a discussion of the confusion surrounding floodplain classification, see Janet M. Chernela, "Managing Rivers of Hunger: The Tukano of Brazil," in *Resource Management in Amazonia: Indigenous and Folk Strategies,* ed. Darrell A. Posey and William Balée (New York: New York Botanical Garden, 1989), 238–48.

28. Harald Sioli, "Tropical Rivers as Expressions of Their Terrestrial Environments," in *Tropical Ecological Systems: Trends in Terrestrial and Aquatic Research,* ed. Frank B. Golley and Ernesto Medina (New York: Springer-Verlag, 1975), 275–88.

29. Harald Sioli, "The Amazon and Its Main Affluents: Hydrography, Morphology of the River Courses, and River Types," in *The Amazon: Limnology and Landscape Ecology of a Mighty Tropical River and Its Basin,* ed. Harald Sioli (Dordrecht: Dr. W. Junk, 1984), 127–65; Wolfgang J. Junk and Karin Furch, "The Physical and Chemical Properties of Amazonian Waters," in Prance and Lovejoy, *Key Environments,* 3–17.

30. Junk and Furch, "Physical and Chemical Properties," 15. Other authors have pointed out that lower fluvial productivity is not absolute and is subject to increase through management. See Chernela, "Managing Rivers of Hunger"; Oliver T. Coomes, "Blackwater Rivers, Adaptation, and Environmen-

tal Heterogeneity in Amazonia," *American Anthropologist* 94, no. 3 (1992): 698–701.

31. Curt Nimuendajú, "Os Tapajo," *Boletim do Museu Paraense Emílio Goeldi* 10 (1949): 93–106.

32. See Joseph M. McCann, " 'Extinct' Cultures and Persistent Landscapes of the Lower Tapajos Region, Brazilian Amazonia," paper presented at the Annual Meetings of the Association of American Geographers, New York, February 27–March 3, 2000. For comments on modern uses of *terra preta*, see Nigel J. H. Smith, "Anthrosols and Human Carrying Capacity in the Amazon," *Annals of the American Association of Geographers* 70 (1980): 553–66; William I. Woods and Joseph M. McCann, "The Anthropogenic Origin and Persistence of Amazonian Dark Earths," *Conference of Latin Americanist Geographers Yearbook* 25 (1999): 7–14.

33. Bates, *Naturalist*, 254.

34. Sioli, "Tropical Rivers," 278.

35. Another common term is *varação*.

36. Vicente Chermont de Miranda, *Glossário Paraense ou coleção de vocábulos peculiares á Amazônia e especialmente á Ilha do Marajó* (Belém: Universidade Federal do Pará, 1968).

37. William Henry Hudson, *Green Mansions: A Romance of the Tropical Forest* (New York: Random House, 1944), 33–34.

38. Chermont de Miranda, *Glossário Paraense*, 74–75.

39. Paulo Jacob's *Dicionário da língua popular da Amazônia* (Rio de Janeiro: Liv. Ed. Cátedra, 1985) is a valuable recent work that covers similar ground.

40. V. N. Vološinov, *Marxism and the Philosophy of Language*, trans. Ladislav Matejka and Irwin R. Titunik (Cambridge, Mass.: Harvard University Press, 1986), 79–80.

41. Ibid., 80.

42. See Arun Agrawal, "Dismantling the Divide Between Indigenous and Scientific Knowledge," *Development and Change* 26, no. 3 (1995): 413–39.

43. *Varadouro* is a word widely used for terrestrial trails in the western Amazon. See Susanna Hecht's excellent translation of the great Brazilian essayist, Euclides da Cunha (from his collection *Um paraíso perdido: Ensaios, estudos e pronunciamentos sobre a Amazônia*, ed. Leandro Tocantins, 2nd ed. [Rio de Janeiro: José Olympio, 1994]). Da Cunha writes: "The *varadouro*, a legacy of the heroic Paulista, is today shared by the people in Amazonas, Bolivia, Peru. It is the path, the short cut which goes from one fluvial slope to the next. At first tortuous and short, suffocating, down in the forest thickness, the *varadouro* reflected the indecisive steps of an emerging vacillating society which abandoned the comforting laps of the rivers, and chose instead to walk for itself. . . . Taking to the trails, man in fact is not submissive. He is an insurgent against affectionate and treacherous nature which enriches and kills him" (in Susanna B. Hecht and Alexander Cockburn, *The Fate of the Forest: Developers, Destroyers, and Defenders of the Amazon* [London: Penguin, 1989], 303–4).

44. For an example of a socio-ecological model of this type, see Philip M.

Fearnside, *Human Carrying Capacity of the Brazilian Rainforest* (New York: Columbia University Press, 1986).

45. These Arapiuns *varadores* are all access routes or shortcuts. At least two other types of anthropogenic channel have been identified near Santarém: (i) pools and backwaters made in upland streams by damming with trees and other debris, and used for soaking bitter manioc, washing clothes, bathing, or fishing (Joe McCann, personal communication, September 1996); (ii) channels known as *carvados*, cut to allow sediment-laden floodwaters slowly to fill in backswamps for agricultural land, pasture, or football pitches (Antoinette M.A.G. WinklerPrins, "Land-Use Decision Making Using Local Soil Knowledge on the Lower Amazon Floodplain," *Geographical Review* 87, no. 1 [1997]: 105–8).

46. Letter from Santarém to Samuel Stevens, August 18, 1853, "Proceedings of Natural-History Collectors in Foreign Countries," *Zoologist* 12 (1854): 4320.

47. Leopold H. Myers, *The Clio* (London: Robin Clark, 1990). There actually was a *Clio* caught up in the carnage of the Cabanagem civil war. It was carrying arms for the president of Pará, Bernardo Lobo de Souza, but was captured by rebels and its crew killed. Oddly, this is not the story Myers tells, even though his novel is set during a generic revolution. See John Hemming, *Amazon Frontier: The Defeat of the Brazilian Indians* (London: Macmillan, 1987), 232.

48. John Berger and Jean Mohr, *A Fortunate Man: The Story of a Country Doctor* (London: Writers and Readers Cooperative Press, 1969), 13. For foundational work on landscape as ideology and text, see Raymond Williams, *The Country and the City* (Oxford: Oxford University Press, 1973); John Berger, *Ways of Seeing* (London: Penguin/BBC, 1972); Stephen Daniels, "Marxism, Culture, and the Duplicity of Landscape," in *New Models in Geography: The Political-Economy Perspective*, ed. Richard Peet and Nigel Thrift, vol. 1 (London: Unwin Hyman, 1989), 196–220; Denis E. Cosgrove, *Social Formation and Symbolic Landscape* (London: Croom Helm, 1984); Denis E. Cosgrove and Stephen Daniels, eds., *The Iconography of Landscape: Essays on the Symbolic Representation, Design and Use of Past Environments* (Cambridge: Cambridge University Press, 1988); James S. Duncan, *The City as Text: The Politics of Landscape Interpretation in the Kandyan Kingdom* (Cambridge: Cambridge University Press, 1990); Trevor J. Barnes and James S. Duncan, eds., *Writing Worlds: Discourse, Text and Metaphor in the Representation of Landscape* (London: Routledge, 1992).

49. Mary Poovey, *A History of the Modern Fact: Problems of Knowledge in the Sciences of Wealth and Society* (Chicago: University of Chicago Press, 1998).

50. Julian H. Steward, ed., *Handbook of South American Indians*, 6 vols., Bureau of American Ethnology, bulletin no. 143 (Washington, D.C.: U.S. Government Printing Office, 1946–50). With regard to evolutionary theorizing, the key figure is Steward's associate Leslie White. See, for example, Leslie A. White, "Energy and the Evolution of Culture," *American Anthropologist* 45, no. 3 (1943): 335–56; and Leslie A. White and Beth Dillingham, *The Concept of*

Culture (Minneapolis: Burgess, 1973). Note also the association between cultural-ecological evolutionary models of social development and the rise of modernization theory in the 1960s. See Walter W. Rostow, *The Stages of Economic Growth: A Non-Communist Manifesto* (Cambridge: Cambridge University Press, 1971).

51. Julian H. Steward and Louis C. Faron, *Native Peoples of South America* (New York: McGraw-Hill, 1959), 291. On Steward, see Robert F. Murphy, "The Anthropological Theories of Julian Steward," in Julian H. Steward, *Evolution and Ecology: Essays on Social Transformation*, ed. Jane C. Steward and Robert F. Murphy (Urbana: University of Illinois Press, 1977); and Robert A. Manners, "Julian Haynes Steward 1902–1972," *American Anthropologist* 75, no. 3 (1973): 886–903.

52. See the insightful discussion by Peter Hulme, *Colonial Encounters: Europe and the Native Caribbean 1492–1797* (New York: Routledge, 1986), 50–61.

53. See David N. Livingstone, *The Geographical Tradition: Episodes in the History of a Contested Enterprise* (Oxford: Blackwell, 1993). Also, John H. Zammito, *Kant, Herder, and the Birth of Anthropology* (Chicago: University of Chicago Press, 2002); Mark Bassin, "Friedrich Ratzel's Travels in the United States: A Study in the Genesis of his Anthropogeography," *History of Geography Newsletter* 4 (1984): 11–22; idem, "Imperialism and the Nation-State in Friedrich Ratzel's Political Geography," *Progress in Human Geography* 11, no. 3 (1987): 473–95.

54. This preoccupation continued through the 1980s. See, for example, Raymond B. Hames and William T. Vickers, eds., *Adaptive Responses of Native Amazonians* (New York: Academic Press, 1983).

55. The generative text here was Daniel R. Gross, "Protein Capture and Cultural Development in the Amazon Basin," *American Anthropologist* 77 (1975): 526–49. See also the now-infamous work of Napoleon Chagnon. For an overview of these debates, see Leslie E. Sponsel, "Amazon Ecology and Adaptation," *Annual Review of Anthropology* 15 (1986): 67–97.

56. Betty J. Meggers, "Environmental Limitations on the Development of Culture," *American Anthropologist* 56 (1954): 801–24. Also, idem, "Environment and Culture in the Amazon Basin: An Appraisal of the Theory of Environmental Determinism," in Angel Palerm, Eric R. Wolf, Waldo R. Wedel, Betty J. Meggers, Jacques M. May, and Lawrence Krader, *Studies in Human Ecology* (Washington, D.C.: Pan American Union, 1957), 71–89.

57. Although Meggers' limiting factor architecture anticipates Harris, an even more direct parallel is between Gross' notions of regional protein deficiency and Harris' speculations on Aztec cannibalism. See Marvin Harris, *Cannibals and Kings: The Origins of Cultures* (New York: Random House, 1977).

58. Meggers, "Environmental Limitations," 803.

59. Betty J. Meggers and Clifford Evans, *Archaeological Investigations at the Mouth of the Amazon*, Bureau of American Ethnology, bulletin no. 167 (Washington, D.C.: Smithsonian Institution, 1957).

60. The diffusionary model is a characteristic of her work, but see, as rep-

resentative, Betty J. Meggers, *Amazonia: Man and Culture in a Counterfeit Paradise* (Chicago: Aldine, 1971), 36–38, 146–48, 165–67; and, more recently, "Pre-Columbian Amazonia," *National Geographic Research & Exploration* 10, no. 4 (1994): 398–421.

61. For an effective critique of Meggers' devolutionism, see Anna C. Roosevelt, *Parmana: Prehistoric Maize and Manioc Subsistence Along the Amazon and Orinoco* (New York: Academic Press, 1980), 1–56; and idem, *Moundbuilders of the Amazon: Geophysical Archaeology on Marajó Island, Brazil* (New York: Academic Press, 1991), 100–111.

62. See, for example, William M. Denevan, *The Aboriginal Cultural Geography of the Llanos de Mojos of Bolivia*, Ibero-Americana 48 (Berkeley: University of California Press, 1966); idem, "Aboriginal Drained-Field Cultivation in the Americas," *Science* 169 (1970): 647–54; and also Denevan's recent overview, *Cultivated Landscapes of Native Amazonia and the Andes: Triumph Over the Soil* (Oxford: Oxford University Press, 2001); James J. Parsons and William M. Denevan, "Pre-Columbian Ridged Fields," *Scientific American* 217, no. 1 (1967): 93–100; Donald Lathrap, "The Antiquity and Importance of Long-Distance Trade Relationships in the Moist Tropics of Pre-Columbian South America," *World Archaeology* 5, no. 2 (1973): 170–86.

63. A valuable recent collection edited by Balée is explicitly focused on the reconfiguration of these legacies. See particularly William Balée, "Introduction," in *Advances in Historical Ecology*, ed. William Balée (New York: Columbia University Press, 1998), 1–10, and Neil L. Whitehead, "Ecological History and Historical Ecology: Diachronic Modeling Versus Historical Explanation," in Balée, *Advances in Historical Ecology*, 30–41. Other key references are William Balée, "Indigenous Adaptation to Amazonian Palm Forests," *Principes* 32, no. 2 (1988): 47–54; idem, "The Culture of Amazonian Forests," in Posey and Balée, *Resource Management in Amazonia*, 1–21; idem, "Indigenous Transformation of Amazonian Forests: An Example from Maranhão, Brazil," *L'Homme* 33, nos. 2–4 (1993): 231–54; idem, *Footprints of the Forest: Ka'apor Ethnobotany — The Historical Ecology of Plant Utilization by an Amazonian People* (New York: Columbia University Press, 1994); William M. Denevan, "Ecological Heterogeneity and Horizontal Zonation of Agriculture in the Amazonian Floodplain," in *Frontier Expansion in Amazonia*, ed. Marianne Schmink and Charles H. Wood (Gainesville: University of Florida Press, 1984), 311–36; William M. Denevan and Christine Padoch, eds., *Swidden-Fallow Agroforestry in the Peruvian Amazon* (New York: New York Botanical Garden, 1987); Darrell A. Posey, "Indigenous Management of Tropical Forest Ecosystems: The Case of the Kayapó Indians of the Brazilian Amazon," *Agroforestry Systems* 3 (1985): 139–58; Susanna B. Hecht and Darrell A. Posey, "Indigenous Soil Management in the Latin American Tropics: Some Implications for the Amazon Basin," in *Ethnobiology: Implications and Applications*, ed. Darrell A. Posey and William L. Overal, Proceedings of the First International Congress of Ethnobiology, vol. 2 (Belém: Museu Paraense Emílio Goeldi, 1990), 73–86; Anna C. Roosevelt, "Chiefdoms in the Amazon and Orinoco," in *Chiefdoms in the Americas*, ed. Robert D. Drennan and Carlos A. Uribe (Lanham, Md.: University Press of

America, 1987), 153–84; idem, "Natural Resource Management in Amazonia Before the Conquest: Beyond Ethnographic Projection," in Posey and Balée, *Resource Management in Amazonia*, 30–62; idem, "Lost Civilizations of the Lower Amazon," *Natural History* 95, no. 2 (1989): 74–83; idem, "The Rise and Fall of the Amazon Chiefdoms," *L'Homme* 33, nos. 2–4 (1993): 255–83; idem, "Ancient and Modern Hunter-Gatherers of Lowland South America," in Balée, *Advances in Historical Ecology*, 190–212; idem, *Parmana*; and idem, *Moundbuilders*. Other recent and sophisticated contributions to this literature include Philippe Descola, *In the Society of Nature: A Native Ecology of Amazonia*, trans. Nora Scott (Cambridge: Cambridge University Press, 1994); Laura Rival, "Domestication as a Historical and Symbolic Process: Wild Gardens and Cultivated Forests in the Ecuadorian Amazon," in Balée, *Advances in Historical Ecology*, 232–50; and David Cleary, "Towards an Environmental History of the Amazon: From Prehistory to the Nineteenth Century," *Latin American Research Review* 36, no. 2 (2001): 65–96. For a prescient statement of the problematic, see Stephen Nugent, "Amazonia: Ecosystem and Social System," *Man* N.S. 16 (1981): 62–74.

64. Rather than a thoroughgoing break with its logic, Roosevelt's critique of Meggers has rested on a re-evaluation of the resource potential of the várzea; that is, on a finer-grained appreciation of the "carrying capacity" of particular sites. See Eduardo Viveiros de Castro, "Images of Nature and Society in Amazonian Ethnology," *Annual Review of Anthropology* 25 (1996): 179–200; and Balée, "The Culture of Amazonian Forests." Roosevelt's key precursor was Donald Lathrap, see his *The Upper Amazon* (London: Thames and Hudson, 1970). For a description of large-scale settlement in the upland forest, see Michael J. Heckenberger, *War and Peace in the Shadow of Empire: Sociopolitical Change in the Upper Xingu of Southeastern Amazonia, A.D. 1250–2000* (unpbl. Ph.D. dissertation, Department of Anthropology, University of Pittsburgh, 1996).

65. Roosevelt, "Resource Management in Amazonia."

66. A. C. Roosevelt, M. Lima da Costa, C. Lopes Machado, M. Michab, N. Mercier, H. Valladas, J. Feathers, W. Barnett, M. Imazio da Silveira, A. Henderson, J. Sliva, B. Chernoff, D. S. Reese, J. A. Holma, N. Toth, and K. Schick, "Paleoindian Cave Dwellers in the Amazon: The Peopling of the Americas," *Science* 272 (1996): 373–84; and Richard E. Reanier, William P. Barse, Anna C. Roosevelt, Marconales Lima de Costa, Linda J. Brown, John E. Douglas, Matthew O'Donnell, Ellen Quinn, Judy Kemp, Christiane Lopes Machado, Maura Imazio da Silveira, James Feathers, and Andrew Henderson, "Dating a Paleoindian Site in the Amazon in Comparison with Clovis Culture," *Science* 275 (1997): 1948–52. Roosevelt's excavations also suggest that pottery-making began up to 2,000 years earlier in Amazonia than elsewhere in the hemisphere; see, A. C. Roosevelt, R. A. Housley, M. Imazio da Silveira, S. Maranca, and R. Johnson, "Eighth Millennium Pottery from a Prehistoric Shell Midden in the Brazilian Amazon," *Science* 254 (1991): 1621–24. Other sites have produced evidence of early Amazon maize domestication: M. B. Bush, D. R. Piperno, and P. A. Colinvaux, "A 6,000 Year History of Amazonian Maize Cultivation," *Nature* 340 (1989): 303–5.

67. Posey, "Indigenous Management of Tropical Forest Ecosystems." For other work on the material construction of microenvironments, see Hecht and Posey, "Indigenous Soil Management"; Dominique Irvine, "Succession Management and Resource Distribution in an Amazonian Rain Forest," in Posey and Balée, *Resource Management in Amazonia*, 223–37; Chernela, "Managing Rivers of Hunger"; Christine Padoch and Miguel Pinedo-Vásquez, "Farming Above the Flood in the Várzea of Amapá," in *Várzea: Diversity, Development, and Conservation of Amazonia's Whitewater Floodplains*, ed. Christine Padoch, J. Márcio Ayres, Miguel Pinedo-Vásquez, and Anthony Henderson (New York: New York Botanical Garden, 1999), 345–54; and Hugh Raffles, "Exploring the Anthropogenic Amazon: Estuarine Landscape Transformations in Amapá, Brazil," in Padoch et al., *Várzea*, 355–70.

68. Balée, "The Culture of Amazonian Forests"; idem, "Indigenous Adaptation"; and see my account above of colonist use of ancient terra preta sites. Also, William M. Denevan, "The Pristine Myth: The Landscape of the Americas in 1492," *Annals of the Association of American Geographers* 82, no. 3 (1992): 369–85. An important recent collection on this theme is *Unknown Amazon: Culture in Nature in Ancient Brazil*, ed. Colin McEwan, Christiana Barreto, and Edwardo Neves (London: British Museum, 2001).

69. Alfred Métraux, "Tribes of Eastern Bolivia and the Madeira Headwaters," in Steward, *Handbook*, vol. 3: *The Tropical Forest Tribes*, 381–454, 416. Métraux was preceded by the Swedish anthropologist Erland Nordenskiöld, who worked in the Bolivian Amazon from 1904 to 1914. Nordenskiöld documented a large number of indigenous earthworks in this area, including canals. See Erland Nordenskiöld, "Die anpassung der Indianer an die verhältnisse in den überschwemmungsgebieten in Südamerika," *Ymer* 36, no. 2 (1916): 138–55, in which Nordenskiöld cites correspondence from his German colleague Teodor Koch-Grünberg suggesting that the lower reaches of the famous Casiquiare Canal linking the Amazon (via the Rio Negro) and Orinoco river systems may have been opened by Arawak labor (153–55). My thanks to William Denevan for this reference and the invaluable translation.

70. Rival, "Domestication," 245.

71. For an image of a similar channel taken in 1983 at Teso dos Bichos on Marajó, see Roosevelt, *Moundbuilders*, photograph C, 24. See also, the description of an important canal opened by government mechanical diggers at Anajás on Marajó in Luxardo, *Marajó*, 65–67.

72. Isa Adonias, *A cartografia da região Amazônica: Catálogo descritivo (1500–1961)*, vol. 2 (Rio de Janeiro: INPA, 1963), 347. On damming on Marajó and the widespread use of barrages, see Helen C. Palmatary, "The Pottery of Marajó Island, Brazil," *Transactions of the American Philosophical Society* N.S. 39, no. 3 (1949): 260–470, 265–66.

73. See the work of Keith Basso, for example, *Wisdom Sits in Places: Landscape and Language Among the Western Apache* (Albuquerque: University of New Mexico Press, 1996); and Julie Cruikshank, "Getting the Words Right: Perspectives on Naming and Places in Athapaskan Oral History," *Arctic Anthropology* 27, no. 1 (1990): 52–65.

74. Smaller-scale canals cut for timber extraction similar to some of those in Igarapé Guariba have been noted elsewhere in the estuary. See Domingo S. Macedo and Anthony B. Anderson, "Early Ecological Changes Associated with Logging in an Amazon Floodplain," *Biotropica* 25, no. 2 (1993): 151–63; and Anthony B. Anderson, Igor Mousasticoshvily Jr., and Domingo S. Macedo, "Logging of *Virola surinamensis* in the Amazon Floodplain: Impacts and Alternatives," in Padoch et al., *Várzea*, 119–34. For the grandest fluvial engineering scheme of all—a continuous waterway linking the Caribbean to the Rio de la Plata via the Orinoco and the Amazon—see Hilgard O'Reilly Sternberg's fascinating "Proposals for a South American Waterway," in *Proceedings of the 48th International Congress of Americanists*, ed. Magnus Mörner and Mona Rosendahl (Stockholm: Stockholm University/Institute of Latin American Studies, 1995), 99–125. My thanks to Antoinette WinklerPrins for this reference.

CHAPTER 3

1. "Now let us, by a flight of the imagination, suppose that Rome is not a human habitation but a psychical entity with a similarly long and copious past—an entity, that is to say, in which nothing that has once come into existence will have passed away and all the earlier phases of development continue to exist alongside the later one." Sigmund Freud, *Civilization and Its Discontents*, trans. and ed. James Strachey (New York: W. W. Norton, 1962), 18.

2. Jamaica Kincaid, *A Small Place* (New York: Penguin, 1988).

3. Making of it, in fact, the same kind of carceral local that Arjun Appadurai finds in much ethnography. See his "Introduction: Place and Voice in Anthropological Theory," *Cultural Anthropology* 3, no. 1 (1988): 16–20.

4. "The term origin does not mean the process of becoming of that which has emerged, but much more, that which emerges out of the process of becoming and disappearing. The origin stands in the flow of becoming as a whirlpool." Walter Benjamin, *Ursprung des deutschen Trauerspiels*. Cited in Susan Buck-Morss, *The Dialectics of Seeing: Walter Benjamin and the Arcades Project* (Cambridge, Mass.: MIT Press, 1991), 8.

5. David Spurr, *The Rhetoric of Empire: Colonial Discourse in Journalism, Travel Writing, and Imperial Administration* (Durham: Duke University Press, 1996), 158. For an elaboration of this point, see Chapter 5, n. 36 below.

6. For an exploration of this theme, see James C. Scott, *Seeing Like a State: How Certain Schemes to Improve the Human Condition Have Failed* (New Haven: Yale University Press, 1998).

7. An important account of Amazon river traders is José Alípio Goulart, *O regatão: Mascate fluvial da Amazônia* (Rio de Janeiro: Conquista, 1967). Also see David Gibbs McGrath, *The Paraense Traders: Small-scale, Long-distance Trade in the Brazilian Amazon* (unpbd. Ph.D. dissertation, Department of Geography, University of Wisconsin, 1989); Arthur Cézar Ferreira Reis, *O seringal e o seringueiro*, documentário da vida rural, no. 5 (Rio de Janeiro: Ministério da Agricultura, 1953), 124–26; John C. Yungjohann, *White Gold, The Diary of a*

Rubber Cutter in the Amazon, 1906–1916, ed. Ghillean T. Prance (Oracle: Synergetic Press, 1989); and Raymundo Moraes, *Na planície Amazônica*, 7th ed. (São Paulo: Editora Itatiaia, 1987), 71–75. Moraes writes with venom toward both Jewish and Islamic traders (who "spread like rats," 72). This rhetoric reflects widespread xenophobia in the Amazon during the early twentieth century that manifested in periodic explosive violence directed against Jewish regatões and Jewish-owned aviamento houses. This interdigitation of race and political economy points to major gaps in Amazonianist scholarship. For brief comments, see Barbara Weinstein, *The Amazon Rubber Boom, 1850–1920* (Stanford: Stanford University Press, 1983), 50–51, 306 n. 4. Compelling and detailed accounts of Jews who succeeded in establishing themselves as significant commercial figures can be found in Samuel Benchimol's generously illustrated and important *Manáos-do-Amazonas: Memória empresarial*, vol. 1 (Manaus: Universidade do Amazonas, 1994).

8. For a detailed account of such transaction in Igarapé Guariba and for citations on aviamento, see Chapter 7.

9. A regional resonance here is with the pioneer *bandeirantes* (lit., flag-bearers) of the seventeenth century, who led brutalizing expeditions of primitive accumulation into the forest in what is now widely celebrated as a key moment in Brazilian nation-making. Both in the account of his friend Gomes and in the memories of his close family, Viega emerges as a modern (in its fullest sense) pioneer-explorer, a contemporary bandeirante. There is an ambivalence to the foundational Brazilian mythologies that is, of course, absent from these tellings in which authority is expressed in the language of collaborative paternalism. For a useful introduction to the bandeirante, see John Hemming, *Red Gold: The Conquest of the Brazilian Indians* (London: Macmillan, 1978), 238–82. As will be seen, the trope of wilderness on which Gomes is drawing recurs frequently in accounts of Igarapé Guariba. For definitive, although quite distinct, historical treatments in relation to European settler frontier discourse, see Paul Carter, *The Road to Botany Bay: An Exploration of Landscape and History* (Chicago: University of Chicago Press, 1989) and William Cronon, "The Trouble with Wilderness: Or, Getting Back to the Wrong Nature," in *Uncommon Ground: Rethinking the Human Place in Nature*, ed. William Cronon (New York: W. W. Norton, 1996), 69–90. For Amazonia, see Candace Slater, "Amazonia as Edenic Narrative," in Cronon, *Uncommon Ground*, 114–31.

10. Reis, *O seringal*, 113.

11. Ibid., 114.

12. Raymond Williams, *Marxism and Literature* (Oxford: Oxford University Press, 1977), 128–35. Also, Avery F. Gordon, *Ghostly Matters: Haunting and the Sociological Imagination* (Minneapolis: University of Minnesota Press, 1997), 198–202. Structures of feeling are best thought of as multiple, overlapping, processual, and located. As I am suggesting, localization of this type has contradictory political implications. See Steven Gregory, *Black Corona: Race and the Politics of Place in an Urban Community* (Princeton: Princeton University Press, 1998). For critiques of the unmarked parochialism of Williams' work in relation to race and colonialism, see Paul Gilroy, *There Ain't No Black in the*

Union Jack: The Cultural Politics of Race and Nation (London: Hutchinson, 1987), 49–50; Benita Parry, "Review: *In Theory: Classes, Nations, Literatures* by Aijaz Ahmad," *History Workshop Journal* 36 (1993): 232–42. For broader assessments, see Dennis L. Dworkin and Leslie G. Roman, eds., *Views Beyond the Border Country: Raymond Williams and Cultural Politics* (New York: Routledge, 1993).

13. See Chapter 7 for a fuller description of this episode.

14. The anaconda (*sucuriju*) grows to fabulous proportions in stories of the unpredictable and highly mobile *Cobra Grande* (Great Snake). For discussions, see Candace Slater, *Dance of the Dolphin: Transformation and Disenchantment in the Amazonian Imagination* (Chicago: University of Chicago Press, 1994); João de Jesus Paes Loureiro, *Cultura Amazônica: Um poética do imaginário* (Belém: CEJUP, 1995); Nigel J. H. Smith, *Man, Fishes, and the Amazon* (New York: Columbia University Press, 1981); and Roberto M. Rodrigues, *A fauna da Amazônia* (Belém: CEJUP, 1992).

15. For important recent discussion of the regional implications of the term "caboclo," see Stephen Nugent, *Amazonian Caboclo Society: An Essay in Invisibility* (Oxford: Berg, 1996); idem, "The Coordinates of Identity in Amazonia: At Play in the Fields of Culture," *Critique of Anthropology* 17, no. 1 (1997): 33–51; and Mark Harris, " 'What It Means to Be *Caboclo*': Some Critical Notes on the Construction of Amazonian *Caboclo* Society as an Anthropological Object," *Critique of Anthropology* 18, no. 1 (1998): 83–95.

16. Such a term seems to embody processual imaginaries: a past in which the closely vegetated area was once open water and a future in which it becomes the expansive "lake." I owe this insight to Daniel Zarin, who first pointed out the history instantiated in the term "lago."

17. For accounts of similar genderings of landscape spaces through a division of labor into that based around the home and that based on expeditionary travel, see Louise Fortmann, "Gendered Knowledge: Rights and Space in Two Zimbabwe Villages," in *Feminist Political Ecology: Global Issues and Local Experiences*, ed. Dianne Rocheleau, Barbara Thomas-Slayter, and Esther Wangari (New York: Routledge, 1996), 211–23; and Stacy Leigh Pigg, "Constructing Social Categories Through Place: Social Representations and Development in Nepal," *Comparative Studies in Society and History* 34, no. 3 (1992): 491–513.

18. Raymond Williams, *The Country and the City* (Oxford: Oxford University Press, 1973), 120.

19. These images are directly comparable. Seasonal variation has been eliminated by using images from the same months of different years (October/November). Diurnal tidal variation has been controlled for by the reading of exposed mudflats as water (Daniel Zarin, personal communication). For a comprehensive analysis of images from this area, see Valeria F. G. Pereira, *Spatial and Temporal Analysis of Floodplain Ecosystems — Amapá, Brazil — Using Geographic Information Systems (GIS) and Remote Sensing* (unpbd. M.Sc. thesis, Department of Natural Resources, University of New Hampshire, 1998).

20. "O centro" translates literally as "the center," but Paulo Jacob pins down its meaning in the present context: "The heart of the forest. A place remote from settlement" ("Âmago da mata. Lugar afastado da povoação"). There

is room here for revelatory interpretative analysis of comparative notions of "centrality." Paulo Jacob, *Dicionário da língua popular da Amazônia* (Rio de Janeiro: Liv. Ed. Cátedra, 1985), 43.

21. "I think it was a curiosity to see what was there ["curiosidade de ver"]," Lene told me. "In those days, you didn't have airplanes. He thought that the way to see farther would be to open a stream and go have a look." Dona Rita joined in: "Yes, it really was curiosity, without studying or anything . . . real curiosity."

22. On the role of traveling leaders in constituting rural communities, see Anna L. Tsing, *In the Realm of the Diamond Queen: Marginality in an Out-of-the-Way Place* (Princeton: Princeton University Press, 1993), 72–76. On the Comunidades de Base and church politics during this period, see Scott Mainwaring, *The Catholic Church and Politics in Brazil, 1916–1985* (Stanford: Stanford University Press, 1986), and, for an interesting sociological case study from the Amazon, see Thomas C. Bruneau, "Brazil: The Catholic Church and Basic Christian Communities," in *Religion and Political Conflict in Latin America*, ed. Daniel H. Levine (Chapel Hill: University of North Carolina Press, 1986), 106–23.

23. In a protracted if often surprisingly straightforward (at least in Amapá) process, title to terra requerida is available by demonstrating to INCRA that the area in question is currently unused or uninhabited. Terra requerida cannot normally be sold, as the definitive title remains with the state. It can, however, be inherited.

24. For a graphic account of land violence in the south of Pará during this period, see Sue Branford and Oriel Glock, *The Last Frontier: Fighting for Land in the Amazon* (London: Zed Press, 1985). Also, Chapter 6 below.

25. See Chapter 6 for a discussion of recent theoretical developments in ecology that have emphasized the stochastic dynamism of natural systems, foregrounding "disturbance regimes" in a break with notions of stability, climax, and the teleologies of measured succession.

26. Of course, the symbolic value of some of these foods has only appreciated since bans on their trade and urban consumption were imposed by the federal state through the federal environmental agency, the Instituto Brasileiro do Meio Ambiente e dos Recursos Naturais Renováveis (IBAMA).

27. Here I am using "glamour" as a gloss on Pierre Bourdieu's concepts of cultural and symbolic capital. See Pierre Bourdieu, *Language and Symbolic Power*, ed. John B. Thompson, trans. Gino Raymond and Matthew Adamson (Cambridge: Polity, 1991). In their account of the failure of the Partido dos Trabalhadores (PT/Workers' Party) to capture the Brazilian presidency in the 1989 national elections, Emil Sader and Ken Silverstein suggest that Lula's unwillingness to embody such cultural resources—his strategic self-presentation as a self-consciously working-class figure—lost him critical support among an urban and rural poor accustomed to clientalist political modes. Emil Sader and Ken Silverstein, *Without Fear of Being Happy: Lula, the Workers Party and Brazil* (London: Verso, 1991). For a richer ethnographic discussion of the Brazilian political process in these terms, see Daniel T. Linger, "The Hegemony of Discontent," *American Ethnologist* 20, no. 1 (1993): 3–25.

28. This intimation of Amazonian impermanence echoes David Cleary's important analysis of the instabilities of regional political economy — work that stands as a powerful critique of the conventional use of the frontier metaphor in the Amazonianist literature. David Cleary, "After the Frontier: Problems With Political Economy in the Modern Brazilian Amazon," *Journal of Latin American Studies* 25, no. 2 (1993): 331–50.

29. There is a growing literature on the impact of transnational environmental discourse on Amazonian politics. Much of this focuses on the ambivalence of co-optation: the complications that ensue from the attempt — often highly sophisticated — of indigenous groups to (counter-) appropriate discursive space created by narratives of deforestation. For recent discussions, see Beth A. Conklin and Laura R. Graham, "The Shifting Middle-Ground: Amazonian Indians and Eco-Politics," *American Anthropologist* 97, no. 4 (1995): 695–710; Beth A. Conklin, "Body Paint, Feathers, and VCRs: Aesthetics and Authenticity in Amazonian Activism," *American Ethnologist* 24, no. 4 (1997): 711–37; and Terence Turner, "Indigenous Rights, Indigenous Cultures and Environmental Conservation: Convergence or Divergence? The Case of the Brazilian Kayapó," in *Earth, Air, Fire, Water: Humanistic Studies of the Environment*, ed. Jill Ker Conway, Kenneth Keniston, and Leo Marx (Amherst: University of Massachusetts Press, 1999) 145–69. Discussions of these issues in relation to ribeirinho actors are much rarer. For an intervention that focuses on the perceived attempts of U.S. environmentalists to reconfigure Amazonian class politics in environmental terms, see Susanna B. Hecht and Alexander Cockburn, "Defenders of the Amazon," *The Nation*, May 22, 1989, 695–702, September 18, 1989, 262, 291–92.

30. Other words applied in this context are *acabado* (finished) and *parado* (stopped), definitive comments on local "development."

31. It is likely that an aggregate longitudinal analysis of ecological change in the area would support their claims — some of which are at least partly echoed by Macedo loyalists. There can be little doubt that the long-term hydrological effects of stream-cutting have resulted in a net loss of available cultivable area and other key resources both upstream and downstream in Igarapé Guariba. Yet the notion of *access* is key to local understandings of the changing landscape, and an analysis in aggregate terms overlooks intra-Guariba relations of power, assuming an idealized "community" in which resources and incomes are equitably partitioned. In contrast, the analysis presented here emphasizes the historical and power-laden processes of allocation through which present-day social relations are constituted and reconfigured (this type of argument has now been effectively staked out by political ecologists — see, for example, Nancy Lee Peluso, *Rich Forests, Poor People: Resource Control and Resistance in Java* [Berkeley: University of California Press, 1992]).

CHAPTER 4

1. Pablo Ojer, S.J., *La formación del Oriente Venezolano: I. Creación de las gobernaciones* (Caracas: Universidade Católica Andres Bello, 1966), 109,

grants first usage of "Guiana" to the conquistador Diego de Ordaz in 1531. John W. Shirley, "Sir Walter Raleigh's Guiana Finances," *Huntington Library Quarterly* 13 (1949): 55–69, 67, suggests that Ralegh is responsible for the word's entry into English.

2. Kenneth R. Andrews, *Trade, Plunder and Settlement: Maritime Enterprise and the Genesis of the British Empire, 1480–1630* (Cambridge: Cambridge University Press, 1984); James A. Williamson, *English Colonies in Guiana and on the Amazon, 1604–1668* (Oxford: Clarendon Press, 1923); and David B. Quinn, *Raleigh and the British Empire* (London: Hodder and Stoughton, 1947), 163ff. For a particularly fine graphic representation, see P. du Val D'Abbeville's 1654 map of the coastline from Trinidad to Pará entitled "La Gvaiane ov Coste Sauuage, autrement El Dorado, et Pais des Amazones," reproduced as Map B in Robert Harcourt, *A Relation of a Voyage to Guiana*, ed. Sir C. Alexander Harris (Hakluyt Society Second Series No. 60. London: Hakluyt Society, 1926 [1613]).

3. Edmund Spenser, *The Faerie Queene*, ed. A. C. Hamilton (Harlow, Essex: Longman, 1977), Book IV, Canto xi, stanzas 22, 21. I follow Robert Schomburgk and most contemporary scholars in my spelling of Ralegh.

4. Joyce Lorimer, *English and Irish Settlement on the River Amazon, 1550–1646* (Hakluyt Society Second Series No. 171. London: Hakluyt Society, 1989) is the indispensable source. Also Williamson, *English Colonies*; Andrews, *Trade, Plunder and Settlement*, 294–300; and Vincent T. Harlow, "Introduction," in *Colonising Expeditions to the West Indies and Guiana, 1623–1667*, ed. Vincent T. Harlow (Hakluyt Society Second Series No. 56. London: Hakluyt Society, 1925), xiii–xcv. Key texts on which I have drawn that focus on other national histories include Cornelis Ch. Goslinga, *The Dutch in the Caribbean and on the Wild Coast, 1580–1680* (Gainesville: University of Florida Press, 1971); Walter Norman Breymann, *The Opening of the Amazon 1540–1640* (unpbd. Ph.D. dissertation, Department of History, University of Illinois, 1950); and Ojer, *La formación*.

5. Sir Walter Ralegh, "The Apology," in *Last Voyages — Cavendish, Hudson, Ralegh: The Original Narratives*, ed. Philip Edwards (Oxford: Clarendon Press, 1988), 226–48, 240.

6. See Neil L. Whitehead, "Introduction," in Sir Walter Ralegh, *The Discoverie of the Large, Rich and Bewtiful Empyre of Guiana*, ed. Neil L. Whitehead (Manchester: Manchester University Press, 1997), 69. Henceforth, Whitehead, *Discoverie*. Although Whitehead argues that the Pakaraima mountains formed a "frontier" — a cultural as well as a physical watershed — his data suggest the extent to which this boundary was porous, uneven, and contingent, both spatially and temporally. Much of the ethnohistorical recuperation of the early modern indigenous polity to which I refer here is due to Whitehead's detailed scholarship. In addition to the extensive introductory essays to his recent edition of *The Discoverie*, see Neil L. Whitehead, "Tribes Make States and States Make Tribes: Warfare and the Creation of Colonial Tribe and State in Northeastern South America," in *War in the Tribal Zone: Expanding States and Indigenous Warfare*, ed. R. Brian Ferguson and Neil L. Whitehead (Sante Fe:

School of American Research Press, 1992), 127–50; idem, "Ethnic Transformation and Historical Discontinuity in Native Amazonia and Guayana, 1500–1900," *L'Homme* 33, nos. 2–4 (1993): 289–309; and idem, "The Ancient Amerindian Polities of the Amazon, the Orinoco, and the Atlantic Coast: A Preliminary Analysis of Their Passing," in *Amazonian Indians from Prehistory to the Present: Anthropological Perspectives*, ed. Anna C. Roosevelt (Tucson: University of Arizona Press, 1994), 33–54. Also of importance are Simone Dreyfus, "Historical and Political Anthropological Inter-Connections: The Multilinguistic Indigenous Polity of the Carib Islands and Mainland Coast from the 16th to the 18th Century," *Antropológica* 59–62 (1983–84): 39–55; idem, "Os empreendimentos coloniais e os espaços políticos indígenas no interior da Guiana ocidental (entre o Orenoco e o Corentino) de 1613–1796," in *Amazônia: Etnologia e história indígena*, org. Eduardo Viveiros de Castro e Manuela Carneiro da Cunha (São Paulo: NHII-USP/FAPESP, 1993), 19–41; Arie Boomert, "Gifts of the Amazons: Greenstone Pendants and Beads as Items of Ceremonial Exchange," *Antropológica* 67 (1987): 33–54; and Nelly Arvello-Jiménez and Horacio Biord, "The Impact of Conquest on Contemporary Indigenous Peoples of the Guiana Shield: The System of Orinoco Regional Interdependence," in Roosevelt, *Amazonian Indians*, 55–78.

7. Whitehead, "Introduction," 106, and Map II, 61.

8. See Thomas Hariot to Robert Cecil, July 11, 1596, in Edward Edwards, *The Life of Sir Walter Ralegh*, vol. 2 (London: Macmillan, 1868), 420, on Ralegh's chart of Guiana which "was don but by intelligence from the Indians." Also, Paul Carter, *The Road to Botany Bay: An Exploration of Landscape and History* (Chicago: University of Chicago Press, 1989).

9. On expeditionary "metalepsis," see D. Graham Burnett, *Masters of All They Surveyed: Exploration, Geography, and a British El Dorado* (Chicago: University of Chicago Press, 2000), 37–66; Rolena Adorno, "The Discursive Encounter of Spain and America: The Authority of Eyewitness Testimony in the Writing of History," *The William and Mary Quarterly* 49, no. 2 (1992): 210–28; and Stephen Greenblatt, "Foreword," in Frank Lestringant, *Mapping the Renaissance World: The Geographical Imagination in the Age of Discovery*, trans. David Fausett (Berkeley: University of California Press, 1994), vii–xv. This discursive practice was often constitutive of the spatial practice of routed exploration. Its citationality can also usefully be considered in the terms elaborated by Judith Butler, following Austin and Derrida, in *Bodies That Matter: On the Discursive Limits of "Sex"* (New York: Routledge, 1993).

10. This familiar story has been the focus of a vast historiography. See, *inter alia*, Richard H. Tawney, *Business and Politics under James I: Lionel Cranfield as Merchant and Minister* (Cambridge: Cambridge University Press, 1958); Theodore K. Rabb, *Enterprise and Empire: Merchant and Gentry Investment in the Expansion of England, 1575–1630* (Cambridge, Mass.: Harvard University Press, 1967); Eva G. R. Taylor, *Tudor Geography, 1485–1583* (London: Methuen, 1930); idem, *Late Tudor and Early Stuart Geography, 1583–1650* (New York: Octagon, 1968); Richard Helgerson, *Forms of Nationhood: The Eliza-*

bethan Writing of England (Chicago: University of Chicago Press, 1992); Christopher Hill, *Intellectual Origins of the English Revolution Revisited* (Oxford: Clarendon Press, 1997); and Andrews, *Trade, Plunder and Settlement*.

11. Sir Walter Ralegh, *The Discoverie of the Large, Rich, and Bewtiful Empire of Guiana, with a Relation of the Great and Golden City of Manoa (which the Spaniards call El Dorado) And the provinces of Emeria, Arromaia, Amapaia and other Countries, with their rivers, adioyning. Performed in the Year 1595 by Sir W. Ralegh, Knight, Captaine of her Maiesties Guard, Lo. Warden of the Stanneries, and her Highnesse Lieutenant generall of the Countie of Cornewall,* ed. Robert H. Schomburgk (Hakluyt Society First Series No. 3. London: Hakluyt Society, 1848), 228. Henceforth, Schomburgk, *Discoverie*.

12. Vincent T. Harlow, "Introduction," in Sir Walter Ralegh, *The Discoverie of the Large and Bewtiful Empire of Guiana,* ed. V. T. Harlow (London: The Argonaut Press, 1928), xv–cvi, xcvii.

13. Ojer, *La formación,* 541.

14. On British Guiana, see Burnett, *Masters,* 25–27, and, on the Raleigh Club, a precursor to the Royal Geographic Society, see David R. Stoddart, "The RGS and the 'New Geography': Changing Aims and Roles in Nineteenth-Century Science," *Geographical Journal* 146, no. 3 (1980): 191–202.

15. *The Discoverie* has been an important text for literary scholars, particularly for "new historicists." I have drawn heavily on this work in this chapter, but understand my project as generating readings driven by anthropological rather than literary preoccupations. Among the recent literary discussions of Ralegh's text that I have found most helpful are Mary B. Campbell, *The Witness and the Other World: Exotic European Travel Writing, 400–1600* (Ithaca: Cornell University Press, 1988); Louis Montrose, "The Work of Gender in the Discourse of Discovery," *Representations* 33 (1991): 1–41; and Mary C. Fuller, "Ralegh's Fugitive Gold: Reference and Deferral in *The Discoverie of Guiana,*" *Representations* 33 (1991): 42–64. Neil L. Whitehead's valuable explorations of *The Discoverie* represent a third way in which Ralegh's rich text can be mined: ethnohistorically. See Neil L. Whitehead, "The Historical Anthropology of Text: The Interpretation of Ralegh's *Discoverie of Guiana,*" *Current Anthropology* 36, no. 1 (1995): 53–74, and, further elaborated, Whitehead, "Introduction."

16. Kenneth R. Andrews, *Elizabethan Privateering: English Privateering During the Spanish War 1585–1603* (Cambridge: Cambridge University Press, 1964); idem, ed., *English Privateering Voyages to the West Indies, 1588–1595* (Hakluyt Society Second Series No. 111. London: Hakluyt Society, 1956); Joyce Lorimer, "The English Contraband Tobacco Trade in Trinidad and Guiana 1590–1617," in *The Westward Enterprise: English Activities in Ireland, the Atlantic, and America 1480–1650,* ed. Kenneth R. Andrews, Nicholas P. Canny, and Paul E. H. Hair (Liverpool: University of Liverpool Press, 1978), 124–50.

17. Richard Hakluyt, *A Particular Discourse Concerning the Greate Necessitie and Manifolde Commodyties That Are Like to Growe to this Realme of Englande by the Westerne Discoueries Lately Attempted, Written in the Yere 1584 by Richard Hakluyt of Oxforde Known as Discourse of Western Planting,*

ed. David B. Quinn and Alison M. Quinn (Hakluyt Society Extra Series No. 45. London: Hakluyt Society, 1993), 51. The Quinns, ibid., 161, take the "River of Saint Augustine" to be the Amazon.

18. For descriptions of the Ralegh circle, see Hill, *Intellectual Origins*, 125–30, and Shannon Miller, *Invested With Meaning: The Raleigh Circle in the New World* (Philadelphia: University of Pennsylvania Press, 1998).

19. Lorimer, "Contraband Tobacco," 126; idem, "The Location of Ralegh's Guiana Gold Mine," *Terrae Incognitae* 14 (1982): 77–95.

20. For the drama, see Robert Lacey, *Sir Walter Ralegh* (London: Weidenfeld and Nicholson, 1973), 369–82; and Edmund Gosse, *Raleigh* (New York: D. Appleton, 1886), 202ff. For a text of Ralegh's final speech, see Vincent T. Harlow, ed., *Ralegh's Last Voyage* (London: The Argonaut Press, 1932), 305–11. For a smart survey of Ralegh's shifting reputation, see Robert Lawson-Peebles, "The Many Faces of Sir Walter Ralegh," *History Today* 48, no. 3 (1998): 17–24.

21. A challenge of historical writing is to resist the certainty of hindsight when reimagining the possibilities of the lived moment. This point is elegantly elaborated in relation to the conquest of America by Jonathan Goldberg, "The History That Will Be," in *Premodern Sexualities*, ed. Louise Fradenberg and Carla Freccero (New York: Routledge, 1996), 3–21.

22. Whitehead, *Discoverie*, 138. All emphases in this and other quotations from *The Discoverie* are present in the original text.

23. Even when this strategy met with its greatest success—the capture and looting of the treasure-laden Portuguese carrack, the *Madre de Dios*, in 1592—most of the profit scattered with the sailors on their return to Dorset. See Edwards, *The Life*, vol. 1, 155–58.

24. Cited in Murdo J. Macloed, "Spain and America: The Atlantic Trade, 1492–1720," in *The Cambridge History of Latin America*, vol. I: *Colonial Latin America*, ed. Leslie Bethell (Cambridge: Cambridge University Press, 1984), 314–88, 387. Also, see John H. Elliott, *The Old World and the New, 1492–1650* (Cambridge: Cambridge University Press, 1970), 54–78.

25. Helgerson, *Forms of Nationhood*, 151–91; Taylor, *Late Tudor*, 1–38; Rabb, *Enterprise and Empire*, 19–92; William R. Scott, *The Constitution and Finance of English, Scottish and Irish Joint-Stock Companies to 1720* (Cambridge: Cambridge University Press, 1910–12), vol. 2.

26. David B. Quinn, *Explorers and Colonies: America, 1500–1625* (London: The Hambledon Press, 1990); Helgerson, *Forms of Nationhood*.

27. "The Letters Patents, Granted by the Queenes Majestie to M. Walter Ralegh, now Knight, for the Discovering and Planting of New Lands and Countries, to Continue the Space of 6. Yeeres and No More," in *The Portable Hakluyt's Voyages*, ed. Irwin R. Blacker (New York: Viking, 1965), 279–85, 279.

28. See Lacey, *Ralegh*, 15–17. John Aubrey, in his *Brief Lives* ed. Oliver Lawson Dick (London: Secker & Warburg, 1949) informs us both that Ralegh "spake broad Devonshire to his dying day" (255) and that "In his youth for several yeares he was under streights for want of money. I remember that Mr. Thomas Child, of Worcestershire, told me that Sir Walter borrowed a Gowne of

him when he was at Oxford (they were both of the same College) which he never restored, nor money for it" (253).

29. "Epistle Dedicatorie," in Whitehead, *Discoverie*, 121.

30. William H. Sherman, *John Dee: The Politics of Reading and Writing in the English Renaissance* (Amherst: University of Massachusetts Press, 1995), 182–92.

31. Whitehead, *Discoverie*, 135.

32. Ibid., 156.

33. Ibid., 158, 179, 148.

34. Antonello Gerbi, *Nature in the New World: From Christopher Columbus to Gonzalo Fernández de Oviedo*, trans. Jeremy Moyle (Pittsburgh: University of Pittsburgh Press, 1985), 93. Also, Jonathan Goldberg, *Sodometries: Renaissance Texts, Modern Sexualities* (Stanford: Stanford University Press, 1992), 179–222.

35. Joyce Lorimer, "Ralegh's First Reconnaissance of Guiana? An English Survey of the Orinoco in 1587," *Terra Incognitae* 9 (1977): 7–21. Dom Antonio was the aggrieved king-in-exile whose accession in 1580 had been pre-empted by his cousin, Philip II, thus cementing a Spanish control of the Iberian peninsula that lasted until 1640.

36. Andrews, *Elizabethan Privateering*, 173.

37. On Spanish concerns about such vulnerabilities, see Ojer, *La formación*, 353–96.

38. See Eva G. R. Taylor, "Introduction," in *The Original Writings and Correspondence of the Two Richard Hakluyts*, ed. Eva G. R. Taylor, vol. 1 (Hakluyt Society Second Series No. 76. London: Hakluyt Society, 1935), 47; and Charles Nicholl, *The Creature in the Map: A Journey to El Dorado* (New York: Morrow, 1995), 32–37.

39. This was the pre-existing narrative context within which Ralegh interpreted Topiawari's tales of crimson-hatted foreigners attacking from the west (see below, n. 53). It is worth noting the correspondence between this story of Andean invasion and the diffusionary models of cultural development in the Americas that came to dominate Amazonian studies in the early and mid-twentieth century. As we know, scholars such as Julian Steward and Betty Meggers explained the presence of "complex" societies in Amazonia by positing an early migration from the Andes. Burdened with a developmentalist theory of culture that rested on a close causative relationship between the ecological potential of an area and the societies that could emerge there, Steward, Meggers, and others fell back on speculation about Andean migration to account for "anomalous" evidence of large-scale settlements. These scholars were extremely cautious about regarding narratives such as *The Discoverie* as historical sources and thereby giving credence to accounts of substantial floodplain chiefdoms. Nevertheless, it is in Ralegh's account that we find the first explicit statement of what would become a hegemonic Andean diffusionary hypothesis.

40. José Toribio Medina, ed., *The Discovery of the Amazon According to the Account of Friar Gaspar de Carvajal and Other Documents*, trans. Bertram T. Lee (New York: Dover, 1988).

41. Pedro Simón, *The Expedition of Pedro de Ursua and Lope de Aguirre in Search of El Dorado and Omagua in 1560–1*, trans. William Bollaert (Works issued by the Hakluyt Society, No. 28. London: Hakluyt Society, 1861), 194.

42. Whitehead, *Discoverie*, 141.

43. Simón, "*The Expedition*," xi – xii.

44. Lorimer, *Settlement*, 10. For broad El Dorado histories, see John Hemming, *The Search for El Dorado* (New York: E. P. Dutton, 1978); and Robert Silverberg, *The Golden Dream: Seekers of El Dorado* (Athens: University of Ohio Press, 1996).

45. A preliminary to Ralegh's own voyage was his sponsorship of John Burgh's belligerent voyage to La Margarita, Cumaná, and probably Guiana in 1593. See Andrews, *English Privateering*, 225–35.

46. Shirley, "Raleigh's Guiana Finances." Rabb, *Enterprise and Empire*, 35–92, delineates distinct agenda within the coalition of merchant and gentry investors in the colonial voyages. His data on the Guiana campaign are in Table 5, 66.

47. Alfred L. Rowse, *Sir Walter Ralegh, His Family and Private Life* (New York: Harper & Brothers, 1962), 183. More detail is offered by Ojer, *La formación*, 539–63.

48. Patricia Seed, "Taking Possession and Reading Texts: Establishing the Authority of Overseas Empires," *The William and Mary Quarterly* 49, no. 2 (1992): 183–209, 186.

49. See John Hemming, *Red Gold: The Conquest of the Brazilian Indians* (London: Macmillan, 1978).

50. Whitehead, *Discoverie*, 165–66.

51. See Hakluyt, *Discourse of Western Planting*, 52–61.

52. Campbell, *The Witness*, 242.

53. Whitehead, *Discoverie*, 173.

54. This was not an unprecedented sentiment, but it does situate Ralegh in a particular New World tradition. Las Casas, for example, "stated explicitly in the very last work he wrote, *On Royal Power*, [that] the 'kings' and 'princes' of the Americas enjoyed the same status as the nobility in Naples and Milan." Anthony Pagden, "Introduction," in Bartolomé de Las Casas, *A Short Account of the Destruction of the Indies*, ed. and trans. Nigel Griffin (Harmondsworth: Penguin, 1992), xiii–li, xvi.

55. For a brilliantly sustained discussion of this tension in the texts of New World discovery, see Anthony Pagden, *European Encounters with the New World: From Renaissance to Romanticism* (New Haven:Yale University Press, 1993), 17–49.

56. Whitehead, *Discoverie*, 174.

57. Ibid., 181.

58. Ibid., 185.

59. And, of course, with each other. Ralegh avoids homogenizing Americans into undifferentiated "Indianness." The political affiliations of particular groups are of paramount importance to him.

60. Harcourt, *Relation*, 73; Whitehead, "Introduction," 30–31.

61. Lawrence Keymis, "A Relation of the Second Voyage to Guiana, Performed and Written in the Yeere 1696. by Lawrence Keymis Gent.," in Richard Hakluyt, *The Principal Navigations, Voyages, Traffiques & Discoveries of the English Nation Made by Sea or Over-land to the Remote and Farthest Distant Quarters of the Earth at Any Time Within the Compasse of These 1600 Yeeres*, vol. 10 (Glasgow: James MacLehose, 1903–5), 462–67.

62. Stephen Greenblatt, *Marvelous Possessions: The Wonder of the New World* (Chicago: University of Chicago Press, 1991), 12–13.

63. Michel de Certeau, *The Writing of History*, trans. Tom Conley (New York: Columbia University Press, 1988), xxv; emphasis in original.

64. Whitehead, *Discoverie*, 196.

65. George Chapman, "De Guiana carmen Epicum," in Hakluyt, *Principal Navigations*, vol. 10, 451.

66. Keymis, "Relation," 487.

67. Carolyn Merchant, *The Death of Nature: Women, Ecology, and the Scientific Revolution* (New York: Harper & Row, 1980). Seamus Heaney has written powerfully on this tripartite connection in direct relation to Ralegh. In his poem "Ocean's Love to Ireland," Heaney revisits the famous "Sweet Sir Walter" episode from Aubrey's *Brief Lives*, an episode Aubrey narrates in a comic register. Taking his cue from Ralegh's "The Ocean to Cynthia," Heaney writes water as the medium that fuses Ralegh's rape of a maid of honor with the colonial violence of the Irish campaigns. He ties the material historicity of bodies, rivers, puddles, swamps, and oceans, bringing into view hierarchies of sex, race, and nation, and holding Raleigh to account as the agent through whom Ireland is "possessed and repossessed." Heaney's Ralegh is cynical and brutal, far removed from the national-heroic rogue of Aubrey's gossip, and the retold story is bitter and deadening: "Ralegh has backed the maid to a tree / As Ireland is backed to England / And drives inland / Till her strands are all breathless / 'Sweesir, Swatter! Sweesir, Swatter!'" Seamus Heaney, *North* (London: Faber, 1975), 41. This, of course, is a radically different metaphorics of water from that of Gaston Bachelard, which I consider in Chapter 7.

68. For a perceptive discussion of *The Discoverie* in these terms, see Montrose, "The Work of Gender."

69. Whitehead, *Discoverie*, 199.

70. Keymis, "Relation," 487.

71. As the Brazilian military would put it in the 1970s when encouraging migration to Amazonia from the hardscrabble northeast: "a land without people for a people without land."

72. See Anthony Pagden, *The Fall of Natural Man: The American Indian and the Origins of Comparative Ethnology* (New York: Cambridge University Press, 1982); and, more generally, Manuela Carneiro da Cunha, "Introdução a uma história indígena," in *História dos índios no Brasil*, org. Manuela Carneiro da Cunha (São Paulo: Companhia das Letras, 1992), 9–24. On nature, see Antonello Gerbi, *The Dispute of the New World: The History of a Polemic, 1750–1900*, trans. Jeremy Moyle (Pittsburgh: University of Pittsburgh Press, 1973); idem, *Nature in the New World*; and Clarence J. Glacken, *Traces on the Rho-*

dian Shore: Nature and Culture in Western Thought from Ancient Times to the End of the Eighteenth Century (Berkeley: University of California Press, 1967).

73. Viz. Michel de Certeau: "Discourse about the other is a means of constructing a discourse authorized by the other." *Heterologies: Discourse on the Other* (Minneapolis: University of Minnesota Press, 1986), 68. Cf. Michael T. Ryan, "Assimilating New Worlds in the Sixteenth and Seventeenth Centuries," *Comparative Studies in Society and History* 23 (1981): 519–38, 521: "Neither Montaigne nor any other sceptic was particularly interested in seeing the world through the eyes of an exotic: That would simply be exchanging custom for custom, folly for folly."

74. John H. Elliott, *The Old World and the New*; Ryan, "Assimilating New Worlds"; Anthony Grafton, *New Worlds, Ancient Texts: The Power of Tradition and the Shock of Discovery* (Cambridge, Mass.: Harvard University Press, 1992); Anthony Pagden, "'The Impact of the New World on the Old': The History of an Idea," *Renaissance and Modern Studies* 30 (1986): 1–11; idem, *The Fall of Natural Man*; Gerbi, *Nature in the New World*; and Glacken, *Traces on the Rhodian Shore*.

75. Grafton, *New Worlds*, 65–68; Lorraine Daston and Katherine Park, *Wonders and the Order of Nature, 1150–1750* (New York: Zone Books, 1998), 63.

76. Daston and Park, *Wonders*, 220. Although, given the limits of a discursive practice that failed to encompass atheism, for example, we should understand "free-for-all" in rather relative terms. My thanks to Carla Freccero for this observation.

77. Roy Porter, "The Terraqueous Globe," in *The Ferment of Knowledge: Studies in the Historiography of Eighteenth-Century Science*, ed. George S. Rousseau and Roy Porter (Cambridge: Cambridge University Press, 1980), 285–324; Grafton, *New Worlds*, 147, 207–12; Glacken, *Traces on the Rhodian Shore*, 357–66. A key question given little attention in these texts is the active opposition between Protestant and Catholic interpretations and experiences of the New World. This theme is explored more often in readings of French accounts (see, most famously, Jean de Léry, *History of a Voyage to the Land of Brazil, Otherwise Called America*, trans. Janet Whatley [Berkeley: University of California Press, 1990], and, for important commentary, de Certeau, *The Writing of History*, 209–43; also Lestringant, *Mapping the Renaissance World*, on André Thévet). Clearly, though, the competition between religions and the associated national politics formed a complex strategic field of action for Ralegh. His treatment of the conquistadores as both source and inspiration for the Guiana campaign (*The Discoverie* as a "Spanish" text), his marriage into the suspect Throckmortons, and the whispers of atheism that hung around his inner circle were all fodder for his detractors—and ultimately the stuff from which the fatal charges of pro-Spanish conspiracy were manufactured.

78. Gerbi, *Nature in the New World*, 61.

79. Michel Foucault, *The Order of Things: An Archaeology of the Human Sciences* (New York: Vintage, 1994), 17–45, argues suggestively but schematically for similitude as the ordering principle of an early modern European episteme.

80. Whitehead, *Discoverie*, 146; emphasis in original.

81. Ibid., 145.

82. Cf. Greenblatt, "Introduction," xi, on "one of the key principles of the Renaissance geographical imagination: eye-witness testimony, [which] for all its vaunted importance, sits as a very small edifice on top of an enormous mountain of hearsay, rumor, convention, and endlessly recycled fable."

83. Johannes Kepler, *Kepler's Conversation with Galileo's Sidereal Messenger*, ed. and trans. Edward Rosen (New York: Johnson Reprint Corp., 1965), 17, cited in Pagden, "'The Impact,'" 4.

84. Andrews, *Trade, Plunder, and Settlement*, 27–31; Sherman, *John Dee*, 182–92.

85. Hugh Honour, *The New Golden Land: European Images of America from the Discoveries to the Present Time* (New York: Pantheon, 1975), 71–78; Grafton, *New Worlds*, 126.

86. Hill, *Intellectual Origins*, 125.

87. As the botanist John Ellis wrote, rather tartly, to Linnaeus in August 1768: "No people ever went to sea better fitted out for the purpose of Natural History, nor more elegantly. They have got a fine library of Natural History; they have all sorts of machines for catching and preserving insects; all kinds of nets, trawls, drags and hooks for coral fishing; they have even a curious contrivance of a telescope by which, put into the water, you can see the bottom to a great depth, where it is clear. . . . They have two painters and draughtsmen, several volunteers who have a tolerable notion of Natural History, in short Solander assured me this expedition would cost Mr Banks 10000 pounds." Quoted in Ray Desmond, *Kew: The History of the Royal Botanic Gardens* (London: Harvill Press with the Royal Botanic Gardens, Kew, 1995), 87.

88. For a sense of the distinctiveness of these projects, see Allen J. Grieco, "The Social Politics of Pre-Linnean Botanical Classification," *I Tatti Studies: Essays in the Renaissance* 4 (1991): 131–49.

89. Ralegh also experimented with brewing the famous "Guiana balsam" that, in 1612, failed to revive Prince Henry Stuart, his only significant protector at the Jacobean Court. See John W. Shirley, "The Scientific Experiments of Sir Walter Ralegh, the Wizard Earl, and the Three Magi in the Tower 1603–1617," *Ambix* 4, nos. 1–2 (1949): 52–66; Whitehead, "Introduction," 30–31; Hill, *Intellectual Origins*, 131–32.

90. Hill, *Intellectual Origins*, 16.

91. Ibid., 66–67.

92. Cambridge University did not have a chair of mathematics until 1663. A fine account of the history of Gresham College can be found in Hill, *Intellectual Origins*, 31–60.

93. Eustace M. W. Tillyard, *The Elizabethan World Picture* (London: Chatto & Windus, 1943), 93; Paula Findlen, *Possessing Nature: Museums, Collecting, and Scientific Culture in Early Modern Italy* (Berkeley: University of California Press, 1994); Porter, "The Terraqueous Globe," 289–90. For a sophisticated elaboration of this point, see Lorraine Daston, "The Nature of Nature in Early Modern Europe," *Configurations* 6, no. 2 (1998): 149–72.

94. Among outstanding works that pay attention to the relationship between early modern natural history, overseas discovery, and collecting, see Daston and Park, *Wonders*; Findlen, *Possessing Nature*; Krzysztof Pomian, *Collectors and Curiosities: Paris and Venice, 1500–1800* (Cambridge: Polity, 1990); Oliver Impey and Arthur MacGregor, eds., *The Origins of Museums: The Cabinet of Curiosities in Sixteenth- and Seventeenth-Century Europe* (New York: Clarendon Press, 1985); Pamela H. Smith and Paula Findlen, eds., *Merchants and Marvels: Commerce, Science, and Art in Early Modern Europe* (New York: Routledge, 2001); and Horst Bredekamp, *The Lure of Antiquity and the Cult of the Machine: The Kunstkammer and the Evolution of Nature, Art and Technology*, trans. Allison Brown (Princeton: Markus Wiener, 1995). Scott Atran, *Cognitive Foundations of Natural History: Towards an Understanding of Science* (Cambridge: Cambridge University Press, 1989).

95. Stephen Greenblatt, *Sir Walter Ralegh: The Renaissance Man and His Roles* (New Haven: Yale University Press, 1973), 103.

96. On Dee, see Taylor, *Tudor Geography*; Sherman, *John Dee*; and, for the initial and effective revision, Nicholas H. Clulee, *John Dee's Natural Philosophy: Between Science and Religion* (London: Routledge, 1988).

97. Deborah E. Harkness, *John Dee's Conversations With Angels: Cabala, Alchemy, and the End of Nature* (Cambridge: Cambridge University Press, 1999); Taylor, *Tudor Geography*, 77; Clulee, *John Dee*, 179–80.

98. Agnes M. C. Latham, *Sir Walter Ralegh* (Writers and Their Work, No. 177. London: The British Council, 1964), 20–26. For a sustained attempt at empirical justification of Ralegh's claims, see Whitehead, "Introduction."

99. Campbell, *The Witness*, 219–54.

100. Grafton, *New Worlds*, 37. See Hakluyt's marginal note on Keymis' refusal to describe "a sorte of people more monstrous" than the Ewaipanoma: "They have eminent heads like dogs, and live all the day time in the sea" (Keymis, "Relation," 465).

101. Daston and Park, *Wonders*, 149.

102. For more detailed publishing histories, see Schomburgk, "Introduction," *Discoverie*, lxvii, n. 1, and Whitehead, "Introduction," 10–11.

103. Campbell, *The Witness*, 226.

104. Whitehead, *Discoverie*, 176; Campbell, *The Witness*, 227.

105. Peter Hulme, *Colonial Encounters: Europe and the Native Caribbean, 1492–1797* (London: Routledge, 1992), 94–101, 99–100.

106. Tillyard, *The Elizabethan World Picture*, 93.

107. Whitehead, *Discoverie*, 158.

108. Ibid., 191.

109. Ibid., 160.

110. Ibid., 161.

111. Ibid.

112. Campbell, *The Witness*, 247.

113. On Montaigne and the good savage, see Honour, *New Golden Land*, 66; on Mandeville and paradise, Greenblatt, *Marvelous Possessions*, 28–30.

114. Whitehead, *Discoverie*, 161.

115. David Arnold, *The Problem of Nature: Environment, Culture and European Expansion* (Oxford: Blackwell, 1996). See also Chapter 5 below.

116. Whitehead, *Discoverie*, 162.

117. Ibid.

118. Ibid., 162–63. For a sustained analysis of the "ecstasis" of encounter, see Johannes Fabian, *Out of Our Minds: Reason and Madness in the Exploration of Central Africa* (Berkeley: University of California Press, 2000). Thanks to Annie Gray for making this connection.

119. Edmund Spenser, *The Complete Works in Verse and Prose of Edmund Spenser*, 10 vols., ed. Alexander B. Grosart (London: Hazell, Watson, and Viney, 1882–84), vol. IV, 200.

120. Raymond Williams, *The Country and the City* (Oxford: Oxford University Press, 1973), 22.

121. Carter, *The Road to Botany Bay*, 243.

122. Whitehead, *Discoverie*, 186–87.

123. Ibid., 188, 168.

124. Ibid., 163. This is a complicated moment. Ralegh describes the sacrificial crew member as a "negro." Whitehead points out that no records mention a "negro" on this voyage, and, following V. S. Naipaul, argues that Ralegh fabricated the incident "to validate [his] experience in Orinoco as truly exotic." Ibid., 104; V. S. Naipaul, *A Way in the World* (New York: Knopf, 1994).

125. Whitehead, "Introduction," 4–5; idem, *Discoverie*, 170, 163, n. 70. William M. Denevan, "Aboriginal Drained-field Cultivation in the Americas," *Science* 169 (1970): 647–54; William M. Denevan and Alberta Zucchi, "Ridged Field Excavations in the Central Orinoco Llanos," in *Advances in Andean Archaeology*, ed. D. L. Browman (The Hague: Mouton, 1978), 235–46.

126. Michael J. Eden, *Ecology and Land Management in Amazonia* (London: Belhaven, 1990), 49.

127. João Murça Pires and Ghillean T. Prance, "The Vegetation Types of the Brazilian Amazon," in *Key Environments: Amazonia*, ed. Ghillean T. Prance and Thomas E. Lovejoy (London: Pergamon, 1985), 131–39; Otto Huber, "Significance of Savanna Vegetation in the Amazon Territory of Venezuela," in *Biological Diversification in the Tropics*, ed. Ghillean T. Prance (New York: Columbia University Press, 1982), 221–24.

128. Keymis, "Relation," 475.

129. Nineteenth-century British colonists in Australia similarly used Aboriginal tracks and trails as settler roads. However, Aboriginal land management was widely recognized and discussed by Europeans at the time. See Carter, *The Road to Botany Bay*, 335–45.

130. Philip Amadas and Arthur Barlow, "The First Voyage Made to the Coasts of *America*, with Two Barks, Where in Were Captaines M. *Philip Amadas*, and M. *Arthur Barlowe*, who Discovered Part of the Countrey now called *Virginia*, Anno 1584. Written by One of the Said Captaines, and Sent to Sir *Walter Ralegh*, Knight, At Whose Charge and direction the Said Voyage was Set

Forth," in Richard Hakluyt, *The Principal Navigations, Voiages and Discoveries of the English Nation*, ed. David B. Quinn and Raleigh A. Skelton, vol. 3 (Hakluyt Society Extra Series No. 39. London: Hakluyt Society, 1965 [1589]), 728–33, 731. For reasons that remain a mystery to me, this line was excised from the edition of 1600 and consequently does not appear in the definitive modern MacLehose edition of 1903–5.

131. Michel de Montaigne, *Selected Essays*, trans. Charles Cotton and William C. Hazlitt, ed. Blanchard Bates (New York: Random House, 1949), 80.

132. Whitehead, *Discoverie*, 159.

133. Ibid., 176.

134. Williamson, *English Colonies*, 147.

135. Lorimer, "Contraband Tobacco."

136. Williamson, *English Colonies*, 147–49; Lorimer, *Settlement*, 10–59.

137. John Wilson, "The Relation of Master John Wilson of Wansteed in Essex, One of the Last Ten That Returned into England from Wiapoco in Guiana 1606," in Samuel Purchas, *Hakluytus Posthumus or Purchas His Pilgrimes, Contayning a History of the World in Sea Voyages and Lande Travells by Englishmen and Others*, 20 vols. (Glasgow: James MacLehose, 1905–7), vol. 16, 349–50.

138. Lorimer, *Settlement*, 19–26.

139. João Capistrano de Abreu, *Chapters of Brazil's Colonial History, 1500–1800*, trans. Arthur Brakel (Oxford: Oxford University Press, 1997), 102–3; Lorimer, *Settlement*, 56–57.

140. Antonio Porro, *O povo das águas: Ensaios de etno-história Amazônica* (São Paulo: Vozes, 1996), 45; Hemming, *Red Gold*, 213–37; Lorimer, *Settlement*, 80–102, Dreyfus, "Os empreendimentos coloniais."

141. My thanks to Gary Miles for his clarification that "sive" is the non-exclusive "or." For a detailed, contextualized discussion of the extant English maps of this period, see Sarah Tyacke, "English Charting of the River Amazon c. 1595–c. 1630," *Imago Mundi* 32 (1980): 73–89.

142. "Guiana" persisted in popular geographies into the seventeenth century, past the Treaty of Breda of 1667 at which the colonial boundaries of Suriname and French Guiana were drawn and a lived regionalism made subject to cartographic displacement (see, for example, Aphra Behn's key novella *Oroonoko, or, The Royal Slave*, ed. Lore Metzger [New York: Norton Library, 1973 (1688)]). Only much later, with Humboldt and Bonpland's voyage of 1800 through the Casiquiare Canal — at a moment when the preoccupation with state boundaries had effaced competing spatialities — did Europe discover that the two basins were hydrologically as well as imaginatively conjoined. For cartography, see Isa Adonias, *A cartografia da região Amazônica: Catálogo descritivo (1500–1961)*, 2 vols. (Rio de Janeiro: INPA, 1963); on the regional disciplining that took place around Brazil's border with French Guiana, see Arthur Cézar Ferreira Reis, *Limites e demarcações na Amazônia Brasileira*, 2 vols. (Rio de Janeiro: Imprensa Nacional, 1947); and for the ethnohistorical unit, see John Gillin, "Tribes of the Guianas," in *Handbook of South American Indians*, ed. Julian Steward (Bureau of American Ethnology, bulletin no. 143. Washington,

D.C.: Smithsonian Institution, 1948), vol. 3, 699–860. As David Cleary points out, Guyana, French Guiana, and Suriname are today considered Amazonian countries in geopolitical discourse "even though regional hydrography clearly shows that between them they do not muster a single river which drains into the Amazon" ("Towards an Environmental History of the Amazon: From Prehistory to the Nineteenth Century," *Latin American Research Review* 36, no. 2 [2001]: 65–96, 66).

CHAPTER 5

1. David Cleary, "'Lost Altogether to the Civilized World': Race and the Cabanagem in Northern Brazil, 1750 to 1850," *Comparative Studies in Society and History* 40 (1998): 109–35, 114.
2. Alexander von Humboldt and Aimé Bonpland, *Voyage aux régions équinoxiales du nouveau continent, fait en 1799, 1800, 1801, 1802, 1803 et 1804*, 12 vols. (Paris, 1816–34). Citations below are from the abridged English translation of 1895: *Personal Narrative of Travels to the Equinoctial Regions of the New Continent During the Years 1799–1804*, 3 vols., trans. and ed. Thomasina Ross (London: George Routledge and Sons, 1895). Humboldt's title was not merely formulaic. As he wrote to his brother Wilhelm, the philologist, in July 1799, the excitement of arrival amid such novelty had Bonpland and him "running around like a couple of mad things." Quoted in Douglas Botting, *Humboldt and the Cosmos* (London: Sphere Books, 1973), 76.
3. More than 20,000 people were to die in the six years it took for the Rio government's brutal pacification campaign finally to take hold, and I would not want to gloss the very real and decisive intraregional contradictions of race and class around which the Cabanagem coalesced (see Luís Balkar Pinheiro, "Do Mocambeiro a Cabano: Notas sobre a presença negra na Amazônia na primeira metade do século XIX," *Terra das águas* 1 [1999]: 148–72; Cleary, "'Lost Altogether'"). Nevertheless, it also stands as a rare moment of northern political assertion in a tense history of national ambition and regional recalcitrance. The regional consciousness (in the region-*for*-itself sense) presupposed by the early moments of the Cabanagem may well have been a preoccupation primarily of the liberal elite, but it quickly generalized, and in radicalized form. Although strongly derivative of European republicanism, such politics had a distinctively local cast and are an important reminder that my concern with the dynamics of metropolitan region-making does not substitute for analyses focused more squarely on the development of regional identities and region-making practices among elite and subaltern Amazonian populations. Political and cultural regionalisms in Amazonia were made and remade in oblique and reciprocal relation to metropolitan projects, not simply through them or in response to them. On the centrifugal tendencies of this period, see Sérgio Buarque de Holanda, *História geral da civilização Brasileira*, 3rd ed. (São Paulo: Difusão Européia do Livro, 1970), tomo II, vol. 1, 9–39.
4. Carolus Linnaeus, *Systema naturae*, 2 vols. (New York: Stechert-Hafner, 1964 [1735]). See, *inter alia*, Clarence J. Glacken, *Traces on the Rhodian Shore:*

Nature and Culture in Western Thought from Ancient Times to the End of the Eighteenth Century (Berkeley: University of California Press, 1967); Keith Thomas, *Man and the Natural World: A History of the Modern Sensibility* (New York: Pantheon, 1983); Carolyn Merchant, *The Death of Nature: Women, Ecology, and the Scientific Revolution* (New York: Harper & Row, 1980); Mary Louise Pratt, *Imperial Eyes: Travel Literature and Transculturation* (New York: Routledge, 1992); and Harriet Ritvo, "At the Edge of the Garden: Nature and Domestication in Eighteenth- and Nineteenth-Century Britain," *Huntington Library Quarterly* 55, no. 3 (1992): 363–78.

5. For productive links among zoological taxonomy, race, and empire, see Harriet Ritvo, *The Animal Estate: The English and Other Creatures in the Victorian Age* (Cambridge, Mass.: Harvard University Press, 1987); idem, *The Platypus and the Mermaid and Other Figments of the Classifying Imagination* (Cambridge, Mass.: Harvard University Press, 1998).

6. Bates to Brown, Pará, June 17, 1848, *Zoologist* 8 (1849): 2837.

7. Until very recently, there has been little writing on this topic that has escaped a pervasively heroic mode of presentation. As prominent examples, see Victor Wolfgang von Hagen, *South America Called Them: Explorations of the Great Naturalists; La Condamine, Darwin, Humboldt, Spruce* (New York: Alfred A. Knopf, 1945); John Ure, *Trespassers of the Amazon* (London: Constable, 1990); Anthony Smith, *Explorers of the Amazon* (London: Viking, 1986); Peter Raby, *Bright Paradise: Victorian Scientific Travellers* (London: Pimlico Press, 1996); George Woodcock, *Henry Walter Bates, Naturalist of the Amazons* (London: Faber, 1968); and, although couched in a more natural-scientific register, many of the papers collected in Mark R. D. Seaward and Sylvia M. D. FitzGerald, eds., *Richard Spruce (1817–1893): Botanist and Explorer* (London: Royal Botanic Gardens, Kew, 1996).

8. Henry Walter Bates, "Contributions to an Insect Fauna of the Amazon Valley. Lepidoptera: Heliconidae," *Transactions of the Linnaean Society* 23 (1862): 495–566, 513. Darwin's enthusiastic response to this paper was expressed in his correspondence with Bates. See Robert M. Stecher, "The Darwin–Bates Letters: Correspondence Between Two Nineteenth-Century Travellers and Naturalists," *Annals of Science* 25, no. 1 (1969): 1–47, no. 2 (1969): 95–125. For recent assessments, see Stephen Jay Gould, "Here Goes Nothing," *Natural History* 94, no. 7 (1985): 12–19; and James Mallet and Mathieu Joron, "Evolution of Diversity in Warning Color and Mimicry: Polymorphisms, Shifting Balance, and Speciation," *Annual Review of Ecology and Systematics* 30 (1999): 201–33.

9. Even though professional training in science did not exist at the time in Britain, the scientific establishment was, inevitably, filled by men with Oxbridge credentials. Academic training opened careers in medicine, law, or the clergy. Darwin, for instance, had studied medicine and then switched to theology. Hooker and Huxley were both trained in medicine, Lyell in law. An additional restriction was the imposition of orthodox religious examinations for matriculation or fellowships. Barbara G. Beddall, ed., *Wallace and Bates in the Tropics:*

An Introduction to the Theory of Natural Selection (London: Macmillan, 1969), 6–7.

10. Frederick Bates in M. E. Grant Duff, "Obituary. Henry Walter Bates, F.R.S.," *Proceedings of the Royal Geographical Society* 14 (1892): 245–57, 245–46.

11. Some of their views on Lyell, Chambers, Darwin, and Humboldt can be gauged from letters extracted by Wallace in his autobiography. Humboldt had extended an irresistible challenge: "America offers an ample field for the labours of the naturalist. On no other part of the globe is he called upon more powerfully by nature to raise himself to general ideas on the cause of phenomena and their mutual connection" (Humboldt and Bonpland, *Personal Narrative*, vol. 1, xxi). Thomas R. Malthus, *An Essay on the Principle of Population; or, A View of Its Past and Present Effect on Human Happiness; With an Inquiry into our Prospects Respecting the Future Removal or Mitigation of the Evils which it Occasions*, 2nd ed. (London: J. Johnson, 1803); Charles Lyell, *Principles of Geology; Being an Attempt to Explain the Former Changes of the Earth's Surface, by Reference to Causes now in Operation*, 3 vols. (London: John Murray, 1830–33); Robert Chambers, *Vestiges of the Natural History of Creation* (London: J. Churchill, 1844); Charles Darwin, *Journal of Researches into the Geology and Natural History of the Various Countries Visited by H.M.S. Beagle, Under the Command of Captain FitzRoy, R.N., from 1832 to 1836* (London: H. Colburn, 1839); William H. Edwards, *A Voyage Up the River Amazon, Including a Residence at Pará* (London: John Murray, 1847).

12. See Arnold Thackray, "The Industrial Revolution and the Image of Science," in *Science and Values*, ed. Arnold Thackray and Everett Mendelsohn (New York: Humanities Press, 1974), 5–22.

13. Extensive Bates bibliographies can be found in John Dickenson, "Henry Walter Bates and the Study of Latin America in the Late Nineteenth Century; A Bibliographic Essay," *Revista interamericana de bibliografía* 40 (1990): 570–80; idem, "Henry Walter Bates—The Naturalist of the River Amazons," *Archives of Natural History* 19 (1992): 209–18; and James E. O'Hara, "Henry Walter Bates—His Life and Contributions to Biology," *Archives of Natural History* 22 (1995): 195–219. On the RGS years, see H. P. Moon, *Henry Walter Bates F.R.S. 1825–1892: Explorer, Scientist and Darwinian* (Leicester: Leicestershire Museums, 1976), 54–71.

14. Alfred Russel Wallace, "Obituary: H. W. Bates. The Naturalist of the Amazons," *Nature* 45, no. 1165 (1892): 398–99, 399. According to Grant Allen, "Bates of the Amazons," *Fortnightly Review* 58 (1892): 798–809, Bates apparently viewed this narrowing of focus as an inevitable accommodation to the increasing specialization of biological science. However, Wallace's bitter obituary of Bates suggests—as do his own career and those of Darwin and Huxley—that there were alternative intellectual roads for scientists of Bates' status and talent to walk. As Woodcock, *Henry Walter Bates*, points out, though, the RGS job was certainly not to be sneered at by a man under pressure to support a growing family.

15. E. P. Thompson, *The Making of the English Working Class*, 2nd ed. (Harmondsworth: Penguin, 1968), 781–82.

16. David Elliston Allen, *The Naturalist in Britain: A Social History*, 2nd ed. (Princeton: Princeton University Press, 1994), 145–47. Also, Anne Secord, "Science in the Pub: Artisan Botanists in Early Nineteenth-Century Lancashire," *History of Science* 32, no. 3 (1994): 269–315.

17. Frederick Bates in Grant Duff, "Obituary," 247.

18. See John Seed, "Theologies of Power: Unitarianism and the Social Relations of Religious Discourse, 1800–50," in *Class, Power and Social Structure in British Nineteenth-Century Towns*, ed. Robert J. Morris (Leicester: Leicester University Press, 1986), 107–56; Thackray, "The Industrial Revolution and the Image of Science"; Woodcock, *Henry Walter Bates*, 16; Thompson, *The Making*, 28–58, 781ff.

19. Eric Hobsbawm, *Industry and Empire* (London: Pelican, 1969), 91.

20. Ian Inkster, "Aspects of the History of Science and Science Culture in Britain: 1780–1850 and Beyond," in *Metropolis and Province: Science in British Culture, 1780–1850*, ed. Ian Inkster and Jack Morrell (Philadelphia: University of Pennsylvania Press, 1983), 11–54, 31–33.

21. Thompson, *The Making*, 819.

22. Journal entry, February 11, 1864, cited in Edward Clodd, "Memoir," in Henry Walter Bates, *The Naturalist on the River Amazons: A Record of Adventures, Habits of Animals, Sketches of Brazilian and Indian Life, and Aspects of Nature Under the Equator, During Eleven Years of Travel*, unabridged commemorative ed. (London: John Murray, 1892), lxxiv.

23. According to Kropotkin, Bates responded enthusiastically to the thesis of *Mutual Aid*, exclaiming: "That is true Darwinism. It is a shame to think what they have made of Darwin's ideas." Peter Kropotkin, *Memoirs of a Revolutionist*, ed. James Allen Rogers (London: Century Hutchinson, 1988 [1899]), 300. We should note, also, that at one time contradictions within these circles were less apparent, and that Bates had named one of his sons Herbert Spencer Bates (and another Darwin Bates).

24. Alfred Russel Wallace, *A Narrative of Travels on the Amazon and Rio Negro, with an Account of the Native Tribes, and Observations on the Climate, Geology, and Natural History of the Amazon Valley* (London: Reeve, 1853), 231, 232.

25. Bates, *The Naturalist*, 406.

26. See Susan Thorne, "'The Conversion of Englishmen and the Conversion of the World Inseparable': Missionary Imperialism and the Language of Class in Early Industrial Britain," in *Tensions of Empire: Colonial Cultures in a Colonial World*, ed. Frederick Cooper and Ann Laura Stoler (Berkeley: University of California Press, 1997), 238–62.

27. Bates, *The Naturalist*, 406–7.

28. Clifford Geertz, *Works and Lives: The Anthropologist as Author* (Stanford: Stanford University Press, 1988), 1–24.

29. See Antonello Gerbi, *The Dispute of the New World: The History of a Polemic, 1750–1900*, trans. Jeremy Moyle (Pittsburgh: University of Pittsburgh

Press, 1973); and idem, *Nature in the New World: From Christopher Columbus to Gonzalo Fernández de Ovideo*, trans. Jeremy Moyle (Pittsburgh: University of Pittsburgh Press, 1985), on the persistent belief—expounded most famously by Hegel and Buffon—that the New World is inferior to the Old and, specifically, that American animal life (including human) "suffers from degeneration and arrested development" (Gerbi, *Nature*, 3). On ties between race and climate, see David N. Livingstone, "The Moral Discourse of Climate: Historical Considerations on Race, Place and Virtue," *Journal of Historical Geography* 17, no. 4 (1991): 413–34; idem, *The Geographical Tradition: Episodes in the History of a Contested Enterprise* (Oxford: Blackwell, 1993).

30. Bates, *The Naturalist*, 278. I have suppressed a paragraph break. Racial theorizing in Brazil was indelibly complicated by the hybridity of categories, and Bates was generally disapproving of the existing solution to his race problem. Occasionally, however, he is open to ambivalence: "It is interesting," he notes in Cametá, "to find the mamelucos displaying talent and enterprise, for it shows that degeneracy does not necessarily result from the mixture of white and Indian blood" (ibid., 77). "Degeneracy" continued to be a preoccupation of Brazilian elites as well as foreign visitors. Nancy Leys Stepan, *The Hour of Eugenics: Race, Gender, and Nation in Latin America* (Ithaca: Cornell University Press, 1996) provides an important account of the assemblage of race, sex, science, and nation that was to cohere later in the century. For the race politics that animated the Cabanagem, see Cleary, "Lost Altogether"; and, for sharp commentary that follows race and nation into the era of *mestiçagem*, idem, "Race, Nationalism and Social Theory in Brazil: Rethinking Gilberto Freyre," Economic and Social Research Council Transnational Communities Programme, Working Papers Series: WPTC-99-09, Oxford, 1999.

31. Bates to Frederick Bates, Ega, May 30, 1856, *Zoologist* 15 (1856): 5658–59.

32. Humboldt and Bonpland, *Personal Narrative*, vol. 1, xxi.

33. Henry Walter Bates, "Some Account of the Country of the River Solimoens, or Upper Amazons," *Zoologist* 10 (1852): 3592; Bates to Stevens, Santarém, April 12, 1852, *Zoologist* 11 (1852): 3726; Bates to Brown, Pará, October 19, 1848, *Zoologist* 8 (1849): 2840; Bates to Brown, Pará, June 17, 1848, *Zoologist* 8 (1849): 2837; Bates, "Some Account," 3597.

34. Bates, *Naturalist*, 197–98. I have suppressed a paragraph break.

35. Foucault's observation that natural historical modes of representation are characterized by the "nomination of the visible" is apposite here. See Michel Foucault, *The Order of Things: An Archaeology of the Human Sciences* (New York: Vintage, 1994), 132. In this context we can also think about Bates' mobilization of racial typing. Note, for example, the seamless move from observed, surface traits to correlative innate characteristics in the following passage: "The cheek-bones are not generally prominent; the eyes are black, and seldom oblique like those of the Tatar races of Eastern Asia, which are supposed to have sprung from the same original stock as the American red man. The features exhibit scarcely any mobility of expression; this is connected with the apathetic and undemonstrative character of the race. They never betray, *in fact they do not*

feel keenly, the emotions of joy, grief, wonder, fear, and so forth" (Bates, *Naturalist*, 39–40; emphasis added).

36. Bates, *Naturalist*, 77. It was Wallace who expressed these ideas in their most polemical form and who most clearly theorized the intersection of race and environment. See, particularly, Alfred Russel Wallace, "The Development of Human Races Under the Law of Natural Selection," in *Natural Selection and Tropical Nature: Essays on Descriptive and Theoretical Biology* (London: Macmillan, 1891 [1864]), 167–85. David Spurr, *The Rhetoric of Empire: Colonial Discourse in Journalism, Travel Writing, and Imperial Administration* (Durham: Duke University Press, 1996), 61–75, 156–65, discusses scientifically supported racial hierarchization and the malleability of the European tradition of environmental determinism that "identifies non-European peoples with the forces of nature and then places nature in opposition to culture" (158). Wallace, though, was more rigorous in also allowing for the effects of such a binarism on *European* development. He and Bates are able at times to share in the Rousseauian fantasy of the indolent, sensual native as innocent primitive, but they read it through the prism of scientific selection in which intellectual and moral capacity is judged by the ability of a race to transform nature in the name of progress. Spurr finds explicit and convincing links between evolutionary science and the rather non-specific "colonial discourse" he is concerned to delineate. See George W. Stocking Jr., *Victorian Anthropology* (New York: The Free Press, 1987), 96–102; Nancy Leys Stepan, *Picturing Tropical Nature* (Ithaca: Cornell University Press, 2001), 57–84 (both on Wallace); and Adam Kuper, "On Human Nature: Darwin and the Anthropologists," in *Nature and Society in Historical Context*, ed. Mikulás Teich, Roy Porter, and Bo Gustafsson (Cambridge: Cambridge University Press, 1997), 274–90.

37. Michael Taussig, *Mimesis and Alterity: A Particular History of the Senses* (New York: Routledge, 1993).

38. Bates, *Naturalist*, 280.

39. Bates to Frederick Bates, Ega, May 30, 1856, *Zoologist* 15 (1857): 5658.

40. Bates to Frederick Bates, Ega, September 1, 1855, *Zoologist* 14 (1856): 5018. Bates' relativism was not always *positively* humanist in the terms I am suggesting: it could also be inflected by a class snobbery that ascribed negative characteristics to the uneducated.

41. Controversial, that is, because of the humanity it afforded the child. See Bates, *Naturalist*, 275–77.

42. Bates, *Naturalist*, 75–76. I have suppressed a paragraph break.

43. For a useful discussion of Joseph Banks' efforts to establish a global network of botanical collectors during the late eighteenth century, see David MacKay, "Agents of Empire: The Banksian Collectors and Evaluation of New Lands," in *Visions of Empire: Voyages, Botany, and Representations of Nature*, ed. David Philip Miller and Peter Hanns Reill (Cambridge: Cambridge University Press, 1996), 38–57. Adequate consideration of Joseph Banks' pivotal role in the story of colonial science would require a supplementary essay. Harold B. Carter, *Sir Joseph Banks, 1743–1820* (London: British Museum [Natural His-

tory], 1988), breathed new life into Banks scholarship, rehabilitating a figure that historians of science had tended to overlook largely because he wrote little. Important discussions can be found in Mackay, "A Presiding Genius of Exploration: Banks, Cook and Empire, 1767–1805," in *Captain James Cook and His Times*, ed. Robin Fisher and Hugh Johnston (Seattle: University of Washington Press, 1979), 20–39; idem, *In the Wake of Cook: Exploration, Science, and Empire, 1780–1801* (London: Croom Helm, 1985); and John Gascoigne, *Joseph Banks and the English Enlightenment: Useful Knowledge and Polite Culture* (Cambridge: Cambridge University Press, 1994).

44. Extended fragments of Bates' letters to Stevens as well as of others to his family and friends were published in the *Zoologist* between 1850 and 1857 (vols. 8–15) under the heading "Extracts from the Correspondence of Mr. H. W. Bates Now Forming Entomological Collections in South America," or the more general "Proceedings of Natural-History Collectors in Foreign Countries." Bates also submitted (via Stevens) several detailed accounts of short excursions. On Wallace's relations with Stevens, see Jane Camerini, "Wallace in the Field," in *Science in the Field*, ed. Henrika Kuklick and Robert E. Kohler, *Osiris* 11 (1996): 44–65.

45. Botanist Richard Spruce, for example, in an 1849[?] diary entry, writes: "How often I have regretted that England did not possess the magnificent Amazon valley instead of India! If that booby James, instead of putting Raleigh in prison and finally cutting off his head, had persevered in supplying him with ships, money and men until he had formed a permanent establishment on one of the great American rivers, I have no doubt but that the whole American continent would have been at this moment in the hands of the English race!" (quoted in Smith, *Explorers of the Amazon*, 254–55). Schomburgk's 1848 edition of Ralegh's *Discoverie* was also an inspiration to a generation of North American artists; see Katherine Emma Manthorne, *Tropical Renaissance: North American Artists Exploring Latin America, 1839–1879* (Washington, D.C.: Smithsonian Institution, 1989). The institutional centers I am referring to are the Raleigh Club and the still-flourishing Hakluyt Society.

46. See Bernard S. Cohn, *Colonialism and Its Forms of Knowledge: The British in India* (Princeton: Princeton University Press, 1996), 3–15. Obviously enough, in an early-nineteenth-century Latin American context of newly independent nation-states, much of the administrative technology Cohn describes for India fell outside a formally colonial context. However, there can be little doubt as to the depth of penetration of British capital into the region, the excited interest of British entrepreneurs and scientists once access became available, and the application of modalities of data collection and management that correspond in large measure to those mobilized in other regions of the world and circulated through the same institutional calculating centers. See Richard Graham, *Britain and the Onset of Modernization in Brazil, 1850–1914* (Cambridge: Cambridge University Press, 1968); Buarque de Holanda, *História geral*, 64–99. Also: Henry Lister Maw, *Journal of a Passage from the Pacific to the Atlantic, Crossing the Andes in the Northern Provinces of Peru, and Descending the River Marañon or Amazon* (London: John Murray, 1829); William Smyth

and Frederick Lowe, *Narrative of a Journey from Lima to Para, Across the Andes and Down the Amazon, Undertaken with a View of Ascertaining the Practicability of a Navigable Communication with the Atlantic by the Rivers Pachitea, Ucayali, and Amazon* (London: John Murray, 1836); John Dickenson, "Bates, Wallace and Economic Botany in Mid-19th Century Amazonia," in Seaward and FitzGerald, *Richard Spruce*, 65–80, 66–67.

47. See the important historiographical recuperation of this work by Antonio Porro, *O povo das águas* (São Paulo: Vozes, 1995), especially 181–98; and David Cleary, "Tristes Trope-iques: Science and the Representation of Nature in Amazonia Since the Eighteenth Century," paper presented to the Department of Anthropology, University of Chicago, May 11, 2000. The key primary texts — long ignored by English-language scholars — are Padre João Daniel, *Tesouro descoberto no Rio Amazonas*, Anais da Biblioteca Nacional, vol. 95, 2 vols. (Rio de Janeiro: Biblioteca Nacional, 1975), and Alexandre Rodrigues Ferreira, *Viagem filosófica pelas Capitanias do Grão-Pará, Rio Negro, Mato Grosso e Cuiabá* (Rio de Janeiro: Conselho Federal de Cultura, 1971–74). Cleary accurately describes the latter's expedition, which lasted from 1783 to 1792, as "the beginning of professionalised natural science in the Amazon basin" ("Tristes Trope-iques," 5). Daniel was a Jesuit priest resident in the Amazon from 1741 until the Pombaline expulsion of the order in 1757.

48. Distant in Grant Duff, "Obituary," 251.

49. I am drawing here on Bruno Latour's notion of "cycles of accumulation," *Science in Action: How to Follow Scientists and Engineers through Society* (Cambridge, Mass.: Harvard University Press, 1987), 215–57. Also, Bruce Braun, "Producing Vertical Territory: Geology and Governmentality in Late Victorian Canada," *Ecumene* 7 (2000): 7–46. See C. Barrington Brown and William Lidstone, *Fifteen Thousand Miles on the Amazon and Its Tributaries* (London: Edward Stanford, 1878); William Chandless, "Ascent of the River Purûs, and Notes on the River Aquiry," *Journal of the Royal Geographical Society* 35 (1866): 86–118; idem, "Notes on a Journey up the River Jurúa," *Journal of the Royal Geographical Society* 39 (1869): 296–310; idem, "Notes on the Rivers Maué-Assú, Abacaxis and Canuma," *Journal of the Royal Geographical Society* 40 (1870): 411–32.

50. Prior to leaving London, Bates and Wallace met with William H. Edwards — a recent graduate of the new "natural history" courses at Williams College and author of *A Voyage Up the River Amazon*. Edwards provided valuable letters of introduction to Europeans and North Americans in Belém and the interior. The book had made a powerful impression on the two friends. In his autobiography, Wallace writes that "[it] gave such a pleasing account of the people, their kindness and hospitality to strangers, and especially of the English and American merchants in Pará, while expenses of living and of travelling were both very moderate, that Bates and myself at once agreed that this was the very place to go to" (Alfred Russel Wallace, *My Life: A Record of Events and Opinions*, vol. 1 [New York: Dodd, Mead, 1905], 264).

51. On the often clandestine instrumentalities of British botany in Latin America — the most notorious South American examples of which were the

transfer of rubber and cinchona to Asia—see Richard Drayton, *Nature's Government: Science, Imperial Britain, and the 'Improvement' of the World* (New Haven: Yale University Press, 2000); and Lucile H. Brockway, *Science and Colonial Expansion: The Role of the British Royal Botanic Gardens* (New York: Academic Press, 1979). The professionalization of botany and zoology occurred concurrently with that of other emerging sciences. See, for example, Robert A. Stafford, *Scientist of Empire: Sir Roderick Murchison, Scientific Exploration and Victorian Imperialism* (Cambridge: Cambridge University Press, 1989).

52. Distant in Grant Duff, "Obituary," 251.

53. For example, a cataloguing entry from his field notebooks: "Probably new species of the genus—at any rate I have the descriptions of 5 out of the 7 sp^s known and it does not agree," Bates, [*The Amazon Expeditions*], manuscript in collections of Entomology Library of the British Museum of Natural History, London, 1851–59), vol. 1, 183. Or, Bates to Stevens, April 30, 1851, *Zoologist* 9 (1852): 3232: "My great objection is, that I cannot mention any animal, or insect, or plant, under a name by which it will be recognized."

54. Linnaeus cast himself as Adam in the frontispiece of the 1760 edition of the *Systema naturae*. Interestingly, the trope points to the restricted nature of the field collectors' Eden: they could wander there, but the political economy of natural history prevented them from exercising the critical authority. This hierarchical division of labor between collector and theorist is present even in Bacon's *Novum organum* of 1620 (Francis Bacon, *The New Organon*, ed. Lisa Jardine and Michael Silverthorne [Cambridge: Cambridge University Press, 2000]). See Mary Poovey, *A History of the Modern Fact: Problems of Knowledge in the Sciences of Wealth and Society* (Chicago: University of Chicago Press, 1998), 99.

55. Bates to Darwin, October 17, 1862; in Stecher, "Darwin–Bates Letters," 35 [letter 32]. Contemporary social scientists find themselves making a very similar case in relation to the hermeneutics of fieldwork: see, for example, Geertz, *Works and Lives*.

56. Bates to Darwin, May 2, 1863; in Stecher, "Darwin–Bates Letters," 45 [letter 48]; idem, November 24, 1862(?); in ibid., 38 [letter 35].

57. For an introduction to Humboldt's geography, see the lucid discussion by Malcolm Nicolson, "Alexander von Humboldt and the Geography of Vegetation," in *Romanticism and the Sciences*, ed. Andrew Cunningham and Nicholas Jardine (Cambridge: Cambridge University Press, 1990), 169–85. Susan Cannon, *Science in Culture: The Early Victorian Period* (New York: Neale Watson, 1978), was responsible for the rediscovery and configuration of "Humboldtian science" in the history of science and includes a useful commentary on Darwin. For an important recent reassessment, see Michael Dettelbach, "Humboldtian Science," in *Cultures of Natural History*, ed. Nicholas Jardine, James A. Secord, and Emma C. Spary (Cambridge: Cambridge University Press, 1996), 287–304.

58. Nicolson, "Humboldt," 170.

59. Ibid., 180. For a discussion of the inverse relationship—the impact of voyages of exploration such as Humboldt's on the Romantic poets—see Alan

Frost, "New Geographical Perspectives and the Emergence of the Romantic Imagination," in Fisher and Johnston, *Captain James Cook and His Times*, 5–19.

60. See Cannon, *Science in Culture*, 16–24, for an elegant discussion of Ruskin and Dickens in this context.

61. The key work here remains Foucault, *The Order of Things*. As I argue below, however, there were contradictory imperatives enforcing a reliance on these very specificities, and locality—in a broad sense—was a crucial supplement to the specimen.

62. A point made by Humboldt himself: "The progress of the geography of plants depends in a great measure on that of descriptive botany; and it would be injurious to the advancement of science, to attempt rising to general ideas, whilst neglecting the knowledge of particular facts," Humboldt and Bonpland, *Personal Narrative*, vol. 1, x.

63. On competition between the state and collectors, see Satpal Sangwan, "The Strength of a Scientific Culture: Interpreting Disorder in Colonial Science," *The Indian Economic and Social History Review* 34 (1997): 217–50.

64. For example, the colonial foresters described by K. Sivaramakrishnan, *Modern Forests: Statemaking and Environmental Change in Colonial Eastern India* (Stanford: Stanford Univesity Press, 1999).

65. Hooker to Bates, May 13, 1863, cited by Clodd, "Memoir," lxvi; emphasis in original.

66. Francis Galton, "Reminiscences of Mr. H. W. Bates," *Proceedings of the Royal Geographical Society* 14 (1892): 256. Moon, *Henry Walter Bates*, 63, suggests that Darwin was also a key player in this appointment, for which the only other candidate was Wallace.

67. See William D. Paden, "Arthur O'Shaughnessy in the British Museum; Or, The Case of the Misplaced Fusees and the Reluctant Zoologist," *Victorian Studies* 8 (1964): 7–30.

68. See Jacques Derrida, *Of Grammatology*, trans. Gayatri Chakravorty Spivak (Baltimore: Johns Hopkins University Press, 1976), for a discussion of the double function of the supplement as something that completes at the same time as it betrays inadequacy.

69. Stevens, *Zoologist* 8 (1849): 2663–64.

70. For example, in a note attached to one shipment to Stevens, Bates writes: "You can send me the names &c. of the species; say whether rare, the price of each specimen, and if I should send more." Bates to Stevens, Santarém, January 8, 1852, *Zoologist* 10 (1852): 3449–50.

71. E.g., Ritvo, "At the Edge of the Garden," 371–75.

72. On spatial practice, see Henri Lefebvre, *The Production of Space*, trans. Donald Nicholson-Smith (Oxford: Blackwell, 1991); and Donald Moore, "Subaltern Struggles and the Politics of Place: Remapping Resistance in Zimbabwe's Eastern Highlands," *Cultural Anthropology* 13 (1998): 344–75.

73. Bates to Stevens, Santarém, January 8, 1852, *Zoologist* 10 (1852): 3450; emphasis in original.

74. And by depending on Stevens' efficiency: "I now see by the books sent,

how little is known of Diurnes, &c. Besides the notes sent, I find I can add a great deal of information from memory; thus you see it is important that I should find my collection complete, with all the Nos. attached, when I return," Bates to Stevens, Santarém, June 4, 1852, *Zoologist* 11 (1853): 3728.

75. Cf. Pratt, *Imperial Eyes*, following Foucault.

76. Bates, "Preface," in *Naturalist*, viii. Mary Poovey has tracked the ambiguity of the statistical fact in the mid-nineteenth century: its deracinated facticity and its contradictory status as evidence, necessarily theorized. Bates' practice can be read usefully in relation to this tension. An inductionist with an activist commitment to theory, he relies on the evidentiary fact, yet also finds himself and his Amazons caught up in the deductive logic and representational aesthetics of number. One way to understand this tension more specifically is in light of the long-term struggle between natural history (as aggregation of the deracinated particular) and natural philosophy (as systematic knowledge) — and as an indication of the persistence of the former. Poovey, *The Modern Fact*, especially 9, 315–17, and Chapter 4 above. My thanks to Bill Maurer for encouraging this line of inquiry.

77. Clodd, "Memoir," lxxxiv.

78. Ibid., ix; emphasis in original.

79. Which is not to ignore the domestic vernacular sources. See, for example, Gillian Feeley-Harnik, " 'Pigeons, If You Please': An Avian Perspective on Darwin and *The Origin of Species*," paper presented to the 99th Annual Meeting of the American Anthropological Association, San Francisco, Calif., November 15–19, 2000.

80. Bates to Brown, Pará, June 17, 1848, *Zoologist* 8 (1849): 2838.

81. Homi Bhabha has argued that we should look for the effects of colonial power in "the production of hybridization rather than the noisy command of colonialist authority or the silent repression of native traditions." Homi K. Bhabha, *The Location of Culture* (New York: Routledge, 1994), 112; emphasis removed. Hybridization, a process of subjectivation and appropriation within a complexly overdetermined field of power, does not imply the joining of stable, unitary, or equivalent objects, nor the absence of domination. In this sense, Bhabha's insight undergirds my understanding of Bates' representational practice as a site in which non-Europeans participated in the metropolitan regionalization of the Amazon and intervened in the emergent logics of metropolitan science. However, this is not to privilege hybridity in the process of encounter, nor to displace attention from mimesis and the work of a clutch of simultaneous traveling practices, including dialogue, performance, parody, and articulation.

82. Perhaps it is this preoccupying difficulty which forces Bates to confront Amazonian politics and devote extensive passages to discussions of the Cabanagem and other issues of regional history. However, we should also acknowledge his self-consciously wide-ranging intellectual interests. Bates' encompassing strategy of investigation could be contrasted with the narrowly commercial and dehistoricizing narratives of his contemporaries traveling in Argentina. Kristine L. Jones, "Nineteenth Century British Travel Accounts of Argentina," *Ethnohistory* 33 (1986): 195–211.

83. Bates to Stevens, Aveyros, August 1, 1852, *Zoologist* 11 (1853): 3801–2.

84. Bates to Stevens, Santarém, October 18, 1852, *Zoologist* 11 (1853): 3841.

85. E.g., Alfred Russel Wallace, *Travels*, 237: "The temptation of being left alone for nearly a day, with a garafão of caxaça, was too strong for them. Of course I passed all over in silence, appearing to be perfectly ignorant of what had taken place, as, had I done otherwise, they would probably both have left me, after having received the greater part of their payment beforehand, and I should have been unable to proceed on my voyage."

86. Bates to Stevens, June 3, 1851, *Zoologist* 10 (1852): 3321; emphasis in original.

87. Or so Spruce tells it. He certainly does seem to have provoked considerable hostility, including that of an elderly and rather Shakespearean nurse who — he reports — would shout at her near-to-death patient, that is, at Spruce: "Die, you English dog, that we might have a merry watch-night with your dollars!" Richard Spruce, *Notes of a Botanist on the Amazon and Andes. Being Records of Travel on the Amazon and Its Tributaries, the Trombetas, Rio Negro, Uaupés, Casiquiari, Pacimoni, Huallaga, and Pastasa; as also to the Cataract of the Orinoco, along the Eastern Side of the Andes of Peru and Ecuador, and the Shore of the Pacific, During the Years 1849–1864*, ed. A. R. Wallace (London: Macmillan, 1908), vol. 1, 487–93, 465.

88. Thanks to David Cleary for clarifying this point. In the period from the disintegration of the Directorate in 1798 until the 1830s, conditions for populations of the Amazon interior were notable for their autarkic lack of regulation. See Cleary, " 'Lost Altogether' "; Pinheiro, "Do Mocambeiro a Cabano"; Pasquale di Paolo, *Cabanagem: A revolução popular da Amazônia* (Belém: CEJUP 1986).

89. It "looks very like compulsion," writes Edwards of forced labor, "but it is little more than jury duty" (*A Voyage Up the River Amazon*, 81).

90. For one example, see Bates to Stevens, Pará, April 30, 1851, *Zoologist* 9 (1851): 3230. For the inhibiting effects of a *quilombo* of escaped slaves, see Bates, *Naturalist*, 202. Also David Sweet, "Native Resistance in Eighteenth Century Amazonia: The 'Abominable Muras' in War and Peace," *Radical History Review* 53 (1992): 49–80.

91. It is only fair to draw attention to Bates' (rather pedagogical) humor, which could no doubt enliven an excursion. On one occasion, for example, he lined up himself and his companions holding hands, and, by repeatedly touching an electric eel with the tip of his hunting-knife, sent shocks passing through the five of them — to the general amusement of all (Bates, *Naturalist*, 324).

92. Bates to Stevens, Pará, June 3, 1851, *Zoologist* 9 (1852): 3321.

93. And raise issues that are now very familiar to anthropologists. See, as foundational, James Clifford's question: "Who is actually the author of fieldnotes?" James Clifford, *The Predicament of Culture: Twentieth-Century Ethnography, Literature, and Art* (Cambridge, Mass.: Harvard University Press, 1988), 45.

94. See, in addition, Richard H. Grove, *Green Imperialism: Colonial Expansion, Tropical Island Edens and the Origin of Environmentalism, 1600–1860* (Cambridge: Cambridge University Press, 1995), 73–90. Lisbet Koerner describes connections between Linnaeus and "indigenous knowledge" that were even more direct — forged by the taxonomist's own philosophical commitment to a hybrid "new science" to be formed through his "cross-cultural mediation between high and folk/tribal knowledges." These arose through Linnaeus' own traveling science as well as via his emphatic instructions to his students to prioritize the study of local practices ("Carl Linnaeus in His Time and Place," in Jardine et al., *Cultures of Natural History*, 145–62, 152, 158–59).

95. Albert Howard, *Crop-Production in India* (Oxford: Oxford University Press, 1924); Paolo Palladino and Michael Worboys, "Science and Imperialism," *Isis* 84 (1993): 91–102.

96. Pratt *Imperial Eyes*, 143; Alexander von Humboldt and Aimé Bonpland, *Essai sur la géographie des plantes; Accompagné d'un tableau physique des régions équinoxiales* (London: Society for the Bibliography of Natural History, 1959 [1807]); John V. Murra, *The Economic Organization of the Inca State* (Greenwich, Conn.: JAI Press, 1979).

97. See, for example, his near-astonished reaction on being told a chrysalis would soon become a butterfly (Bates, *Naturalist*, 371–72).

98. As were Wallace and Spruce. As a paradigmatic example of the convergence of systematics and utilitarian ethnology in economic botany, see Alfred Russel Wallace, *Palm-Trees of the Amazon and Their Uses* (London: John van Voorst, 1853).

99. Bate to Stevens, Santarém, March 27, 1854, *Zoologist* 13 (1855): 4550.

100. As Bates' comment below indicates, northern Europeans were most familiar with two Amazonian collecting expeditions at the time, both of which were large-scale, state-sponsored affairs. The first was that of the Bavarians Spix and Martius, who collected in the Amazon in 1819–20 and who had spent ten days at Ega in November–December 1819. The other, just preceding the visit of Bates and Wallace in 1848, was that of Comte Francis de Castelnau, a correspondent of the Muséum National d'Histoire Naturelle in Paris. Castelnau traveled through Brazil and the Andes in 1843–47, before being appointed French consul to Brazil in 1848.

101. See Grove, *Green Imperialism*, 88–90. This is by no means to imply a homogeneity of Amazonian ideas of nature and local knowledges.

102. Bates, *Naturalist*, 288. I have suppressed a paragraph break.

103. Nicholas Thomas, *Colonialism's Culture: Anthropology, Travel and Government* (Princeton: Princeton University Press, 1994), 7.

104. Bates, *Naturalist*, 331.

105. See the comments by Clements Markham and Francis Galton in Grant Duff, "Obituary," 255, 256. In this methodological vein, Bates contributed to the Society's important "Hints to Travellers" series with "Hints on the Collection of Objects of Natural History," *Proceedings of the Royal Geographical Society* 16 (1871): 67–78.

106. Stafford, *Scientist of Empire*, 22.

107. John Dickenson, "The Naturalist on the River Amazons and a Wider World: Reflections on the Centenary of Henry Walter Bates," *The Geographical Journal* 158 (1992): 207–14.

108. All preceding quotations in this section are from Allen, "Bates of the Amazons," 802–3.

109. Bates, [*The Amazon Expeditions*], vol. 1, 192.

CHAPTER 6

1. There are several compelling accounts of the chaotic occupation of this area and its extreme effects. Particularly gripping — possibly because it is written with a journalistic eye from the midst of the storm — is Sue Branford and Oriel Glock's *The Last Frontier: Fighting Over Land in the Amazon* (London: Zed Books, 1985). See also Padre Ricardo Resende, *Posseiros e padres do Araguaia: A justiça do lobo* (Pétropolis, RJ: Vozes, 1986). Thanks to Michael Reynolds for this reference. Adrian Cowell's film *Killing for Land* (1990) graphically documents some of the events of the late 1980s in the general locale in which this chapter is set.

2. On the events at Serra Pelada to which I refer here, see Susanna B. Hecht and Alexander Cockburn, *The Fate of the Forest: Developers, Destroyers and Defenders of the Amazon* (London: Penguin, 1989); and Marianne Schmink and Charles H. Wood, *Contested Frontiers in Amazonia* (New York: Columbia University Press, 1992). For a broader and more textured analysis of the general trajectory from "informal" to state-captured mining, see David Cleary, *Anatomy of the Amazon Gold Rush* (London: Macmillan, 1990).

3. Michael J. Reynolds, "When Good Intentions Go Up in Smoke: Environmental Politics in the Brazilian Amazon," paper presented at the Annual Meetings of the Society for the Study of Social Problems, Chicago, August 5, 2000.

4. Indeed, such camps are popularly known as *fofocas*, a colloquial Brazilian Portuguese word for gossip.

5. For an excellent summary of the enduring debates over Turner's "The Significance of the Frontier in American History" (1893), see David Arnold, *The Problem of Nature: Environment, Culture and European Expansion* (Oxford: Blackwell, 1996), 98–118.

6. Although it almost goes without saying that in Brazilian popular and elite discourse the Amazon frontier is interpellated in a radically different set of narratives — most potently, in a history of nation-building and national security that celebrates the adventures of the pioneering *bandeirantes* (lit. flag-bearers). Juscelino Kubitschek, the president who initiated post–World War II opening of the region, made the connection explicitly in a 1960 election slogan: "Juscelino: O grande bandeirante do século" ("Juscelino: the century's great bandeirante").

7. For thoroughgoing critiques of the deployment of the frontier metaphor in relation to Amazonia, see Stephen G. Bunker, *Underdeveloping the Amazon: Extraction, Unequal Exchange and the Failure of the Modern State* (Chicago:

University of Chicago Press, 1988); and David Cleary, "After the Frontier: Problems with Political Economy in the Modern Brazilian Amazon," *Journal of Latin American Studies* 25, no. 2 (1993): 331–50.

8. On the characteristic structure of the environmental declension narrative, see William Cronon, "A Place for Stories: Nature, History and Narrative," *Journal of American History*, 78, no. 4 (1992): 1347–76.

9. For an excellent mapping of the divergent lineages in Amazonianist anthropology, see Eduardo Viveiros de Castro, "Images of Nature and Society in Amazonian Ethnology," *Annual Review of Anthropology* 25 (1996): 179–200.

10. For a useful discussion, see J. Peter Brosius, "Endangered Forest, Endangered People: Environmentalist Representations of Indigenous Knowledge," *Human Ecology* 25, no. 1 (1997): 47–69. Also interesting for its attention to a moment of contradiction is Patricia Pierce Erikson's "A-Whaling We Will Go: Encounters of Knowledge and Memory at the Makah Cultural Research Center," *Cultural Anthropology* 14, no. 4 (1999): 556–83.

11. Which have, quite logically, become the objects of critique. On indigenous strategic essentialisms, see, for example, Beth A. Conklin, "Body Paint, Feathers, and VCRs: Aesthetics and Authenticity in Amazonian Activism," *American Ethnologist* 24, no. 4 (1997): 711–37.

12. Here I am wondering how Benedict Anderson's suggestive idea might look from a traveling metropolitan standpoint. See *The Specter of Comparisons: Nationalism, Southeast Asia and the World* (London: Verso, 1998).

13. The phrase in this context is from Daniel H. Janzen, "The Future of Tropical Ecology," *Annual Review of Ecology and Systematics* 17 (1986): 305–24. Many thanks to Jimmy Grogan for this citation.

14. See Antonio Gramsci, *Selections from the Prison Notebooks*, ed. and trans. Quintin Hoare and Geoffrey Nowell-Smith (New York: International Publishers, 1971); Judith Butler, *Bodies That Matter: On the Discursive Limits of "Sex"* (New York: Routledge, 1993); Saba Mahmood, "Feminist Theory, Embodiment, and the Docile Agent: Some Reflections on the Egyptian Islamic Revival," *Cultural Anthropology* 16, no. 2 (2001): 202–36; and, for a critical intervention on the question of "experience," Joan W. Scott, "The Evidence of Experience," *Critical Inquiry* 17, no. 4 (1991): 773–97. And note also Steven Gregory's critical supplement: "What makes the hegemonic process effective is less its 'taken for grantedness' . . . than its capacity as an ensemble of political relations and practices to command the social processes through which meanings are publicly articulated, communicated, and invested with contextual authority and social legitimacy" (*Black Corona: Race and the Politics of Place in an Urban Community* [Princeton: Princeton University Press, 1998], 246).

15. For the prior studies, see R. E. Gullison, S. N. Panfil, J. J. Strouse, and S. P. Hubbell, "Ecology and Management of Mahogany (*Swietenia macrophylla* King) in the Chimanes Forest, Beni, Bolivia," *Botanical Journal of the Linnean Society* 122 (1996): 9–34; and Laura K. Snook, *Stand Dynamics of Mahogany (Swietenia macrophylla King) and Associated Species After Fire and Hurricane in the Tropical Forests of the Yucatán Peninsula* (unpbd. doctoral dissertation, Yale School of Forestry, 1993).

16. On this, see the pioneering work of Susanna Hecht, particularly "Deforestation in the Amazon Basin: Magnitude, Dynamics, and Soil Resource Effects," *Studies in Third World Societies* 13 (1981): 61–110; and idem, "Environment, Development and Politics: Capital Accumulation and the Livestock Sector in Eastern Amazonia," *World Development* 13, no. 6 (1985): 663–84.

17. Useful accounts here are Marianne Schmink and Charles H. Wood, eds., *Frontier Expansion in Amazonia* (Gainesville: University of Florida Press, 1984); idem, *Contested Frontiers*; John O. Browder, "Lumber Production and Economic Development in the Brazilian Amazon: Regional Trends and a Case Study," *Journal of World Forest Resource Management* 4 (1989): 1–19; and Hecht, "Environment, Development, and Politics."

18. There are also a number of regional plantation projects, of varying sophistication, commitment, and success.

19. On the Kayapó's complicated relationship to timber money, see Reynolds, "Good Intentions"; and Terence Turner, "Indigenous Rights, Indigenous Cultures and Environmental Conservation: Convergence or Divergence? The Case of the Brazilian Kayapó," in *Earth, Air, Fire, Water: Humanistic Studies of the Environment*, ed. Jill Ker Conway, Kenneth Keniston, and Leo Marx (Amherst: University of Massachusetts Press, 1999), 145–69. Also of importance for its attention to social history is William H. Fisher, "Native Amazonians and the Making of the Amazon Wilderness: From Discourse of Riches and Sloth to Underdevelopment," in *Creating the Countryside: The Politics of Rural and Environmental Discourse*, ed. E. Melanie DuPuis and Peter Vandergeest (Philadelphia: Temple University Press, 1996), 166–203.

20. Information on the MST can be found at either their Portuguese- or English-language Web sites (www.mst.org.br and www.mstbrazil.org). Powerful commentary on the situation of the landless in this country with the most skewed land distribution in the world is provided by the photographer Sebastião Salgado in *Terra: Struggle of the Landless* (London: Phaidon, 1997).

21. Or, at least, under the cover of this explanation. Media reporting of the MST's campaign of land invasions has highlighted the cutting and selling of timber on occupied land. This figure is from Adalberto Veríssimo, Paulo Barreto, Ricardo Tarifa, and Christopher Uhl, "Extraction of a High-Value Resource in Amazonia: The Case of Mahogany," *Forest Ecology and Management* 72, no. 1 (1995): 39–60.

22. For a historical account of this methodology, see Henry E. Lowood, "The Calculating Forester: Quantification, Cameral Science, and the Emergence of Scientific Forestry Management in Germany," in *The Quantifying Spirit in the Eighteenth Century*, ed. Tore Frangsmyr, J. L. Heilbron, and Robin E. Rider (Berkeley: University of California Press, 1991), 315–42.

23. And the extraction of large trees removes a disproportionate amount of germplasm from the forest — as larger/mature individuals produce an exponentially greater number of flowers and seeds.

24. On this, see Alfredo Kingo Oyama Homma, *Extrativismo vegetal na Amazônia: Limites e oportunidades* (Brasília: EMBRAPA-SPI, 1993); idem, "The Dynamics of Extraction in Amazonia: A Historical Perspective," in *Non-*

Timber Products from Tropical Forests: Evaluation of a Conservation and Development Strategy, ed. Daniel C. Nepstad and Stephen Schwartzman (New York: New York Botanical Garden, 1992), 23–32. For the paradigmatic tale of Amazonian rubber, Warren Dean, *Brazil and the Struggle for Rubber: A Study in Environmental History* (Cambridge: Cambridge University Press, 1987).

25. See, for example, Ana Cristina Barros and Adalberto Veríssimo, eds., *A expansão da atividade madeireira na Amazônia: Impactos e perspectivas para o desenvolvimento do setor florestal no Pará* (Belém: IMAZON, 1996); Veríssimo et al., "Extraction of a High-Value Resource"; Ana Cristina Barros and Christopher Uhl, "Logging Along the Amazon River and Estuary: Patterns, Problems and Potential," *Forest Ecology and Management* 77, nos. 1–3 (1995): 87–105; Jennifer Johns, Paulo Barreto, and Christopher Uhl, "Logging Damage During Planned and Unplanned Logging Operations in the Eastern Amazon," *Forest Ecology and Management* 89, nos. 1–3 (1996): 59–77; Paulo Barreto, Paulo Amaral, Edson Vidal, and Christopher Uhl, "Costs and Benefits of Forest Management for Timber Production in Eastern Amazonia," *Forest Ecology and Management* 108, nos. 1–2 (1998): 9–26; Adalberto Veríssimo, Carlos Souza Jr., Steve Stone, and Christopher Uhl, "Zoning of Timber Extraction in the Brazilian Amazon," *Conservation Biology* 12, no. 1 (1998): 18–36.

26. Yrjö Haila, "Measuring Nature: Quantitative Data in Field Biology," in *The Right Tools for the Job: At Work in Twentieth-Century Life Sciences*, ed. Adele E. Clark and Joan H. Fujimura (Princeton: Princeton University Press, 1992), 233–53, 240.

27. Appendix II is the second-most restrictive of the three available listings under the Convention. For detailed descriptions, visit www.cites.org/CITES/eng/index.shtm. Background to the failed 1994 proposal to list bigleaf mahogany under CITES—a repeat of the campaign of 1991, and an attempt to prevent the extraction of the species from unmanaged forests—is discussed by John Bonner, "Battle for Brazilian Mahogany," *New Scientist* 144, no. 1948 (1994): 16–17. For more recent developments, see "Compromise on Mahogany Reached," *Los Angeles Times*, June 21, 1997, A9.

28. On the scientist as modest witness, see Stephen Shapin and Simon Shaffer, *Leviathan and the Air-Pump: Hobbes, Boyle, and the Experimental Life* (Princeton: Princeton University Press, 1989); also Donna J. Haraway, *Modest_Witness@Second_Millennium. FemaleMan© Meets OncoMouse™: Feminism and Technoscience* (New York: Routledge, 1997).

29. An argument made by technically minded observers for some time. In addition to the work of the IMAZON researchers cited above, see John R. Palmer, "Forestry in Brazil—Amazonia," *Commonwealth Forestry Review* 56, no. 2 (1977): 115–30, an early critical analysis of regional practices by a British forester.

30. Veríssimo et al., "Extraction of a High-Value Natural Resource." A useful discussion of the early phases of this process can be found in Bunker, *Underdeveloping the Amazon*, 91–93.

31. The range of bigleaf mahogany is huge: a continuous swathe from Tampico, Mexico, as far south as Pará and west across the entire Amazon basin

to Bolivia. See F. Bruce Lamb, *Mahogany of Tropical America: Its Ecology and Management* (Ann Arbor: University of Michigan Press, 1966), figs. 5 and 6, 53–54.

32. See, as a well-known example, P. A. Sanchez, D. E. Bandy, J. H. Villachica, and J. J. Nicholaides, "Amazon Basin Soils: Management for Continuous Crop Production," *Science* 216 (1982): 821–27, and the self-critical revision in P. A. Sanchez and J. R. Benites, "Low-Input Cropping for Acid Soils of the Humid Tropics," *Science* 238 (1987): 1521–27.

33. For an early attempt to map such circulations, see Ann Hawkins, "Contested Ground: International Environmentalisms and Global Climate Change," in *The State and Social Power in Global Environmental Politics*, ed. Ronnie D. Lipschutz and Ken Conca (New York: Columbia University Press, 1993), 221–45. As an overview of competing positions on the mahogany debate and a sense of the official U.S. position, see Ariel E. Lugo, "Point-Counterpoints on the Conservation of Big-Leaf Mahogany" (Washington, D.C.: U.S. Department of Agriculture, Forest Service, 1999).

34. Allan Carman, *Monarch of Mahogany Visits Schmieg-Hungate & Kotzian, Being The History, Travels and Eventual Life of Perhaps the Oldest Living and Grandest King of the Wood of Woods* (New York: Scribner, 190?).

35. Ibid., 10.

36. The brief account that follows is drawn from the following sources: William Farquhar Payson, ed., *Mahogany Antique and Modern: A Study of Its History and Use in the Decorative Arts* (New York: E. P. Dutton, 1926); B. J. Rendle, *Commerical Mahoganies and Allied Timbers*, Forest Products Research Bulletin No. 18. Department of Scientific and Industrial Research (London: HMSO, 1938); Samuel J. Record and Robert W. Hess, *Timbers of the New World* (New Haven: Yale University Press, 1943); George N. Lamb, *The Mahogany Book*, 5th ed. (Chicago: Mahogany Association Inc., 1946); Committee on Interstate and Foreign Commerce, *Decorative Wood Labeling and Use of the Term "Mahogany,"* Hearings Before a Subcommittee of the Committee on Interstate and Foreign Commerce (House of Representatives. Washington, D.C.: U.S. Government Printing Office, 1964); Lamb, *Mahogany of Tropical America*; Jan de Vos, *Oro verde: La conquista de la Selva Lacandona por los madereros tabasqueños* (México, D.F.: Fondo de Cultura Económica, 1988).

37. Of these, particular energy was directed against the so-called Philippine mahogany (*Shorea* spp., a Dipterocarp).

38. The initial binomial was bestowed by Linnaeus: *Cedrela mahogani*. *Cedrela*, denoting the cedars, was soon revised. But *mahogani* stuck. Apparently a corruption of the Yoruba for African mahogany that was used by slaves to denote the Jamaican relative, "mahogany" became the specific name for the Cuban *Swietenia* and the common name denoting *Swietenia* and its allies.

39. A particular irony here is that in this period tropical nature is conventionally figured as sensuously feminine. Of course, in this case, the king's masculinity — given the inevitability of his conquest — only serves to heighten the achievement of his master. On "tropicality," see Arnold, *The Problem of Nature;* Nancy Leys Stepan, *Picturing Tropical Nature* (Ithaca: Cornell University

Press, 2001); and the papers collected in the special issue of the *Singapore Journal of Tropical Geography* 21, no. 1 (2000).

40. Payson, *Mahogany Antique and Modern*, 3.

41. Ibid., 5.

42. Notable contributions to what is now a large and expanding literature on the historical intersections of conservation and colonialism include David Anderson and Richard Grove, eds., *Conservation in Africa: People, Policies, and Practice* (Cambridge: Cambridge University Press, 1987); John M. MacKenzie, ed., *Imperialism and the Natural World* (New York: Manchester University Press, 1990); Richard H. Grove, *Green Imperialism: Colonial Expansion, Tropical Island Edens and the Origin of Environmentalism, 1600–1860* (Cambridge: Cambridge University Press, 1995); Tom Griffiths and Libby Robin, eds., *Ecology and Empire: Environmental History of Settler Societies* (Seattle: University of Washington Press, 1997); William Beinart and Peter Coates, *Environment and History: The Taming of Nature in the USA and South Africa* (London: Routledge, 1995); Roderick P. Neumann, *Imposing Wilderness: Struggles over Livelihood and Nature Preservation in Africa* (Berkeley: University of California Press, 1998); and K. Sivaramakrishnan, *Modern Forests: Statemaking and Environmental Change in Colonial Eastern India* (Stanford: Stanford University Press, 1999).

43. Geoffrey C. Bowker and Susan Leigh Star, *Sorting Things Out: Classification and Its Consequences* (Cambridge, Mass.: MIT Press, 1999), 31–32.

44. Although Bruno Latour has more confidence in commensurability and less interest in constitutive "context" than I am proposing here, his "The 'Pédofil' of Boa Vista: A Photo-Philosophical Montage," *Common Knowledge* 4, no. 1 (1995): 144–87, offers a brilliantly precise account of the logic and practice of translation in a similar setting.

45. That is, where the individual tree stands in the cycle of leaf shedding, flush, and subsequent flowering.

46. For varied and insightful histories, see Sharon Kingsland, *Modeling Nature: Episodes in the History of Population Ecology*, 2nd ed. (Chicago: University of Chicago Press, 1995); Joel B. Hagen, *An Entangled Bank: The Origins of Ecosystem Ecology* (New Brunswick: Rutgers University Press, 1992); Robert P. McIntosh, *The Background of Ecology: Concept and Theory* (Cambridge: Cambridge University Press, 1985).

47. On this, see S. H. Hurlbert's hugely influential "Pseudoreplication and the Design of Ecological Field Experiments," *Ecological Monographs* 54, no. 2 (1984): 187–212, and, *inter alia*, the creative response from W. W. Hargrove and J. Pickering, "Pseudoreplication: A *sine qua non* for Regional Ecology," *Landscape Ecology* 6, no. 4 (1992): 251–58. In drawing attention to the sloppiness of much of what passed for replication in ecology, Hurlbert's essential point was that the discipline had to tighten up its statistics if it wanted to be taken seriously. The effects of this argument can be seen in the current emphasis on experimental design and data handling. Thanks to Greg Balza for drawing my attention to this literature.

48. At certain times, replicates can effectively enable the elimination of experimental noise. But, at others, they merely multiply the possibilities.

49. On the emergence and proliferating significance of quantitative precision as an agent of state-making and in social and scientific life, see the essays collected in M. Norton Wise, ed., *The Values of Precision* (Princeton: Princeton University Press, 1995).

50. At the time, one Brazilian *real* was more or less equivalent to U.S. $1. The payment applies to all trees found and marked. All marked trees are cut and the explorador is paid whether these yield useful timber or not. Productive and mature seed trees that are, for example, split and of little commercial value, are therefore also marked and felled.

51. On the history of Conceição, see Schmink and Wood, *Contested Frontiers*, 141–63.

52. The classic statement here is Bruno Latour's *Science in Action: How to Follow Scientists and Engineers through Society* (Cambridge, Mass.: Harvard University Press, 1987).

53. The convergence may be less harmonic than the social science commentators would wish (see n. 57 below). Non-equilibrium ecology continues to emphasize a holistic approach to an albeit heterogeneous ecosystem; it retains a commitment to experimental method, and, as I describe here, it is still highly parsimonious in its criteria of relevance.

54. See David M. Smith, *The Practice of Silviculture: Applied Forest Ecology*, 9th ed. (New York: Wiley, 1997); Harold K. Steen, *David M. Smith and the History of Silviculture: An Interview* (Durham: Forest History Society, 1990). The key statement of the Hubble Brook research is F. Herbert Bormann and Gene E. Likens, *Pattern and Process in a Forested Ecosystem: Disturbance, Development and the Steady State* (New York: Springer-Verlag, 1979), a book that closes with a discussion of its implications for landscape management.

55. For a comprehensive temperate study that uses non-equilibrium and processual models of forest patchiness as a basis for the development of detailed silvicultural practice, see Chadwick D. Oliver and Bruce C. Larson, *Forest Stand Dynamics* (New York: McGraw-Hill, 1990).

56. See, for example, Karl Zimmerer, "Human Geography and the New Ecology: The Prospect and Promise of Integration," *Annals of the Association of American Geographers* 84, no. 1 (1994): 108–25, Ian Scoones, "New Ecology and the Social Sciences: What Prospects for a Fruitful Engagement?" *Annual Review of Anthropology* 28 (1999): 479–507, and, as an earlier alert, Donald Worster's *Nature's Economy: A History of Ecological Ideas*, 2nd ed. (Cambridge: Cambridge University Press, 1985). A less sanguine appraisal is offered by William M. Adams, "Rationalization and Conservation: Ecology and the Management of Nature in the United Kingdom," *Transactions of the Institute of British Geographers* N.S. 22 (1997): 277–91. For a succinct summary of the non-equilibrium model, see Peggy L. Fiedler, Peter S. White, and Robert A. Leidy, "The Paradigm Shift in Ecology and Its Implications for Conservation," in *The Ecological Basis of Conservation: Heterogeneity, Ecosystems, and Biodiversity*, ed. S.T.A. Pickett, R. S. Ostfield, M. Shachak, and G. E. Likens (New

York: Chapman and Hall, 1997), 83–92. Influential and interesting as a detailed polemic for non-equilibrium theory is *Discordant Harmonies: A New Ecology for the Twenty-First Century* (New York: Clarendon Press, 1990) by Daniel Botkin, an ecological modeler who worked at Hubble Brook (and, for a sharp critique of Botkin's bifurcated history, see Hagen, *An Entangled Bank*, 1–14, 189–97).

57. See Bormann and Likens, *Pattern and Process*, 164–212. On Odum, see Peter J. Taylor, "Technocratic Optimism, H. T. Odum, and the Partial Transformation of Ecological Metaphor After World War II," *Journal of the History of Biology* 21, no. 2 (1988): 213–44; and Peter J. Taylor and Ann S. Blum, "Ecosystems as Circuits: Diagrams and the Limits of Physical Analogies," *Biology and Philosophy* 6 (1991): 275–94. Zimmerer and Scoones are absolutely correct to lament the baleful impact of systems ecology on environmental anthropology and its cognate fields. Odum's influence persisted unacknowledged in the social sciences long after it was unpopular in ecology, to the extent that it provided theoretical architecture for the foundational texts of political ecology. See, for example, Piers Blaikie, *The Political Economy of Soil Degradation in Developing Countries* (London: Longman, 1987).

58. For useful discussions of Hubbard Brook, see McIntosh, *Background of Ecology*, 204–8; and Hagen, *An Entangled Bank*, 181–88.

59. This is well expressed by Laura Cameron in the context of non-equilibrium theories. See her "Histories of Disturbance," *Radical History Review* 74 (1999): 4–24.

60. As an increasingly familiar variant, work in Amazonian restoration ecology (in which the landscape is by definition an already vitiated site of human activity) offers the region as a corrupted space of nature. See, as an early and important example, Daniel Nepstad, Christopher Uhl, and E.A.S. Serrão, "Recuperation of a Degraded Amazonian Landscape: Forest Recovery and Agricultural Restoration," *Ambio* 20, no. 6 (1991): 248–55.

61. See Oliver T. Coomes, "Blackwater Rivers, Adaptation, and Environmental Heterogeneity in Amazonia," *American Anthropologist* 94, no. 3 (1992): 698–701; and João Murça Pires and Ghillean T. Prance, "The Vegetation Types of the Brazilian Amazon," in *Key Environments: Amazonia*, ed. Ghillean T. Prance and Thomas E. Lovejoy (London: Pergamon, 1985), 126–31.

62. Viveiros de Castro, "Images of Nature and Society." And see Chapter 2 above.

63. On governmentality, see Michel Foucault, "Governmentality," in *The Foucault Effect: Studies in Governmentality*, ed. Graham Burchill, Colin Gordon, and Peter Miller (London: Harvester Wheatsheaf, 1991), 87–104; Nikolas Rose, *Powers of Freedom: Reframing Political Thought* (Cambridge: Cambridge University Press, 1999). On environmental regulation, see Adams, "Rationalization and Conservation," and, for notions of "environmentality," Timothy Luke, *Ecocritique: Contesting the Politics of Nature, Economy, and Culture* (Minneapolis: University of Minnesota Press, 1997); Akhil Gupta, *Postcolonial Developments: Agriculture in the Making of Modern India* (Durham: Duke Univer-

sity Press, 1998); and Arun Agrawal, "State Formation in Community Spaces? Decentralization of Control Over Forests in the Kumaon Himalaya, India," *Journal of Asian Studies* 60, no. 1 (2001): 9–40.

64. For an example of this type of work, see Daniel C. Nepstad, Claudio R. de Carvalho, Eric A. Davidson, Peter H. Jipp, Paul A. Lefebvre, Gustavo H. Negreiros, Elson D. da Silva, Thomas A. Stone, Susan E. Trumbore, and Simone Vieira, "The Role of Deep Roots in the Hydrological and Carbon Cycles of Amazonian Forests and Pastures," *Nature* 372, no. 6507 (1994): 666–69. For the definitive statement of the closed rain forest system, see Paul W. Richards, *The Tropical Rain Forest: An Ecological Study* (Cambridge: Cambridge University Press, 1952), who describes a "closed cycle of plant nutrients" (219). Richards places much of the emphasis in his highly influential account on the thick root mat characteristic of nutrient-poor ecosystems. The concentration of tree roots near or on top of the soil surface confers a competitive advantage in relation to decomposer litter organisms, as well as increasing surface area to volume ratio between root surface and soil. In its most developed form the Amazonian root mat is composed of a complex of interlaced humus and feeder roots forming a surface layer up to 45 centimeters thick and consisting of over 35 percent of total root biomass. See Carl F. Jordan, ed., *An Amazonian Rain Forest: The Structure and Function of a Nutrient Stressed Ecosystem and the Impact of Slash-and-Burn Agriculture* (Paris: UNESCO, 1989); Carl F. Jordan and Gladys Escalante, "Root Productivity in an Amazonian Rain Forest," *Ecology* 61, no. 1 (1980): 14–18.

65. This is, as Sharon Simpson and Donald Moore have pointed out to me, an inversion of the liberal dreams of both the grassroots development worker and the applied anthropologist, dreams in which the outside expert withers away after conferring the technical skills that create local autonomy.

66. Johann Wolfgang von Goethe, *Italian Journey [1786–1788]*, trans. W. H. Auden and Elizabeth Mayer (London: Penguin 1970), 112.

67. For a potent recent example of these types of narratives at play, see Mike Davis' *Ecology of Fear: Los Angeles and the Imagination of Disaster* (New York: Metropolitan Books, 1998). For a broader discussion of the apocalyptic in contemporary culture, see Kathleen Stewart and Susan Harding, "Bad Endings: American Apocalypsis," *Annual Review of Anthropology* 28 (1999): 285–310.

68. The principal exception is the late Alwyn H. Gentry's *A Field Guide to the Families and Genera of Woody Plants of Northwest South America (Colombia, Ecuador, Peru), With Supplementary Notes on Herbaceous Taxa* (Washington, D.C.: Conservation International, 1993).

CHAPTER 7

1. Gaston Bachelard, *Water and Dreams: An Essay on the Imagination of Matter*, trans. Edith R. Farrell (Dallas: The Pegasus Foundation, 1983), 8; ellipses present in original.

2. Ibid., 6; emphasis in original.

3. Ibid., 15; emphasis in original.

4. Ludwig Wittgenstein, *Philosophical Investigations*, trans. Gertrude E. M. Anscombe (New York: Prentice Hall, 1999), §129.

5. Bruno Latour, *We Have Never Been Modern*, trans. Catherine Porter (Cambridge, Mass.: Harvard University Press, 1993), 117. See the incisive discussion by Marilyn Strathern, "Afterword: Relocations," in *Shifting Contexts: Transformations in Anthropological Knowledge* (New York: Routledge, 1995), 177–85.

6. See Hugh Raffles, "Local Theory: Nature and the Making of an Amazonian Place," *Cultural Anthropology* 14, no. 3 (1999): 323–60; Liisa H. Malkki, *Purity and Exile: Violence, Memory, and National Cosmology Among Hutu Refugees in Tanzania* (Chicago: University of Chicago Press, 1995); and James Ferguson and Akhil Gupta, eds., *Culture, Power, Place: Explorations in Critical Anthropology* (Durham: Duke University Press, 1997).

7. All kinds of earthly paradises and El Dorados fall into this category: see Alberto Manguel and Gianni Guadalupi's seductive *Dictionary of Imaginary Places* (New York: Harcourt Brace, 1999).

8. On the plurality of the "now," see Dipesh Chakrabarty, *Provincializing Europe: Postcolonial Thought and Historical Difference* (Princeton: Princeton University Press, 2000), 243. And see note 67, Chapter 4 above.

9. Joan Scott, "The Evidence of Experience," *Critical Inquiry* 17, no. 4 (Summer 1991), 773–97; Raymond Williams, *Marxism and Literature* (Oxford: Oxford University Press, 1977), 128–35.

10. Alphonso Lingis, *Abuses* (Berkeley: University of California Press, 1994); idem, *Dangerous Emotions* (Berkeley: University of California Press, 2000). For a useful discussion of Lingis' earlier work in relation to body politics, see Elizabeth Grosz, *Volatile Bodies: Towards a Corporeal Feminism* (Bloomington: University of Indiana Press, 1994).

11. Doreen Massey, *Space, Place, and Gender* (Minneapolis: University of Minnesota Press, 1994), 120. Also, idem, "Spatial Disruptions," in *The Eight Technologies of Otherness*, ed. Sue Golding (London: Routledge, 1997), 217–25, and idem, "Travelling Thoughts," in *Without Guarantees: In Honour of Stuart Hall*, ed. Paul Gilroy, Lawrence Grossberg, and Angela McRobbie (London: Verso, 2000), 225–32. For important work in geography and anthropology that pays close attention to the co-production of difference and place, see Michael Keith and Steve Pile, eds., *Place and the Politics of Identity* (London: Routledge, 1993); Steve Pile and Michael Keith, eds., *Geographies of Resistance* (London: Routledge, 1997); Steven Feld and Keith H. Basso, eds., *Senses of Place* (Santa Fe: SAR Press, 1996); James Ferguson and Akhil Gupta, eds., *Culture, Power, Place: Explorations in Critical Anthropology* (Durham: Duke University Press, 1997); Steven Gregory, *Black Corona: Race and the Politics of Place in an Urban Community* (Princeton: Princeton University Press, 1998); Jacqueline Nassy Brown, "Black Liverpool, Black America and the Gendering of Diasporic Space," *Cultural Anthropology* 13, no. 3 (1998): 291–325; idem, "Enslaving History: Narratives on Local Whiteness in a Black Atlantic Port," *American Ethnologist* 27, no. 2 (2000): 340–70; and Donald Moore, "Sub-

altern Struggles and the Politics of Place: Remapping Resistance in Zimbabwe's Eastern Highlands," *Cultural Anthropology* 13, no. 3 (1998): 344–81.

12. I am introducing "effective geographies" in order to draw out the spatial dimension of Foucault's work on Nietzsche's *wirkliche Historie* (effective history). Foucault's intervention helps oppose the tendency to identify space with atemporal homogeneity and radically problematizes the question of (temporal and spatial) scale. At the same time, through his attention to the affective and the embodied, Foucault points us toward historical and spatial understandings of intimacy. For Foucault, as for Nietzsche, "history becomes 'effective' to the degree that it introduces discontinuity into our very being—as it divides our emotions, dramatizes our instincts, multiplies our body and sets it against itself. 'Effective' history deprives the self of the reassuring stability of life and nature, and it will not permit itself to be transported by a voiceless obstinacy toward a millennial ending. It will uproot its traditional foundations and relentlessly disrupt its pretended continuity." He continues: "The world we know is not this ultimately simple configuration where events are reduced to accentuate their essential traits, their final meaning, or their initial and final value. On the contrary, it is a profusion of entangled events. . . . We want historians to confirm our belief that the present rests upon profound intentions and immutable necessities. But the true historical sense confirms our existence among countless lost events, without a landmark or a point of reference." Michel Foucault, "Nietzsche, Genealogy, History," in *Language, Counter-Memory, Practice: Selected Essays and Interviews*, ed. Donald F. Bouchard, trans. Donald F. Bouchard and Sherry Simon (Ithaca: Cornell University Press, 1980), 139–64, 154–55. My thanks to Donald Moore for securing this connection.

13. Gilles Deleuze and Félix Guattari, *A Thousand Plateaus: Capitalism and Schizophrenia*, trans. Brian Massumi (Minneapolis: University of Minnesota Press, 1987), 25.

14. Foucault, "Nietzsche, Genealogy, History," 155.

15. See Latour, *We Have Never Been Modern*.

16. Getúlio Vargas inaugurated the "March to the West" in 1940 and launched the SPVEA in 1953 during a later term. In 1966, SPVEA was reinvented as the *Superintendência de Desenvolvimento da Amazônia* (SUDAM) in an effort to cleanse the integration process of the most obvious signs of corruption. Although Vargas committed suicide before the highways had carved their way into the Amazon, as Browder and Godfrey put it, "he articulated a nationalist ideology that subsequently propelled the forces of popular and corporate expansion into the northern frontier" (John D. Browder and Brian J. Godfrey, *Rainforest Cities: Urbanization, Development, and Globalization of the Brazilian Amazon* [New York: Columbia University Press, 1997], 64). Also, Seth Garfield, *Indigenous Struggle at the Heart of Brazil: State Policy, Frontier Expansion, and the Xavante Indians, 1937–1988* (Durham: Duke University Press, 2001). For a useful account of SPVEA and SUDAM, see Martin T. Katzman, "Paradoxes of Amazonian Development in a 'Resource-Starved' World," *Journal of Developing Areas* 10 (1975): 445–60; also, Marianne Schmink and Charles H. Wood, *Contested Frontiers in Amazonia* (New York: Columbia Uni-

versity Press, 1992), especially 46–94; and Sue Branford and Oriel Glock, *The Last Frontier: Fighting Over Land in the Amazon* (London: Zed Books, 1985).

17. Small-scale operations still characterize the Amazonian industry. See the useful analysis of the structure of the logging trade in the eastern Amazon by Christopher Uhl, Paulo Barreto, Adalberto Veríssimo, Ana Cristina Barros, Paulo Amaral, Edson Vidal, and Carlos Souza Jr., "Uma abordagem integrada de pesquisa sobre o manejo dos recursos naturais na Amazônia," in *A expansão da atividade madeireira na Amazônia: Impactos e perspectivas para o desenvolvimento do setor florestal no Pará*, ed. Ana Cristina Barros and Adalberto Veríssimo (Belém: IMAZON, 1996), 143–64.

18. Mikhail Bakhtin, *The Dialogic Imagination*, ed. Michael Holquist, trans. Caryl Emerson and Michael Holquist (Austin: University of Texas Press, 1981), 84. On oral history as narrative, see the work of Alessandro Portelli, particularly, *The Death of Luigi Trastulli and Other Stories: Form and Meaning in Oral History* (New York: SUNY Press, 1991).

19. Bakhtin, *The Dialogic Imagination*, 250. I have suppressed a paragraph break.

20. Ibid.

21. An honorific. On the implications of *Coronelismo* in Brazil, see Victor Nunes Leal, *Coronelismo, enxada e voto: O município e o regime representativo no Brasil*, 2nd ed. (São Paulo: Alfa-Omega, 1975). For a contemporary Amazonian account that is highly germane to the current discussion, see Jacky Picard, "O clientalismo nas colônias agrícolas do sudeste do Pará," in *Amazônia e a crise da modernização*, org. Maria Angela D'Inção and Isolda Maciel da Silveira (Belém: Museu Paraense Emílio Goeldi, 1994), 279–99.

22. See Harrison Pollak, Marli Mattos, and Christopher Uhl, "A Profile of Palm Heart Extraction in the Amazon Estuary," *Human Ecology* 23, no. 3 (1995): 357–85, and Jeremy Strudwick, "Commercial Management for Palm Heart from *Euterpe oleracea* Mart. Palmae in the Amazon Estuary," in *New Directions in the Study of Plants and People: Research Contributions from the Institute of Economic Botany*, ed. Ghillean T. Prance and Michael J. Balick (New York: New York Botanical Garden, 1990), 241–48.

23. Given its regional importance, there has been remarkably little written on aviamento directly. For descriptions—from which one can get a sense of a regional diversity of political-economic form—see, particularly Stephen Hugh-Jones' exceptional "Yesterday's Luxuries, Tomorrow's Necessities: Business and Barter in Northwest Amazonia," in *Barter, Exchange and Value: An Anthropological Approach*, ed. Caroline Humphrey and Stephen Hugh-Jones (Cambridge: Cambridge University Press, 1992), 42–74; David Gibbs McGrath, *The Paraense Traders: Small-scale, Long-distance Trade in the Brazilian Amazon* (unpbd. Ph.D. dissertation, Department of Geography, University of Wisconsin. Ann Arbor: UMI Microfilms, 1989); Arthur Cézar Ferreira Reis, *O seringal e o seringueiro*, documentário da vida rural, no. 5 (Rio de Janeiro: Ministério da Agricultura, 1953); Roberto Santos, *História econômica da Amazônia (1800–1920)* (São Paulo: T. A. Queiroz, 1980); Morio Ono and Nobue Miyazaki, "O aviamento na Amazônia: Estudo sócio-econômico sôbre a produção de juta,"

262 NOTES TO CHAPTER SEVEN

Sociologia 20, nos. 3–4 (1958): 366–96, 530–63; João Pacheco de Oliveira Filho, "O caboclo e o brabo: Notas sobre duas modalidades de força-de-trabalho na expansão da fronteira Amazônica no século XIX," *Encontros com a civilização Brasileira* 11 (1979): 101–40; Barbara Weinstein, *The Amazon Rubber Boom, 1850–1920* (Stanford: Stanford University Press, 1983); Michael Taussig, *Shamanism, Colonialism, and the Wild Man: A Study in Terror and Healing* (Chicago: University of Chicago Press, 1987); and Blanca Muratorio, *The Life and Times of Grandfather Alonso: Culture and History in the Upper Amazon* (New Brunswick: Rutgers University Press, 1991).

24. The "modernizing" narrative is central to arguments made by Marianne Schmink and Charles H. Wood, for example. See their *Contested Frontiers in Amazonia*, in which they describe the waning of aviamento in southern Pará in the face of the rapid expansion of wage labor. While a useful corrective to general accounts of Amazonian economic organization that over-emphasize historical continuity, their case should not be generalized too readily. Heterogeneity of political-economic relations is a more reliable definitive character of regional realities. For a useful discussion of this point, see David Cleary, "After the Frontier: Problems With Political Economy in the Modern Brazilian Amazon," *Journal of Latin American Studies* 25, no. 2 (1993): 331–49.

25. This argument is made by several members of the Viega family and by McGrath, *The Paraense Traders*, 95–105. For an illuminating discussion of gift and commodity exchange, see Charles Piot, *Remotely Global: Village Modernity in West Africa* (Durham: Duke University Press, 1999), 62–66.

26. Despite the endurance of the boom in açaí and the success of the fruit in penetrating potentially huge markets in the south of Brazil, there are at this point relatively few published social science studies. Most focus on management of the plant as a resource and technical possibilities for increasing income from its marketing. Among currently available discussions, see Mário Hiraoka, "Land Use Changes in the Amazon Estuary," *Global Environmental Change* 5, no. 4 (1995): 323–36; Anthony B. Anderson and Mário Augusto G. Jardim, "Costs and Benefits of Floodplain Forest Management by Rural Inhabitants in the Amazon Estuary: A Case Study of Açaí Palm Production," in *Fragile Lands of Latin America: The Search for Sustainable Uses*, ed. John O. Browder (Boulder: Westview, 1989), 114–29; Stephen Nugent, "The Limitations of 'Environmental Management': Forest Utilization in the Lower Amazon," in *Environment and Development in Latin America: The Politics of Sustainability*, ed. David Goodman and Michael Redclift (Manchester: Manchester University Press, 1991), 141–54; N. Miret Muñiz, R. Vamos, M. Hiraoka, F. Montagnini, and R. O. Mendelsohn, "The Economic Value of Managing *Açaí* Palm (*Euterpe oleracea* Mart.) in the Floodplains of the Amazon Estuary, Pará, Brazil," *Forest Ecology and Management* 87, nos. 1–3 (1996): 163–73; Batista B. G. Calzavara, "As possibilidades do açaizeiro no estuário Amazônico," *Boletim da Faculdade de Ciências Agrárias do Pará* 5, 1972. NAEA/UFPa, MPEG, EMBRAPA, and SECTAM organized the important and timely conference *Seminário açaí: Possibilidades e limites em processos de desenvolvimento sustentável no estuário Amazônico* held at the Museu Goeldi, Belém, in October 1996.

27. See Christine Padoch and Miguel Pinedo-Vásquez, "Farming Above the Flood in the Várzea of Amapá," in *Várzea: Diversity, Development, and Conservation of Amazonia's Whitewater Floodplains*, ed. Christine Padoch, J. Márcio Ayres, Miguel Pinedo-Vásquez, and Anthony Henderson (New York: New York Botanical Garden, 1999), 345–54; Hiraoka, "Land Use Changes in the Amazon Estuary"; Mário Augusto G. Jardim and John S. Rumbold, "Effects of Adubation and Thinning on *Açaí* Palm (*Euterpe oleracea* Mart.): Fruit Yield from a Natural Population," *Boletim do Museu Paraense Emílio Goeldi*, Série Botânica 10, no. 2 (1994): 283–93.

28. There is, inevitably, an entire series of class-based codes associated with açaí: when and how often it is eaten, at what point in the meal, with what utensils, with which additives. This becomes complex when we consider the questions of subject formation tied up in this urban appropriation of a distinctive aspect of rural life.

29. For accounts of Amazonian urbanization, see Bertha K. Becker, "Fronteira e urbanização repensadas," *Revista Brasileira de Geografia* 47, nos. 3–4 (1985): 357–71; Browder and Godfrey, *Rainforest Cities*.

30. A sack is measured out of four *latas*—rectangular, catering-size margarine tins.

31. In Macapá, the *zona franca* free-trade zone is popularly known as the *zona fraca*, the weak/pathetic zone, because of its failure to emulate the (temporary) success of the Manaus model. In Belém, the pull of the zona franca is replaced by the push of extreme land conflict and violence in the south of Pará and Maranhão.

32. For a fascinating discussion of the urban marketing of a very similar forest product that considers additional questions—for example, the fruit's significance in ancillary trades such as icecream manufacture—see Christine Padoch's "Aguaje (*Mauritia flexuosa* L.f.) in the economy of Iquitos, Peru," in *The Palm—Tree of Life: Biology, Utilization and Conservation*, ed. Michael J. Balick (New York: New York Botanical Garden, 1988), 214–24.

33. In times of shortfall in either Belém or Macapá, well-capitalized buyers like Jacaré make short-term profits by shipping fruit across the bay. They make a deal for a boat, pay someone to travel, pack the açaí in ice, and earn as much as R $120 per sack for the first few loads of açaí to arrive—although prices drop quickly as others enter the market.

34. For valuable discussions of the politics of "talk," see Linda Alcoff and Laura Gray, "Survivor Discourse: Transgression or Recuperation?" *Signs: Journal of Women in Culture and Society* 18, no. 2 (1993): 260–90; and Kathleen Stewart, *A Space on the Side of the Road: Cultural Poetics in an "Other" America* (Princeton: Princeton University Press, 1996).

35. Other, less economically important, produce is generally sold at a 30 percent markup (e.g., limes, *graviola*, oranges, bananas, *maxixe*, and watermelon).

BIBLIOGRAPHY

Adams, William M. "Rationalization and Conservation: Ecology and the Management of Nature in the United Kingdom." *Transactions of the Institute of British Geographers* N.S. 22 (1997): 277–91.

Adonias, Isa. *A cartografia da região Amazônica: Catálogo descritivo (1500–1961)*. 2 vols. Rio de Janeiro: INPA, 1963.

Adorno, Rolena. "The Discursive Encounter of Spain and America: The Authority of Eyewitness Testimony in the Writing of History." *The William and Mary Quarterly* 49, no. 2 (1992): 210–28.

Agrawal, Arun. "Dismantling the Divide Between Indigenous and Scientific Knowledge." *Development and Change* 26, no. 3 (1995): 413–39.

———. "State Formation in Community Spaces? Decentralization of Control Over Forests in the Kumaon Himalaya, India." *Journal of Asian Studies* 60, no. 1 (2001): 9–40.

Alcoff, Linda, and Laura Gray. "Survivor Discourse: Transgression or Recuperation?" *Signs: Journal of Women in Culture and Society* 18, no. 2 (1993): 260–90.

Allen, David Elliston. *The Naturalist in Britain: A Social History*. 2nd ed. Princeton: Princeton University Press, 1994.

Allen, Grant. "Bates of the Amazons." *Fortnightly Review* 58 (1892): 798–809.

Amadas, Philip, and Arthur Barlow. "The First Voyage Made to the Coasts of *America*, with Two Barks, Where in Were Captaines M. *Philip Amadas*, and M. *Arthur Barlowe*, who Discovered Part of the Countrey now called Virginia, Anno 1584. Written by One of the Said Captaines, and Sent to Sir *Walter Ralegh*, Knight, At Whose Charge and direction the Said Voyage was Set Forth." In Richard Hakluyt, *The Principal Navigations, Voiages and Discoveries of the English Nation*, ed. David B. Quinn and Raleigh A. Skelton, vol. 3, 728–33. Hakluyt Society Extra Series No. 39. London: Hakluyt Society, 1965 [1589].

Anderson, Anthony B., and Mário Augusto G. Jardim, "Costs and Benefits of Floodplain Forest Management by Rural Inhabitants in the Amazon Estuary: A Case Study of Açaí Palm Production." In *Fragile Lands of Latin America: The Search for Sustainable Uses*, ed. John O. Browder, 114–29. Boulder: Westview, 1989.

Anderson, Anthony B., Igor Mousasticoshvily Jr., and Domingo S. Macedo. "Logging of *Virola surinamensis* in the Amazon Floodplain: Impacts and Alternatives." In *Várzea: Diversity, Development, and Conservation of Amazonia's Whitewater Floodplains*, ed. Christine Padoch, J. Márcio Ayres, Miguel Pinedo-Vásquez, and Anthony Henderson, 119–34. New York: New York Botanical Garden, 1999.

Anderson, Benedict. *The Specter of Comparisons: Nationalism, Southeast Asia and the World*. London: Verso, 1998.

Anderson, David, and Richard Grove, eds. *Conservation in Africa: People, Policies, and Practice.* Cambridge: Cambridge University Press, 1987.

Anderson, S. D. "Engenhos na várzea: uma analise do declinio de uma sistema de produção tradicional na Amazônia." In *Amazônia: A fronteira agrícola 20 anos depois,* org. Philippe Lenna and Adelia Engracia de Oliveira, 114–26. Belém: Museu Paraense Emílio Goeldi/ORSTOM, 1991.

Andrews, Kenneth R. *Elizabethan Privateering: English Privateering During the Spanish War 1585–1603.* Cambridge: Cambridge University Press, 1964.

———. *Trade, Plunder and Settlement: Maritime Enterprise and the Genesis of the British Empire, 1480–1630.* Cambridge: Cambridge University Press, 1984.

Andrews, Kenneth R., ed. *English Privateering Voyages to the West Indies, 1588–1595.* Hakluyt Society Second Series No. 111. London: Hakluyt Society, 1956.

Appadurai, Arjun. "Introduction: Place and Voice in Anthropological Theory." *Cultural Anthropology* 3, no. 1 (1988): 16–20.

Arnold, David. *The Problem of Nature: Environment, Culture and European Expansion.* Oxford: Blackwell, 1996.

Arvello-Jiménez, Nelly, and Horacio Biord. "The Impact of Conquest on Contemporary Indigenous Peoples of the Guiana Shield: The System of Orinoco Regional Interdependence." In *Amazonian Indians: From Prehistory to the Present,* ed. Anna C. Roosevelt, 55–78. Tucson: University of Arizona Press, 1994.

Atran, Scott. *Cognitive Foundations of Natural History: Towards an Understanding of Science.* Cambridge: Cambridge University Press, 1989.

Aubrey, John. *Brief Lives.* Ed. Oliver Lawson Dick. London: Secker & Warburg, 1949.

Bachelard, Gaston. *Water and Dreams: An Essay on the Imagination of Matter.* Trans. Edith R. Farrell. Dallas: The Pegasus Foundation, 1983.

Bacon, Francis. *The New Organon.* Ed. Lisa Jardine and Michael Silverthorne. Cambridge: Cambridge University Press, 2000 [1620].

Bakhtin, Mikhail. *The Dialogic Imagination.* Ed. Michael Holquist, trans. Caryl Emerson and Michael Holquist. Austin: University of Texas Press, 1981.

Balée, William. "Indigenous Adaptation to Amazonian Palm Forests." *Principes* 32, no. 2 (1988): 47–54.

———. "The Culture of Amazonian Forests." In *Resource Management in Amazonia: Indigenous and Folk Strategies,* ed. Darrell A. Posey and William Balée, 1–21. New York: New York Botanical Garden, 1989.

———. "Indigenous Transformation of Amazonian Forests: An Example from Maranhão, Brazil." *L'Homme* 33, nos. 2–4 (1993): 231–54.

———. *Footprints of the Forest: Ka'apor Ethnobotany—The Historical Ecology of Plant Utilization by an Amazonian People.* New York: Columbia University Press, 1994.

———. "Introduction." In *Advances in Historical Ecology,* ed. William Balée, 1–10. New York: Columbia University Press, 1998.

Balée, William, ed. *Advances in Historical Ecology.* New York: Columbia University Press, 1998.

Baptista de Moura, Ignácio. *De Belém a São João do Araguaia, Vale do Rio Tocantins.* Belém: Fundação Cultural do Pará Tancredo Neves/Secretaria de Estado da Cultura, 1989.

Barnes, Trevor J., and James S. Duncan, eds. *Writing Worlds: Discourse, Text and Metaphor in the Representation of Landscape.* London: Routledge, 1992.

Barreto, Paulo, Paulo Amaral, Edson Vidal, and Christopher Uhl. "Costs and Benefits of Forest Management for Timber Production in Eastern Amazonia." *Forest Ecology and Management* 108, nos. 1–2 (1998): 9–26.

Barros, Ana Cristina, and Christopher Uhl. "Logging Along the Amazon River and Estuary: Patterns, Problems and Potential." *Forest Ecology and Management* 77, nos. 1–3 (1995): 87–105.

Barros, Ana Cristina, and Adalberto Veríssimo, eds. *A expansão da atividade madeireira na Amazônia: Impactos e perspectivas para o desenvolvimento do setor florestal no Pará.* Belém: IMAZON, 1996.

Bassin, Mark. "Friedrich Ratzel's Travels in the United States: A Study in the Genesis of His Anthropogeography." In *History of Geography Newsletter* 4 (1984): 11–22.

———. "Imperialism and the Nation-State in Friedrich Ratzel's Political Geography." In *Progress in Human Geography* 11, no. 3 (1987): 473–95.

Basso, Keith. *Wisdom Sits in Places: Landscape and Language Among the Western Apache.* Albuquerque: University of New Mexico Press, 1996.

Bates, Henry Walter, "Extracts from the Correspondence of Mr. H. W. Bates, Now Forming Entomological Collections in South America." *Zoologist* 8: 2663–68; 2715–19; 2789–93; 2836–41; 2940–44; 2965–66; 9: 3142–44; 3230–32; 10: 3321–24; 3352–53; 3449–50; 14: 5016–19; 15: 5651–62; 1849–56.

———. [The Amazon Expeditions] Manuscript. Vol. 1. In manuscript collections of the Entomology Library of the British Museum of Natural History, London, 1851–59.

———. "Some Account of the Country of the River Solimoens, or Upper Amazons." *Zoologist* 10 (1852): 3592.

———. "Proceedings of Natural-History Collectors in Foreign Countries." *Zoologist* 11: 3726–29; 3801–04; 3841–43; 3897–3900; 4111–17; 12: 4200–4202; 4318–21; 4397–98; 13: 4549–53; 14: 5012–16; 15: 5557–59; 1852–56.

———. "Contributions to an Insect Fauna of the Amazon Valley. Lepidoptera: Heliconidae." *Transactions of the Linnaean Society* 23 (1862): 495–566.

———. "Hints on the Collection of Objects of Natural History." *Proceedings of the Royal Geographical Society* 16 (1871): 67–78.

———. *The Naturalist on the River Amazons: A Record of Adventures, Habits of Animals, Sketches of Brazilian and Indian Life, and Aspects of Nature under the Equator, during Eleven Years of Travel.* Unabridged commemorative ed. London: John Murray, 1892 [1863].

Becker, Bertha K. "Fronteira e urbanização repensadas." *Revista Brasileira de Geografia* 47, nos. 3–4 (1985): 357–71.

Beddall, Barbara G., ed. *Wallace and Bates in the Tropics: An Introduction to the Theory of Natural Selection.* London: Macmillan, 1969.

Behn, Aphra. *Oroonoko, or, The Royal Slave.* Ed. Lore Metzger. New York: Norton Library, 1973 [1688].

Beinart, William, and Peter Coates. *Environment and History: The Taming of Nature in the USA and South Africa.* London: Routledge, 1995.

Benchimol, Samuel. *Manáos-do-Amazonas: Memória empresarial.* Vol. 1. Manaus: Universidade do Amazonas, 1994.

Benjamin, Walter. *Illuminations.* Ed. Hannah Arendt, trans. Harry Zohn. New York: Fontana, 1973.

———. *One-Way Street, and Other Writings.* Trans. Edmund Jephcott and Kingsley Shorter. London: New Left Books, 1979.

———. *The Arcades Project.* Trans. Howard Eiland and Kevin McLaughlin. Cambridge, Mass.: Belknap Press of Harvard University Press, 1999.

Berger, John. *Ways of Seeing.* London: Penguin/BBC, 1972.

Berger, John, and Jean Mohr. *A Fortunate Man: The Story of a Country Doctor.* London: Writers and Readers Cooperative Press, 1969.

Berlant, Laurent. "Intimacy: A Special Issue." *Critical Inquiry* 24, no. 2 (Winter 1998): 281–88.

Bhabha, Homi K. *The Location of Culture.* New York: Routledge, 1994.

Blaikie, Piers. *The Political Economy of Soil Degradation in Developing Countries.* London: Longman, 1987.

Bonner, John. "Battle for Brazilian Mahogany." *New Scientist* 144, no. 1948 (1994): 16–17.

Boomert, Arie. "Gifts of the Amazons: Greenstone Pendants and Beads as Items of Ceremonial Exchange." *Antropológica* 67 (1987): 33–54.

Bormann, F. Herbert, and Gene E. Likens. *Pattern and Process in a Forested Ecosystem: Disturbance, Development and the Steady State.* New York: Springer-Verlag, 1979.

Botkin, Daniel. *Discordant Harmonies: A New Ecology for the Twenty-First Century.* New York: Clarendon Press, 1990.

Botting, Douglas. *Humboldt and the Cosmos.* London: Sphere Books, 1973.

Bourdieu, Pierre. *Outline of a Theory of Practice.* Trans. Richard Nice. Cambridge: Cambridge University Press, 1977.

———. *Language and Symbolic Power.* Ed. John B. Thompson, trans. Gino Raymond and Matthew Adamson. Cambridge: Polity, 1991.

Bowker, Geoffrey C., and Susan Leigh Star. *Sorting Things Out: Classification and Its Consequences.* Cambridge, Mass.: MIT Press, 1999.

Branford, Sue, and Oriel Glock. *The Last Frontier: Fighting for Land in the Amazon.* London: Zed Press, 1985.

Braun, Bruce. "Producing Vertical Territory: Geology and Governmentality in Late Victorian Canada." *Ecumene* 7 (2000): 7–46.

Braun, Bruce, and Noel Castree, eds. *Remaking Reality: Nature at the Millennium.* New York: Routledge, 1998.

Bredekamp, Horst. *The Lure of Antiquity and the Cult of the Machine: The Kunstkammer and the Evolution of Nature, Art and Technology.* Trans. Allison Brown. Princeton: Markus Wiener, 1995.

Breymann, Walter Norman. *The Opening of the Amazon 1540–1640.* Unpbd. Ph.D. dissertation, Department of History, University of Illinois, 1950.

Brockway, Lucile H. *Science and Colonial Expansion: The Role of the British Royal Botanic Gardens.* New York: Academic Press, 1979.

Brosius, J. Peter. "Endangered Forest, Endangered People: Environmentalist Representations of Indigenous Knowledge." *Human Ecology* 25, no. 1 (1997): 47–69.

Browder, John O. "Lumber Production and Economic Development in the Brazilian Amazon: Regional Trends and a Case Study." *Journal of World Forest Resource Management* 4 (1989): 1–19.

Browder, John O., and Brian J. Godfrey. *Rainforest Cities: Urbanization, Development, and Globalization of the Brazilian Amazon.* New York: Columbia University Press, 1997.

Brown, C. Barrington, and William Lidstone. *Fifteen Thousand Miles on the Amazon and Its Tributaries.* London: Edward Stanford, 1878.

Brown, Jacqueline Nassy. "Black Liverpool, Black America and the Gendering of Diasporic Space." *Cultural Anthropology* 13, no. 3 (1998): 291–325.

————. "Enslaving History: Narratives on Local Whiteness in a Black Atlantic Port." *American Ethnologist* 27, no. 2 (2000): 340–70.

Bruneau, Thomas C. "Brazil: The Catholic Church and Basic Christian Communities." In *Religion and Political Conflict in Latin America,* ed. Daniel H. Levine, 106–23. Chapel Hill: University of North Carolina Press, 1986.

Buarque de Holanda, Sérgio. *História geral da civilização Brasileira.* 3rd ed. São Paulo: Difusão Européia do Livro, 1970.

Buarque, Manoel. *Tocantins e Araguaya.* Belém: Imprensa Oficial do Estado do Pará, 1919.

Buck-Morss, Susan. *The Dialectics of Seeing: Walter Benjamin and the Arcades Project.* Cambridge, Mass.: MIT Press, 1989.

Bunker, Stephen G. *Underdeveloping the Amazon: Extraction, Unequal Exchange and the Failure of the Modern State.* Chicago: University of Chicago Press, 1988.

Bush, M. B., D. R. Piperno, and P. A. Colinvaux, "A 6,000 Year History of Amazonian Maize Cultivation." *Nature* 340 (1989): 303–5.

Burnett, D. Graham. *Masters of All They Surveyed: Exploration, Geography, and a British El Dorado.* Chicago: University of Chicago Press, 2000.

Butler, Judith. *Bodies That Matter: On the Discursive Limits of "Sex."* New York: Routledge, 1993.

Calzavara, Batista B. G. "As possibilidades do açaizeiro no estuário Amazônico." *Boletim da Faculdade de Ciências Agrárias do Pará* 5 (1972).

Camerini, Jane. "Wallace in the Field." *Osiris* 11 (1996): 44–65.

Cameron, Laura. "Histories of Disturbance." *Radical History Review* 74 (1999): 4–24.

Campbell, Mary B. *The Witness and the Other World: Exotic European Travel Writing, 400–1600.* Ithaca: Cornell University Press, 1988.

Cannon, Susan. *Science in Culture: The Early Victorian Period*. New York: Neale Watson, 1978.

Capistrano de Abreu, João. *Chapters of Brazil's Colonial History, 1500–1800*. Trans. Arthur Brakel. Oxford: Oxford University Press, 1997.

Carman, Allan. *Monarch of Mahogany Visits Schmieg-Hungate & Kotzian, Being The History, Travels and Eventual Life of Perhaps the Oldest Living and Grandest King of the Wood of Woods*. New York: Scribner, 190?.

Carneiro da Cunha, Manuela. "Introdução a uma história indígena." In *História dos índios no Brasil*, org. Manuela Carneiro da Cunha, 9–24. São Paulo: Companhia das Letras, 1992.

Carter, Harold B. *Sir Joseph Banks, 1743–1820*. London: British Museum (Natural History), 1988.

Carter, Paul. *The Road to Botany Bay: An Exploration of Landscape and History*. Chicago: University of Chicago Press, 1989.

Casas, Bartoloméo de las. *Breuissima relacion de la destruycion de las Indias*. Seville: Sebastian Trugillo, 1552.

Chakrabarty, Dipesh. *Provincializing Europe: Postcolonial Thought and Historical Difference*. Princeton: Princeton University Press, 2000.

Chambers, Robert. *Vestiges of the Natural History of Creation*. London: J. Churchill, 1844.

Chandless, William. "Ascent of the River Purûs, and Notes on the River Aquiry." *Journal of the Royal Geographical Society* 35 (1866): 86–118.

———. "Notes on a Journey up the River Jurúa." *Journal of the Royal Geographical Society* 39 (1869): 296–310.

———. "Notes on the Rivers Maué-Assú, Abacaxis and Canuma." *Journal of the Royal Geographical Society* 40 (1870): 411–32.

Chapman, George. "De Guiana carmen Epicum." In Richard Hakluyt, *The Principal Navigations, Voyages, Traffiques & Discoveries of the English Nation Made by Sea or Over-land to the Remote and Farthest Distant Quarters of the Earth at Any Time Within the Compasse of These 1600 Yeeres*. Vol. 10, 451. Glasgow: James MacLehose, 1903–5.

Chermont de Miranda, Vicente. *Glossário Paraense ou coleção de vocábulos peculiares á Amazônia e especialmente á Ilha do Marajó*. Belém: Universidade Federal do Pará, 1968.

Chernela, Janet M. "Managing Rivers of Hunger: The Tukano of Brazil." In *Resource Management in Amazonia: Indigenous and Folk Strategies*, ed. Darrell A. Posey and William Balée, 238–48. New York: New York Botanical Garden, 1989.

Cleary, David. *Anatomy of the Amazon Gold Rush*. London: Macmillan, 1990.

———. "After the Frontier: Problems With Political Economy in the Modern Brazilian Amazon." *Journal of Latin American Studies* 25, no. 2 (1993): 331–50.

———. " 'Lost Altogether to the Civilized World': Race and the Cabanagem in Northern Brazil, 1750 to 1850." *Comparative Studies in Society and History* 40 (1998): 109–35.

———. "Race, Nationalism and Social Theory in Brazil: Rethinking Gilberto

Freyre." Economic and Social Research Council Transnational Communities Programme, Working Papers Series: WPTC-99-09, Oxford, 1999.

———. "Tristes Trope-iques: Science and the Representation of Nature in Amazonia Since the Eighteenth Century." Paper presented to the Department of Anthropology, University of Chicago, May 11, 2000.

———. "Towards an Environmental History of the Amazon: From Prehistory to the Nineteenth Century." *Latin American Research Review* 36, no. 2 (2001): 65–96.

Clements, Harry. *Alfred Russel Wallace: Biologist and Social Reformer*. London: Hutchinson, 1983.

Clifford, James. *The Predicament of Culture: Twentieth-Century Ethnography, Literature, and Art*. Cambridge, Mass.: Harvard University Press, 1988.

Clodd, Edward. "Memoir." In Henry Walter Bates, *The Naturalist on the River Amazons: A Record of Adventures, Habits of Animals, Sketches of Brazilian and Indian Life, and Aspects of Nature Under the Equator, During Eleven Years of Travel*, xvii–lxxxix. Unabridged commemorative ed. London: John Murray, 1892.

Clulee, Nicholas H. *John Dee's Natural Philosophy: Between Science and Religion*. London: Routledge, 1988.

Cohn, Bernard S. *Colonialism and Its Forms of Knowledge: The British in India*. Princeton: Princeton University Press, 1996.

Colp, Ralph, Jr. "'I Will Gladly Do My Best.' How Charles Darwin Obtained a Civil List Pension for Alfred Russel Wallace." *Isis* 83 (1992): 3–26.

Committee on Interstate and Foreign Commerce. *Decorative Wood Labeling and Use of the Term "Mahogany,"* Hearings Before a Subcommittee of the Committee on Interstate and Foreign Commerce, House of Representatives. Washington, D.C.: U.S. Government Printing Office, 1964.

Conklin, Beth A. "Body Paint, Feathers, and VCRs: Aesthetics and Authenticity in Amazonian Activism." *American Ethnologist* 24, no. 4 (1997): 711–37.

Conklin, Beth A., and Laura R. Graham. "The Shifting Middle-Ground: Amazonian Indians and and Eco-politics." *American Anthropologist* 97, no. 4 (1995): 695–710.

Coomes, Oliver T. "Blackwater Rivers, Adaptation, and Environmental Heterogeneity in Amazonia." *American Anthropologist* 94, no. 3 (1992): 698–701.

Cosgrove, Denis E. *Social Formation and Symbolic Landscape*. London: Croom Helm, 1984.

Cosgrove, Denis E., and Stephen Daniels, eds. *The Iconography of Landscape: Essays on the Symbolic Representation, Design and Use of Past Environments*. Cambridge: Cambridge University Press, 1988.

Cronon, William. "A Place for Stories: Nature, History, and Narrative." *Journal of American History* 78, no. 4 (1992): 1347–76.

———. "The Trouble with Wilderness: Or, Getting Back to the Wrong Nature." In *Uncommon Ground: Rethinking the Human Place in Nature*, ed. William Cronon, 69–90. New York: W. W. Norton, 1996.

Cruikshank, Julie. "Getting the Words Right: Perspectives on Naming and Places in Athapaskan Oral History." *Arctic Anthropology* 27, no. 1 (1990): 52–65.

da Cunha, Euclides. *Um paraíso perdido: Ensaios, estudos e pronunciamentos sobre a Amazônia.* Ed. Leandro Tocantins. 2nd ed. Rio de Janeiro: José Olympio, 1994.

da Silva, Maria de Fátima P. *Assunto: Vila de Mazagão Velho.* Mimeograph. Macapá: Universidade Federal do Amapá, 1992.

Daniel, Padre João. *Tesouro descoberto no Rio Amazonas.* Anais da Biblioteca Nacional, vol. 95, 2 vols. Rio de Janeiro, Brasil: Biblioteca Nacional, 1975.

Daniels, Stephen. "Marxism, Culture, and the Duplicity of Landscape." In *New Models in Geography: The Political-Economy Perspective,* ed. Richard Peet and Nigel Thrift, vol. 1, 337–64. London: Unwin Hyman, 1989.

Darwin, Charles. *Journal of Researches into the Geology and Natural History of the Various Countries Visited by H.M.S. Beagle, Under the Command of Captain FitzRoy, R.N., from 1832 to 1836.* London: H. Colburn, 1839.

Daston, Lorraine. "Baconian Facts, Academic Civility, and the Prehistory of Objectivity." *Annals of Scholarship* 8, nos. 3–4 (1991): 337–64.

———. "The Nature of Nature in Early Modern Europe." In *Configurations* 6, no. 2 (1998): 149–72.

Daston, Lorraine, and Katherine Park. *Wonders and the Order of Nature, 1150–1750.* New York: Zone Books, 1998.

Davis, Mike. *Ecology of Fear: Los Angeles and the Imagination of Disaster.* New York: Metropolitan Books, 1998.

de Certeau, Michel. *Heterologies: Discourse on the Other.* Minneapolis: University of Minnesota Press, 1986.

———. *The Writing of History.* Trans. Tom Conley. New York: Columbia University Press, 1988.

de Vos, Jan. *Oro verde: La conquista de la Selva Lacandona por los madereros tabasqueños.* México, D.F.: Fondo de Cultura Económica, 1988.

Dean, Warren. *Brazil and the Struggle for Rubber: A Study in Environmental History.* Cambridge: Cambridge University Press, 1987.

Deleuze, Gilles, and Félix Guattari. *A Thousand Plateaus: Capitalism and Schizophrenia.* Trans. Brian Massumi. Minneapolis: University of Minnesota Press, 1987.

Delson, Roberta Marx. *New Towns for Colonial Brazil.* Ann Arbor: UMI, 1979.

Demerritt, David. "The Nature of Metaphors in Cultural Geography and Environmental History." *Progress in Human Geography* 18, no. 2 (1994): 163–85.

Denevan, William M. *The Aboriginal Cultural Geography of the Llanos de Mojos of Bolivia.* Ibero-Americana 48. Berkeley: University of California Press, 1966.

———. "Aboriginal Drained-Field Cultivation in the Americas." *Science* 169 (1970): 647–54.

———. "Ecological Heterogeneity and Horizontal Zonation of Agriculture in the Amazonian Floodplain." In *Frontier Expansion in Amazonia,* ed. Marianne Schmink and Charles H. Wood, 311–36. Gainesville: University of Florida Press, 1984.

―――. "The Pristine Myth: The Landscape of the Americas in 1492." *Annals of the Association of American Geographers* 82, no. 3 (1992): 369–85.

―――. *Cultivated Landscapes of Native Amazonia and the Andes: Triumph Over the Soil.* Oxford: Oxford University Press, 2001.

Denevan, William M., and Alberta Zucchi. "Ridged Field Excavations in the Central Orinoco Llanos." In *Advances in Andean Archaeology*, ed. David L. Browman, 235–46. The Hague: Mouton, 1978.

Denevan, William M., and Christine Padoch, eds. *Swidden-Fallow Agroforestry in the Peruvian Amazon.* New York: New York Botanical Garden, 1987.

Derrida, Jacques. *Of Grammatology.* Trans. Gayatri Chakravorty Spivak. Baltimore: Johns Hopkins University Press, 1976.

Descola, Philippe. *In the Society of Nature: A Native Ecology of Amazonia.* Trans. Nora Scott. Cambridge: Cambridge University Press, 1994.

Descola, Philippe, and Gísli Pálsson, eds. *Nature and Society: Anthropological Perspectives.* New York: Routledge, 1996.

Desmond, Ray. *Kew: The History of the Royal Botanic Gardens.* London: Royal Botanic Gardens, Kew, 1995.

Dettelbach, Michael. "Humboldtian Science." In *Cultures of Natural History*, ed. Nicholas Jardine, James A. Secord, and Emma C. Spary, 287–304. Cambridge: Cambridge University Press, 1996.

di Paolo, Pasquale. *Cabanagem: A revolução popular da Amazônia.* Belém: CE-JUP, 1986.

Dickenson, John. "Henry Walter Bates and the Study of Latin America in the Late Nineteenth Century; A Bibliographic Essay." *Revista interamericana de bibliografía* 40 (1990): 570–80.

―――. "Henry Walter Bates ― The Naturalist of the River Amazons." *Archives of Natural History* 19 (1992): 209–18.

―――. "The Naturalist on the River Amazons and a Wider World: Reflections on the Centenary of Henry Walter Bates." *The Geographical Journal* 158 (1992): 207–14.

―――. "Bates, Wallace and Economic Botany in Mid-19th Century Amazonia." In *Richard Spruce (1817–1893): Botanist and Explorer*, ed. Mark R. D. Seaward and Sylvia M. D. FitzGerald, 65–80. London: Royal Botanic Gardens, Kew, 1996.

Drayton, Richard. *Nature's Government: Science, Imperial Britain, and the 'Improvement' of the World.* New Haven: Yale University Press, 2000.

Dreyfus, Simone. "Historical and Political Anthropological Inter-Connections: The Multilinguistic Indigenous Polity of the Carib Islands and Mainland Coast from the 16th to the 18th Century." *Antropológica* 59–62 (1983–84): 39–55.

―――. "Os empreendimentos coloniais e os espaços políticos indígenas no interior da Guiana ocidental (entre o Orenoco e o Corentino) de 1613–1796." In *Amazônia: Etnologia e história indígena*, org. Eduardo Viveiros de Castro e Manuela Carneiro da Cunha, 19–41. São Paulo: NHII-USP/FAPESP, 1993.

Duncan, James S. *The City as Text: The Politics of Landscape Interpretation in the Kandyan Kingdom.* Cambridge: Cambridge University Press, 1990.

Dworkin, Dennis L., and Leslie G. Roman, ed. *Views Beyond the Border Country: Raymond Williams and Cultural Politics*. New York: Routledge, 1993.

Eden, Michael J. *Ecology and Land Management in Amazonia*. London: Belhaven, 1990.

Edwards, Edward. *The Life of Sir Walter Ralegh*. 2 vols. London: Macmillan, 1868.

Edwards, William H. *A Voyage Up the River Amazon, Including a Residence at Pará*. London: John Murray, 1847.

Elliott, John H. *The Old World and the New, 1492–1650*. Cambridge: Cambridge University Press, 1970.

Erikson, Patricia Pierce. "A-Whaling We Will Go: Encounters of Knowledge and Memory at the Makah Cultural Research Center." *Cultural Anthropology* 14, no. 4 (1999): 556–83.

Fabian, Johannes. *Out of Our Minds: Reason and Madness in the Exploration of Central Africa*. Berkeley: University of California Press, 2000.

Fearnside, Philip M. *Human Carrying Capacity of the Brazilian Rainforest*. New York: Columbia University Press, 1986.

Feeley-Harnik, Gillian. " 'Pigeons, If You Please': An Avian Perspective on Darwin and *The Origin of Species*." Paper presented to the 99th Annual Meeting of the American Anthropological Association, San Francisco, Calif., November 15–19, 2000.

Feld, Steven, and Keith H. Basso, eds. *Senses of Place*. Santa Fe: SAR Press, 1996.

Ferguson, James, and Akhil Gupta, eds. *Culture, Power, Place: Explorations in Critical Anthropology*. Durham: Duke University Press, 1997.

Ferreira, Alexandre Rodrigues. *Viagem filosófica pelas Capitanias do Grão-Pará, Rio Negro, Mato Grosso e Cuiabá*. Rio de Janeiro, Brasil: Conselho Federal de Cultura, 1971–74.

Fiedler, Peggy L., Peter S. White, and Robert A. Leidy. "The Paradigm Shift in Ecology and Its Implications for Conservation." In *The Ecological Basis of Conservation: Heterogeneity, Ecosystems, and Biodiversity*, ed. S.T.A. Pickett, R. S. Ostfield, M. Shachak, and G. E. Likens, 83–92. New York: Chapman and Hall, 1997.

Findlen, Paula. *Possessing Nature: Museums, Collecting, and Scientific Culture in Early Modern Italy*. Berkeley: University of California Press, 1994.

Fisher, William H. "Native Amazonians and the Making of the Amazon Wilderness: From Discourse of Riches and Sloth to Underdevelopment." In *Creating the Countryside: The Politics of Rural and Environmental Discourse*, ed. E. Melanie DuPuis and Peter Vandergeest. Philadelphia: Temple University Press, 1996, 166–203.

Fortmann, Louise. "Gendered Knowledge: Rights and Space in Two Zimbabwe Villages." In *Feminist Political Ecology: Global Issues and Local Experiences*, ed. Dianne Rocheleau, Barbara Thomas-Slayter, and Esther Wangari, 211–23. New York: Routledge, 1996.

Foucault, Michel. *The Order of Things: An Archaeology of the Human Sciences*. New York: Vintage, 1994.

———. "Nietzsche, Genealogy, History." *Language, Counter-Memory, Practice: Selected Essays and Interviews*, ed. Donald F. Bouchard, trans. Donald F. Bouchard and Sherry Simon, 139–64. Ithaca: Cornell University Press, 1980.

———. "Governmentality." In *The Foucault Effect: Studies in Governmentality*, ed. Graham Burchill, Colin Gordon, and Peter Miller, 87–104. London: Harvester Wheatsheaf, 1991.

Freud, Sigmund. *Civilization and Its Discontents*. Trans. and ed. James Strachey. New York: W. W. Norton, 1962.

Frost, Alan. "New Geographical Perspectives and the Emergence of the Romantic Imagination." In *Captain James Cook and His Times*, ed. Robin Fisher and Hugh Johnston, 5–19. Seattle: University of Washington Press, 1979.

Fuller, Mary C. "Ralegh's Fugitive Gold: Reference and Deferral in *The Discoverie of Guiana*." *Representations* 33 (1991): 42–64.

Galton, Francis. "Reminiscences of Mr. H. W. Bates." *Proceedings of the Royal Geographical Society* 14 (1892): 256.

Garfield, Seth. *Indigenous Struggle at the Heart of Brazil: State Policy, Frontier Expansion, and the Xavante Indians, 1937–1988*. Durham: Duke University Press, 2001.

Gascoigne, John. *Joseph Banks and the English Enlightenment: Useful Knowledge and Polite Culture*. Cambridge: Cambridge University Press, 1994.

Geertz, Clifford. *Works and Lives: The Anthropologist as Author*. Stanford: Stanford University Press, 1988.

Gentil, Janete. "A juta na agricultura de várzea na área de Santarém-Médio Amazonas." *Boletim do Museu Paraense Emílio Goeldi: Série Antropologia* 4, no. 2 (1988): 118–99.

Gentry, Alwyn H. *A Field Guide to the Families and Genera of Woody Plants of Northwest South America (Colombia, Ecuador, Peru), With Supplementary Notes on Herbaceous Taxa*. Washington, D.C.: Conservation International, 1993.

George, Wilma. *Biologist Philosopher: A Study of the Life and Writings of Alfred Russel Wallace*. London: Abelard-Schuman, 1964.

Gerbi, Antonello. *The Dispute of the New World: The History of a Polemic, 1750–1900*. Trans. Jeremy Moyle. Pittsburgh: University of Pittsburgh Press, 1973.

———. *Nature in the New World: From Christopher Columbus to Gonzalo Fernández de Oviedo*. Trans. Jeremy Moyle. Pittsburgh: University of Pittsburgh Press, 1985.

Gillin, John. "Tribes of the Guianas." In *Handbook of South American Indians*, vol. 3: *The Tropical Forest Tribes*, ed. Julian Steward, 699–860. Bureau of American Ethnology, bulletin no. 143. Washington, D.C.: Smithsonian Institution, 1948.

Gilroy, Paul. *There Ain't No Black in the Union Jack: The Cultural Politics of Race and Nation*. London: Hutchinson, 1987, 49–50.

Glacken, Clarence J. *Traces on the Rhodian Shore: Nature and Culture in Western Thought from Ancient Times to the End of the Eighteenth Century*. Berkeley: University of California Press, 1967.

Goethe, Johann Wolfgang von. *Italian Journey [1786–1788]*. Trans. W. H. Auden and Elizabeth Mayer. London: Penguin, 1970.

Goldberg, Jonathan. "The History That Will Be." In *Premodern Sexualities*, ed. Louise Fradenburg and Carla Freccero, 3–21. New York: Routledge, 1996.

———. *Sodometries: Renaissance Texts, Modern Sexualities*. Stanford: Stanford University Press, 1992.

Gondim, Neide. *A invenção da Amazônia*. São Paulo: Marco Zero, 1994.

Gordon, Avery F. *Ghostly Matters: Haunting and the Sociological Imagination*. Minneapolis: University of Minnesota Press, 1997.

Goslinga, Cornelis Ch. *The Dutch in the Caribbean and on the Wild Coast, 1580–1680*. Gainesville: University of Florida Press, 1971.

Gosse, Edmund. *Raleigh*. New York: D. Appleton, 1886.

Goulart, José Alípio. *O regatão: Mascate fluvial da Amazônia*. Rio de Janeiro: Conquista, 1967.

Gould, Stephen Jay. "Here Goes Nothing." *Natural History* 94, no. 7 (1985): 12–19.

Grafton, Anthony. *New Worlds, Ancient Texts: The Power of Tradition and the Shock of Discovery*. Cambridge, Mass.: Harvard University Press, 1992.

Graham, Richard. *Britain and the Onset of Modernization in Brazil, 1850–1914*. Cambridge: Cambridge University Press, 1968.

Gramsci, Antonio. *Selections from the Prison Notebooks*. Ed. and trans. Quintin Hoare and Geoffrey Nowell-Smith. New York: International Publishers, 1971.

Grant Duff, Mountstuart E. "Obituary. Henry Walter Bates, F.R.S." *Proceedings of the Royal Geographical Society* 14 (1892): 245–57.

Greenblatt, Stephen. *Sir Walter Ralegh: The Renaissance Man and His Roles*. New Haven: Yale University Press, 1973.

———. *Marvelous Possessions: The Wonder of the New World*. Chicago: University of Chicago Press, 1991.

———. "Foreword." In Frank Lestringant, *Mapping the Renaissance World: The Geographical Imagination in the Age of Discovery*, trans. David Fausett, vii–xv. Berkeley: University of California Press, 1994.

Gregory, Steven. *Black Corona: Race and the Politics of Place in an Urban Community*. Princeton: Princeton University Press, 1998.

Grieco, Allen J. "The Social Politics of Pre-Linnean Botanical Classification." *I Tatti Studies: Essays in the Renaissance* 4 (1991): 131–49.

Griffiths, Tom, and Libby Robin, eds. *Ecology and Empire: Environmental History of Settler Societies*. Seattle: University of Washington Press, 1997.

Gross, Daniel R. "Protein Capture and Cultural Development in the Amazon Basin." *American Anthropologist* 77 (1975): 526–49.

Grosz, Elizabeth. *Volatile Bodies: Towards a Corporeal Feminism*. Bloomington: University of Indiana Press, 1994.

Grove, Richard H. *Green Imperialism: Colonial Expansion, Tropical Island Edens and the Origin of Environmentalism, 1600–1860*. Cambridge: Cambridge University Press, 1995.

Gullison, R. E., S. N. Panfil, J. J. Strouse, and S. P. Hubbell. "Ecology and

Management of Mahogany (*Swietenia macrophylla* King) in the Chimanes Forest, Beni, Bolivia." *Botanical Journal of the Linnean Society* 122 (1996): 9–34.

Gupta, Akhil. *Postcolonial Developments: Agriculture in the Making of Modern India.* Durham: Duke University Press, 1998.

Hagen, Joel B. *An Entangled Bank: The Origins of Ecosystem Ecology.* New Brunswick: Rutgers University Press, 1992.

Hagen, Victor Wolfgang von. *South America Called Them: Explorations of the Great Naturalists; La Condamine, Darwin, Humboldt, Spruce.* New York: Alfred A. Knopf, 1945.

Haila, Yrjö. "Measuring Nature: Quantitative Data in Field Biology." In *The Right Tools for the Job: At Work in Twentieth-Century Life Sciences*, ed. Adele E. Clark and Joan H. Fujimura, 233–53. Princeton: Princeton University Press, 1992.

Hakluyt, Richard. *A Particular Discourse Concerning the Greate Necessitie and Manifolde Commodyties That Are Like to Growe to this Realme of Englande by the Westerne Discoueries Lately Attempted, Written in the Yere 1584 by Richard Hakluyt of Oxforde Known as Discourse of Western Planting.* Ed. David B. Quinn and Alison M. Quinn. Hakluyt Society Extra Series No. 45. London: Hakluyt Society, 1993.

Hall, Stuart. "Introduction: Who Needs Identity?" In *Questions of Identity*, ed. Stuart Hall and Paul Du Gay, 1–17. Thousand Oaks, Calif.: Sage, 1996.

Hames, Raymond B., and William T. Vickers, eds. *Adaptive Responses of Native Amazonians.* New York: Academic Press, 1983.

Haraway, Donna. J. *Modest Witness@Second Millennium. FemaleMan© Meets OncoMouse™: Feminism and Technoscience.* New York: Routledge, 1997.

Harcourt, Robert. *A Relation of a Voyage to Guiana.* Ed. Sir C. Alexander Harris. Hakluyt Society Second Series No. 60. London: Hakluyt Society, 1926 [1613].

Hargrove, W. W., and J. Pickering. "Pseudoreplication: A *sine qua non* for Regional Ecology." *Landscape Ecology* 6, no. 4 (1992): 251–58.

Harkness, Deborah E. *John Dee's Conversations With Angels: Cabala, Alchemy, and the End of Nature.* Cambridge: Cambridge University Press, 1999.

Harlow, Vincent T. "Introduction." In *Colonising Expeditions to the West Indies and Guiana, 1623–1667*, ed. Vernon T. Harlow, xiii–xcv. Hakluyt Society Second Series No. 56. London: Hakluyt Society, 1925.

———. "Introduction." In Sir Walter Ralegh, *The Discoverie of the Large and Bewtiful Empire of Guiana*, ed. V. T. Harlow, xv–cvi. London: The Argonaut Press, 1928.

Harlow, Vincent T., ed. *Ralegh's Last Voyage.* London: The Argonaut Press, 1932.

Harris, Mark. "'What It Means to Be *Caboclo*': Some Critical Notes on the Construction of Amazonian *Caboclo* Society as an Anthropological Object." *Critique of Anthropology* 18, no. 1 (1998): 83–95.

Harris, Marvin. *Cannibals and Kings: The Origins of Cultures.* New York: Random House, 1977.

Hawkins, Ann. "Contested Ground: International Environmentalisms and Global Climate Change." In *The State and Social Power in Global Environmental Politics*, ed. Ronnie D. Lipschutz and Ken Conca, 221–45. New York: Columbia University Press, 1993.

Heaney, Seamus. *North*. London: Faber, 1975.

Hecht, Susanna B. "Deforestation in the Amazon Basin: Magnitude, Dynamics, and Soil Resource Effects." *Studies in Third World Societies* 13 (1981): 61–110.

————. "Environment, Development and Politics: Capital Accumulation and the Livestock Sector in Eastern Amazonia." *World Development* 13, no. 6 (1985): 663–84.

Hecht, Susanna B., and Alexander Cockburn. *The Fate of the Forest: Developers, Destroyers and Defenders of the Amazon*. London: Penguin, 1989.

————. "Defenders of the Amazon." *The Nation*, May 22, 1989, 695–702, September 18, 1989, 262, 291–92.

Hecht, Susanna B., and Darrell A. Posey. "Indigenous Soil Management in the Latin American Tropics: Some Implications for the Amazon Basin." In *Ethnobiology: Implications and Applications*, ed. Darrell A. Posey and William L. Overal, Proceedings of the First International Congress of Ethnobiology, vol. 2, 73–86. Belém: Museu Paraense Emílio Goeldi, 1990.

Heckenberger, Michael J. *War and Peace in the Shadow of Empire: Sociopolitical Change in the Upper Xingu of Southeastern Amazonia, A.D. 1250–2000*. Unpbd. Ph.D. dissertation, Department of Anthropology, University of Pittsburgh, 1996.

Helgerson, Richard. *Forms of Nationhood: The Elizabethan Writing of England*. Chicago: University of Chicago Press, 1992.

Hemming, John. *Red Gold: The Conquest of the Brazilian Indians*. London: Macmillan, 1978.

————. *The Search for El Dorado*. New York: E. P. Dutton, 1978.

————. *Amazon Frontier: The Defeat of the Brazilian Indians*. London: Macmillan, 1987.

Hill, Christopher. *Intellectual Origins of the English Revolution Revisited*. Oxford: Clarendon Press, 1997.

Hiraoka, Mário. "Land Use Changes in the Amazon Estuary." *Global Environmental Change* 5, no. 4 (1995): 323–36.

Hobsbawm, Eric. *Industry and Empire*. London: Pelican, 1969.

Homma, Alfredo Kingo Oyama. "The Dynamics of Extraction in Amazonia: A Historical Perspective." In *Non-Timber Products from Tropical Forests: Evaluation of a Conservation and Development Strategy*, ed. Daniel C. Nepstad and Stephen Schwartzman, 23–32. New York: New York Botanical Garden, 1992.

————. *Extrativismo vegetal na Amazônia: Limites e oportunidades*. Brasília: EMBRAPA-SPI, 1993.

Honour, Hugh. *The New Golden Land: European Images of America from the Discoveries to the Present Time*. New York: Pantheon, 1975.

Howard, Albert. *Crop-Production in India*. Oxford: Oxford University Press, 1924.

Huber, Otto. "Significance of Savanna Vegetation in the Amazon Territory of Venezuela." In *Biological Diversification in the Tropics*, ed. Ghillean T. Prance, 221–24. New York: Columbia University Press, 1982.

Hudson, William Henry. *Green Mansions: A Romance of the Tropical Forest*. New York: Random House, 1944.

Hugh-Jones, Stephen. "Yesterday's Luxuries, Tomorrow's Necessities: Business and Barter in Northwest Amazonia." In *Barter, Exchange and Value: An Anthropological Approach*, ed. Caroline Humphrey and Stephen Hugh-Jones, 42–74. Cambridge: Cambridge University Press, 1992.

Hulme, Peter. *Colonial Encounters: Europe and the Native Caribbean, 1492–1797*. London: Routledge, 1992.

Humboldt, Alexander von, and Aimé Bonpland. *Essai sur la géographie des plantes; Accompagné d'un tableau physique des régions équinoxiales*. London: Society for the Bibliography of Natural History, 1959 [1807].

———. *Voyage aux régions équinoxiales du nouveau continent, fait en 1799, 1800, 1801, 1802, 1803 et 1804*. 12 vols. Paris, 1816–34.

———. *Personal Narrative of Travels to the Equinoctial Regions of the New Continent During the Years 1799–1804*. 3 vols. Trans. and ed. Thomasina Ross. London: George Routledge and Sons, 1895.

Hurlbert, Stuart H. "Pseudoreplication and the Design of Ecological Field Experiments." *Ecological Monographs* 54, no. 2 (1984): 187–212.

Impey, Oliver, and Arthur MacGregor, ed. *The Origins of Museums: The Cabinet of Curiosities in Sixteenth- and Seventeenth-Century Europe*. New York: Clarendon Press, 1985.

Inkster, Ian. "Aspects of the History of Science and Science Culture in Britain: 1780–1850 and Beyond." In *Metropolis and Province: Science in British Culture, 1780–1850*, ed. Ian Inkster and Jack Morrell, 11–54. Philadelphia: University of Pennsylvania Press, 1983.

Jacob, Paulo. *Dicionário da língua popular da Amazônia*. Rio de Janeiro: Liv. Ed. Cátedra, 1985.

Janzen, Daniel H. "The Future of Tropical Ecology." *Annual Review of Ecology and Systematics* 17 (1986): 305–24.

Jardim, Mário Augusto G., and John S. Rumbold. "Effects of Adubation and Thinning on *Açaí* Palm (*Euterpe oleracea* Mart.): Fruit Yield from a Natural Population." *Boletim do Museu Paraense Emílio Goeldi*. Série Botânica 10, no. 2 (1994): 283–93.

Jardine, Nicholas, James A. Secord, and Emma C. Spary, ed. *Cultures of Natural History*. Cambridge: Cambridge University Press, 1996.

Johns, Jennifer, Paulo Barreto, and Christopher Uhl. "Logging Damage During Planned and Unplanned Logging Operations in the Eastern Amazon." *Forest Ecology and Management* 89, nos. 1–3 (1996): 59–77.

Jones, Kristine L. "Nineteenth Century British Travel Accounts of Argentina." *Ethnohistory* 33 (1986): 195–211.

Jordan, Carl F., and Gladys Escalante. "Root Productivity in an Amazonian Rain Forest." *Ecology* 61, no. 1 (1980): 14–18.

Jordan, Carl F., ed. *An Amazonian Rain Forest: The Structure and Function of a Nutrient Stressed Ecosystem and the Impact of Slash-and-Burn Agriculture.* Paris: UNESCO, 1989.

Junk, Wolfgang J., and Karin Furch. "The Physical and Chemical Properties of Amazonian Waters." In *Key Environments: Amazonia,* ed. Ghillean T. Prance and Thomas E. Lovejoy, 3–17. London: Pergamon, 1985.

Katzman, Martin T. "Paradoxes of Amazonian Development in a 'Resource-Starved' World." *Journal of Developing Areas* 10 (1975): 445–60.

Keith, Michael, and Steve Pile, eds. *Place and the Politics of Identity.* London: Routledge, 1993.

Kepler, Johannes. *Kepler's Conversation with Galileo's Sidereal Messenger.* Ed. and trans. Edward Rosen. New York: Johnson Reprint Corp., 1965.

Keymis, Lawrence. "A Relation of the Second Voyage to Guiana, Performed and Written in theYeere 1696. by Lawrence Keymis Gent." In Richard Hakluyt, *The Principal Navigations, Voyages, Traffiques & Discoveries of the English Nation Made by Sea or Over-land to the Remote and Farthest Distant Quarters of the Earth at Any Time Within the Compasse of These 1600 Yeeres.* Vol. 10, 462–67. Glasgow: James MacLehose, 1903–5.

Kincaid, Jamaica. *A Small Place.* New York: Penguin, 1988.

Kingsland, Sharon. *Modeling Nature: Episodes in the History of Population Ecology.* 2nd ed. Chicago: University of Chicago Press, 1995.

Koerner, Lisbet. "Carl Linnaeus in His Time and Place." In *Cultures of Natural History,* ed. Nicholas Jardine, James A. Secord, and Emma C. Spary, 145–62. Cambridge: Cambridge University Press, 1996.

Kropotkin, Peter. *Memoirs of a Revolutionist.* Ed. James Allen Rogers. London: Century Hutchinson, 1988 [1899].

Kuper, Adam. "On Human Nature: Darwin and the Anthropologists." In *Nature and Society in Historical Context,* ed. Mikulás Teich, Roy Porter, and Bo Gustafsson, 274–90. Cambridge: Cambridge University Press, 1997.

Lacey, Robert. *Sir Walter Ralegh.* London: Weidenfeld and Nicholson, 1973.

Lamb, F. Bruce. *Mahogany of Tropical America: Its Ecology and Management.* Ann Arbor: University of Michigan, 1966.

Lamb, George N. *The Mahogany Book.* 5th ed. Chicago: Mahogany Association Inc., 1946.

Latham, Agnes M. C. *Sir Walter Ralegh.* Writers and Their Work, No. 177. London: The British Council, 1964.

Lathrap, Donald. *The Upper Amazon.* London: Thames and Hudson, 1970.

Lathrap, Donald. "The Antiquity and Importance of Long-Distance Trade Relationships in the Moist Tropics of Pre-Columbian South America." *World Archaeology* 5, no. 2 (1973): 170–86.

Latour, Bruno. *Science in Action: How to Follow Scientists and Engineers through Society* Cambridge, Mass.: Harvard University Press, 1987.

———. *We Have Never Been Modern.* Trans. Catherine Porter. Cambridge, Mass.: Harvard University Press, 1993.

———. "The 'Pédofil' of Boa Vista: A Photo-Philosophical Montage." *Common Knowledge* 4, no. 1 (1995): 144–87.

Lawson-Peebles, Robert. "The Many Faces of Sir Walter Ralegh." *History Today* 48, no. 3 (1998): 17–24.

Leal, Victor Nunes. *Coronelismo, enxada e voto: O município e o regime representativo no Brasil.* 2nd ed. São Paulo: Alfa-Omega, 1975.

Lefebvre, Henri. *The Production of Space.* Trans. Donald Nicholson-Smith. Oxford: Blackwell, 1991.

Léry, Jean de. *History of a Voyage to the Land of Brazil, Otherwise Called America.* Trans. Janet Whatley. Berkeley: University of California Press, 1990.

Lestringant, Frank. *Mapping the Renaissance World: The Geographical Imagination in the Age of Discovery.* Trans. David Fausett. Berkeley: University of California Press, 1994.

Linger, Daniel T. "The Hegemony of Discontent." *American Ethnologist* 20, no. 1 (1993): 3–25.

Lingis, Alphonso. *Abuses.* Berkeley: University of California Press, 1994.

———. *Dangerous Emotions.* Berkeley: University of California Press, 2000.

Linnaeus, Carolus. *Systema naturae.* 2 vols. New York: Stechert-Hafner, 1964 [1735].

Livingstone, David N., "The Moral Discourse of Climate: Historical Considerations on Race, Place and Virtue." In *Journal of Historical Geography* 17, no. 4 (1991): 413–34.

———. *The Geographical Tradition: Episodes in the History of a Contested Enterprise.* Oxford: Blackwell, 1993.

Lobato, Eladio. *Caminho de canoa pequena: História do município de Igarapé-Miri.* 2nd ed. Belém: Imprensa Oficial, 1985.

Lorimer, Joyce. "Ralegh's First Reconnaissance of Guiana? An English Survey of the Orinoco in 1587." *Terra Incognitae* 9 (1977): 7–21.

———. "The English Contraband Tobacco Trade in Trinidad and Guiana 1590–1617." In *The Westward Enterprise: English Activities in Ireland, the Atlantic, and America 1480–1650,* ed. Kenneth R. Andrews, Nicholas P. Canny, and Paul E. H. Hair, 124–50. Liverpool: University of Liverpool Press, 1978.

———. "The Location of Ralegh's Guiana Gold Mine." *Terrae Incognitae* 14 (1982): 77–95.

Lorimer, Joyce, ed. *English and Irish Settlement on the River Amazon, 1550–1646.* Hakluyt Society Second Series No. 171. London: Hakluyt Society, 1989.

Los Angeles Times. "Compromise on Mahogany Reached," June 21, 1997, A9.

Lowood, Henry E. "The Calculating Forester: Quantification, Cameral Science, and the Emergence of Scientific Forestry Management in Germany." In *The Quantifying Spirit in the Eighteenth Century,* ed. Tore Frangsmyr, J. L. Heilbron, and Robin E. Rider, 315–42. Berkeley: University of California Press, 1991.

Lugo, Ariel E. "Point-Counterpoints on the Conservation of Big-Leaf Mahogany." Washington, D.C.: U.S. Department of Agriculture, Forest Service, 1999.

Luke, Timothy. *Ecocritique: Contesting the Politics of Nature, Economy, and Culture.* Minneapolis: University of Minnesota Press, 1997.

Luxardo, Líbero. *Marajó: Terra anfíbia*. Belém: Grafisa, 1977.

Lyell, Charles. *Principles of Geology; Being an Attempt to Explain the Former Changes of the Earth's Surface, by Reference to Causes now in Operation*. 3 vols. London: John Murray, 1830–33.

Macedo, Domingo S., and Anthony B. Anderson. "Early Ecological Changes Associated with Logging in an Amazon Floodplain." *Biotropica* 25, no. 2 (1993): 151–63.

Mackay, David. "A Presiding Genius of Exploration: Banks, Cook and Empire, 1767–1805." In *Captain James Cook and His Times*, ed. Robin Fisher and Hugh Johnston, 20–39. Seattle: University of Washington Press, 1979.

———. *In the Wake of Cook: Exploration, Science, and Empire, 1780–1801*. London: Croom Helm, 1985.

———. "Agents of Empire: The Banksian Collectors and Evaluation of New Lands." In *Visions of Empire: Voyages, Botany, and Representations of Nature*, ed. David Philip Miller and Peter Hanns Reill, 38–57. Cambridge: Cambridge University Press, 1996.

MacKenzie, John M., ed. *Imperialism and the Natural World*. New York: Manchester University Press, 1990.

Macloed, Murdo J. "Spain and America: The Atlantic Trade, 1492–1720." In *The Cambridge History of Latin America*, vol. I: *Colonial Latin America*, ed. Leslie Bethell, 314–88. Cambridge: Cambridge University Press, 1984.

Mahmood, Saba. "Feminist Theory, Embodiment, and the Docile Agent: Some Reflections on the Egyptian Islamic Revival." *Cultural Anthropology* 16, no. 2 (2001): 202–36.

Mainwaring, Scott. *The Catholic Church and Politics in Brazil, 1916–1985*. Stanford: Stanford University Press, 1986.

Maligo, Pedro. *Land of Metaphorical Desires: The Representation of Amazonia in Brazilian Literature*. New York: Peter Lang, 1998.

Malkki, Liisa H. *Purity and Exile: Violence, Memory, and National Cosmology Among Hutu Refugees in Tanzania*. Chicago: University of Chicago Press, 1995.

Mallet, James, and Mathieu Joron. "Evolution of Diversity in Warning Color and Mimicry: Polymorphisms, Shifting Balance, and Speciation." *Annual Review of Ecology and Systematics* 30 (1999): 201–33.

Malthus, Thomas R. *An Essay on the Principle of Population; or, A View of Its Past and Present Effect on Human Happiness; With an Inquiry into our Prospects Respecting the Future Removal or Mitigation of the Evils which it Occasions*. 2nd ed. London: J. Johnson, 1803.

Manguel, Alberto, and Gianni Guadalupi. *Dictionary of Imaginary Places*. New York: Harcourt Brace, 1999.

Manners, Robert A. "Julian Haynes Steward 1902–1972." *American Anthropologist* 75, no. 3 (1973): 886–903.

Manthorne, Katherine Emma. *Tropical Renaissance: North American Artists Exploring Latin America, 1839–1879*. Washington, D.C.: Smithsonian Institution, 1989.

Massey, Doreen. *Space, Place, and Gender*. Minneapolis: University of Minnesota Press, 1994.

———. "Spatial Disruptions." In *The Eight Technologies of Otherness*, ed. Sue Golding, 217–25. London: Routledge, 1997.

———. "Travelling Thoughts." In *Without Guarantees: In Honour of Stuart Hall*, ed. Paul Gilroy, Lawrence Grossberg, and Angela McRobbie, 225–32. London: Verso, 2000.

Maurer, Bill. "Uncanny Exchanges: The Possibilities and Failures of 'Making Change' with Alternative Monetary Forms." *Environment and Planning 'D': Society and Space*, forthcoming.

Maw, Henry Lister. *Journal of a Passage from the Pacific to the Atlantic, Crossing the Andes in the Northern Provinces of Peru, and Descending the River Marañon or Amazon*. London: John Murray, 1829.

McCann, Joseph M. " 'Extinct' Cultures and Persistent Landscapes of the Lower Tapajos Region, Brazilian Amazonia." Paper presented at the Annual Meetings of the Association of American Geographers, New York, February 27–March 3, 2000.

McEwan, Colin, Christiana Barreto, and Eduardo Neves, eds. *Unknown Amazon: Culture in Nature in Ancient Brazil*. London: British Museum, 2001.

McGrath, David G. *The Paraense Traders: Small-scale, Long-distance Trade in the Brazilian Amazon*. Unpbd. Ph.D. dissertation, Department of Geography, University of Wisconsin, 1989.

McGrath, David G., F. de Castro, C. Futemma, B. D. do Amaral, and J. Calabria. "Fisheries and the Evolution of Resource Management on the Lower Amazon Floodplain." *Human Ecology* 21, no. 2 (1993): 167–95.

McIntosh, Robert P. *The Background of Ecology: Concept and Theory*. Cambridge: Cambridge University Press, 1985.

Medina, José Toribio, ed. *The Discovery of the Amazon According to the Account of Friar Gaspar de Carvajal and Other Documents*. Trans. Bertram T. Lee. New York: Dover, 1988.

Meggers, Betty J. "Environmental Limitations on the Development of Culture." *American Anthropologist* 56 (1954): 801–24.

———. "Environment and Culture in the Amazon Basin: An Appraisal of the Theory of Environmental Determinism." In *Studies in Human Ecology*, Angel Palerm, Eric R. Wolf, Waldo R. Wedel, Betty J. Meggers, Jacques M. May, and Lawrence Krader, 71–89. Washington, D.C.: Pan American Union, 1957.

———. *Amazonia: Man and Culture in a Counterfeit Paradise*. Chicago: Aldine, 1971.

———. "Pre-Columbian Amazonia." *National Geographic Research & Exploration* 10, no. 4 (1994): 398–421.

Meggers, Betty J., and Clifford Evans. *Archaeological Investigations at the Mouth of the Amazon*, Bureau of American Ethnology, bulletin no. 167. Washington, D.C.: Smithsonian Institution, 1957.

Merchant, Carolyn. *The Death of Nature: Women, Ecology, and the Scientific Revolution*. New York: Harper & Row, 1980.

Métraux, Alfred. "Tribes of Eastern Bolivia and the Madeira Headwaters." In *Handbook of South American Indians*, vol. 3: *The Tropical Forest Tribes*, ed., Julian H. Steward, 381–454. Bureau of American Ethnology, bulletin no. 143. Washington, D.C.: U.S. Government Printing Office, 1948.

Michaux, Henri. *Ecuador: A Travel Journal*. Trans. Robin Magowan. London: Owen, 1970.

Miller, Shannon. *Invested With Meaning: The Raleigh Circle in the New World*. Philadelphia: University of Pennsylvania Press, 1998.

Montaigne, Michel de. *Selected Essays*. Trans. Charles Cotton and William Carew Hazlitt, ed. Blanchard Bates. New York: Random House, 1949.

Montrose, Louis. "The Work of Gender in the Discourse of Discovery." *Representations* 33 (1991): 1–41.

Moon, H. P. *Henry Walter Bates F.R.S. 1825–1892: Explorer, Scientist and Darwinian*. Leicester: Leicestershire Museums, 1976.

Moore, Donald. "Subaltern Struggles and the Politics of Place: Remapping Resistance in Zimbabwe's Eastern Highlands." *Cultural Anthropology* 13 (1998): 344–75.

Moore, Donald, Anand Pandian, and Jake Kosek, eds. *Race, Nature, and the Politics of Difference*. Durham: Duke University Press, forthcoming.

Moraes, Raymundo. *Na planície Amazônica*. 7th ed. São Paulo: Editora Itatiaia, 1987.

Muniz, João da Palma. "Limites municipais do estado do Pará." *Annaes da bibliotheca e archivo publico do Pará*. Tomo IX, 383–515. Belém: Imprensa de Alfredo Augusto Silva, 1916.

Muñiz, N. Miret, R. Vamos, Mário Hiraoka, Florencia Montagnini, and Robert O. Mendelsohn. "The Economic Value of Managing *Açaí* Palm (*Euterpe oleracea* Mart.) in the Floodplains of the Amazon Estuary, Pará, Brazil." *Forest Ecology and Management* 87, nos. 1–3 (1996): 163–73.

Muratorio, Blanca. *The Life and Times of Grandfather Alonso: Culture and History in the Upper Amazon*. New Brunswick: Rutgers University Press, 1991.

Murphy, Robert F. "The Anthropological Theories of Julian Steward." In Julian H. Steward, *Evolution and Ecology: Essays on Social Transformation*. Ed. Jane C. Steward and Robert F. Murphy. Urbana: University of Illinois Press, 1977.

Murra, John V. *The Economic Organization of the Inca State*. Greenwich, Conn.: JAI Press, 1979.

Myers, Leopold H. *The Clio*. London: Robin Clark, 1990.

Naipaul, V. S. *A Way in the World*. New York: Knopf, 1994.

Nepstad, Daniel C., Claudio R. de Carvalho, Eric A. Davidson, Peter H. Jipp, Paul A. Lefebvre, Gustavo H. Negreiros, Elson D. da Silva, Thomas A. Stone, Susan E. Trumbore, and Simone Vieira. "The Role of Deep Roots in the Hydrological and Carbon Cycles of Amazonian Forests and Pastures." *Nature* 372, no. 6507 (1994): 666–69.

Nepstad, Daniel C., Christopher Uhl, and E.A.S. Serrão. "Recuperation of a Degraded Amazonian Landscape: Forest Recovery and Agricultural Restoration." *Ambio* 20, no. 6 (1991): 248–55.

Neumann, Roderick P. *Imposing Wilderness: Struggles over Livelihood and Nature Preservation in Africa.* Berkeley: University of California Press, 1998.

Nicholl, Charles. *The Creature in the Map: A Journey to El Dorado.* New York: Morrow, 1995.

Nicolson, Malcolm. "Alexander von Humboldt and the Geography of Vegetation." In *Romanticism and the Sciences,* ed. Andrew Cunningham and Nicholas Jardine, 169–85. Cambridge: Cambridge University Press, 1990.

Nimuendajú, Curt. "Os Tapajo." *Boletim do Museu Paraense Emílio Goeldi* 10 (1949): 93–106.

Nordenskiöld, Erland. "Die anpassung der Indianer an die verhältnisse in den überschwemmungsgebieten in Südamerika." *Ymer* 36, no. 2 (1916): 138–55.

Nugent, Stephen. "Amazonia: Ecosystem and Social System." *Man* N.S. 16 (1981): 62–74.

———. "The Limitations of 'Environmental Management': Forest Utilization in the Lower Amazon." In *Environment and Development in Latin America: The Politics of Sustainability,* ed. David Goodman and Michael Redclift, 141–54. Manchester: Manchester University Press, 1991.

———. *Amazonian Caboclo Society: An Essay in Invisibility.* Oxford: Berg, 1996.

———. "The Coordinates of Identity in Amazonia: At Play in the Fields of Culture." *Critique of Anthropology* 17, no. 1 (1997): 33–51.

O'Hara, James E. "Henry Walter Bates—His Life and Contributions to Biology." *Archives of Natural History* 22 (1995): 195–219.

Ojer, Pablo, S.J. *La formación del Oriente Venezolano: I. Creación de las gobernaciones.* Caracas: Universidade Católica Andres Bello, 1966.

Oliver, Chadwick D., and Bruce C. Larson. *Forest Stand Dynamics.* New York: McGraw-Hill, 1990.

Ono, Morio, and Nobue Miyazaki. "O aviamento na Amazônia: Estudo sócio-econômico sôbre a produção de juta." *Sociologia* 20, nos. 3–4 (1958): 366–96, 530–63.

Pacheco de Oliveira Filho, João. "O caboclo e o brabo: Notas sobre duas modalidades de força-de-trabalho na expansão da fronteira Amazônica no século XIX." *Encontros com a civilização Brasileira* 11 (1979): 101–40.

Paden, William D. "Arthur O'Shaughnessy in the British Museum; Or, The Case of the Misplaced Fusees and the Reluctant Zoologist." *Victorian Studies* 8 (1964): 7–30.

Padoch, Christine. "Aguaje (*Mauritia flexuosa* L.f.) in the economy of Iquitos, Peru." In *The Palm—Tree of Life: Biology, Utilization and Conservation,* ed. Michael J. Balick, 214–24. New York: New York Botanical Garden, 1988.

Padoch, Christine, and Miguel Pinedo-Vásquez. "Farming Above the Flood in the Várzea of Amapá." In *Várzea: Diversity, Development, and Conservation of Amazonia's Whitewater Floodplains,* ed. Christine Padoch, J. Márcio Ayres, Miguel Pinedo-Vásquez, and Anthony Henderson, 345–54. New York: New York Botanical Garden, 1999.

Paes Loureiro, João de Jesus. *Cultura Amazônica: Um poética do imaginário.* Belém: CEJUP, 1995.

Pagden, Anthony. *The Fall of Natural Man: The American Indian and the Origins of Comparative Ethnology.* New York: Cambridge University Press, 1982.

———. " 'The Impact of the New World on the Old': The History of an Idea." *Renaissance and Modern Studies* 30 (1986): 1–11.

———. "Introduction." In Bartolomé de Las Casas, *A Short Account of the Destruction of the Indies.* Ed. and trans. Nigel Griffin, xiii–li. Harmondsworth: Penguin, 1992.

———. *European Encounters with the New World: From Renaissance to Romanticism.* New Haven: Yale University Press, 1993.

Palladino, Paolo, and Michael Worboys. "Science and Imperialism." *Isis* 84 (1993): 91–102.

Palmatary, Helen C. "The Pottery of Marajó Island, Brazil." *Transactions of the American Philosophical Society* N.S. 39, no. 3 (1949): 260–470.

Palmer, John R. "Forestry in Brazil—Amazonia." *Commonwealth Forestry Review* 56, no. 2 (1977): 115–30.

Parry, Benita. "Review: *In Theory: Classes, Nations, Literatures* by Aijaz Ahmad." In *History Workshop Journal* 36 (1993): 232–42.

Parsons, James J., and William M. Denevan. "Pre-Columbian Ridged Fields." *Scientific American* 217, no. 1 (1967): 93–100.

Payson, William Farquhar, ed. *Mahogany Antique and Modern: A Study of Its History and Use in the Decorative Arts.* New York: E. P. Dutton, 1926.

Peluso, Nancy Lee. *Rich Forests, Poor People: Resource Control and Resistance in Java.* Berkeley: University of California Press, 1992.

Pereira, Valeria F. G. *Spatial and Temporal Analysis of Floodplain Ecosystems—Amapá, Brazil—Using Geographic Information Systems (GIS) and Remote Sensing.* Unpbd. M.Sc. thesis, Department of Natural Resources, University of New Hampshire, 1998.

Picard, Jacky. "O clientalismo nas colônias agrícolas do sudeste do Pará." In *Amazônia e a crise da modernização*, org. Maria Angela D'Ínção and Isolda Maciel da Silveira, 279–99. Belém: Museu Paraense Emílio Goeldi, 1994.

Pigg, Stacy Leigh. "Constructing Social Categories Through Place: Social Representations and Development in Nepal." *Comparative Studies in Society and History* 34, no. 3 (1992): 491–513.

Pile, Steve, and Michael Keith, eds. *Geographies of Resistance.* London: Routledge, 1997.

Pinheiro, Luís Balkar. "Do Mocambeiro a Cabano: Notas sobre a presença negra na Amazônia na primeira metade do século XIX." *Terra das águas* 1 (1999): 148–72.

Piot, Charles. *Remotely Global: Village Modernity in West Africa.* Durham: Duke University Press, 1999.

Pires, João Murça, and Ghillean T. Prance. "The Vegetation Types of the Brazilian Amazon." In *Key Environments: Amazonia*, ed. Ghillean T. Prance and Thomas E. Lovejoy, 109–45. London: Pergamon, 1985.

Pollak, Harrison, Marli Mattos, and Christopher Uhl. "A Profile of Palm Heart Extraction in the Amazon Estuary." *Human Ecology* 23, no. 3 (1995): 357–85.

Pomian, Krzysztof. *Collectors and Curiosities: Paris and Venice, 1500–1800.* Cambridge: Polity, 1990.

Poovey, Mary. *A History of the Modern Fact: Problems of Knowledge in the Sciences of Wealth and Society*. Chicago: University of Chicago Press, 1998.

Porro, Antonio. *O povo das águas: Ensaios de etno-história Amazônica*. São Paulo: Vozes, 1996.

Portelli, Alessandro. *The Death of Luigi Trastulli and Other Stories: Form and Meaning in Oral History*. New York: SUNY Press, 1991.

Porter, Roy. "The Terraqueous Globe." In *The Ferment of Knowledge: Studies in the Historiography of Eighteenth-Century Science*, ed. George S. Rousseau and Roy Porter, 285–324. Cambridge: Cambridge University Press, 1980.

Posey, Darrell A. "Indigenous Management of Tropical Forest Ecosystems: The Case of the Kayapó Indians of the Brazilian Amazon." *Agroforestry Systems* 3 (1985): 139–58.

Povinelli, Elizabeth A. "Notes on Gridlock: Genealogy, Intimacy, Sexuality." In *Public Culture*, forthcoming.

Prance, Ghillean. "Notes on the Typology of Amazonia III. The Terminology of Amazonian Forest Types Subject to Inundation." *Brittonia* 31, no. 1 (1979): 26–38.

Pratt, Mary Louise. *Imperial Eyes: Travel Literature and Transculturation*. New York: Routledge, 1992.

Quinn, David B. *Raleigh and the British Empire*. London: Hodder & Stoughton, 1947.

———. *Explorers and Colonies: America, 1500–1625*. London: The Hambledon Press, 1990.

Rabb, Theodore K. *Enterprise and Empire: Merchant and Gentry Investment in the Expansion of England, 1575–1630*. Cambridge, Mass.: Harvard University Press, 1967.

Raby, Peter. *Bright Paradise: Victorian Scientific Travellers*. London: Pimlico Press, 1996.

Raffles, Hugh. "Exploring the Anthropogenic Amazon: Estuarine Landscape Transformations in Amapá, Brazil." In *Várzea: Diversity, Development, and Conservation of Amazonia's Whitewater Floodplains*, ed. Christine Padoch, J. Márcio Ayres, Miguel Pinedo-Vásquez, and Anthony Henderson, 355–70. New York: New York Botanical Garden, 1999.

———. "Local Theory: Nature and the Making of an Amazonian Place." *Cultural Anthropology* 14, no. 3 (1999): 323–60.

Raffles, Hugh, and Antoinette M.A.G. WinklerPrins. "Anthropogenic Fluvial Landscape Transformation in the Amazon Basin," manuscript.

Ralegh, Sir Walter. "The Apology." In *Last Voyages—Cavendish, Hudson, Ralegh: The Original Narratives*, ed. Philip Edwards, 226–48. Oxford: Clarendon Press, 1988.

———. *The Discoverie of the Large, Rich, and Bewtiful Empire of Guiana, with a Relation of the Great and Golden City of Manoa (which the Spaniards call El Dorado) And the provinces of Emeria, Arromaia, Amapaia and other Countries, with their rivers, adioyning. Performed in the Year 1595 by Sir W. Ralegh, Knight, Captaine of her Maiesties Guard, Lo. Warden of the Stanneries, and her Highnesse Lieutenant generall of the Countie of Cornewall*. Ed.

Robert H. Schomburgk. Hakluyt Society First Series No. 3. London: Hakluyt Society, 1848.

———. *The Discoverie of the Large and Bewtiful Empire of Guiana*. Ed. Vincent T. Harlow. London: The Argonaut Press, 1928.

———. *The Discoverie of the Large, Rich and Bewtiful Empyre of Guiana*. Ed. Neil L. Whitehead. Manchester: Manchester University Press, 1997.

Ramos, Alcida Rita. "The Indigenous Movement in Brazil: A Quarter Century of Ups and Downs." *Cultural Survival Quarterly* 21, no. 2 (1997): 50–53.

Reanier, Richard E., William P. Barse, Anna C. Roosevelt, Marconales Lima de Costa, Linda J. Brown, John E. Douglas, Matthew O'Donnell, Ellen Quinn, Judy Kemp, Christiane Lopes Machado, Maura Imazio da Silveira, James Feathers, and Andrew Henderson. "Dating a Paleoindian Site in the Amazon in Comparison with Clovis Culture." *Science* 275 (1997): 1948–52.

Record, Samuel J., and Robert W. Hess. *Timbers of the New World*. New Haven: Yale University Press, 1943.

Reeds, Karen. "Renaissance Humanism and Botany." In *Annals of Science* 33 (1976): 519–42.

Reis, Arthur Cézar Ferreira. *Limites e demarcações na Amazônia Brasileira*. 2 vols. Rio de Janeiro: Imprensa Nacional, 1947.

———. *O seringal e o seringueiro*. Documentário da vida rural, no. 5. Rio de Janeiro: Ministério da Agricultura, 1953.

Rendle, B. J. *Commerical Mahoganies and Allied Timbers*, Forest Products Research Bulletin No. 18. Department of Scientific and Industrial Research. London: HMSO, 1938.

Resende, Padre Ricardo. *Posseiros e padres do Araguaia: A justiça do lobo*. Pétropolis, RJ: Vozes, 1986.

Reynolds, Michael J. "When Good Intentions Go Up in Smoke: Environmental Politics in the Brazilian Amazon." Paper presented at the Annual Meetings of the Society for the Study of Social Problems, Chicago, August 5, 2000.

Richards, Paul W. *The Tropical Forest: An Ecological Study*. Cambridge: Cambridge University Press, 1952.

Ritvo, Harriet. *The Animal Estate: The English and Other Creatures in the Victorian Age*. Cambridge, Mass.: Harvard University Press, 1987.

———. "At the Edge of the Garden: Nature and Domestication in Eighteenth- and Nineteenth-Century Britain." *Huntington Library Quarterly* 55, no. 3 (1992): 363–78.

———. *The Platypus and the Mermaid and Other Figments of the Classifying Imagination*. Cambridge, Mass.: Harvard University Press, 1998.

Rival, Laura. "Domestication as a Historical and Symbolic Process: Wild Gardens and Cultivated Forests in the Ecuadorian Amazon." In *Advances in Historical Ecology*, ed. William Balée, 232–50. New York: Columbia University Press, 1998.

Rodrigues, Roberto M. *A fauna da Amazônia*. Belém: CEJUP, 1992.

Roosevelt, Anna C. *Parmana: Prehistoric Maize and Manioc Subsistence Along the Amazon and Orinoco*. New York: Academic Press, 1980.

———. "Chiefdoms in the Amazon and Orinoco." In *Chiefdoms in the Amer-*

icas, ed. Robert D. Drennan and Carlos A. Uribe, 153–84. Lanham, Md.: University Press of America, 1987.

————. "Lost Civilizations of the Lower Amazon." *Natural History* 95, no. 2 (1989): 74–83.

————. "Natural Resource Management in Amazonia Before the Conquest: Beyond Ethnographic Projection." In *Resource Management in Amazonia: Indigenous and Folk Strategies*, ed. Darrell A. Posey and William Balée, 30–62. New York: New York Botanical Garden, 1989.

————. *Moundbuilders of the Amazon: Geophysical Archaeology on Marajó Island, Brazil*. New York: Academic Press, 1991.

————. "The Rise and Fall of the Amazon Chiefdoms." *L'Homme* 33, nos. 2–4 (1993): 255–83.

————. "Ancient and Modern Hunter-Gatherers of Lowland South America." In *Advances in Historical Ecology*, ed. William Balée, 190–212. New York: Columbia University Press, 1998.

Roosevelt, Anna C., R. A. Housley, M. Imazio da Silveira, S. Maranca, and R. Johnson. "Eighth Millennium Pottery from a Prehistoric Shell Midden in the Brazilian Amazon." *Science* 254 (1991): 1621–24.

Roosevelt, Anna C., M. Lima da Costa, C. Lopes Machado, M. Michab, N. Mercier, H. Valladas, J. Feathers, W. Barnett, M. Imazio da Silveira, A. Henderson, J. Sliva, B. Chernoff, D. S. Reese, J. A. Holma, N. Toth, and K. Schick. "Paleoindian Cave Dwellers in the Amazon: The Peopling of the Americas." *Science* 272 (1996): 373–84.

Rose, Nikolas. *Powers of Freedom: Reframing Political Thought*. Cambridge: Cambridge University Press, 1999.

Rostow, Walter W. *The Stages of Economic Growth: A Non-Communist Manifesto*. Cambridge: Cambridge University Press, 1971.

Rowse, Alfred Leslie. *Sir Walter Ralegh, His Family and Private Life*. New York: Harper & Brothers, 1962.

Ryan, Michael T. "Assimilating New Worlds in the Sixteenth and Seventeenth Centuries." *Comparative Studies in Society and History* 23 (1981): 519–38.

Sader, Emil, and Ken Silverstein. *Without Fear of Being Happy: Lula, the Workers Party and Brazil*. London: Verso, 1991.

Salgado, Sebastião. *Terra: Struggle of the Landless*. London: Phaidon, 1997.

Sanchez, P. A., D. E. Bandy, J. H. Villachica, and J. J. Nicholaides. "Amazon Basin Soils: Management for Continuous Crop Production." *Science* 216 (1982): 821–27.

Sanchez, P. A., and J. R. Benites. "Low-Input Cropping for Acid Soils of the Humid Tropics." *Science* 238 (1987): 1521–27.

Sangwan, Satpal. "The Strength of a Scientific Culture: Interpreting Disorder in Colonial Science." *The Indian Economic and Social History Review* 34 (1997): 217–50.

Santos, Roberto. *História econômica da Amazônia (1800–1920)*. São Paulo: T. A. Queiroz, 1980.

Schmink, Marianne, and Charles H. Wood. *Contested Frontiers in Amazonia*. New York: Columbia University Press, 1992.

Schmink, Marianne, and Charles H. Wood, eds. *Frontier Expansion in Amazonia*. Gainesville: University of Florida Press, 1984.

Scoones, Ian. "New Ecology and the Social Sciences: What Prospects for a Fruitful Engagement?" *Annual Review of Anthropology* 28 (1999): 479–507.

Scott, James C. *Seeing Like a State: How Certain Schemes to Improve the Human Condition Have Failed*. New Haven: Yale University Press, 1998.

Scott, Joan W. "The Evidence of Experience." *Critical Inquiry* 17, no. 4 (1991): 773–97.

Scott, William R. *The Constitution and Finance of English, Scottish and Irish Joint-Stock Companies to 1720*. 3 vols. Cambridge: Cambridge University Press, 1910–12.

Seaward, Mark R. D., and Sylvia M. D. FitzGerald, eds. *Richard Spruce (1817–1893): Botanist and Explorer*. London: Royal Botanic Gardens, Kew, 1996.

Sebald, W. G. *Austerlitz*. New York: Random House, 2001.

Secord, Anne. "Science in the Pub: Artisan Botanists in Early Nineteenth-Century Lancashire." *History of Science* 32, no. 3 (1994): 269–315.

Seed, John. "Theologies of Power: Unitarianism and the Social Relations of Religious Discourse, 1800–50." In *Class, Power and Social Structure in British Nineteenth-Century Towns*, ed. Robert J. Morris, 107–56. Leicester: Leicester University Press, 1986.

Seed, Patricia. "Taking Possession and Reading Texts: Establishing the Authority of Overseas Empires." *The William and Mary Quarterly* 49, no. 2 (1992): 183–209.

Shapin, Stephen, and Simon Shaffer. *Leviathan and the Air-Pump: Hobbes, Boyle, and the Experimental Life*. Princeton: Princeton University Press, 1989.

Sherman, William H. *John Dee: The Politics of Reading and Writing in the English Renaissance*. Amherst: University of Massachusetts Press, 1995.

Shirley, John W. "Sir Walter Raleigh's Guiana Finances." *Huntington Library Quarterly* 13 (1949): 55–69.

———. "The Scientific Experiments of Sir Walter Ralegh, the Wizard Earl, and the Three Magi in the Tower 1603–1617." *Ambix* 4, nos. 1–2 (1949): 52–66.

Silverberg, Robert. *The Golden Dream: Seekers of El Dorado*. Athens: University of Ohio Press, 1996.

Simón, Pedro. *The Expedition of Pedro de Ursua and Lope de Aguirre in Search of El Dorado and Omagua in 1560–1*. Trans. William Bollaert. Works issued by the Hakluyt Society, No. 28. London: Hakluyt Society, 1861.

Singapore Journal of Tropical Geography 21, no. 1 (2000). "Special Issue: Constructing the Tropics," ed. Felix Driver and Brenda S. A. Yeoh.

Sioli, Harald. "Tropical Rivers as Expressions of Their Terrestrial Environments." In *Tropical Ecological Systems: Trends in Terrestrial and Aquatic Research*, ed. Frank B. Golley and Ernesto Medina, 275–88. New York: Springer-Verlag, 1975.

———. "The Amazon and Its Main Affluents: Hydrography, Morphology of the River Courses, and River Types." In *The Amazon: Limnology and Landscape Ecology of a Mighty Tropical River and its Basin*, ed. Harald Sioli, 127–65. Dordrecht: Dr. W. Junk, 1984.

Sivaramakrishnan, K. *Modern Forests: Statemaking and Environmental Change in Colonial Eastern India.* Stanford: Stanford University Press, 1999.

Slater, Candace. *Dance of the Dolphin: Transformation and Disenchantment in the Amazonian Imagination.* Chicago: University of Chicago Press, 1994.

———. "Amazonia as Edenic Narrative." In *Uncommon Ground: Rethinking the Human Place in Nature*, ed. William Cronon, 114–31. New York: W. W. Norton, 1996.

———. *Entangled Edens: Visions of the Amazon.* Berkeley: University of California Press, 2002.

Smith, Anthony. *Explorers of the Amazon.* London: Viking, 1986.

Smith, David M. *The Practice of Silviculture: Applied Forest Ecology.* 9th ed. New York: Wiley, 1997.

Smith, Nigel J. H. "Anthrosols and Human Carrying Capacity in the Amazon." *Annals of the American Association of Geographers* 70 (1980): 553–66.

———. *Man, Fishes, and the Amazon.* New York: Columbia University Press, 1981.

Smith, Pamela H., and Paula Findlen, ed. *Merchants and Marvels: Commerce, Science, and Art in Early Modern Europe.* New York: Routledge, 2001.

Smyth, William, and Frederick Lowe. *Narrative of a Journey from Lima to Para, Across the Andes and Down the Amazon, Undertaken with a View of Ascertaining the Practicability of a Navigable Communication with the Atlantic by the Rivers Pachitea, Ucayali, and Amazon.* London: John Murray, 1836.

Snook, Laura K. *Stand Dynamics of Mahogany* (Swietenia macrophylla *King) and Associated Species After Fire and Hurricane in the Tropical Forests of the Yucatán Peninsula.* Unpbd. Ph.D. dissertation, Yale School of Forestry, 1993.

Souza, Márcio. *Mad Maria.* Trans. Thomas Colchie. New York: Avon Books, 1985.

Spenser, Edmund. *The Complete Works in Verse and Prose of Edmund Spenser.* 10 vols. Ed. Alexander B. Grosart. London: Hazell, Watson, and Viney, 1882–84.

———. *The Faerie Queene.* Ed. A. C. Hamilton. Harlow, Essex: Longman, 1977.

Sponsel, Leslie E. "Amazon Ecology and Adaptation." *Annual Review of Anthropology* 15 (1986): 67–97.

Spruce, Richard. *Notes of a Botanist on the Amazon and Andes. Being Records of Travel on the Amazon and Its Tributaries, the Trombetas, Rio Negro, Uaupés, Casiquiari, Pacimoni, Huallaga, and Pastasa; as also to the Cataract of the Orinoco, along the Eastern Side of the Andes of Peru and Ecuador, and the Shore of the Pacific, During the Years 1849–1864.* 2 vols. Ed. A. R. Wallace. London: Macmillan, 1908.

Spurr, David. *The Rhetoric of Empire: Colonial Discourse in Journalism, Travel Writing, and Imperial Administration.* Durham: Duke University Press, 1996.

Stafford, Robert A. *Scientist of Empire: Sir Roderick Murchison, Scientific Exploration and Victorian Imperialism.* Cambridge: Cambridge University Press, 1989.

Stecher, Robert M. "The Darwin–Bates Letters: Correspondence Between Two Nineteenth-Century Travellers and Naturalists." *Annals of Science* 25, no. 1(1969): 1–47, and 25, no. 2(1969): 95–125.

Steen, Harold K. *David M. Smith and the History of Silviculture: An Interview.* Durham: Forest History Society, 1990.

Stepan, Nancy Leys, *The Hour of Eugenics: Race, Gender, and Nation in Latin America.* Cornell University Press, 1996.

———. *Picturing Tropical Nature.* Ithaca: Cornell University Press, 2001.

Sternberg, Hilgard O'Reilly. "Proposals for a South American Waterway." In *Proceedings of the 48th International Congress of Americanists,* ed. Magnus Mörner and Mona Rosendahl, 99–125. Stockholm: Stockholm University/Institute of Latin American Studies, 1995.

Steward, Julian H., and Louis C. Faron. *Native Peoples of South America.* New York: McGraw-Hill, 1959.

Steward, Julian H., ed. *Handbook of South American Indians.* 6 vols. Bureau of American Ethnology, bulletin no. 143. Washington, D.C.: U.S. Government Printing Office, 1946–50.

Stewart, Kathleen. *A Space on the Side of the Road: Cultural Poetics in an "Other" America.* Princeton: Princeton University Press, 1996.

Stewart, Kathleen, and Susan Harding. "Bad Endings: American Apocalypsis." *Annual Review of Anthropology* 28 (1999): 285–310.

Stocking, George W., Jr. *Victorian Anthropology.* New York: The Free Press, 1987.

Stoddart, David R. "The RGS and the 'New Geography': Changing Aims and Roles in Nineteenth-Century Science." *Geographical Journal* 146, no. 3 (1980): 191–202.

Stoler, Ann Laura. "Tense and Tender Ties: Intimacies of Empire in North American History and (Post) Colonial Studies." *Journal of American History* 88, no. 3 (2001): 829–65.

Strathern, Marilyn. "Afterword: Relocations." In *Shifting Contexts: Transformations in Anthropological Knowledge,* ed. Marilyn Strathern, 177–85. New York: Routledge, 1995.

Strudwick, Jeremy. "Commercial Management for Palm Heart from *Euterpe oleracea* Mart. Palmae in the Amazon Estuary." In *New Directions in the Study of Plants and People: Research Contributions from the Institute of Economic Botany,* ed. Ghillean T. Prance and Michael J. Balick, 241–48. New York: New York Botanical Garden, 1990.

Sweet, David. "Native Resistance in Eighteenth Century Amazonia: The 'Abominable Muras' in War and Peace." *Radical History Review* 53 (1992): 49–80.

Taussig, Michael. *Shamanism, Colonialism, and the Wild Man: A Study in Terror and Healing.* Chicago: University of Chicago Press, 1987.

———. *Mimesis and Alterity: A Particular History of the Senses.* New York: Routledge, 1993.

Tawney, Richard Henry. *Business and Politics under James I: Lionel Cranfield as Merchant and Minister.* Cambridge: Cambridge University Press, 1958.

Taylor, Eva Germaine Rimington. *Tudor Geography, 1485–1583.* London: Methuen, 1930.

———. "Introduction." In *The Original Writings and Correspondence of the Two Richard Hakluyts*, ed. Eva Germaine Rimington Taylor, vol. 1, 1–66. Hakluyt Society Second Series No. 76. London: Hakluyt Society, 1935.

———. *Late Tudor and Early Stuart Geography, 1583–1650*. New York: Octagon, 1968.

Taylor, Peter J. "Technocratic Optimism, H. T. Odum, and the Partial Transformation of Ecological Metaphor After World War II." *Journal of the History of Biology* 21, no. 2 (1988): 213–44.

Taylor, Peter J., and Ann S. Blum. "Ecosystems as Circuits: Diagrams and the Limits of Physical Analogies." *Biology and Philosophy* 6 (1991): 275–94.

Thackray, Arnold. "The Industrial Revolution and the Image of Science." In *Science and Values*, ed. Arnold Thackray and Everett Mendelsohn, 5–22. New York: Humanities Press, 1974.

"The Letters Patents, Granted by the Queenes Majestie to M. Walter Ralegh, now Knight, for the Discovering and Planting of New Lands and Countries, to Continue the Space of 6. Yeeres and No More." In *The Portable Hakluyt's Voyages*, ed. Irwin R. Blacker, 279–85. New York: Viking, 1965.

Thomas, Keith. *Man and the Natural World: A History of the Modern Sensibility*. New York: Pantheon, 1983.

Thomas, Nicholas. *Colonialism's Culture: Anthropology, Travel and Government*. Princeton: Princeton University Press, 1994.

Thompson, Edward P. *The Making of the English Working Class*. 2nd ed. Harmondsworth: Penguin, 1968.

Thorne, Susan. "'The Conversion of Englishmen and the Conversion of the World Inseparable': Missionary Imperialism and the Language of Class in Early Industrial Britain." In *Tensions of Empire: Colonial Cultures in a Colonial World*, ed. Frederick Cooper and Ann Laura Stoler, 238–62. Berkeley: University of California Press, 1997.

Tillyard, Eustace Mandeville Wetenhall. *The Elizabethan World Picture*. London: Chatto & Windus, 1943.

Tomlinson, Henry M. *The Sea and the Jungle*. London: Duckworth, 1912.

Tsing, Anna L. *In the Realm of the Diamond Queen: Marginality in an Out-of-the-Way Place*. Princeton: Princeton University Press, 1993.

Turner, Terence. "Indigenous Rights, Indigenous Cultures and Environmental Conservation: Convergence or Divergence? The Case of the Brazilian Kayapó." In *Earth, Air, Fire, Water: Humanistic Studies of the Environment*, ed. Jill Ker Conway, Kenneth Keniston, and Leo Marx, 145–69. Amherst: University of Massachusetts Press, 1999.

Tyacke, Sarah. "English Charting of the River Amazon c. 1595–c. 1630." *Imago Mundi* 32 (1980): 73–89.

Uhl, Christopher, Paulo Barreto, Adalberto Veríssimo, Ana Cristina Barros, Paulo Amaral, Edson Vidal, and Carlos Souza Jr. "Uma abordagem integrada de pesquisa sobre o manejo dos recursos naturais na Amazônia." In *A expansão da atividade madeireira na Amazônia: Impactos e perspectivas para o desenvolvimento do setor florestal no Pará*, ed. Ana Cristina Barros and Adalberto Veríssimo, 143–64. Belém: IMAZON, 1996.

Ure, John. *Trespassers of the Amazon*. London: Constable, 1990.

Veríssimo, Adalberto, Paulo Barreto, Ricardo Tarifa, and Christopher Uhl. "Extraction of a High-Value Resource in Amazonia: The Case of Mahogany." *Forest Ecology and Management* 72, no. 1 (1995): 39–60.

Veríssimo, Adalberto, Carlos Souza Jr., Steve Stone, and Christopher Uhl. "Zoning of Timber Extraction in the Brazilian Amazon." *Conservation Biology* 12, no. 1 (1998): 18–36.

Viveiros de Castro, Eduardo. "Images of Nature and Society in Amazonian Ethnology." *Annual Review of Anthropology* 25 (1996): 179–200.

Vološinov, Valentin N. *Marxism and the Philosophy of Language*. Trans. Ladislav Matejka and Irwin R. Titunik. Cambridge, Mass.: Harvard University Press, 1986.

Wallace, Alfred Russel. *A Narrative of Travels on the Amazon and Rio Negro, with an Account of the Native Tribes, and Observations on the Climate, Geology, and Natural History of the Amazon Valley*. London: Reeve, 1853.

———. *Palm-Trees of the Amazon and Their Uses*. London: John van Voorst, 1853.

———. "The Development of Human Races Under the Law of Natural Selection." In Alfred Russel Wallace, *Natural Selection and Tropical Nature: Essays on Descriptive and Theoretical Biology*, 167–85. London: Macmillan, 1891 [1864].

———. *The Malay Archipelago: The Land of the Orang-Utan, and the Bird of Paradise. A Narrative of Travel, with Studies of Man and Nature*. New York: Harper and Brothers, 1869.

———. "Obituary: H. W. Bates. The Naturalist of the Amazons." *Nature* 45, no. 1165 (1892): 398–99.

———. *My Life: A Record of Events and Opinions*. 2 vols. New York: Dodd, Mead, 1905.

Weinstein, Barbara. *The Amazon Rubber Boom, 1850–1920*. Stanford: Stanford University Press, 1983.

White, Leslie A. "Energy and the Evolution of Culture." *American Anthropologist* 45, no. 3 (1943): 335–56.

White, Leslie A., and Beth Dillingham. *The Concept of Culture*. Minneapolis: Burgess, 1973.

Whitehead, Neil L. "Tribes Make States and States Make Tribes: Warfare and the Creation of Colonial Tribe and State in Northeastern South America." In *War in the Tribal Zone: Expanding States and Indigenous Warfare*, ed. R. Brian Ferguson and Neil L. Whitehead, 127–50. Sante Fe: School of American Research Press, 1992.

———. "Ethnic Transformation and Historical Discontinuity in Native Amazonia and Guayana, 1500–1900." *L'Homme* 33, nos. 2–4 (1993): 289–309.

———. "The Ancient Amerindian Polities of the Amazon, the Orinoco, and the Atlantic Coast: A Preliminary Analysis of Their Passing." In *Amazonian Indians from Prehistory to the Present: Anthropological Perspectives*, ed. Anna C. Roosevelt, 33–54. Tucson: University of Arizona Press, 1994.

———. "The Historical Anthropology of Text: The Interpretation of Ralegh's *Discoverie of Guiana*." *Current Anthropology* 36, no. 1 (1995): 53–74.

———. "Introduction." In Sir Walter Ralegh, *The Discoverie of the Large, Rich and Bewtiful Empyre of Guiana*, ed. Neil L. Whitehead, 3–116. Manchester: Manchester University Press, 1997.

———. "Ecological History and Historical Ecology: Diachronic Modeling Versus Historical Explanation." In *Advances in Historical Ecology*, ed. William Balée. New York: Columbia University Press, 1998.

Williams, Raymond. *The Country and the City*. Oxford: Oxford University Press, 1973.

———. *Marxism and Literature*. Oxford: Oxford University Press, 1977.

Williams-Ellis, Amabel. *Darwin's Moon: A Biography of Alfred Russel Wallace*. London: Blackie, 1966.

Williamson, James A. *English Colonies in Guiana and on the Amazon, 1604–1668*. Oxford: Clarendon Press, 1923.

Wilson, Edward O. *The Diversity of Life*. Cambridge, Mass.: Belknap Press of Harvard University Press, 1992.

Wilson, John. "The Relation of Master John Wilson of Wansteed in Essex, One of the Last Ten That Returned into England from Wiapoco in Guiana 1606." In Samuel Purchas, *Hakluytus Posthumus or Purchas His Pilgrimes, Contayning a History of the World in Sea Voyages and Lande Travells by Englishmen and Others*. Vol. 16, 349–50. Glasgow: James MacLehose, 1905–7.

WinklerPrins, Antoinette M. A. G. "Land-Use Decision Making Using Local Soil Knowledge on the Lower Amazon Floodplain." *Geographical Review* 87, no. 1 (1997): 105–8.

Wise, M. Norton, ed. *The Values of Precision*. Princeton: Princeton University Press, 1995.

Wittgenstein, Ludwig. *Philosophical Investigations*. Trans. Gertrude E. M. Anscombe. New York: Prentice Hall, 1999.

Woodcock, George. *Henry Walter Bates, Naturalist of the Amazons*. London: Faber, 1968.

Woods, William I., and Joseph M. McCann. "The Anthropogenic Origin and Persistence of Amazonian Dark Earths." *Conference of Latin Americanist Geographers Yearbook* 25 (1999): 7–14.

Worster, Donald. *Nature's Economy: A History of Ecological Ideas*. 2nd ed. Cambridge: Cambridge University Press, 1985.

Yungjohann, John C. *White Gold, The Diary of a Rubber Cutter in the Amazon, 1906–1916*. Ed. Ghillean T. Prance. Oracle: Synergetic Press, 1989.

Zammito, John H. *Kant, Herder, and the Birth of Anthropology*. Chicago: University of Chicago Press, 2002.

Zedong Mao. "Where Do Correct Ideas Come From?" In *Selected Readings from the Works of Mao Tsetung*, 502–4. Beijing: Foreign Languages Press, 1971.

Zimmerer, Karl. "Human Geography and the New Ecology: The Prospect and Promise of Integration." *Annals of the Association of American Geographers* 84, no. 1 (1994): 108–25.

Žižek, Slavoj. *The Sublime Object of Ideology*. London: Verso, 1989.

CREDITS

An earlier version of Chapter 3 was published as "Local Theory: Nature and the Making of an Amazonian Place" in *Cultural Anthropology* 14, no. 3 (1999). An earlier version of Chapter 5 appeared in *American Ethnologist* 28, no. 3 (2001). I am indebted to the American Anthropological Association for permission to include this material.

The images listed below appear in the chapters indicated. I am grateful to the institutions and individuals concerned for their willingness to allow reproduction. Any photographs not described here were taken by the author in Brazil between 1995 and 1999. The maps in Chapters 2, 3, and 4 were drawn by Patricia Wynne.

Chapter 1: Infrared aerial photograph taken by the Companhia de Pesquisas e Recursos Minerais (also reproduced in Chapter 3) appears courtesy of Daniel Zarin. The "generic" Amazonia aerial view is of the Rio Tigre in the Peruvian Amazon and is ©Layne Kennedy/Corbis. "Stag Beetle with Fruits, Flowers, and Animals" from *Archetypa studiaque patris Georgii Hoefnagelii* (Frankfurt am Main, 1592) by Jacob Hoefnagel, is reproduced courtesy of the Library, Getty Research Institute, Los Angeles.

Chapter 3: LandSat TM image appears courtesy of Daniel Zarin.

Chapter 4: *Sir Walter Ralegh* (c. 1585) by Nicholas Hilliard is reproduced by courtesy of the National Portrait Gallery, London. The frontispiece to Ralegh's *Discoverie* is from Hulsius' *Voyages* (Nuremberg, 1599). Both this and the engraving from Theodor de Bry's *Americae* (Frankfurt am Main, 1617) are reproduced courtesy of Rare Books Division, The New York Public Library, Astor, Lenox, and Tilden Foundations. *Portrait of a Man* (1603–15) by the circle of Marc Gheeraerts is reproduced courtesy of the North Carolina Museum of Art, Raleigh, North Carolina, purchased with funds from the North Carolina Art Society (Robert F. Phifer Bequest). "Guiana sive Amazonum regio" (Amsterdam, 1638) by Willem Janszoon Blaeu is from the collection of FairWinds Antique Maps, New York (www.fairmaps.com).

Chapter 5: The hydrographic map of the Amazon Basin and the engraving *Turtle-fishing and adventure with Alligator* by J. W. Whymper after J. B. Zwecker are reproduced from Henry Walter Bates, *The*

Naturalist on the River Amazons (London, 1892). *Henry Walter Bates* (c. 1859) by Thomas Sims and the photograph of Bates (c. 1892) by J. Thomson are both ©Royal Geographical Society, London.

Chapter 6: The two Monarch of Mahogany images are reproduced from Allan Carman, *Monarch of Mahogany Visits Schmieg-Hungate & Kotzian* (New York, 190?).

Chapter 7: Engraving of açaí palm is reproduced from Alfred Russel Wallace, *Palm-Trees of the Amazon and Their Uses* (London, 1853).

For their help in locating these images I am particularly grateful to Clive Coward at the Royal Geographical Society, Joseph Gonzalez at FairWinds Maps, Erika Ingham at the National Portrait Gallery, Virginia Funkhouser and Wim de Wit at the Getty Library, John Rathe at the New York Public Library, and Dennis Weller at the North Carolina Museum of Art.

Unless otherwise noted, all translations are my own. I have retained original spellings in all quotations.

INDEX